Film Cartoons

Film Cartoons

*A Guide to
20th Century American
Animated Features
and Shorts*

by
Douglas L. McCall

McFarland & Company, Inc., Publishers
Jefferson, North Carolina, and London

The present work is a reprint of the library bound edition
of Film Cartoons: A Guide to 20th Century American
Animated Features and Shorts, first published in 1998
by McFarland.

LIBRARY OF CONGRESS CATALOGUING-IN-PUBLICATION DATA

McCall, Douglas L., 1971–
     Film cartoons : a guide to 20th century American animated
features and shorts / by Douglas L. McCall.
          p.   cm.
     Includes bibliographical references and index.

     ISBN 0-7864-2450-8 (softcover : 50# alkaline paper) ∞

     1. Animated films—United States.   I. Title.
NC1766.U5M38   2005
016.79143'3—dc21   98-26404

British Library cataloguing data are available

©1998 Douglas L. McCall. All rights reserved

No part of this book may be reproduced or transmitted in any form
or by any means, electronic or mechanical, including photocopying
or recording, or by any information storage and retrieval system,
without permission in writing from the publisher.

Cover art by Sarah Sanders

Manufactured in the United States of America

McFarland & Company, Inc., Publishers
   Box 611, Jefferson, North Carolina 28640
   www.mcfarlandpub.com

Contents

Preface

From J. Stuart Blackton's landmark short, *Humorous Phases of Funny Faces* (1906), to *Anastasia* (1997), Don Bluth's latest feature-length challenge to Walt Disney Studios (leaders in the field since the debut of a certain mouse in 1928), animated films have entertained and amazed audiences by bringing to life characters, stories and whole worlds born in — and limited only by — the artist's imagination. Like so many others, I have loved these films since I was kid, and this book is the result of that love and the need to know more about them.

My main goal when starting *Film Cartoons* was to compile a guide that would help me and others to know these films better. I wanted to learn the who, what and when behind them, more than the how and why, which can be better explored in animation histories, biographies and technical studies. It was the names, titles and dates that I was most concerned with, finding the correct ones and making them easier to find for others.

This guide is divided into three main parts: Part 1 covers 180 animated feature films; Part 2 lists feature films that have short animation sequences; Part 3 covers over 1,500 animated shorts. For the more comprehensive first part I have focused mainly on American titles, but have also included many significant English-language foreign films and English-dubbed foreign films to give this part greater scope. Credit information (on direction, story, music, cast/voices, awards) is given for each film along with production information, additional notes of interest, and brief critiques (with star ratings, from no star for poor, to *** for excellent).

In deciding what should be included in Part 3, however, a more selective process had to be used, as it would have been impossible and impractical to include all shorts. I concentrated primarily on the sound shorts released by the major cartoon studios (Warner Bros., Walt Disney, MGM, Walter Lantz, and so on), and then, more specifically, on series or character debuts, Academy Award winners and nominees, and technical innovations. There are bound to be some noticeable omissions; I only hope they are few.

To put these films and their origins in better perspective, I have compiled an appendix of the top animation studios, both past and present, which looks at the individual histories, films and personnel of these remarkable movie factories.

It is my greatest hope that whether one is young or old, a recent convert or longtime devotee, this book will be considered a valuable reference for all lovers of these very special films in the history of American motion pictures.

D.L.M., *Summer 1998*

1

PART 1: Animated Feature Films

1 *The Adventures of Ichabod and Mr. Toad* (1949) ****½**
U.S.; Rated G; 68 mins.; Released October 5, 1949; Walt Disney.

Synopsis: Two Disney featurettes—Kenneth Grahame's *The Wind in the Willows*, narrated by Basil Rathbone, and Washington Irving's *The Legend of Sleepy Hollow*, narrated by Bing Crosby (see SHORTS).

Notes: Two classic stories superbly rendered by Disney Studios; Aka *Ichabod and Mr. Toad*; Last of the segmented animated features Disney made during the '40s; Working title—*Two Fabulous Characters*.

Highlight: Ichabod Crane's harrowing ride on Halloween night.

Credits: Supervisor—Ben Sharpsteen; Directors—Jack Kinney, Clyde Geronimi, James Algar; Directing Animators—Frank Thomas, Ollie Johnston, Wolfgang Reitherman, Milt Kahl, John Lounsbery, Ward Kimball; Screenplay by Erdman Penner, Winston Hibler, Joe Rinaldi, Ted Sears, Homer Brightman and Harry Reeves, based on stories by Kenneth Grahame and Washington Irving; Musical Director—Oliver Wallace; Songs by Don Raye, Gene De Paul, Frank Churchill, Charles Wolcott, Larry Morey and Ray Gilbert; Songs—"Ichabod," "Katrina," "The Headless Horseman" and "Merrily on Our Way."

Voices: Basil Rathbone and Bing Crosby (Narrators), Eric Blore, Pat O'Malley, John McLeish (aka John Ployardt), Colin Campbell, Campbell Grant, Claud Allister, Alec Harford, The Rhythmaires.

2 *The Adventures of Mark Twain* (1986) ******
U.S.; Rated G; 86 mins.; Released January 1986 (Video: December 1986, Paramount); Will Vinton Productions.

Synopsis: In 1910, Mark Twain travels with his characters Tom Sawyer, Huck Finn and Becky Thatcher on a magic balloon ride to Halley's Comet.

Notes: Imaginative, impressively-produced Claymation feature, the first from Oscar-winner Will Vinton (*Closed Mondays*). Vinton, who coined the term "Claymation" for his technique of animating clay figures, may be best known for his California Raisins TV commercials and specials; Two tons of plasticine were used in the film's production; Produced by Vinton.

Credits: Director—Will Vinton; Principal Character Claymation—William L. Fiesterman, Tom Gasek, Mark Gustafson, Barry Bruce, Craig Bartlett, Bruce McKean; Screenplay by Susan Shadburne (wife of director Vinton); Music by Billy Scream; Song—"Heroes" (performed by The Billy Scream Band) by Scream, Paul Jamison and Susan Shadburne.

Voices: James Whitmore (Mark Twain), Chris Ritchie (Tom Sawyer), Gary Krug (Huck Finn), Michele Mariana (Becky Thatcher/Mysterious Stranger/Girl in Crowd), John Morrison (Adam), Carol Edelman (Eve), Dallas McKennon (Jim Smiley/Newspaper Boy), Herb Smith (Stranger), Marley Stone (Aunt Polly), Wilbur Vincent (Mysterious Stranger), Wally Newman (Captain Stormfield), Tim Conner (Three-Headed Alien), Todd Tolces

3

(Saint Peter), Billy Scream (Indexivator/Animal), Bob Griggs (First Heckler), Coward Wholesale (Second Heckler), Tomasek (Man in Crowd), Sally Sopwith (Woman in Crowd), Wilf Innton (Dan'l Webster), Tom Gasek (Homer/Calaveras Miner), Andrew Edwards (First Miner), Harvey Brown (Second Miner), Craig Bartlett, Mark Gustafson, Bruce McKean (Calaveras Miners), Billy Victor (God), Compton Downs (Injun Joe), Nell Suza (Animal/Mud Person), Tim Kahn, Stashu Beencof (Animals), Kesag Mot, Kim Tonner (Mud People), Gary Thompson (Baby Cain).

The Adventures of Milo in the Phantom Tollbooth **see** *The Phantom Tollbooth*

3 *The Adventures of the American Rabbit* (1986) *
U.S.; Rated G; 85 mins.; Released February 1986 (Video: January 1987, Paramount); Toei Animation.

Synopsis: Mild-mannered Rob Rabbit is transformed into the American Rabbit—protector of the animals—after inheriting the Legacy.

Notes: Minor kids film, presented by Clubhouse Pictures; The American Rabbit was chosen as a "Special Friend" of the March of Dimes.

Credits: Directors—Fred Wolf, Nobutaka Nishizawa; Chief Animator—Takashi Abe; Screenplay by Norm Lenzer, based on characters created by Stewart Moskowitz; Music and lyrics written and performed by Mark Volman and Howard Kaylan, with John Hoier.

Voices: Barry Gordon (Rob/American Rabbit), Pat Fraley (Tini Meeny), Ken Mars (Vultor/Buzzard), Lorenzo Music (Ping Pong), Bob Arbogast (Theo), Bob Holt (Rodney), Lew Horn (Dip/various characters), Norm Lenzer (Bruno), John Mayer (Too Loose), Maitzi Morgan (Lady Pig), Laurie O'Brien (Bunny O'Hare), Hal Smith (Mentor), Russi Taylor (Mother), Fred Wolf (Fred Red).

The Adventures of the Great Mouse Detective **see** *The Great Mouse Detective*

4 *Aladdin* (1992) ***
U.S.; Rated G; 90 mins.; Released November 25, 1992 (Video: September 1993, Walt Disney); Walt Disney.

Synopsis: Aladdin, a misunderstood street urchin, tries to win the love of the beautiful Princess Jasmine with the aid of a Genie from a magic lamp, while the evil sorcerer Jafar schemes against them.

Notes: Superbly-animated, hilarious Disney version of the *Arabian Nights* tales deftly mixes classic adventure-romance with irreverent, contemporary humor; Disney's 31st animated feature; 600 artists and animators worked on the film for four years; Cost of film— $35 million; The Oscar-winning songwriting team of Alan Menken and Howard Ashman (who died of AIDS in March 1991) worked together for the last time on this film (following *The Little Mermaid* and *Beauty and the Beast*), writing three of the songs used; The drawing of the Genie was inspired by the artwork of caricaturist Al Hirschfeld; Comedian-actor Robin Williams (as the Genie) does vocal impersonations of over 60 famous personalities, including Jack Nicholson, William F. Buckley, Ed Sullivan and Peter Lorre; Spawned a Saturday morning cartoon series (1994–); Followed by two made-for-video sequels, *The Return of Jafar* (1994) and *Aladdin and the King of Thieves* (1996), with Williams returning as the Genie in the latter; Produced by John Musker and Ron Clements (the directing team behind *The Little Mermaid*).

Highlights: Robin Williams' funny, fast-paced vocal performance as the Genie, Aladdin's flying carpet escape from the Cave of Wonders, and the "Friend Like Me" and "Prince Ali" production numbers.

Credits: Directors—John Musker, Ron Clements; Supervising Animators—Glen Keane, Eric Goldberg, Mark Henn, Andreas Deja, Duncan Marjoribanks, Randy Cartwright, Will Finn, David Pruiksma; Screenplay by Ron Clements and John Musker, Ted Elliott and Terry Rossio, based on the Arabian Nights tales; Musical score by Alan Menken; Songs (Menken-Howard Ashman)— "Arabian Nights," "Friend Like Me" and "Prince Ali"; Songs (Menken-Tim Rice)— "One Jump Ahead," "A Whole New World" and "Prince Ali Reprise"; **Note:** Tony-winning lyricist Rice is best known for his collaborations with Andrew Lloyd Webber (*Jesus Christ Superstar, Evita*).

Voices: Scott Weinger (Aladdin), Brad Kane (Aladdin's singing voice), Robin Williams (Genie), Linda Larkin (Jasmine), Lea Salonga (Jasmine's singing voice), Jonathan Freeman (Jafar), Frank Welker (Abu), Gilbert Gottfried (Iago), Douglas Seale (Sultan); **Notes:** Weinger played Steve Hale (1992–94) on TV's *Full House*. Salonga won a Tony as star of the hit musical *Miss Saigon* (1990).

Honors: Academy Awards— Original Score and Song ("A Whole New World"), also nominated for Sound (Terry Porter, Mel Metcalfe, David J. Hudson, Doc Kane), Sound Effects Editing (Mark Mangini) and Song ("Friend Like Me"); Other awards— Golden Globe Awards (Best Original Score, Best Song— "A Whole New World," Special Achievement Award— Robin Williams), MTV Movie Awards (Best Comedic Performance— Robin Williams).

5 *Alakazam the Great!* (1961) $*\frac{1}{2}$
Japanese-U.S.; Not Rated; 84 mins.; Released in Japan in 1960; Toei Animation.

Synopsis: Alakazam, a shy monkey who becomes arrogant and selfish after being made king of the animals, is humbled while on an arduous journey across the country-side.

Notes: Fine adventure-morality tale for kids; American version of a Japanese film— originally titled *Saiyu-ki*; Presented by James H. Nicholson and Samuel Z. Arkoff.

Credits: Directors— Lee Kresel (American version), Taiji Yabushita, Osamu Tezuka, Daisaku Shirakawa; **Note:** Tezuka (1928–89) created the popular comic-strip superhero "Astro Boy" (originally called "Tetsuwan Atom"— or "The Mighty Atom") in 1951, which became a U.S. TV hit in 1963; Screenplay by Lou Rusoff, Lee Kresel, Osamu Tezuka and Keinosuke Uekusa; Music and lyrics by Les Baxter; Songs— "Ali the Great," "Bluebird in the Cherry Tree," "Under the Waterfall" and "Aliki-Aliko-Alakazam."

Voices: Frankie Avalon (Alakazam), Dodie Stevens (De De), Jonathan Winters (Sir Quigley Broken Bottom), Arnold Stang (Lulipopo), Sterling Holloway (Narrator).

6 *Alice in Wonderland* (1950) $*\frac{1}{2}$
U.S./French/British; Not Rated; 83 mins.; Premiered in New York Aug. 1951 (opening in the same week as Disney's *Alice*); Lou Bunin/Union Générale Cinématographie/Rank.

Synopsis: On the day of Queen Victoria's visit to Oxford, math professor Charles Dodgson takes the Dean's three daughters (including Alice) for a row on the river where he tells them the story of "Alice in Wonderland."

Notes: Faithful, fairly-entertaining telling of the Lewis Carroll tale, mixing live-action with stop-motion animated puppets (Lou Bunin's Film Puppets); Bunin, who created the puppet-animated opening for MGM's *Ziegfeld Follies* (1946), worked on the film for five years. One hundred twenty-eight puppets (modeled after the original John Tenniel drawings) were constructed for its production; Premiered in France as *Alice en pays des merveilles*; Disney veteran Art Babbitt acted as animation consultant on the film; Unreleased in Great Britain until 1985, owing to the film's possibly offensive caricaturing of Queen Victoria; Produced by Bunin.

Credits: Directors— Dallas Bower (live action), Lou Bunin (puppet animation); Puppet Animation— William King, Ben Radin, Oscar Fessler; Screenplay by Henry Myers,

Albert E. Lewin and Edward Eliscu, based on *Alice's Adventures in Wonderland* by Lewis Carroll; Music by Sol Kaplan, performed by The London Symphony Orchestra; Lyrics by Henry Myers and Edward Eliscu.

Cast/Voices: Carol Marsh (Alice Liddell), Stephen Murray (Rev. Charles Dodgson, aka Lewis Carroll/Knave of Hearts), Pamela Brown (The Queen/Queen of Hearts), Felix Aylmer (Dr. Liddell/Cheshire Cat), Ernest Milton (Vice Chancellor/ White Rabbit), David Read (The Prince Consort/King of Hearts), Raymond Bussieres (Tailor/Mad Hatter), Elizabeth Henson (Lorina Liddell), Joan Dale (Edith Liddell), Joyce Grenfell (Ugly Duchess), Jack Train, Ivan Staff.

7 *Alice in Wonderland* (1951) ***
U.S.; Rated G; 75 mins.; Released July 28, 1951; Walt Disney.

Synopsis: Young Alice falls down a rabbit hole and into a bizarre, nonsensical world where she meets a variety of strange characters, including the Cheshire Cat, the Queen of Hearts and the Mad Hatter.

Notes: Certainly the best screen version of the beloved Lewis Carroll tale, this Disney classic boasts great, colorful animation and superb voice characterizations; Walt Disney first brought *Alice* to the screen with his Lewis Carrol–inspired silent series "Alice Comedies" (1924–27), which placed a live-action Alice in a cartoon world, and he first considered making an *Alice* feature back in the early '30s; Cost of film—$3 million; A behind-the-scenes look at the film, titled *One Hour in Wonderland*, was the first Disney TV special (it aired Dec. 25, 1950 on NBC); Though not a great commercial success when first released, the film, with its surrealist images, became a major hit in rerelease during the late '60s and early '70s.

Highlights: the Cheshire Cat, the tea party sequence (with the Mad Hatter and March Hare), and the courtroom finale.

Credits: Supervisor—Ben Sharpsteen; Directors—Clyde Geronimi, Hamilton Luske, Wilfred Jackson; Directing Animators—Milt Kahl, Ward Kimball, Frank Thomas, Eric Larson, John Lounsbery, Ollie Johnston, Wolfgang Reitherman, Marc Davis, Les Clark, Norm Ferguson; Story by Winston Hibler, Ted Sears, Bill Peet, Erdman Penner, Joe Rinaldi, Milt Banta, Bill Cottrell, Dick Kelsey, Joe Grant, Dick Huemer, Del Connell, Tom Oreb and John Walbridge, based on *Alice's Adventures in Wonderland* (1865) and *Through the Looking-Glass* (1871) by Lewis Carroll (Charles Dodgson, 1832–98); Music score by Oliver Wallace; Songs by Bob Hilliard, Sammy Fain, Don Raye, Gene DePaul, Mack David, Jerry Livingston and Al Hoffman; Songs—"I'm Late," "The Unbirthday Song," "All in the Golden Afternoon," "Very Good Advice," "In a World of My Own," "Painting the Roses Red" and "Alice in Wonderland."

Voices: Kathryn Beaumont (Alice), Ed Wynn (Mad Hatter), Richard Haydn (Caterpillar), Sterling Holloway (Cheshire Cat), Jerry Colonna (March Hare), Verna Felton (Queen of Hearts), Pat O'Malley (Walrus/Carpenter/Dee/Dum), Bill Thompson (White Rabbit/Dodo), Heather Angel (Alice's Sister), Joseph Kearns (Doorknob), Larry Grey (Bill), Queenie Leonard (Bird in the Tree), Dink Trout (King of Hearts), Doris Lloyd (The Rose), James MacDonald (Dormouse), The Mellomen (Card Painters); Notes: Comedian-actor Wynn (1886–1966) later played Uncle Albert in Disney's *Mary Poppins* (1964). Thompson was also the voice of MGM's Droopy.

Honors: Academy Award nomination—Musical Score.

8 *All Dogs Go to Heaven* (1989) *½
U.S.; Rated G; 84 mins.; Released November 1989 (Video: August 1990, MGM/UA); Sullivan Bluth.

Synopsis: A con-artist dog is killed by his crooked partner and goes to heaven, but is sent back to Earth to do a good deed.

Notes: Well-animated Don Bluth feature, marred by a dark, convoluted storyline and forgettable songs; The film—Bluth's fourth animated feature—took 19 months, $13 million and 1.5 million drawings to produce; Earned $26 million at the box office; Followed by a sequel in 1996; Produced by Bluth, Gary Goldman and John Pomeroy.

Credits: Director—Don Bluth; Co-Directors—Dan Kuenster, Gary Goldman; Animation Directors—John Pomeroy, Linda Miller, Ralph Zondag, Dick Zondag, Lorna Pomeroy-Cook, Jeff Etter, Ken Duncan; Screenplay by David N. Weiss; Story by Don Bluth, Ken Cromar, Gary Goldman, Larry Leker, Linda Miller, Monica Parker, John Pomeroy, Gary Schulman, David Steinberg and Weiss; Music score by Ralph Burns (Oscar-winning composer/musical director of *Cabaret* and *All That Jazz*); Songs by Charles Strouse (*Bye Bye Birdie, Annie*) and T.J. Kuenster; Songs—"You Can't Keep a Good Dog Down," "Let Me Be Surprised," "What's Mine Is Yours," "Let's Make Music Together," "Soon You'll Come Home," "Hallelujah" and "Love Survives" (by Al Kasha, Joel Hirschhorn and Michael Lloyd/perf by Irene Cara and Freddie Jackson).

Voices: Burt Reynolds (Charlie B. Barkin), Dom DeLuise (Itchy), Loni Anderson (Flo), Vic Tayback (Carface), Judith Barsi (Anne-Marie), Charles Nelson Reilly (Killer), Melba Moore (Whippet Angel), Daryl Gilley (Dog Caster), Candy Devine (Vera), Rob Fuller (Harold), Earleen Carey (Kate), Anna Manahan (Stella Dallas), Nigel Pegram (Sir Reginald), Ken Page (King Gator), Godfrey Quigley (Terrier), Jay Stevens (Mastiff), Cyndi Cozzo, Kelly Briley (Puppies), Thomas Durkin (Gambler Dog), Dana Rifkin (Fat Pup), John Carr, John Eddings, Jeff Etter, Dan Hofstedt, Dan Kuenster, Dan Molina, Mark Swan, Taylor Swanson, David N. Weiss, Dick Zondag; Note: Reynolds and Anderson were married for a time (1988–93). Tayback (1929–90) played Mel on TV's *Alice* (1976–85).

9 *All Dogs Go to Heaven 2* (1996) *

U.S.; Rated G; 82 mins.; Released March 29, 1996 (Video: August 1996, MGM/UA); MGM.

Synopsis: Bored with Dog Heaven, Charlie and his recently-deceased pal Itchy are allowed to return to Earth to retrieve a horn stolen from the angel Gabriel.

Notes: Lesser sequel to the 1989 Don Bluth film; The first feature from MGM's new animation division; Produced by Sabella, Jonathan Dern, Kelly Ward and Mark Young.

Credits: Directors—Paul Sabella, Larry Leker; Animation Director—Todd Waterman; Directing Animator—David Fleiss; Screenplay by Arne Olsen, Kelly Ward and Mark Young; Story by Ward and Young; Music score by Mark Watters; Songs by Barry Mann and Cynthia Weil, including "It Feels So Good to Be Bad."

Voices: Charlie Sheen (Charlie Barkin), Sheena Easton (Sasha La Fleur), Ernest Borgnine (Carface), Dom DeLuise (Itchy Itchiford), George Hearn (Red), Bebe Neuwirth (Anabelle), Adam Wylie (David), Hamilton Camp (Chihuahua), Wallace Shawn (Labradour MC), Bobby DiCicco (Thom), Jesse Corti (Charlie's singing voice); Notes: Sheen replaces Burt Reynolds who voiced Charlie in the original film. DeLuise returns as Itchy.

10 *Allegro Non Troppo* (1976) **$\frac{1}{2}$

Italian; Rated PG; 75 mins.; Bruno Bozzetto.

Synopsis: A collection of cartoon shorts illustrating the following pieces of classical music—"Bolero" (Ravel), "Firebird" (Stravinsky), "Valse Triste" (Sibelius), "Concerto in C Minor" (Vivaldi), "Prelude to the Afternoon of a Faun" (Debussy) and "Slavonic Dance No. 7" (Dvorak).

Notes: Highly-imaginative tribute to Disney's *Fantasia* from Italian animator Bruno Bozzetto; Includes comedic live-action scenes of a conductor (comedian Maurizio Nichetti, who also acted as assistant director) and orchestra between segments; Several noted musical conductors worked on the film, including Hans Stadlmair, Herbert von Karajan and Lorin Maazel; Bozzetto's (b. 1938) third animated feature. He later directed the Oscar-nominated short *Grasshoppers (Cavallette)* (1990).

Highlights: the "Valse Triste" sequence in which a cat wanders the desolate ruins of his former home, and "Bolero" which chronicles evolution on an unknown planet.

Credits: Director—Bruno Bozzetto; Screenplay by Bruno Bozzetto, Guido Manuli and Maurizio Nichetti.

Cast: Maurizio Nichetti, Nestor Garay, Maurizio Micheli, Maria Luisa Giovannini; **Note:** Nichetti later wrote, directed and starred in the film satire *The Icicle Thief* (1989).

11 *American Pop* (1981) *

U.S.; Rated R; 98 mins.; Released February 13, 1981 (Video: April 1998, Columbia TriStar); Ralph Bakshi.

Synopsis: A chronicle of American popular music following the generations of a musical family through the turmoil of the twentieth century.

Notes: Uninspired musical saga from Ralph Bakshi, featuring extensive use of rotoscoping (live-action tracing); Produced by Bakshi and Martin Ransohoff.

Credits: Director—Ralph Bakshi; Screenplay by Ronni Kern; Music by Lee Holdridge; Includes music by Jim Morrison, Bob Dylan, Jimi Hendrix, Janis Joplin, Frank Sinatra, Benny Goodman, Bob Seger, the Sex Pistols, and many others.

Voices: Ron Thompson (Tony/Pete), Marya Small (Frankie), Jerry Holland (Louie), Lisa Jane Persky (Bella), Roz Kelly (Eva Tanguay), Jeffrey Lippa (Zalmie), Frank DeKova (Crisco), Richard Singer (Benny), Elsa Raven (Hannele), Ben Frommer (Palumbo), Amy Levitt (Nancy), Leonard Stone (Leo), Eric Taslitz (Little Pete), Gene Borkan (Izzy), Richard Moll (Poet), Beatrice Colen (Prostitute), Vincent Schiavelli (Theater Owner), Hilary Beane (Showgirl #1).

12 *An American Tail* (1986) **

U.S.; Rated G; 80 mins.; Released November 1986 (Video: August 1987, MCA/Universal); Don Bluth (Sullivan Studios)/Amblin Entertainment.

Synopsis: The adventures of a young mouse who is separated from his family during their journey from Czarist Russia to America.

Notes: Entertaining family film with splendid animation making up for weaknesses in the story; Don Bluth's second animated feature (following 1982's *The Secret of NIMH*); The film's lead mouse, Fievel, was named after the grandfather of executive producer Steven Spielberg; Earned $47.5 million at the box office; Followed by a sequel in 1991; Produced by Bluth, Gary Goldman and John Pomeroy.

Credits: Director—Don Bluth; Directing Animators—John Pomeroy, Dan Kuenster, Linda Miller; Screenplay by Judy Freudberg and Tony Geiss (former writers for TV's *Sesame Street*), from a story created by David Kirschner. Music by James Horner, performed by The London Symphony Orchestra; Songs by Horner, Barry Mann and Cynthia Weil; Songs—"There Are No Cats in America," "Never Say Never," "A Duo" and "Somewhere Out There" (performed by Linda Ronstadt and James Ingrim over end titles).

Voices: Phillip Glasser (Fievel Mousekewitz), Dom DeLuise (Tiger), Madeline Kahn (Gussie Mausheimer), Nehemiah Persoff (Papa Mousekewitz), Christopher Plummer (Henri), John Finnegan (Warren T. Rat), Cathianne Blore (Bridget), Amy Green (Tanya Mousekewitz), Erica Yohn (Mama Mousekewitz), Pat Musick (Tony Toponi), Neil Ross (Honest John), Will Ryan (Digit), Hal Smith (Moe).

Honors: Academy Award nomination—Song ("Somewhere Out There"); Grammy Award—Song of the Year and Best Motion Picture Song ("Somewhere Out There").

13 *An American Tail: Fievel Goes West* (1991) *½

U.S.; Rated G; 74 mins.; Released November 22, 1991 (Video: March, 1992, MCA/Universal); Amblimation.

Synopsis: The Mousekewitz family travels out West where Fievel meets his hero, Sheriff Wylie Burp, and some new enemies.

Notes: Fine sequel to Don Bluth's 1986 hit will appeal more to kids than adults; The first feature from Steven Spielberg's London-based Amblimation Studio; Opened on the same day as Disney's *Beauty and the Beast*; Produced by Spielberg and Robert Watts.

Credits: Directors—Phil Nibbelink, Simon Wells; Supervising Animators—Nancy Beiman, Kristof Serrand, Rob Stevenhagen; Screenplay by Flinte Dille; Story by Charles Swenson; Created by David Kirschner. Music by James Horner; Songs by Horner and Will Jennings; Songs—"The Girl You Left Behind," "Way Out West" and "Dreams to Dream" (performed by Linda Ronstadt).

Voices: Phillip Glasser (Fievel Mousekewitz), James Stewart (Wylie Burp), John Cleese (Cat R. Waul), Dom DeLuise (Tiger), Jon Lovitz (T.R. Chula), Amy Irving (Miss Kitty), Erica Yohn (Mama Mousekewitz), Nehemiah Persoff (Papa Mousekewitz), Cathy Cavadini (Tanya Mousekewitz), Jack Angel, Fausto Bara, Vanna Bonta, Philip Clarke, Jennifer Darling, Annie Holliday, Sherry Lynn, Lev Mailer, Mickie McGowan, Larry Moss, Nigel Pegram, Patrick Pinney, Lisa Raggio, Lawrence Steffan, David Tate, Robert Watts; **Notes:** Film legend Stewart (*Mr. Smith Goes to Washington*, *It's a Wonderful Life*) played his last role in this film (he died in 1997 at 89). Cleese is a member of the British comedy troupe Monty Python.

14 *Anastasia* (1997) **

U.S.; Rated G; 93 mins.; Released November 21, 1997; Premiered in New York November 9, 1997 (Video: April 1998, Fox); Twentieth Century–Fox.

Synopsis: Anastasia, the only surviving child of Russia's doomed last Czar, must overcome the evil Rasputin in order to reclaim her imperial identity and be reunited with her Dowager Empress grandmother in 1920s Paris.

Notes: Lavishly-animated romantic fairy tale, filmed in widescreen CinemaScope, based on the legend of the last surviving member of the Romanov family; The first film from Twentieth Century–Fox's new feature animation division (located in Phoenix, Ariz.) and the ninth effort from Don Bluth and Gary Goldman; A three-year production costing $53 million and requiring some 350,000 drawings; Fox also produced the live-action version of *Anastasia* (1956) starring Ingrid Bergman; In real life, Czar Nicholas Romanov and his family (including 17-year-old Anastasia) were executed by Bolshevik revolutionaries on July 16, 1918 (two years after the assassination of Rasputin). The claim by Anna Anderson (Manahan) (1901–84) that she was Anastasia was disproved by DNA testing in 1992; Produced by Bluth and Goldman.

Credits: Directors—Don Bluth, Gary Goldman; Directing Animators—Len Simon, John Hill, Troy Saliba, Fernando Moro, Sandro Cleuzo, Paul Newberry; Screenplay by Bruce Graham, Bob Tzudiker, Noni White and Susan Gauthier, based on the play by Marcelle Maurette and screenplay by Arthur Laurents; Music by David Newman; Songs by Lynn Ahrens and Stephen Flaherty; Songs include "Journey to the Past," "A Rumor in St. Petersburg," "Learn to Do It" and "Once Upon a December"; **Note:** Ahrens and Flaherty also collaborated on the musical *Ragtime* (which opened on Broadway in 1998).

Voices: Meg Ryan (Anastasia, or "Anya"), Christopher Lloyd (Rasputin), John Cusack (Dimitri), Hank Azaria (Bartok the bat), Angela Lansbury (Dowager Empress Marie), Kelsey Grammer (Vladimir), Liz Callaway (Anya's singing voice), Bernadette Peters (Sophie), Kirsten Dunst (Young Anastasia), Lacey Chabert (Young Anastasia's singing voice), Jim Cummings (Rasputin's singing voice), Jonathan Dokuchitz (Dimitri's singing voice), Rick Jones, Andrea Martin, Glenn Walker Harris, Jr., Debra Mooney, Arthur Malet, Charity James; **Note:** Azaria also voices Moe, Apu and Chief Wiggum on TV's *The Simpsons*.

Honors: Academy Award nominations—Score and Song ("Journey to the Past").

15 *Animal Farm* (1954) **
British; Not Rated; 73 mins.; Halas-Batchelor.

Synopsis: The animals of Manor Farm revolt against their brutal master and set up their own government, which they soon find under the control of tyrannical pigs.

Notes: Powerful, well-produced animated translation of George Orwell's political fable; Britain's first feature-length cartoon was a three-year production which required 70 artists, 750 scenes, and 300,000 drawings; Orwell's original ending was changed to a more optimistic one, which led to some criticism; Produced by Halas-Batchelor Cartoon Films (formed in 1940 by the husband-and-wife animators), and presented by Louis de Rochemont (creator of the *March of Time* newsreel series).

Credits: Directors—John Halas, Joy Batchelor; Animation Director—John F. Reed. Screenplay by John Halas, Joy Batchelor, Lothar Wolff, Borden Mace and Philip Stapp, based on the 1945 novel by George Orwell (1903–50).

Voices: Gordon Heath (Narrator), Maurice Denham (All Animals).

16 *Animalympics* (1979) *½
U.S.; Not Rated; 79 mins.; Lisberger Studios Inc.

Synopsis: Animals from around the world come together to compete in the Animalympic Games.

Notes: Funny—but overlong—spoof of the Olympics and its TV coverage; The film began as a seven-minute short in 1976; Produced by Steven Lisberger and Donald Kushner.

Credits: Director—Steven Lisberger; Animation Director—Bill Kroyer. Screenplay by Michael Fremer and Steven Lisberger; Character Development and Story by Lisberger, Roger Allers and John Norton; Music composed and performed by Graham Gouldman (of the group 10cc).

Voices: Gilda Radner, Billy Crystal, Harry Shearer, Michael Fremer.

17 *Arabian Knight* (1995) *½
U.S.; Rated G; 72 mins.; Released August 25, 1995; Richard Williams/Miramax Films.

Synopsis: In ancient Baghdad, a poor cobbler named Tack becomes involved with a beautiful princess (Yum Yum) and an evil wizard (ZigZag).

Notes: Revamped version of a film originally started by Richard Williams in 1968 as *The Amazing Nasrudin* (he later retitled it *The Thief and the Cobbler* following some copyright problems). The Oscar-winning animator of *Who Framed Roger Rabbit* had worked on it off and on over the years before creditors took control of it in 1992 (Williams had gone over budget and still had about 15 mins. of footage to complete). Three years later Miramax bought the film and added new scenes (animated cheaply by others), songs and voices, changed the title, and released it briefly in theaters; Released on video as *The Thief and the Cobbler*; Produced by Williams and Imogen Sutton.

Credits: Director—Richard Williams; Master Animation—Ken Harris; Animators include Richard Williams, Art Babbitt, Emery Hawkins and Alex Williams (son of Richard); **Note:** Harris, who was a top animator for Chuck Jones at Warner Bros. (1937–64), was also the chief animator on Williams' Oscar-winning short *A Christmas Carol* (1972). Screenplay by Richard Williams and Margaret French; Music score by Robert Folk; Songs by Folk and Norman Gimbel.

Voices: Vincent Price (Zigzag), Matthew Broderick (Tack), Jennifer Beals (Princess Yum Yum), Eric Bogosian (Phido), Toni Collette (Nurse/Good Witch), Jonathan Winters (The Thief), Bobbi Page (Yum Yum's singing voice), Clive Revill (King Nod), Keven Dorsey (One-Eye), Donald Pleasence; **Note:** One of Price's last-released films (he died in October 1993). The actor was one of the film's original voice artists (he was hired back in the late '60s).

18 *The Aristocats* (1970) *½

U.S.; Rated G; 78 mins.; Premiered August 10, 1970, in Los Angeles; Released December 24, 1970 (Video: April, 1996, Walt Disney); Walt Disney.

Synopsis: In Paris in 1910, a cat and her three kittens are abandoned in the country by a conniving butler who wants to keep them from inheriting his employer's wealth.

Notes: Pleasing, but below par, Disney animated feature—the first one produced after Walt Disney's death (in 1966), although he did help conceive the idea for it back in 1963; French actor-singer Maurice Chevalier came out of retirement (at age 80) to sing the film's title song; The film took four years and $4 million to produce; Produced by Wolfgang Reitherman and Winston Hibler.

Credits: Director—Wolfgang Reitherman; Animation Directors—Milt Kahl, Ollie Johnston, Frank Thomas, John Lounsbery; Screenplay by Larry Clemmons, Vance Gerry, Ken Anderson, Frank Thomas, Eric Cleworth, Julius Svendsen and Ralph Wright, based on a story by Tom Rowe and Tom McGowan; Music by George Bruns; Songs by Robert B. and Richard M. Sherman, Terry Gilkyson, Floyd Huddleston and Al Rinker; Songs—"Scales and Arpeggios," "She Never Felt Alone," "Thomas O'Malley Cat," "Ev'rybody Wants to Be a Cat" and the title tune (sung by Maurice Chevalier); **Note:** Chevalier's last film effort (he died in January 1972).

Voices: Eva Gabor (Duchess), Phil Harris (J. Thomas O'Malley), Sterling Holloway (Roquefort), Scatman Crothers (Scatcat), Paul Winchell (Chinese Cat), Lord Tim Hudson (English Cat), Vito Scotti (Italian Cat), Thurl Ravenscroft (Russian Cat), Dean Clark (Berlioz), Liz English (Marie), Gary Dublin (Toulouse), Nancy Kulp (Frou Frou), Pat Buttram (Napoleon), George Lindsey (Lafayette), Monica Evans (Abigail), Carole Shelley (Amelia), Charles Lane (Lawyer), Hermione Baddeley (Madame Bonfamille), Roddy Maude-Roxby (Butler), Bill Thompson (Uncle Waldo), Ruth Buzzi (Frou Frou's singing voice), Pete Renoudet (French Milkman); **Notes:** Gabor (1921–95) was later the voice of Miss Bianca in Disney's *The Rescuers* (1977) and *The Rescuers Down Under* (1990). She and Buttram both starred in TV's *Green Acres* (1965–71). Winchell was also the voice of Tigger in Disney's "Winnie the Pooh" shorts.

19 *Babar: The Movie* (1989) *½

Canadian-French; Rated G; 79 mins.; Released August, 1989; Nelvana/Ellipse.

Synopsis: Babar the elephant king tells his children about when he was a boy king and had to defend Elephantland from marauding rhinos.

Notes: Agreeable animated tale for kids based on the French children's stories (the first of which was published in 1931); 100 French and Canadian animators worked on the film; Produced by Patrick Loubert, Michael Hirsh and Clive A. Smith.

Credits: Director—Alan Bunce; Director of Animation—John Lawrence Collins. Screenplay by Peter Sauder, J.D. Smith, John de Klein, Raymond Jafelice and Alan Bunce; Story by Sauder, Patrick Loubert and Michael Hirsh, based on the children's books by Jean and Laurent de Brunhoff; Music score by Milan Kymlicka; Songs by Maribeth Solomon, Phil Balsam, Kevan Staples, Marvin Dolgay and Carole Pope; Songs—"Elephantland March," "Best We Both Can Be," "Monkey Business," "Committee Song" and "Rataxes Song.".

Voices: Gordon Pinsent (King Babar), Gavin Magrath (Boy Babar), Elizabeth Hanna (Queen Celeste/The Old Lady), Sarah Polley (Young Celeste), Chris Wiggins (Cornelius), Lisa Yamanaka (Isabelle), Marsha Moreau (Flora), Bobby Beckon (Pom), Amos Crawley (Alexander), Stephen Ouimette (Pompadour), John Stocker (Zephir), Charles Kerr (Rataxes), Stuart Stone (Arthur), Carl Banas (Old Tusk), Angela Fusco (Celeste's Mom); **Note:** Polley starred in the award-winning TV series *Avonlea*.

20 *Balto* (1995) * $\frac{1}{2}$

U.S.-British; Rated G; 77 mins.; Released December 22, 1995 (Video: April, 1996, MCA/Universal); Amblimation.

Synopsis: In Alaska in 1925, a half-breed (half-dog, half-wolf) comes to the rescue of a dog sled team bringing antitoxins to Nome, where there has been a diphtheria outbreak.

Notes: Children's adventure tale, based on a true story, helped by Bob Hoskins' comic turn as the snow goose sidekick; Includes some live-action scenes; Produced by Steven Hickner.

Credits: Director—Simon Wells; Supervising Animators—Jeffrey J. Varab, Dick Zondag, Kristof Serrand, Rob Stevenhagen, Sahin Ersoz, Rodolphe Guenoden, Nicolas Marlet, William Salazar, David Bowers, Patrick Mate; Screenplay by Cliff Ruby, Elana Lesser, David Steven Cohen and Roger S.H. Schulman; Music by James Horner.

Cast/Voices: Miriam Margolyes (Grandma Rosy), Lola Bates-Campbell (Granddaughter); Kevin Bacon (Balto), Bob Hoskins (Boris), Bridget Fonda (Jenna), Jim Cummings (Steele), Phil Collins (Muk/Luk), Jack Angel (Nikki), Danny Mann (Kaltag), Robby Rist (Star), Juliette Brewer (Rosy), Sandra Searles Dickinson (Sylvie/Dixie/Rosy's Mother), Donald Sinden (Doc), William Roberts (Rosy's Father), Garrick Hagon (Telegraph Operator), Bill Bailey (Butcher), Big Al (Town Dog), Mike McShane, Miriam Margolyes, Austin Tichenor, Reed Martin, Adam Long (Extra voices).

21 *Bambi* (1942) ***

U.S.; Rated G; 69 mins.; Released August 13, 1942 (Video: September 1989, Walt Disney); Walt Disney.

Synopsis: A coming-of-age tale about a fawn who learns—with the help of his woodland friends—the true meaning of love and friendship and how to survive the dangers that lurk in the forest.

Notes: The Disney Studio's fifth animated feature is a perfect blending of lyrical storytelling and brilliant, detailed animation. A true masterpiece that is both funny and emotionally powerful; The film—said to be Walt Disney's personal favorite—was in production from 1937 to 1942 (while Disney was also working on *Pinocchio*, *Fantasia* and *Dumbo*), and required nearly 50 artists and four million drawings; The forest in the film is based on photographic studies of the Maine woods; In 1942 Disney turned production toward the war effort, making this the studio's last fully-animated, single-story feature until 1950's *Cinderella*.

Highlights: the "Little April Shower" storm sequence, the memorable—and heart-wrenching—death of Bambi's mother, and the thrilling forest fire finale.

Credits: Supervising Director—David Hand; Sequence Directors—James Algar, Bill Roberts, Norman Wright, Sam Armstrong, Paul Satterfield, Graham Heid; Supervising Animators—Franklin Thomas, Milton Kahl, Eric Larson, Oliver M. Johnston, Jr.; Screenplay by Larry Morey, based on a 1928 children's story by Felix Salten; Story Direction by Perce Pearce; Music score by Frank Churchill and Edward H. Plumb; Songs by Churchill and Larry Morey; Songs—"Little April Shower," "The Thumper Song," "Let's Sing a Gay Little Spring Song," "Twitterpated," "Looking for Romance" and "Love Is a Song.".

Voices: Bobby Stewart (Bambi), Peter Behn (Thumper the rabbit), Stan Alexander (Flower the skunk), Cammie King (Faline), Paula Winslowe (Bambi's Mother), Mary Lansing (Aunt Ena/Mrs. Possum), Fred Shields (Prince of the Forest), Bill Wright (Friend Owl), Thelma Boardman (Mrs. Quail), Marjorie Lee (Mrs. Rabbit), Donnie Dunagan, Hardie Albright, John Sutherland, Tim Davis, Sterling Holloway, Ann Gillis, Sam Edwards, Marion Darlington, Thelma Hubbard, Otis Harlan, Jeanne Christy, Janet Chapman, Bobette Audrey, Jack Horner, Francesca Santoro, Babs Nelson, Sandra Lee Richards, Dolyn Bramston Cook, Elouise Woodward; **Note:** Behn was only 4 years old when he provided Thumper's voice, one of the most memorable cartoon voices ever recorded.

Honors: Academy Award nominations—Score, Song ("Love Is a Song") and Sound (C.O. Slyfield).

22 *Batman: Mask of the Phantasm* (1993) $*\frac{1}{2}$
U.S.; Rated PG; 77 mins.; Released December 1993 (Video: April, 1994, Warner); Warner Bros.

Synopsis: Bruce Wayne (aka Batman) must deal with a mysterious, death-masked villain who is killing off mob bosses, as well as the unexpected return of his first love.

Notes: Stylishly-drawn "cartoon noir" from the producers of Fox TV's Emmy-winning *Batman: The Animated Series* (1992–); Aka *Batman: The Animated Movie*; Created by Bob Kane, Batman has appeared in comic books (since 1939), a live-action TV series (1966–68), several cartoon series and 5 films (1966, 89, 92, 95, 97); Produced by Eric Radomski, Bruce W. Timm and Alan Burnett.

Credits: Directors—Eric Radomski, Bruce W. Timm; Sequence Directors—Kevin Altieri, Boyd Kirkland, Frank Paur, Dan Riba; Screenplay by Michael Reaves, Alan Burnett, Paul Dini and Martin Pasko, based on the DC Comics characters created by Bob Kane. Music by Shirley Walker.

Voices: Kevin Conroy (Bruce Wayne/Batman), Mark Hamill (Joker), Dana Delany (Andrea Beaumont), Stacy Keach (Carl Beaumont/The Phantasm), Efram Zimbalist, Jr. (Alfred), Abe Vigoda (Salvatore Valestra), Hart Bochner (Arthur Reeves), Dick Miller (Chuckie Sol), John P. Ryan (Buzz Bronski), Robert Costanzo (Det. Bullock), Bob Hastings (Comm. Gordon).

23 *Beauty and the Beast* (1991) ***
U.S.; Rated G; 84 mins.; Released November 22, 1991 (Video: October 1992, Walt Disney); Walt Disney.

Synopsis: Classic tale about an arrogant prince who is turned into a hideous beast and whose only hope of turning back is by gaining the love of a beautiful maiden.

Notes: First-rate Disney rendering of the 18th-century French fairy tale, beautifully animated, with colorful supporting characters and a great musical score; Disney's 30th animated feature and the first animated film ever to receive an Academy Award nomination for Best Picture; More than 500 animators, artists and technicians worked on the $30 million production; An elaborate stage version of the film opened on Broadway in April, 1994; Made-for-video sequel—*Beauty and the Beast: The Enchanted Christmas* (1997); Produced by Don Hahn.

Highlights: the opening musical number introducing Belle, and the dazzling "Be Our Guest" production number.

Credits: Directors—Gary Trousdale, Kirk Wise; Supervising Animators—James Baxter, Glen Keane, Andreas Deja, Nik Ranieri, Will Finn, David Pruiksma, Ruben A. Aquino, Chris Wahl, Russ Edmonds; Screenplay by Linda Woolverton; Musical score by Alan Menken; Songs by Menken and Howard Ashman (the songwriters for *The Little Mermaid*); Songs—"Belle," "Gaston," "Be Our Guest," "Something There," "Beauty and the Beast" and "The Mob Song"; **Note:** Menken and Ashman's last full score together (Ashman died of AIDS in March, 1991).

Voices: Paige O'Hara (Belle), Robbie Benson (The Beast), Richard White (Gaston), Jerry Orbach (Lumiere the candlestick), David Ogden Stiers (Cogsworth the clock/Narrator), Angela Lansbury (Mrs. Potts the teapot), Bradley Michael Pierce (Chip), Rex Everhart (Maurice), Jesse Corti (Lefou), Hal Smith (Philippe), Jo Anne Worley (Wardrobe), Mary Kay Bergman (Bimbette), Brian Cummings (Stove), Alvin Epstein (Bookseller), Tony Jay (Monsieur D'Arque), Alec Murphy (Baker), Kimmy Robertson (Featherduster), Kath Soucie (Bimbette), Frank Welker (Footstool/Special Vocal Effects); **Note:** Stiers played Major Winchester (1977–83) on TV's *M*A*S*H*.

Honors: Academy Awards—Original Score and Song ("Beauty and the Beast"), also nominated for Best Picture, Sound (Terry Porter, Mel Metcalfe, David J. Hudson and Doc Kane) and Songs ("Belle" and "Be Our Guest"); Other awards—Golden Globe Awards (Best Musical or Comedy Picture, Best Original Score, Best Song).

24 *Beavis and Butt-Head Do America* (1996) $*\frac{1}{2}$

U.S.; Rated PG-13; 80 mins.; Released December 20, 1996 (Video: June, 1997, Paramount); MTV Productions/Geffen Pictures.

Synopsis: While in search of their stolen TV set, Beavis and Butt-Head are mistaken for hired killers and soon find themselves on a cross-country journey and targets of an FBI manhunt.

Notes: Feature debut of the moronic metalhead stars of MTV's popular series (1993–97). For fans; director Mike Judge is also the creator of the hit series *King of the Hill* (which debuted in January 1997); A box-office hit, grossing $63 million (it is the only fully-animated, non–Disney film to gross more than $50 million in North America); Produced by Abby Terkuhle.

Highlights: the opening spoof of '70s TV cop shows, and Beavis' hallucination (based on the artwork of Rob Zombie) in the desert.

Credits: Director—Mike Judge; Animation Director—Yvette Kaplan; Sequence Directors—Mike de Seve, Miguel Martinez Joffre, Geoffrey Johnson, Tony Kluck, Ray Kosarin, Carol Millican, Brian Mulroney, Ilya Skorupsky, Paul Sparagano; Animation Director (hallucination scene)—Chris Prynoski; Screenplay by Mike Judge and Joe Stillman, based on characters created by Judge; Music by John Frizzell; Songs include "Two Cool Guys" (theme song, performed by Isaac Hayes) and "Lesbian Seagull."

Voices: Mike Judge (Beavis/Butt-Head/Tom Anderson/Mr. Van Driessen/Principal McVicker), Robert Stack (Agent Fleming), Cloris Leachman (Old Woman), Demi Moore (Dallas Grimes), Bruce Willis (Muddy Grimes), Greg Kinnear (Agent Bork), Eric Bogosian (Ranger/others), Richard Linklater (Tour Bus Driver), David Letterman (Motley Crue Roadie #1), Jacqueline Barba, Pamela Blair, Kristofor Brown, Tony Darling, John Doman, Francis Dumaurier, Jim Flaherty, Tim Guinee, Toby Huss, Sam Johnson, Rosemary McNamara, Harsh Nayyar, Karen Phillips, Dale Reeves, Michael Ruschak, Gail Thomas; **Note:** Letterman's performance is credited to Earl Hofert.

25 *Bebe's Kids* (1992) *

U.S.; Rated PG-13; 73 mins.; Released July 31, 1992 (Video: March, 1993, Paramount); Hudlin Bros/Hyperion Studio.

Synopsis: Comedian Robin Harris and his girlfriend Jamika baby-sit three mischievous kids at an amusement park.

Notes: Mediocre animated comedy based on the stand-up routine of actor-comedian Robin Harris (who appeared in the films *Do the Right Thing* and *House Party*); Originally planned as a live-action film, it was switched to animation when Harris died suddenly of a heart attack in 1990 at age 36; Produced by Willard Carroll and Thomas L. Wilhite.

Credits: Director—Bruce Smith; Animation Directors—Lennie Graves, Chris Buck, Frans Vischer; Screenplay by Reginald Hudlin, based on characters created by Robin Harris; Music by John Barnes; Songs (18 in all) include "Deeper," "Can't Say Goodbye," "Standing on the Rock of Love" (performed by Aretha Franklin) and "I Want to Thank You for Your Love."

Voices: Faizon Love (Robin Harris), Vanessa Bell Calloway (Jamika), Wayne Collins (Leon), Jonell Green (LaShawn), Marques Houston (Kahlil), Tone-Loc (Pee Wee), Myra J. (Dorothea), Nell Carter (Vivian), John Witherspoon, Chino "Fats" Williams, Rodney Winfield, George Wallace (Card Players), Brad Sanders (Bartender), Reynaldo Rey (Lush), BeBe Drake-Massey (Barfly), Jack Lynch (Richie), Phillip Glasser (Opie), Louie Anderson (Security Guard #1), Tom Everett (Security Guard #2), Kerrigan Mahan (Security Guard #3/Fun World Patrolman), Susan Silo (Ticketlady Saleswoman/Nuclear Mother/ Rodney Rodent), Peter Renaday (Announcer/President Lincoln/Impericon/Tommy Toad), Rich Little (President Nixon), David Robert Cobb (Titanic Captain), Barry Diamond (Nuclear Father/Motorcycle Cop).

26 *Bedknobs and Broomsticks* (1971) **
U.S.; Rated G; 117 mins.; Released October 7, 1971; Walt Disney.

Synopsis: In 1940, an amateur witch and three evacuee children use magic to help the British war effort.

Notes: Live-action Disney fantasy doesn't recreate the magic of *Mary Poppins*, but is still fun, with fine special effects and a 20-minute animation sequence; The film was cut by 20 mins. for its 1979 rerelease (24 mins were restored to the film for its 25th anniversary in 1996); .

Highlight: the animated sequence in which the live-actors visit the Isle of Niboombu.

Credits: Director—Robert Stevenson; **Note:** Stevenson (1905–86) directed 19 live-action Disney films (1957–76), including *The Absent-Minded Professor* (1961) and *Mary Poppins* (1964). Produced by Bill Walsh. Animation Director—Ward Kimball; Screenplay by Bill Walsh and Don DaGradi, based on the book by Mary Norton; Music and lyrics by Richard M. and Robert B. Sherman; Musical Director—Irwin Kostal; Songs—"The Old Home Guard," "The Age of Not Believing," "Eglantine," "Portabello Road," "The Beautiful Briny Sea" and "Substitutiary Locomotion."

Cast: Angela Lansbury (Eglantine Price), David Tomlinson (Mr. Emelius Browne), Ian Weighill (Charlie), Roy Smart (Paul), Cindy O'Callaghan (Carrie), Roddy McDowall (Mr. Jelk), Sam Jaffe (Bookman), John Ericson (Col. Heller), Bruce Forsyth (Swinburne), Tessie O'Shea (Mrs. Hobday), Arthur E. Gould-Porter (Capt. Greer), Ben Wrigley (Street Sweeper), Reginald Owen (Gen. Teagler), Cyril Delevanti, Rick Traeger, Manfred Lating (German Sergeants), John Orchard (Vendor); **Voices:** Lennie Weinrib (Secretary Bird/Lion), Robert Holt (Mr. Codfish), Dal McKennon (Bear); **Notes:** Four-time Tony-winner Lansbury later played Jessica Fletcher on TV's *Murder, She Wrote* (1984–96). Tomlinson played the father in *Mary Poppins*.

Honors: Academy Award—Special Visual Effects (Alan Maley, Eustace Lycett and Danny Lee), also nominated for Art Direction, Score, Song ("The Age of Not Believing") and Costume Design.

27 *The Black Cauldron* (1985) **
U.S.; Rated PG; 80 mins.; Released July 24, 1985; Walt Disney.

Synopsis: In Medieval times, a young boy named Taran sets out on an adventure that pits him against the dark forces of the evil Horned King.

Notes: Disney's 25th animated feature—and the studio's first to receive a PG rating—is a spectacular, lavishly-animated adventure, but lacks the charm and strong characterization of earlier classics; The second Disney animated feature to be photographed in widescreen Technirama 70 (the first was 1959's *Sleeping Beauty*); Released in Dolby Stereo surround sound; The film took five years, more than 200 studio employees (including 68 animators) and 2,519,200 drawings to produce; The first film to utilize Disney's revolutionary Animation Photo Transfer process, which transfers drawings to cells with greater speed and resolution than the usual Xeroxing method; One of Disney's most expensive animated features (it cost $25 million, yet earned less than $10 million in North American release); Produced by Joe Hale.

Credits: Directors—Ted Berman, Richard Rich; Screenplay by David Jonas, Vance Gerry, Ted Berman, Richard Rich, Al Wilson, Roy Morita, Peter Young, Art Stevens and Joe Hale, based on Lloyd Alexander's Newberry Award-winning five-book series *The*

Chronicles of Prydain (1964–68); Music by Elmer Bernstein (*To Kill a Mockingbird, The Great Escape*); Song—"Fflewddur's Song" by Richard Bowden and Richard Rich.

Voices: Grant Bardsley (Taran), John Hurt (Horned King), Susan Sheridan (Eilonwy), Freddy Jones (Dallben), Nigel Hawthorne (Fflewddur), Arthur Malet (King Eidilleg), John Byner (Gurgi/Doli), Eda Reiss Merin (Orddu), Adele Malis-Morey (Orwen), Billie Hayes (Orgoch), Phil Fondacaro (Creeper/Henchman), Lindsay Rich, Brian Call, Gregory Levinson (Fairfolk), Peter Renaday, Wayne Allwine, Steve Hale, James Almanzar, Phil Nibbelink, Jack Laing (Henchmen), John Huston (Narrator).

28 *Bon Voyage, Charlie Brown (and Don't Come Back!)* (1980) * $\frac{1}{2}$
U.S.; Rated G; 75 mins.; Lee Mendelson-Bill Melendez.

Synopsis: The Peanuts gang become exchange students and spend two weeks in France.
Notes: The fourth "Peanuts" feature film is good kids' fare, but not of the same quality as the original specials.
Credits: Director—Bill Melendez; Co-Director—Phil Roman. Screenplay by Charles M. Schulz, based on his comic-strip characters; Music by Ed Bogas and Judy Munsen.
Voices: Daniel Anderson, Scott Beach, Casey Carlson, Debbie Muller, Patricia Patts, Laura Planting, Arrin Skelley, Bill Melendez, Annalisa Bortolin, Roseline Rubens, Pascale de Barolet.

29 *A Boy Named Charlie Brown* (1969) **
U.S.; Rated G; 85 mins.; Lee Mendelson-Bill Melendez.

Synopsis: After failing on the baseball field, Charlie Brown travels to New York City to try his luck in a national spelling bee.
Notes: The first and best feature film based on Charles M. Schulz's "Peanuts" comic-strip. A delight for both kids and adults; The "Peanuts" strip, which debuted in 1950, was brought to TV in 1965 with the Emmy/Peabody Award–winning special *A Charlie Brown Christmas*. The beloved characters have since appeared in some 50 specials, a series (1983–86) and 4 films (1969–80); Followed by *Snoopy, Come Home* (1972); Opened in New York December 4, 1969.
Highlight: Snoopy's elegant ice-skating to Vince Guaraldi's "Skating."
Credits: Director—Bill Melendez; **Note:** Melendez was an animator at Warner Bros. in the '40s and at UPA in the '50s; Screenplay by Charles M. Schulz, based on his comic-strip characters; Music score/adaptation by Vince Guaraldi; Songs by Rod McKuen, John Scott Trotter (also arranger-conductor), Bill Melendez and Al Shean; Songs include "Failure Face," "Champion Charlie Brown," "We Lost Again," "Class Champion," "National Spelling Bee," "B-E-A-G-L-E," "I'm Never Going to School Again," "Big City," "Homecoming," "I Before E" and the title tune (sung by McKuen); Beethoven's "Piano Sonata Opus 13 (Pathetique)" performed by Ingolf Dahl; **Note:** Jazz composer-pianist Guaraldi (1928–76), who won a Grammy for his 1962 hit "Cast Your Fate to the Winds," scored 16 "Peanuts" TV specials (1965–76).
Voices: Peter Robbins (Charlie Brown), Pamelyn Ferdin (Lucy), Glenn Gilger (Linus), Andy Pforsich (Schroeder), Sally Dryer (Patty), Anne Altieri (Violet), Erin Sullivan (Sally), Linda Mendelson (Frieda), Christopher DeFaria (Pig Pen), Bill Melendez (Snoopy), Betty Allan, Loulie Norman, Gloria Wood (singers), David Carey, Guy Pforsich (boys); **Notes:** Robbins provided Charlie Brown's voice for the first 6 "Peanuts" specials (1965–69). He and Ferdin both appeared in the TV series *Blondie* (1968–69).
Honors: Academy Award nomination—Original Song Score (McKuen, Trotter, Melendez, Shean, Guaraldi).

30 *The Brave Little Toaster* (1987) **

U.S.; Rated G; 89 mins.; Released May, 1987; Hyperion/Kushner-Locke.

Synopsis: Five household appliances—Toaster, Lampy, Blanky, Radio and Kirby—travel to the city to find their owners.

Notes: Funny, tuneful adventure for all ages; Disney bought the Thomas Disch story in 1983, originally planning to produce it using computer animation, with John Lasseter as director. When Disney dropped the project, Lasseter left and joined the computer-graphics studio Pixar, where he would later direct the groundbreaking computer-animated feature *Toy Story* (1995); Produced by Tom Wilhite and Willard Carroll.

Credits: Director—Jerry Rees; Directing Animators—Randy Cartwright, Joe Ranft, Rebecca Rees; Screenplay by Jerry Rees and Joe Ranft; Screen Story by Rees, Ranft and Brian McEntee, based on the novella by Thomas M. Disch; Music composed and conducted by David Newman; Original songs by Van Dyke Parks, Bob Walter and Rick Johnston; Songs—"City of Light," "It's a B-Movie," "Cutting Edge," "Worthless" and "Hidden Meadow"; **Note:** Newman is the son of famed film composer Alfred Newman (1901–70) and cousin of singer-songwriter Randy Newman.

Voices: Jon Lovitz (Radio), Tim Stack (Lampy/Zeke), Timothy E. Day (Blanky/Young Master), Thurl Ravenscroft (Kirby), Deanna Oliver (Toaster), Phil Hartman (Air Conditioner/Hanging Lamp), Joe Ranft (Elmo St. Peters), Judy Toll (Mish-Mash/Sewing Machine), Wayne Kaatz (Bob), Colette Savage (Chris), Mindy Stern (Mother/Sewing Machine), Jim Jackman (Pugsy), Randy Cook (Entertainment Complex), Randy Bennett (Computer), Jonathan Benair (Black-and-White TV), Louis Conti (Spanish Announcer); **Note:** Lovitz and Hartman were both cast members of TV's *Saturday Night Live*.

31 *Bravestarr* (1988) $\frac{1}{2}$

U.S.; Rated G; 91 mins.; Released September 1988; Filmation.

Synopsis: Western sci-fi tale about a cowboy named Bravestarr who must save his planet from an evil cattle baron.

Notes: Dull, poorly-animated feature based on the TV series (syndicated, 1987); From Filmation, makers of TV's *He-Man and the Masters of the Universe*; Originally titled *Bravestarr, The Legend*; Given only a limited theatrical release; Produced by Lou Scheimer.

Credits: Director—Tom Tataranowicz; Supervising Animator—Brett Hisey; Screenplay by Bob Forward and Steve Hayes; Music by Frank W. Becker.

Voices: Charlie Adler, Susan Blu, Pat Fraley, Ed Gilbert, Alan Oppenheimer, Erik Gunden, Erika Scheimer.

32 *The Bugs Bunny/Road Runner Movie* (1979) **

U.S.; Rated G; 92 mins.; Released September 30, 1979; Warner Bros.

Synopsis: Bugs Bunny looks back on his career during a tour of his mansion. Includes excerpts from eight cartoons, a compilation of 31 gags (from 16 "Road Runner-Coyote" shorts) and the following five cartoons shown complete: *Hareway to the Stars, What's Opera, Doc?, Duck Amuck, Bully for Bugs* and *Rabbit Fire*. See SHORTS.

Notes: Warner Bros.' first cartoon compilation film is the most satisfying, featuring a number of Chuck Jones classics shorts; Original title—*The Great American Chase*; Contains about 20 minutes of new animation; Features the Warner cartoon stars Bugs Bunny, Daffy Duck, the Road Runner, Wile E. Coyote, Elmer Fudd, Porky Pig, Pepe Le Pew, and others; Followed by Friz Freleng's *The Looney, Looney, Looney Bugs Bunny Movie* (1981); Produced by Jones.

Credits: Director—Chuck Jones; Screenplay by Chuck Jones and Michael Maltese; Music by Carl Stalling, Milt Franklyn and Dean Elliot.

Voices: Mel Blanc (Bugs/Daffy/Porky/Pepe/others), Arthur Q. Bryan (Elmer Fudd).

33 *Bugs Bunny Superstar* (1975) ** $\frac{1}{2}$
U.S.; Not Rated; 90 mins.; Hair Raising Films.

Synopsis: A documentary on Bugs Bunny and other Warner Bros. cartoon creations. Includes interviews with animators, behind-the-scenes footage and nine classic cartoons— *What's Cookin' Doc?*, *A Wild Hare* (Oscar-nominee), *A Corny Concerto*, *I Taw a Putty Tat*, *Rhapsody Rabbit*, *Walky Talky Hawky* (Oscar-nominee), *My Favorite Duck*, *Hair-Raising Hare* and *The Old Grey Hare*. See SHORTS.
Notes: Enjoyable look at the men behind the rabbit, with nine excellent Warner Bros. cartoons (dating from 1940 to 1948); Famed cartoon directors Bob Clampett, Friz Freleng and Tex Avery are interviewed; Produced by Larry Jackson.
Credits: Director—Larry Jackson; Cartoons directed by Bob Clampett, Tex Avery, Friz Freleng, Chuck Jones, Robert McKimson; Narrated by Orson Welles.
Voices: Mel Blanc, Arthur Q. Bryan.

34 *Bugs Bunny's 3rd Movie: 1001 Rabbit Tales* (1982) *
U.S.; Rated G; 76 mins.; Released November 19, 1982; Warner Bros.

Synopsis: In the Arabian Desert, Sultan (Yosemite) Sam forces book salesman Bugs Bunny to read him stories. Cartoons shown— *Ali Baba Bunny*, *Apes of Wrath*, *Bewitched Bunny*, *Cracked Quack*, *Goldimouse and the Three Cats*, *Mexican Boarders*, *One Froggy Evening*, *The Pied Piper of Guadalupe* (Oscar nominee), *Red Riding Hoodwinked*, *Tweety and the Beanstalk* and *Wise Quackers*. See SHORTS.
Notes: Weak Warner Bros. compilation feature (the third), with only a few superior cartoons among the 11 shown (dating from 1949 to 1962); Features Bugs Bunny, Daffy Duck, Porky Pig, Elmer Fudd, Sylvester, Tweety, Speedy Gonzales, Yosemite Sam, and others; Followed by *Daffy Duck's Movie: Fantastic Island* (1983); Produced by Friz Freleng.
Credits: Directors—David Detiege, Art Davis, Bill Perez; Cartoon Directors—Chuck Jones, Friz Freleng; Screenplay by John Dunn, David Detiege and Friz Freleng.; Music by Rob Walsh, Milt Franklyn, Bill Lava and Carl Stalling.
Voices: Mel Blanc, Shep Menken, Lennie Weinrib, June Foray, Arthur Q. Bryan.

35 *The Care Bears Adventure in Wonderland* (1987) $\frac{1}{2}$
Canadian; Rated G; 75 mins.; Released August 1987; Nelvana.

Synopsis: The Care Bears go with Alice through the looking glass to keep an evil wizard from becoming king.
Notes: Third entry in the series of Care Bears features. Strictly for young viewers; Produced by Michael Hirsh, Patrick Loubert and Clive A. Smith.
Credits: Director—Raymond Jafelice; Animation Director—John Lawrence Collins; Screenplay by Susan Snooks and John De Klein, from a story by Peter Sauder; Music by Patricia Cullen; Songs by John Sebastian (former leader of The Lovin' Spoonful) and Maribeth Solomon; Songs—"Have You Seen This Girl," "Mad About Hats," "The King of Wonderland" and "Rise and Shine" (performed by Natalie Cole).
Voices: Tracey Moore (Alice), Keith Knight (White Rabbit), Colin Fox (Wizard), John Stocker (Dim/Cheshire Cat), Don McManus (Caterpillar), Elizabeth Hanna (Queen), Alan Fawcett (Flamingo), Keith Hampshire (Mad Hatter/Jabberwocky), Alyson Court (Princess), Bob Dermer (Grumpy Bear), Eva Almos (Swift Heart Bear), Dan Hennessey (Brave Heart Lion/Dum), Jim Henshaw (Tender Heart Bear), Maria Lukofsky (Good Luck Bear), Luba Goy (Lotsa-Heart Elephant).

36 *The Care Bears Movie* (1985) $\frac{1}{2}$
Canadian; Rated G; 75 mins.; Released March, 1985; Nelvana.

Synopsis: The Care Bears rescue a boy magician under the spell of an evil spirit that is trying to reduce the amount of caring in the world.

Notes: Feature debut of the overly-cute 'n' cuddly bears from the popular children's books, toys and TV series (1985–90); Followed by two sequels (1986, 1987); Produced by Michael Hirsh, Patrick Loubert and Clive A. Smith.

Credits: Director—Arna Selznick; Animation Directors—Charlie Bonifacio, Anne Marie Bradwell; Screenplay by Peter Sauder; Music by Patricia Cullen, with David Bird and Walt Woodward; Songs written and performed by Carole King and John Sebastian; Songs—"Care-a-Lot" and "Home Is in Your Heart.".

Voices: Mickey Rooney (Mr. Cherrywood), Georgia Engel (Love-a-Lot Bear), Jackie Burroughs (The Spirit), Sunny Besen Thrasher (Jason), Harry Dean Stanton (Lion), Eva Almos, Bob Dermer, Gloria Figura, Janet Laine-Green, Dan Hennessey, Maria Lukofsky, Patrice Black, Jayne Eastwood, Cree Summer Francks, Luba Goy, Jim Henshaw, Pauline Rennie, Brent Titcomb, Melleny Brown, Anni Evans, Brian George, Terri Hawkes, Hadley Kay, Billie Mae Richards, Louise Goffin, Sherry Goffin, Robbie Kondor, Levi Larky.

37 *Care Bears Movie II: A New Generation* (1986)

Canadian; Rated G; 77 mins.; Released March 1986 (Video: August 1986, RCA/Columbia); Nelvana.

Synopsis: The Care Bears try to teach the importance of sharing and caring to two selfish youngsters at a summer camp.

Notes: Second Care Bears feature is another bland, poorly-animated affair for kids; Produced by Michael Hirsh, Patrick Loubert and Clive A. Smith.

Credits: Director—Dale Schott; Animation Director—Charles Bonifacio; Screenplay by Peter Sauder; Music by Patricia Cullen; Songs by Dean and Carol Parks, Alan O'Day; Songs—"I Care for You" (performed by Stephen Bishop), "Growing Up" (performed by Bishop), "The Fight Song" (performed by Debbie Allen), "Our Beginning," "Forever Young" and "Flying My Colors."

Voices: Hadley Kay (Dark Heart/The Boy), Chris Wiggins (Great Wishing Star), Cree Summer Francks (Christy), Alyson Court (Dawn), Michael Fatini (John), Sunny Besen Thrasher (Camp Champ), Maxine Miller (True Heart Bear), Pam Hyatt (Noble Heart Horse), Dan Hennessey (Brave Heart Lion), Billie Mae Richards (Tender Heart Bear), Eva Almos (Friend Bear), Bob Dermer (Grumpy Bear), Patrice Black (Share & Funshine Bear), Nonnie Griffin (Harmony Bear), Jim Henshaw (Bright Heart Raccoon), Melleny Brown (Cheer Bear), Janet Laine-Green (Wish Bear), Maria Lukofsky (Playful Heart Monkey), Gloria Figura (Bedtime Bear).

38 *Cats Don't Dance* (1997) **

U.S.; Rated G; 75 mins.; Released March 26, 1997 (Video: August 1997, Warner); Turner Feature Animation/David Kirschner.

Synopsis: In the '30s, a singing and dancing cat goes to Hollywood with dreams of being a movie star, but a vindictive child actress keeps him and other animals playing only extras.

Notes: Fun musical-comedy boasting spirited production numbers and amusing characterizations, particularly that of maniacally-evil child star Darla Dimple; The first and last film from Turner Feature Animation (the studio was absorbed by Warner Bros. Feature Animation in the merger of Time Warner and Turner Broadcasting); Gene Kelly (who died in 1996) acted as a consultant on the dance sequences; Darla's butler in the film is based on Erich von Stroheim's character in the 1950 classic *Sunset Boulevard*; Produced by David Kirschner and Paul Gertz (the team behind 1994's *The Pagemaster*).

Credits: Director—Mark Dindal; Supervising Animators—Jill Culton, Lennie K. Graves, Jay Jackson, Kevin Johnson, Bob Scott, Frans Vischer, Chad Stewart, Steven

Wahl; Screenplay by Roberts Gannaway, Cliff Ruby, Elana Lesser and Theresa Pettengill; Story by Rick Schneider, Robert Lence, Mark Dindal, Brian McEntee, David Womersley and Kelvin Yasuda; Music by Steve Goldstein; Songs by Randy Newman; Songs — "Our Time Has Come" (by Martin Page), "Danny's Arrival Song," "Little Boat on the Sea," "Animal Jam Session," "Big and Loud," "Tell Me Lies," "Nothing's Gonna Stop Us Now" and "I Do Believe" (by Simon Climie and Will Jennings).

Voices: Scott Bakula (Danny), Jasmine Guy (Sawyer), Natalie Cole (Sawyer's singing voice), Ashley Peldon (Darla Dimple), Lindsay Ridgeway (Darla's singing voice), Kathy Najimy (Tillie), John Rhys-Davies (Woolie), George Kennedy (L.B. Mammoth), Rene Auberjonois (Flanigan), Hal Holbrook (Cranston), Don Knotts (T.W. Turtle), Rick Logan (T.W.'s singing voice), Betty Lou Gerson (Francis), Matthew Herried (Pudge), Frank Welker (Farley Wink), David Johansen (Bus Driver), Mark Dindal (Max); **Notes:** Bakula starred in TV's *Quantum Leap* (1989–93). Gerson, 82, voiced Cruella DeVil in Disney's *101 Dalmatians* (1961).

39 *Charlotte's Web* (1973) **
U.S.; Rated G; 94 mins.; Hanna-Barbera.

Synopsis: A special friendship develops between a barnyard spider and a runt pig who is set to be slaughtered for food in winter.

Notes: Hanna-Barbera's animated/musical version of the classic children's story is an enjoyable family film with a fine voice cast; Aka *E. B. White's Charlotte's Web*; Produced by William Hanna and Joseph Barbera.

Credits: Directors — Charles A. Nichols, Iwao Takamoto; Screenplay by Earl Hamner, Jr., based on the 1952 book by E(lwyn) B(rooks) White (1899–1985); **Note:** Hamner was the creator/narrator of TV's *The Waltons* (1972–81); Music and lyrics by Richard M. and Robert B. Sherman; Musical Director — Irwin Kostal; Songs — "A Veritable Smorgasbord," "There Must Be Something More," "I Can Talk," "Mother Earth and Father Time," "We've Got Lots in Common," "Deep in the Dark," "Zuckerman's Famous Pig" and the title song.

Voices: Debbie Reynolds (Charlotte), Henry Gibson (Wilbur), Paul Lynde (Templeton), Rex Allen (Narrator), Martha Scott (Mrs. Arable), Dave Madden (Old Sheep), Danny Bonaduce (Avery), Don Messick (Geoffrey), Herb Vigran (Lurvy), Agnes Moorehead (The Goose), Pam Ferdin (Fern Arable), Joan Gerber (Mrs. Zuckerman/Mrs. Fussy), Robert Holt (Homer Zuckerman), John Stephenson (Arable), William B. White (Henry Fussy); **Notes:** Reynolds has starred in such popular films as *Singin' in the Rain* (1952) and *Tammy and the Bachelor* (1957). Gibson was a regular on TV's *Laugh-in* (1968–71). Madden and Bonaduce both starred in TV's *The Partridge Family* (1970–74). Moorehead's (*Bewitched*) last film role (she died in April, 1974).

Honors: National Board of Review Awards, 1973 (Special Citation).

40 *The Chipmunk Adventure* (1987) *½
U.S.; Rated G; 76 mins.; Released May 22, 1987; Bagdasarian Productions.

Synopsis: The three chipmunks — Alvin, Simon and Theodore — compete with their female friends, The Chipettes, in a hot air balloon race around the world — a race sponsored by diamond smugglers.

Notes: Colorful kids adventure starring the too-cute '80s version of The Chipmunks; The Chipmunks' feature film debut; Produced by Ross Bagdasarian, Jr., husband of the film's director, Janice Karman, and son of original Chipmunks creator Ross Bagdasarian (aka David Saville), who first introduced the trio in 1958 after experimenting with speeding up his voice to record his hit song "Witch Doctor." He died in 1972. Bagdasarian, Jr., and Karmen revived The Chipmunks in the early '80s with new albums (*Chipmunk Punk*, etc.) and the TV series *Alvin and the Chipmunks* (1983–91).

Credits: Director—Janice Karman; Directing Animators—Skip Jones, Don Spencer, Andrew Gaskill, Mitch Rochon, Becky Bristow; Screenplay by Ross Bagdasarian, Jr., and Janice Karman; Music score by Randy Edelman; Original songs by Edelman, Joy Levy, Terry Shaddick, Randy Goodrum, Donna Weiss and Elysee Alexander; Songs—theme song, "I, Yi, Yi, Yi, Yi/Cuanto Le Gusta," "Off to See the World," "The Girls of Rock 'n' Roll," "Getting Lucky," "My Mother," "Woolly Bully," "Diamond Dolls" and the hit novelty songs (sung in the film by Miss Miller) "Come On a My House" (1951) and "Witch Doctor" (1958) by Ross Bagdasarian, Sr.

Voices: Ross Bagdasarian, Jr. (Alvin/Simon/Dave Saville), Janice Karman (Theodore/Brittany/Jeanette/Eleanor), Dody Goodman (Miss Miller), Susan Tyrrell (Claudia Furschtien), Anthony DeLongis (Klaus Furschtien), Frank Welker (Sophie), Nancy Cartwright, Ken Sansom, Charles Adler, Philip Clark, George Poulos, Pat Pinney.

41 *Cinderella* (1950) **½

U.S.; Rated G; 75 mins.; Released February 15, 1950 (Video: October 1988, Walt Disney); Walt Disney.

Synopsis: A beautiful scullery maid, mistreated by her stepmother and two stepsisters, is given a chance to meet her Prince Charming with the help of her Fairy Godmother and some animal friends.

Notes: Disney's animation renaissance of the '50s began with this gorgeously-animated version of the fairy tale. A classic, even if the animals do sometimes overshadow the human characters; This was Disney's first full-length animated feature (with a single story) since the start of World War II (the last one being 1942's *Bambi*), and its huge success at the box office helped the studio out of its bad financial situation; 750 artists and writers worked on the film for six years; The scene in which Cinderella is given her ball gown is said to be Walt Disney's favorite piece of animation.

Highlights: the mending of Cinderella's dress by the mice, and the enchanting Fairy Godmother sequence.

Credits: Supervisor: Ben Sharpsteen; Directors—Wilfred Jackson, Hamilton Luske, Clyde Geronimi; Directing Animators—Eric Larson, Ward Kimball, Norman Ferguson, Marc Davis, John Lounsbery, Milt Kahl, Wolfgang Reitherman, Les Clark, Oliver Johnston, Jr., Franklin Thomas; Story by William Peed, Ted Sears, Homer Brightman, Kenneth Anderson, Erdman Penner, Winston Hibler, Harry Reeves and Joe Rinaldi, based on the 1697 fairy tale by Charles Perrault (1628–1703); Musical score by Oliver Wallace and Paul J. Smith; Songs by Mack David, Jerry Livingston and Al Hoffman; Songs—title song, "A Dream Is a Wish Your Heart Makes," "Sing Sweet Nightingale," "Cinderelly/We Can Do It," "So This is Love" and "Bibbidi-Bobbidi Boo"; **Note:** Composer Livingston (1909–87) also wrote the songs "Mairzy Doats," "It's the Talk of the Town" and TV theme "77 Sunset Strip."

Voices: Ilene Woods (Cinderella), Eleanor Audley (Lady Tremaine, the stepmother), Verna Felton (Fairy Godmother), William Phipps (Prince Charming), Lucille Bliss (Anastasia), Rhoda Williams (Drizella), James Macdonald (Jaq/Gus), Luis Van Rooten (King/Grand Duke), Mike Douglas (The Prince's singing voice), Betty Lou Gerson (Narrator), June Foray (Lucifer), Clint McCauley (Mice); **Note:** Douglas later gained fame as host of his own TV talk show (1961–82).

Honors: Academy Award nominations—Musical Score, Song ("Bibbidi-Bobbidi-Boo") and Sound.

42 *Cool World* (1992) *

U.S.; Rated PG-13; 102 mins.; Released July, 1992 (Video: February 1993, Paramount); Ralph Bakshi.

Synopsis: Cartoonist Jack Deebs is brought into the comic-book world he created by a sexy "doodle" named Holli Would who wants to be human.

Notes: Disappointing combination of live-action and animation has a few fine animated moments but won't make anyone forget *Who Framed Roger Rabbit*; Ralph Bakshi's first animated feature in nearly a decade (his last was 1983's *Fire and Ice*); Cost of film—$30 million; Produced by Frank Mancuso, Jr.

Credits: Director—Ralph Bakshi; Animation Supervisor—Bruce Woodside; Screenplay by Michael Grais and Mark Victor; Story by Ralph Bakshi and Frank Mancuso, Jr.; Music by Mark Isham.

Cast: Kim Basinger (Holli Would), Gabriel Byrne (Jack Deebs), Brad Pitt (Frank Harris), Michele Abrams (Jennifer Malley), Deidre O'Connell (Isabelle Malley), Carrie Hamilton (Comic Bookstore Cashier), Frank Sinatra, Jr. (Himself); **Voices:** Charles Adler (Nails), Maurice LaMarche (Doc Whiskers/Mash), Candi Milo (Lonette/Bob), Michael David Lally (Sparks), Joey Camen (Slash/Holli's Door), Gregory Snegoff (Bash).

43 *Coonskin* (1975) * $\frac{1}{2}$
U.S.; Rated R; 83 mins.; Ralph Bakshi.

Synopsis: The old Uncle Remus tales get an updating in this violent look at ghetto life and black culture.

Notes: Controversial Ralph Bakshi feature (his third) is a gritty, occasionally inspired mix of live-action and animation; The film's black characterizations were denounced as racist by some civil rights activists and caused distributor Paramount Pictures to back out of the project. The film, consequently, received only a brief theatrical run and a title change for its video release; Video title—*Streetfight*; Produced by Albert S. Ruddy.

Credits: Director—Ralph Bakshi; Screenplay by Ralph Bakshi; Music by Chico Hamilton.

Voices: Barry White (Samson/Brother Bear), Charles Gordone (Preacher/Brother Fox), Scatman Crothers (Pappy/Old Man), Philip Michael Thomas (Randy/Brother Rabbit).

44 *The Cosmic Eye* (1985) **
U.S.; Not Rated; 72 mins.; Hubley Studios.

Synopsis: Three jazz musicians from outer space observe the Earth and its evolution.

Notes: Imaginative feature from the Hubley Studios, featuring pieces of John and Faith Hubley's earlier animated shorts—*Moonbird, Windy Day, The Hole, Cockaboody* and *Tijuana Brass Double Feature*. (John died in 1977).

Credits: Directors—Faith Hubley, John Hubley; Animation Directors—Fred Burns, William Littlejohn, Emily Hubley; Music by Dizzy Gillespie, Elizabeth Swados, Benny Carter, Conrad Cummings and William Russo.

Voices: Maureen Stapleton (Mother Earth), Dizzy Gillespie, Sam Hubley, Linda Atkinson.

45 *Daffy Duck's Movie: Fantastic Island* (1983) $\frac{1}{2}$
U.S.; Rated G; 78 mins.; Released August 5, 1983; Warner Bros.

Synopsis: A spoof of TV's *Fantasy Island*, with Daffy Duck and Speedy Gonzales as the island's hosts. Cartoons shown—*Buccaneer Bunny, Stupor Duck, Greedy for Tweety, Banty Raids, Louvre Come Back to Me, Tree for Two, Curtain Razor, A Mouse Divided, Of Rice and Hen* and *From Hare to Heir*. See SHORTS.

Notes: Poor compilation feature (Warner Bros.' fourth) with bland new material and only fair cartoons (dating from 1948 to 1963); Features Daffy Duck, Speedy Gonzales, Bugs Bunny, Yosemite Sam, Sylvester, Tweety, Porky Pig, Pepe Le Pew, Foghorn Leghorn, and the Tasmanian Devil; Daffy's first significant theatrical appearance since his last Warner Bros. cartoon *See Ya Later, Gladiator* in 1968; Produced by Friz Freleng.

Credits: Director—Friz Freleng; Sequence Directors—David Detiege, Friz Freleng, Phil Monroe; Cartoon Directors—Freleng, Chuck Jones, Robert McKimson; Screenplay by John Dunn, David Detiege and Friz Freleng; Music by Rob Walsh, Carl Stalling, Milt Franklyn and Bill Lava.
Voices: Mel Blanc, June Foray, Les Tremayne.

46 *Daffy Duck's Quackbusters* (1988) *
U.S.; Rated G; 76 mins.; Released September 24, 1988; Warner Bros.

Synopsis: After inheriting a million dollars, Daffy Duck sets up a ghost-busting service with Bugs Bunny and Porky Pig. Cartoons shown—*Daffy Dilly Prize Pest, Water Water Every Hare, Hyde and Go Tweet, Claws for Alarm, The Duxorcist, The Abominable Snow Rabbit, Transylvania 6-5000, Punch Trunk* and *Jumpin' Jupiter*. See SHORTS.
Notes: Warner Bros.' fifth compilation film is an adequate effort, featuring nine cartoons (dating from 1948 to 1963) and a new short, *The Duxorcist* (1987), the first theatrical Warner Bros. cartoon since 1969; Features Daffy Duck, Bugs Bunny, Porky Pig, Sylvester and Tweety; Produced by Steven S. Greene and Kathleen Helppie-Shipley.
Credits: Directors—Greg Ford, Terry Lennon; Cartoon Directors—Chuck Jones, Friz Freleng, Robert McKimson, Greg Ford and Terry Lennon; Screenplay by Greg Ford and Terry Lennon; Music by Carl Stalling, Milt Franklyn and Bill Lava.
Voices: Mel Blanc, Roy Firestone, B.J. Ward, Ben Frommer, Julie Bennett.

47 *The Daydreamer* (1966) **
U.S.; Not Rated; 101 mins.; Released summer, 1966; Rankin-Bass.

Synopsis: The adventures of a 13-year-old Hans Christian Andersen, who encounters many of the wonderful characters he would later write of in his fairy tales.
Notes: Entertaining, tuneful combination of live-action and animation, filmed using the Animagic process (stop-motion animation of three-dimensional puppet figures); The first feature film from Rankin-Bass, best known for their TV work (*Rudolph the Red-Nosed Reindeer, The Hobbit*); Filmed in New York, Denmark, Japan, Canada, France and England; Produced by Arthur Rankin, Jr.
Credits: Director—Jules Bass; Live-action scenes staged by Ezra Stone; Animation sequences staged by Don Duga; Screenplay by Arthur Rankin, Jr., based on stories and characters created by Hans Christian Andersen (1805–75); Additional dialogue by Romeo Muller; Music score by Maury Laws; Songs by Laws and Jules Bass; Songs—"Wishes and Teardrops," "Luck to Sell," "Happy Guy," "Who Can Tell," "Simply Wonderful," "Isn't It Cozy Here" and the title song.
Cast: Paul O'Keefe (Chris), Jack Gilford (Papa Andersen), Ray Bolger (The Pieman), Margaret Hamilton (Mrs. Klopplebobbler), Robert Harter (Big Claus); **Voices:** Cyril Ritchard (The Sandman), Hayley Mills (The Little Mermaid), Burl Ives (Father Neptune), Tallulah Bankhead (The Sea Witch), Terry-Thomas, Victor Borge (Tailors), Ed Wynn (The Emperor), Patty Duke (Thumbelina), Boris Karloff (The Rat), Sessue Hayakawa (The Mole), Robert Goulet (Singer); **Note:** Bolger and Hamilton's first screen appearance together since 1939's *The Wizard of Oz*. Bankhead's last film role (she died in 1968).

48 *Dick Deadeye, or Duty Done* (1975) *½
British-U.S.; Rated G; 80 mins.; Bill Melendez.

Synopsis: Dick Deadeye is commissioned by the Queen to rescue the Ultimate Secret from the Sorcerer and Pirate King.
Notes: Interesting, well-drawn animated musical designed by painter Ronald Searle and featuring characters, plot elements and songs (26 modernized versions) from the

Gilbert and Sullivan operettas *H.M.S. Pinafore* (with Dick Deadeye), *The Mikado*, *The Pirates of Penzance*, *The Sorcerer* and *Trial by Jury*; Produced by Steven C. Melendez.

Credits: Director—Bill Melendez; **Note:** Former UPA animator Melendez is best known for his series of "Peanuts" TV specials and films; Animation Director—Dick Horn; Screenplay by Robin Miller and Leo Rost; Music by Jimmy Horowitz; Additional lyrics by Robin Miller.

Voices: Victor Spinetti (Dick Deadeye), Linda Lewis (Yum Yum), Peter Reeves (Sorcerer/Captain of the Pinafore), George A. Cooper (Pirate King), Miriam Karlin (Little Buttercup), John Newton (Nanki Poo), Julia McKenzie (Rose Maybud), Francis Ghent (Monarch of the Sea/Major General), Barry Cryer (Judge), Beth Porter (Princess Zara/Queen Elizabeth), John Baldry (Monarch of the Sea's/Major General's singing voice), Casey Kelley (Nanki Poo's singing voice), Lisa Strike (Rose Maybud's singing voice), Ian Samwell (Pirate King's singing voice); **Note:** British actor Spinetti starred in the Beatles films *A Hard Day's Night* (1964) and *Help!* (1965).

49 *Dirty Duck* (1977) $\frac{1}{2}$

U.S.; Rated X; 75 mins.; Released September 21, 1977; Murakami-Wolf.

Synopsis: Lonely insurance man Willard Eisenbaum meets Dirty Duck and together they go on a sexual journey.

Notes: Low-grade adult animated feature; Produced by Jerry Good.

Credits: Director—Charles Swenson; Animated and Designed by Charles Swenson; Screenplay by Charles Swenson; Songs by Mark Volman and Howard Kaylan (Flo & Eddie).

Voices: Mark Volman, Robert Ridgely, Walker Edmiston, Cynthia Adler, Janet Lee, Lurene Tuttle, Jerry Good, Howard Kaylan.

50 *DuckTales: The Movie—Treasure of the Lost Lamp* (1990) $* \frac{1}{2}$

U.S.; Rated G; 74 mins.; Released August 3, 1990 (Video: March, 1991, Walt Disney); Walt Disney Animation (France) S.A.

Synopsis: Uncle Scrooge McDuck—with his great-nephews Huey, Dewey and Louie and friends—searches the world for the lost treasure of thief Collie Baba.

Notes: Good kids adventure based on *DuckTales* (1987–92), Disney's first daily animated TV series; A Disney Movietoon; The first feature from Disney's animation studio in Paris, headed by twin brothers Paul and Gaetan Brizzi (the brothers' studio, Brizzi Films, was bought by Disney in the late '80s); Produced by Bob Hathcock.

Credits: Director—Bob Hathcock; Sequence Directors—Paul Brizzi, Gaetan Brizzi, Clive Pallant, Mattias Marcos Rodric, Vincent Woodcock; Screenplay by Alan Burnett; Music by David Newman (*The Brave Little Toaster*); Song—"DuckTales Theme" (by Mark Mueller).

Voices: Alan Young (Scrooge), Terence McGovern (Launchpad), Russi Taylor (Huey/Dewey/Louie/Webby), Richard Libertini (Dijon), Christopher Lloyd (Merlock), June Foray (Mrs. Featherby), Chuck McCann (Duckworth), Joan Gerber (Mrs. Beakley), Rip Taylor (Genie), Charlie Adler, Jack Angel, Steve Bulen, Sherry Lynn, Mickie T. McGowan, Patrick Pinney, Frank Welker; **Note:** Young, who starred in TV's *Mr. Ed* (1961–66), last played Uncle Scrooge on film in the short *Mickey's Christmas Carol* (1983).

51 *Dumbo* (1941) ***

U.S.; Rated G; 64 mins.; Released October 23, 1941; Walt Disney.

Synopsis: A pint-sized circus elephant, ridiculed because of his large ears and separated from his mother, learns—with the help of a little mouse friend—that he can fly.

Notes: Classic Disney animated feature (the studio's fourth) is a charming, heartwarming little tale simply—but memorably—told; A modest, inexpensive production (it cost less than $1 million and took only a year and a half to make), Disney made the film to recoup the financial losses of his two previous, bigger films *Pinocchio* and *Fantasia*; A box-office hit when first released (less than two months before the Japanese attack on Pearl Harbor).

Highlights: the tear-jerking "Baby Mine" scene, the surreal "Pink Elephants on Parade" sequence, and the crows' song.

Credits: Supervising Director—Ben Sharpsteen; Sequence Directors—Norm Ferguson, Wilfred Jackson, Bill Roberts, Jack Kinney, Sam Armstrong; Animation Directors— Vladimir Tytla, Fred Moore, Ward Kimball, John Lounsbery, Art Babbitt, Woolie Reitherman; Screenplay by Joe Grant and Dick Huemer, based on the book by Helen Aberson and Harold Pearl; Story Direction by Otto Englander; Musical Score by Oliver Wallace and Frank Churchill; Songs by Churchill and Ned Washington; Songs—"Look Out for Mr. Stork," "Casey Junior," "Song of the Roustabouts," "Baby Mine," "Clown Song," "Pink Elephants on Parade" and "When I See an Elephant Fly (Crows' Song)"; **Note:** Wallace (1887–1963) was a top composer for Disney for the next 20 years.

Voices: Edward Brophy (Timothy Mouse), Sterling Holloway (Stork), Herman Bing (Ringmaster), Cliff Edwards (Jim Crow), Verna Felton, Sarah Selby, Dorothy Scott, Noreen Gamill (Elephants), Billy Sheets (Joe/Clown), Billy Bletcher, Eddie Holden (Clowns), Malcolm Hutton (Skinny), Jim Carmichael, Johnson Choir (Crows), Margaret Wright (Casey Jr.), Harold Manley, Tony Neil, Charles Stubbs (Boys), The King's Men (Roustabouts), John McLeish (Opening Narrator); **Notes:** Character actor Holloway's (1905–92) first voice role in a Disney film. He would go on to do many Disney voices over the next 30 years, his most famous being that of Winnie the Pooh. Edwards is also the voice of Jiminy Cricket.

Honors: Academy Award—Musical Score, also nominated for Song ("Baby Mine"); Other award—Cannes International Film Festival (Grand Prix).

52 *Fantasia* (1940) ***

U.S.; Rated G; 120 mins.; Premiered November 13, 1940 at the Broadway Theater in New York (Video: November 1991, Walt Disney); Walt Disney.

Synopsis: A series of animated short subjects illustrating the following pieces of classical music—*Toccata and Fugue in D Minor* (Bach), *The Nutcracker Suite* (Tchaikovsky), *The Sorcerer's Apprentice* (Dukas), *The Rite of Spring* (Stravinsky), *The Pastoral Symphony* (Beethoven), *Dance of the Hours* (Ponchielli) and *Night on Bald Mountain* (Moussorgsky)/*Ave Maria* (Schubert). See SHORTS.

Notes: Disney's third animated feature film is a brilliant combination of animation and classical music, and considered by many to be the studio's finest artistic achievement; Includes live-action scenes of the conductor, commentator and orchestra in silhouette; The film started in 1937 as a short (*The Sorcerer's Apprentice*), a collaboration between Disney and famed conductor Leopold Stokowski. Too expensive to be profitable as a short, it was expanded into a full-length concert feature, costing a total of $2.28 million; Mickey Mouse's second feature appearance (his first was in the live action 1934 film *Hollywood Party*); The first film with stereophonic sound, or "Fantasound"; German abstract animator Oskar Fischinger contributed to the *Toccata and Fugue* sequence; A sequence visualizing Debussy's "Claire de Lune" was not used (see short *Blue Bayou*); The film received mixed reviews when first released and performed poorly at the box office, but it eventually made money in rerelease and in 1991 became one of the biggest-selling videos of all time; For the film's 1982 reissue, a new digitally-recorded soundtrack was produced by Irwin Kostal; The film was given a major restoration in 1990, the year of its 50th anniversary; Entered in the Library of Congress National Film Registry in 1990.

Highlights: the mushrooms' Chinese dance (*Nutcracker Suite*), Mickey Mouse's memorable performance as *The Sorcerer's Apprentice*, the hilarious ballet dancing of

Hyacinth Hippo and Ben Ali Gator (*Dance of the Hours*), and the devil Chernabog and the swirling demons of *Night on Bald Mountain*.

Credits: Supervisor: Ben Sharpsteen; Sequence Directors—Samuel Armstrong, James Algar, Bill Roberts, Paul Satterfield, Hamilton Luske, Jim Handley, Ford Beebe, T. Hee, Norm Ferguson, Wilfred Jackson; Supervising Animators—Fred Moore, Vladimir Tytla, Wolfgang Reitherman, Joshua Meador, Ward Kimball, Eric Larson, Art Babbitt, Oliver M. Johnston, Jr., Don Towsley, Norm Ferguson; Story Direction by Joe Grant and Dick Huemer; Musical Direction by Edward H. Plumb; Music conducted by Leopold Stokowski and performed by the Philadelphia Orchestra.

Cast: Leopold Stokowski (conductor), the Philadelphia Orchestra, Deems Taylor (commentator); Voices—Walt Disney (Mickey Mouse), Julietta Novis (*Ave Maria* soloist); **Notes:** Stokowski (1882–1977) made two previous film appearances in *The Big Broadcast of 1937* (1936) and the popular *100 Men and a Girl* (1937) with Deanna Durbin. Taylor (1885–1966) was the composer of several operas, including *The King's Henchman* (1927), as well as a writer and radio commentator.

Honors: Academy Awards—Special Awards to Walt Disney, William E. Garrity, John N.A. Hawkins, RCA and Leopold Stokowski, and the Irving Thalberg Award to Walt Disney (for Consistent High-Quality Production).

53 *The Fantastic Planet* (1973) **

Czech-French; Rated PG; 72 mins.; Released in U.S. December 18, 1973; Les Films Armorial/Service De Recherche Ortif.

Synopsis: The struggles between two races—the tiny Oms and the giant Draags—on the alien planet of Ygam.

Notes: Beautifully-drawn (by author-illustrator Roland Topor) sci-fi/fantasy tale, the first feature from French animator Rene Laloux (b. 1929); Original French title—*La Planète Sauvage*; Produced by Simon Damiani and Andre Valio-Cavaglione; Presented by Roger Corman.

Credits: Director—René Laloux; Original artwork by Roland Topor; Graphic Direction by Joseph Kabrt and Joseph Vania; Screenplay by Roland Topor and Rene Laloux, based on Stefan Wul's *Oms en Serie*; Music by Alain Goraguer.

Voices: Barry Bostwick, Marvin Miller, Olan Soule, Cynthia Adler, Nora Heflin, Hal Smith, Mark Gruner, Monika Ramirez, Janet Waldo.

Honors: Awards—Cannes Film Festival, 1973 (Grand Prix); A Grand Prix winner at the film festivals in Atlanta, Barcelona, Trieste and Teheran.

54 *Felix the Cat: The Movie* (1989) *

U.S.; Not Rated; 82 mins.; Felix the Cat Creations, Inc./Animation Film Cologne.

Synopsis: Felix the Cat sets out to rescue the beautiful Princess Oriana from the wicked Duke of Zill.

Notes: Fantasy/adventure for kids starring the updated version of Pat Sullivan's popular silent-screen hero (1919–31); Produced by Don Oriolo (son of the late Joe Oriolo, who produced the *Felix the Cat* TV series in the '60s), Christian Schneider and Janos Schenk.

Credits: Director—Tibor Hernadi; Animation Director—Tibor A. Belay; Directing Animators—Grzegorz Handzlik, Roman Klys, Edit Hernadi, Ryszard Lepiura, Peter Tenkei, Tibor Hernadi; Screenplay by Don Oriolo and Pete Brown; Story by Oriolo; Music by Christopher L. Stone; Songs by Bernd Schonhofen, Don Oriolo, Pete Brown and Christian Schneider; Songs—"Mizzard Shuffle," "Face to the Wind (The Princess Song)," "Sly as a Fox," "Who Is the Boss?," "Something More Than Friends," "Together Again" and "All You Need Is Friends."

Voices: Chris Phillips, Maureen O'Connell, Peter Neuman, Alice Playten, Susan Montanaro, Don Oriolo, Christian Schneider, David Kolin.

55 *FernGully: The Last Rainforest* (1992) * ½

U.S.; Rated G; 76 mins.; Released April 10, 1992 (Video: September 1992, CBS/Fox);
Korty Films Inc.

Synopsis: A young logger in a magical rainforest is enlisted by a fairy sprite to help
save her sylvan home from land developers and an evil forest spirit.

Notes: Environmental musical-fantasy for kids, colorfully animated; Produced by
Wayne Young and Peter Faiman.

Credits: Director—Bill Kroyer; **Note:** Kroyer was Oscar nominated for the short
Technological Threat (1988); Animation Director—Tony Fucile; Sequence Directors—
Bret Haaland, Tim Hauser, Dan Jeup, Susan Kroyer; Screenplay by Jim Cox (*Rescuers
Down Under*), based on the *FernGully* stories by Australian author Diana Young; Music
score by Alan Silvestri; Songs by Silvestri, Jimmy Webb, Thomas Dolby, Jimmy Buffett,
Michael Utley, Guoergui Mintchev, Raffi, Joseph Shabalala, Chris Kenner, Bruce Roberts
and Elton John; Performers include Sheena Easton, Ladysmith Black Mambazo, Johnny
Clegg, Raffi and Elton John; Songs—"Life Is a Magic Thing," "A Dream Worth Keeping," "Batty Rap," "Lithuanian Lullaby," "If I'm Goanna Eat Somebody (It Might As Well
Be You)," "Spis, Li Milke Le," "Toxic Love," "Raining Like Magic," "Bamnqobile," "Land
of a Thousand Dances," "Tri Jetrve" and "Some Other World."

Voices: Tim Curry (Hexxus), Samantha Mathis (Crysta), Christian Slater (Pips),
Jonathan Ward (Zak), Robin Williams (Batty Koda), Grace Zabriskie (Magi Lune),
Geoffrey Blake (Ralph), Robert Pastorelli (Tony), Cheech Marin (Stump), Tommy Chong
(Root), Tone-Loc (The Goanna), Townsend Coleman (Knotty), Brian Cummings (Ock),
Kathleen Freeman (Elder #1), Janet Gilmore (Fairy #1), Naomi Lewis (Elder #2), Danny
Mann (Ash/Voice Dispatch), Neil Ross (Elder #3), Pamela Segall (Fairy #2), Anderson
Wong (Rock), Lauri Hendler, Rosanna Huffman, Harvey Jason, Dave Mallow, Paige Nan
Pollack, Holly Ryan, Gary Schwartz; **Notes:** Comedy partners Cheech (Richard Marin)
and Chong (*Up in Smoke*) broke up in 1985.

56 *Fire and Ice* (1983) * ½

U.S.; Rated PG; 81 mins.; Released September 1983; Ralph Bakshi.

Synopsis: When the beautiful Princess Teegra is kidnapped by Subhumans, a mysterious hero comes to her rescue.

Notes: The artwork of renowned fantasy illustrator Frank Frazetta highlights this
sword-and-sorcery tale; The animation is rotoscoped (traced from live-action footage);
Ralph Bakshi's third film in the sci-fi/fantasy genre (following *Wizards* and *The Lord of
the Rings*) and his last feature effort until 1992's *Cool World*; Working title—*Sword and
the Sorcery*; Produced by Bakshi and Frazetta.

Credits: Director—Ralph Bakshi; Graphic design by Frank Frazetta; Supervising
Animator—Michael Svayko; Screenplay by veteran comic-book writers Roy Thomas and
Gerry Conway, based on characters created by Ralph Bakshi and Frank Frazetta; Music
by William Kraft.

Voices: Susan Tyrrell (Juliana), Maggie Roswell (Teegra), William Ostrander (Larn),
Stephen Mendel (Nekron), Alan Koss (Envoy), Clare Nono (Tutor), Hans Howes (Defender
Captain), Ray Oliver, Nathan Purdee, Le Tari (Subhumans).

57 *The Fox and the Hound* (1981) **

U.S.; Rated G; 83 mins.; Released July 10, 1981 (Video: March 1994, Walt Disney);
Walt Disney.

Synopsis: A puppy and an orphaned fox cub, living on a farm together, form a friendship that is later tested when the pup is a grown hunting dog and the fox is his prey.

Notes: Entertaining parable with a good message about friendship and societal pressures; The first animated feature from a new generation of Disney animators; Cost of film—$12 million; Released in theaters with the compilation short *Once Upon a Mouse* (a retrospective of Disney animation); Produced by Art Stevens and Wolfgang Reitherman (his last film before retiring).

Highlight: the exciting battle between the fox and a ferocious grizzly bear.

Credits: Directors—Art Stevens, Ted Berman, Richard Rich; Supervising Animators—Randy Cartwright, Cliff Nordberg, Frank Thomas, Glen Keane, Ron Clements, Ollie Johnston; **Notes:** The last film from veteran Disney animators (and longtime friends) Thomas and Johnston. The pair later wrote several books together and starred in the delightful documentary *Frank and Ollie* (1995). Keane, who joined Disney in 1974, is the son of *Family Circus* cartoonist Bil Keane. He would become one of the studio's leading animation directors, giving life to Ariel (*The Little Mermaid*) and the Beast (*Beauty and the Beast*), among others; Screenplay by Larry Clemmons, Ted Berman, Peter Young, Steve Hulett, David Michener, Burny Mattinson, Earl Kress and Vance Gerry, based on the book by Daniel P. Mannix; Music by Buddy Baker; Songs by Richard O. Johnston and Stan Fidel, Jim Stafford, Richard Rich and Jeffrey Patch; Songs include "Best of Friends," "Goodbye May Seem Forever" and "A Huntin' Man."

Voices: Kurt Russell (Copper), Mickey Rooney (Tod), Pearl Bailey (Big Mama), Sandy Duncan (Vixey), Pat Buttram (Chief), Jack Albertson (Slade), Jeanette Nolan (Widow Tweed), John Fiedler (Porcupine), John McIntire (Badger), Dick Bakalyan (Dinky), Paul Winchell (Boomer), Keith Mitchell (Young Tod), Corey Feldman (Young Copper); **Notes:** Russell (*Elvis, Escape from New York*) appeared in nine Disney films (1966–75). Albertson's (*Chico and the Man*) last film role (he died in November 1981 at 74).

58 *Freddie as F.R.0.7.* (1992) *$\frac{1}{2}$

British; Rated PG; 90 mins; Released in England August 14, 1992.

Synopsis: A French frog is assigned by the British Secret Service to stop an evil snake from stealing historical monuments.

Notes: Amusing spy spoof for kids; A three-year, $18 million British production from Yugoslav-born producer-director-writer Jon Acevski; Aka *Freddie the Frog*.

Credits: Director—Jon Acevski; Animation Director—Tony Guy (*Watership Down*); Sequence Directors—Dave Unwin, Bill Hajee, Richard Fawdry, Stephen Weston, Roberto Casale, Alain Maindron; Screenplay by Jon Acevski and David Ashton; Music by David Dundas and Rick Wentworth; Lyrics by Don Black, Jon Acevski and David Ashton; Songs sung by George Benson, Patti Austin, Grace Jones, Barbara Dickson, Boy George, Asis, Holly Johnson.

Voices: Ben Kingsley (Freddie), Jenny Agutter (Daphne), Brian Blessed (El Supremo), Nigel Hawthorne (Brigadier G), Sir Michael Hordern (King), Edmund Kingsley (Young Freddie), Phyllis Logan (Nessie), Victor Maddern (Old Gentleman Raven), Jonathan Pryce (Trilby), Prunella Scales (Queen), John Sessions (Scotty), Billie Whitelaw (Messina), David Ashton; **Note:** The voices are supplied by a great British cast—Kingsley (*Gandhi*), Agutter (*Logan's Run*), Blessed (*I, Claudius*), Pryce (*Brazil*), Scales (*Fawlty Towers*), etc.

59 *Fritz the Cat* (1972) **

U.S.; Rated X; 78 mins.; Released April 28, 1972; Ralph Bakshi.

Synopsis: A satirical look at the hippie lifestyles of the 1960s, following the adventures of an alleycat college student in New York.

Notes: Outrageous social satire, best known for being the first animated feature to receive an X-rating; The feature debut of Ralph Bakshi, who had been a cartoon director at the Terrytoon and Paramount Studios in the '60s; Cartoonist Robert Crumb disowned this movie adaptation of his famous "underground" comics character; Sequel—*Nine Lives of Fritz the Cat* (1974); Produced by Steve Krantz.

Credits: Director—Ralph Bakshi; Screenplay by Ralph Bakshi, based on the comic-strip characters created by Robert Crumb; Music by Ed Bogas and Ray Shanklin; Songs performed by B.B. King, Billie Holliday (singing "Yesterdays"), others.

Voices: Skip Hinnant (Fritz), Rosetta LeNoire, John McCurry, Phil Seuling, Judy Engles.

Friz Freleng's Looney, Looney, Looney Bugs Bunny Movie **see** *The Looney, Looney, Looney Bugs Bunny Movie*

60 Fun and Fancy Free (1947) **
U.S.; Rated G; 73 mins.; Released September 27, 1947; Walt Disney.

Synopsis: Jiminy Cricket links two cartoon stories—*Bongo*, about a little circus bear who runs away to the woods, narrated and sung by Dinah Shore; and *Mickey and the Beanstalk*, with Mickey Mouse, Donald Duck and Goofy confronting Willie the Giant, narrated by Edgar Bergen. See SHORTS.

Notes: Mickey's *Beanstalk* adventure highlights this enjoyable Disney double feature; Includes live-action scenes with ventriloquist Bergen and friends; Jiminy Cricket's second feature appearance, following *Pinocchio* (1940).

Credits: Supervisor: Ben Sharpsteen; Directors—Jack Kinney, Bill Roberts, Hamilton Luske; Directing Animators—Ward Kimball, Les Clark, John Lounsbery, Fred Moore, Wolfgang Reitherman; Live-action Director—William Morgan; Screenplay by Homer Brightman, Harry Reeves, Ted Sears, Lance Nolley, Eldon Dedini and Tom Oreb; *Bongo*—based on the story by Sinclair Lewis; Musical Director—Charles Wolcott; Music Score by Paul Smith, Oliver Wallace and Eliot Daniel; Songs by Ray Noble, Buddy Kaye, Bennie Benjamin, William Walsh, Bobby Worth, George Weiss and Arthur Quenzer; Songs—title song, "I'm a Happy-Go-Lucky Fellow," "Lazy Countryside," "Too Good to Be True," "Say It with a Slap," "My, What a Happy Day," "Beanero," "Fee Fi Fo Fum" and "My Favorite Dream"; **Note:** The song "I'm a Happy-Go-Lucky Fellow" (sung by Jiminy Cricket) was originally written for *Pinocchio* (1940), but got cut.

Cast/Voices: Edgar Bergen (with Charlie McCarthy and Mortimer Snerd), Luana Patten, Dinah Shore (Narrator), Anita Gordon (The Singing Harp), Cliff Edwards (Jiminy Cricket), Billy Gilbert (The Giant), Walt Disney/Jim Macdonald (Mickey Mouse), Clarence Nash (Donald Duck), Pinto Colvig (Goofy), The King's Men, The Dinning Sisters, The Starlighters; **Notes:** Child actress Patten (1938–96) also starred in Disney's *Song of the South* and *So Dear to My Heart*. Gilbert was the voice of Sneezy in *Snow White*. Walt Disney's last vocal performance as Mickey (sound-effects man Macdonald voiced the mouse from then until Wayne Allwine took over the role in the '80s).

61 Gay Purr-ee (1962) *$\frac{1}{2}$
U.S.; Rated G; 85 mins.; Premiered November 7, 1962; UPA.

Synopsis: Mewsette, a country cat tired of rural living, travels to Paris where she falls into the sinister hands of city slicker Meowrice.

Notes: Pleasant romantic tale from UPA (United Productions of America); The studio's second (and last) feature, following the Mr. Magoo film *1001 Arabian Nights* (1959); Produced by Henry G. Saperstein.

Credits: Director—Abe Levitow; **Note:** Levitow, a former Warner Bros. animator-director (1953–62), also directed the holiday TV special *Mr. Magoo's Christmas Carol* (1962); Screenplay by Dorothy and Chuck Jones, Ralph Wright; **Note:** Famed Warner cartoon director Chuck Jones and Dorothy (Webster) Jones were husband-and-wife (since

1935); Songs by Harold Arlen and E.Y. Harburg (the songwriting team for *The Wizard of Oz*); Songs—"Mewsette," "Roses Red—Violets Blue," "Take My Hand Paree," "Paris Is a Lonely Town," "The Horses Won't Talk," "The Money Cat," "Little Drops of Rain" and "Bubbles."

Voices: Judy Garland (Mewsette), Robert Goulet (Jaune-Tom), Hermione Gingold (Madame Rubens-Chatte), Red Buttons (Robespier-re), Paul Frees (Meowrice), Morey Amsterdam, Mel Blanc, Julie Bennett, Joan Gardner.

62   *GoBots: Battle of the Rock Lords* (1986) $\frac{1}{2}$

U.S.; Rated G; 75 mins.; Released March, 1986 (Video: January 1987, Paramount); Hanna-Barbera/Tonka Corporation.

Synopsis: The GoBots (intergalactic guardians who can transform into vehicles and spaceships) battle evil Renegades and Rock Lords who want to rule the universe.

Notes: Routine limited-animation feature tied-in with the popular toys and Saturday morning TV series *Challenge of the GoBots* (1984–86); Presented by Clubhouse Pictures; Produced by Kay Wright.

Credits: Director—Ray Patterson; Animation Director—Paul Sabella; Supervising Animator—Janine Dawson; Screenplay by Jeff Segal; Musical Director—Hoyt Curtin.

Voices: Margot Kidder (Solitaire), Roddy McDowall (Nuggit), Michael Nouri (Boulder), Telly Savalas (Magmar), Ike Eisenmann (Nick), Bernard Erhard (Cy-Kill), Marilyn Lightstone (Crasher), Arthur Burghardt (Turbo/Cop-Tur/Talc), Morgan Paul (Matt), Lou Richards (Leader-1), Leslie Speights (A.J.), Frank Welker (Scooter/Zeemon/Rest-Q/Pulver-Eye/Sticks/Narliphant), Michael Bell (Slime/Stone/Granite/Narligator), Foster Brooks (Stone Heart/Fossil Lord), Ken Campbell (Vanguard), Philip Lewis Clarke (Herr Friend/Crack-Pot/Tork), Peter Cullen (Pincher/Tombstone/Stone), Dick Gautier (Brimstone/Klaws/Rock Narlie), Darryl Hickman (Marbles/Hornet), B.J. Ward (Small Foot), Kelly Ward (Fitor), Kirby Ward (Heat Seeker).

63   *A Goofy Movie* (1995) * $\frac{1}{2}$

U.S.; Rated G; 78 mins.; Released April 7, 1995 (Video: September 1995, Walt Disney); Walt Disney Animation (France, Australia).

Synopsis: Goofy attempts to bond with his rebellious teenage son Max during a trip through the country.

Notes: Minor, but enjoyable, Disney film aimed at younger children; Feature version of the Disney TV series *Goof Troop* (1991–93); Goofy's first feature film appearance since *Fun and Fancy Free* (1947); Animated by Disney's teams in Paris, France and Sydney, Australia; Produced by Dan Rounds.

Credits: Director—Kevin Lima; Animation Supervisors—Nancy Beiman, Matias Marcos, Stephane Sainte-Foi, Dominique Monfery; Sequence Director—Steve Moore; Screenplay by Jymn Magon, Brian Pimental and Chris Matheson; Story by Magon; Music by Carter Burwell; Songs by Tom Snow and Jack Feldman, Patrick DeRemer and Roy Freeland; Songs—"After Today," "Stand Out," "Lester's Possum Park" (by Randy Peterson and Kevin Quinn), "On the Open Road," "I-2-I" and "Nobody Else but You."

Voices: Bill Farmer (Goofy), Jason Marsden (Max), Jim Cummings (Pete), Kellie Martin (Roxanne), Rob Paulsen (PJ), Wallace Shawn (Principal Mazur), Jenna Von Oy (Stacey), Frank Welker (Bigfoot), Kevin Lima (Lester), Florence Stanley (Waitress), Jo Anne Worley (Miss Maples), Brittany Alyse Smith (Photo Studio Girl), Robyn Richards (Lester's Grinning Girl), Julie Brown (Lisa), Klee Bragger (Tourist Kid), Joey Lawrence (Chad), Pat Buttram (Possum Park Emcee), Wayne Allwine (Mickey Mouse), Herschel Sparber (Security Guard); **Note:** Buttram's (*Green Acres*) last film role (he died in January 1994).

The Great American Chase **see** *The Bugs Bunny/Road Runner Movie.*

64 *The Great Mouse Detective* (1986) ** ½

U.S.; Rated G; 95 mins.; Released July 2, 1986 (Video: July, 1992, Walt Disney); Walt Disney.

Synopsis: Basil, a mouse detective living beneath the Baker Street residence of Sherlock Holmes, attempts to save the British Empire from an evil genius named Ratigan.

Notes: Good humor and lively animation highlight this delightful Disney adventure, which marked the beginning of the studio's comeback in animated features (this was their 26th); Working title—*Basil of Baker Street* (from the book); 125 animators worked on the $13 million production; Computers assisted in the animation of the climactic clock tower sequence; Disney veteran Eric Larson acted as animation consultant on the film; Video title—*The Adventures of the Great Mouse Detective*; Produced by Burny Mattinson.

Credits: Directors—John Musker, Ron Clements, Dave Michener, Burny Mattinson; Supervising Animators—Mark Henn, Glen Keane, Robert Minkoff, Hendel Butoy; Screenplay by Pete Young, Steve Hulett, John Musker, Matthew O'Callaghan, Dave Michener, Vance Gerry, Ron Clements, Bruce M. Morris, Burny Mattinson and Melvin Shaw, based on the book *Basil of Baker Street* by Eve Titus; Music by Henry Mancini; Songs—"The World's Greatest Criminal Mind" and "Goodbye, So Soon" (by Mancini, Larry Grossman and Ellen Fitzhugh), "Let Me Be Good to You" (written and performed by Melissa Manchester); **Note:** Oscar/Grammy-winning composer Mancini's (1924–94) film credits include *Breakfast at Tiffany's* (1961) and *The Pink Panther* (1964).

Voices: Vincent Price (Professor Ratigan), Barrie Ingham (Basil/Bartholomew), Val Bettin (Dr. David Q. Dawson/Thug Guard), Susanne Pollatschek (Olivia Flaversham), Candy Candido (Fidget), Eve Brenner (Mouse Queen), Diana Chesney (Mrs. Judson), Alan Young (Flaversham), Basil Rathbone (Sherlock Holmes), Laurie Main (Watson), Shani Wallis (Lady Mouse), Ellen Fitzhugh (Bar Maid), Walker Edmiston (Citizen/Thug Guard), Wayne Allwine, Tony Anselmo (Thug Guards); **Note:** Price (1911–93) also voiced—and was the subject of—the Disney animated short *Vincent* (1982), directed by Tim Burton.

65 *The Great Space Chase* (1983) *

U.S.; Rated G; 87 mins.; Filmation.

Synopsis: Mighty Mouse must rescue Pearl Pureheart and finally the universe itself from the villainous feline Harry the Heartless.

Notes: Mediocre sci-fi adventure for kids starring the popular cartoon mouse (who first appeared in Terrytoon shorts, 1942–61); Aka *Mighty Mouse in The Great Space Chase*; The film was edited from 16 episodes of the TV series *The New Adventures of Mighty Mouse and Heckle and Jeckle* (1979–82); Produced by Lou Scheimer, Norm Prescott and Don Christenson.

Credits: Directors—Ed Friedman, Lou Kachivas, Marsh Lamore, Gwen Wetzler, Kay Wright, Lou Zukor; Storyboard Supervisor—Bob Kline; Music by Yvette Blais and Jeff Michael; Title song by Michael and Dean Andre.

Voices: Alan Oppenheimer (Mighty Mouse/Harry), Diane Pershing (Pearl Pureheart).

66 *Grendel, Grendel, Grendel* (1981) * ½

Australian; Not Rated; 90 mins.; Released in U.S. April, 1982.

Synopsis: The story of Grendel, a likable, green-spotted monster in medieval times with a bad habit of eating people now and then.

Notes: Amusing, nicely animated fable based on the classic Beowulf legend; Produced by Alexander Stitt and Phillip Adams.

Credits: Director—Alexander Stitt; Director of Animation—Frank Hellard; Screenplay by Alexander Stitt, based on the 1972 novel *Grendel* by John Grendel; Music by Bruce Smeaton; Lyrics by Alexander Stitt.

Voices: Peter Ustinov, Keith Michell, Arthur Dignam, Julie McKenna, Ed Rosser, Bobby Bright, Ric Stone, Ernie Bourne, Allison Bird, Barry Hill.

67 *Gulliver's Travels* (1939) **

U.S.; Not rated; 77 mins.; Premiered December 18, 1939 at the Sheridan Theater in Miami, FL; Released December 22, 1939; Max Fleischer.

Synopsis: Shipwrecked sailor Lemuel Gulliver lands among the tiny people of Lilliput, who have just gone to war with kingdom of Blefuscu.

Notes: Entertaining romantic-musical version of Jonathan Swift's satirical tale, may appeal more to children; The Fleischers' first feature-length cartoon (and the second ever produced), their answer to Disney's *Snow White* (1937); The animation of Gulliver is rotoscoped, meaning it was traced from live-action footage (a radio announcer named Sam Parker was the model); Gabby, the town crier in the film, later appeared in his own cartoon series (1940–41); Followed by the Fleischers' second (and last) feature *Mr. Bug Goes to Town* (1941); Producer Max Fleischer's studio is best known for its "Betty Boop" and "Popeye" shorts.

Credits: Director—Dave Fleischer; Directors of Animation—Seymour Kneitel, Willard Bowsky, Tom Palmer, Grim Natwick, William Henning, Roland Crandall, Tom Johnson, Robert Leffingwell, Frank Kelling, Winfield Hoskins, Orestes Calpini; Screenplay by Dan Gordon, Cal Howard, Ted Pierce, Isadore Sparber and Edmond Seward; Story adaptation by Seward, from the 1726 book by Jonathan Swift; Music by Victor Young; Songs by Ralph Rainger and Leo Robin; Songs—"All's Well," "It's a Hap-Hap-Happy Day" (by Sammy Timberg, Al Neiburg and Winston Sharples), "Bluebirds in the Moonlight," "I Hear a Dream," "All Together Now" and "Faithful Forever"; **Notes:** Rainger and Robin won the Oscar the year before for "Thanks for the Memory" (Bob Hope's theme) from *The Big Broadcast of 1938*. Timberg (1903–92) wrote many songs for the Fleischer studio over the years.

Voices: Jessica Dragonette (Princess Glory's singing voice), Lanny Ross (Prince David's singing voice), Pinto Colvig (Gabby), Jack Mercer (King Little); **Note:** Dragonette (1900–80) and Ross (1906–88) were both popular radio singers in the '30s.

Honors: Academy Award nominations—Original Score and Song ("Faithful Forever").

68 *Gulliver's Travels Beyond the Moon* (1966) *½

Japanese; Not Rated; 85 mins.; Toei Animation.

Synopsis: Gulliver and his companions travel in a rocket to the planet of Hope where the inhabitants are being held captive by robots.

Notes: Fine sci-fi adventure for kids from Japan's Toei Film Productions; Original Japanese title—*Gulliver No Uchu Ryoko*; Produced by Hiroshi Okawa.

Credits: Director—Yoshio Kuroda; Director of Animation—Hideo Furusawa; Screenplay by Shinichi Sekizawa, based on the character created by Jonathan Swift; Music and songs by Milton and Anne DeLugg; Songs—"I Wanna Be Like Gulliver," "The Earth Sings," "That's the Way It Goes" and "Keep Your Hopes High."

69 *Hans Christian Andersen's Thumbelina* (1994) *½

U.S.; Rated G; 87 mins.; Released March 30, 1994 (Video: August 1994, Warner); Sullivan Bluth.

Synopsis: Thumbelina, a tiny girl longing for her dream prince, falls in with a variety of seedy show biz types and would-be suitors.

Notes: Pleasant, but unexceptional musical fairy tale for kids from the director of *An American Tail* (1986); Produced by Don Bluth, Gary Goldman and John Pomeroy.

Credits: Directors—Don Bluth, Gary Goldman; Supervising Animator—John Pomeroy; Directing Animators—John Hill, Richard Bazley, Jean Morel, Len Simon, Piet Derycker, Dave Kupczyk; Screenplay by Don Bluth, based on the 19th-century story by Hans Christian Andersen; Supervising Composer—Barry Manilow; Underscore by Manilow and William Ross; Songs by Manilow, Jack Feldman and Bruce Sussman; Songs include "Follow Your Heart," "Marry the Mole" and "Let Me Be Your Wings."

Voices: Jodi Benson (Thumbelina), Gino Conforti (Jacquimo), Barbara Cook (Mother), Will Ryan (Hero/Reverand Rat), June Foray (Queen Tabetha), Kenneth Mars (King Colbert), Gary Imhoff (Prince Cornelius), Joe Lynch (Grundel), Charo (Mrs. Delores Toad), Loren Michaels (Gringo), Gilbert Gottfried (Mr. Beetle), Carol Channing (Ms. Fieldmouse), John Hurt (Mr. Mole), Tawny Sunshine Glover (Gnatty), Kendall Cunningham (Baby Bug), Danny Mann (Mozo), Neil Ross (Mr. Fox/Mr. Bear), Pat Musick (Mrs. Rabbit); **Note:** Benson was the voice of Ariel in Disney's *The Little Mermaid* (1989).

70 *Hansel and Gretel* (1954) **½
U.S.; Not Rated; 75 mins.

Synopsis: Two children, lost in the woods, encounter an evil witch and her enticing gingerbread house.

Notes: Wonderful animated version of the famous Engelbert Humperdinck opera featuring Kinemin puppets, electronic figurines that are one-third life-size and capable of making 800,000 expressions; Produced by Michael Myerberg.

Credits: Director—John Paul; Animators—Joseph Horstmann, Inez Anderson, Daniel Diamond, Ralph Emory, Hobart Rosen, Teddy Shepard, Nathalie Schulz; Screenplay by Padraic Colum, based on the libretto by Adelheid Wette (Humperdinck's sister), from the Brothers Grimm fairy tale; Music from the 1893 opera by German composer Engelbert Humperdinck (1854–1921); Orchestra direction and musical treatment by Franz Allers.

Voices: Constance Brigham (Hansel/Gretel), Anna Russell (Rosina Rubylips/The Witch), Mildred Dunnock (Mother), Frank Rogier (Father), Delbert Anderson (Sandman), Helen Boatright (Dew Fairy), Apollo Boys' Choir (Angels/Children).

71 *Happily Ever After* (1990) ½
U.S.; Rated G; 74 mins.; Released June, 1990; Filmation.

Synopsis: Snow White is in danger again, this time from the wicked queen's brother, Lord Maliss, who is seeking revenge for his sister's death.

Notes: Low-grade sequel to the Snow White story, replacing the Dwarfs with the Dwarfelles (their female cousins); The film began production in 1986, as did Filmation's *Pinocchio and the Emperor of the Night* (1987), which is also an unofficial sequel to a Disney animated classic; Rereleased in 1993 to coincide with Disney's eighth rerelease of *Snow White*; Produced by Lou Scheimer.

Credits: Director—John Howley; Sequence Directors—Gian Celestri, Kamoon Song, Lawrence White; Screenplay by Robby London and Martha Moran; Music by Frank W. Becker.

Voices: Irene Cara (Snow White), Edward Asner (Scowl), Carol Channing (Muddy), Dom DeLuise (Looking Glass), Phyllis Diller (Mother Nature), Zsa Zsa Gabor (Blossom), Linda Gary (Critterina/Marina), Jonathan Harris (Sunflower), Michael Horton (Prince), Sally Kellerman (Sunburn), Malcolm McDowell (Lord Maliss), Tracey Ullman (Moonbeam/Thunderella), Frank Welker (Batso).

72 *Heathcliff: The Movie* (1986)
U.S.; Rated G; 73 mins.; Released April 19, 1986; DIC Audiovisuel/LBS Communications/McNaught Syndicate.

Synopsis: Heathcliff tells his three nephews of his youthful exploits.

Notes: Poorly-animated feature starring the orange-striped comic-strip feline Heathcliff, an extension of his Saturday morning TV series (1980–82/86–88); Produced by Jean Chalopin and Denys Heroux, and presented by Clubhouse Pictures.

Credits: Director—Bruno Bianchi; Head Writer—Alan Swayze; Heathcliff created by George Gately; Cats & Co. created by Jean Chalopin and Bruno Bianchi; Music by Shuki Levy and Haim Saban.

Voices: Mel Blanc (Heathcliff), Donna Christie, Peter Cullen, Jeannie Elias, Stanley Jones, Marilyn Lightstone, Danny Mann, Derek McGrath, Marilyn Schreffler, Danny Wells, Ted Ziegler.

73 *Heavy Metal* (1981) *½

Canadian; Rated R; 91 mins.; Released August 7, 1981 (Video: June 1996, Columbia Tri Star); Ivan Reitman/Leonard Mogel.

Synopsis: An anthology of fantasy and science fiction tales. Segments—"Soft Landing," "Grimaldi," "Harry Canyon," "Den," "Captain Sternn," "B-17," "So Beautiful and So Dangerous" and "Taarna."

Notes: Cult favorite inspired by the adult fantasy magazine of the same name (which debuted in 1977). Uneven, but stylishly-drawn at times. For fans; Such top artists as Mike Ploog and Howard Chaykin contributed designs; Released on video after a long delay due to a problem in acquiring music rights; Produced by Ivan Reitman (later the director of *Ghostbusters* and *Twins*).

Credits: Director—Gerald Potterton; **Note:** Potterton (b. 1931), a veteran of the National Film Board of Canada, directed the Oscar-nominated shorts *My Financial Career* (1962) and *The Christmas Cracker* (1963); Sequence Directors—Jack Stokes, Barrie Nelson, Paul Sabella, Pino Van Lamsweerde, Brian Larkin, John Bruno; Screenplay by Dan Goldberg and Len Blum, based on original art and stories by Richard Corben ("Den"), Angus McKie ("So Beautiful and So Dangerous"), Dan O'Bannon ("B-17"), Thomas Warkentin (("Soft Landing") and Berni Wrightson ("Captain Sternn"); Music by Elmer Bernstein, performed by the Royal Philharmonic Orchestra; Features rock songs performed by Blue Oyster Cult, Sammy Hagar, Devo, Black Sabbath, Cheap Trick, Donald Fagen, Don Felder, Grand Funk Railroad, Journey, Nazareth, Stevie Nicks, Riggs, and Trust.

Voices: Richard Romanus (Harry Canyon), John Candy (Den/Desk Sergeant/Dan/Robot), Don Francks (Grimaldi/Co-Pilot/Barbarian), Joe Flaherty (Lawyer/General), Eugene Levy (Sternn/Male Reporter/Edsel), Harold Ramis (Zeks), John Vernon (Prosecutor), Roger Bumpass (Hanover Fiste/Dr. Anrak), Jackie Burroughs (Katherine), Martin Lavut (Ard), Marilyn Lightstone (Whore/Queen), Alice Playten (Gloria), Susan Roman (Girl/Satellite), August Schellenberg (Nort/Taarak), Zal Yanovsky (Navigator/Barbarian); **Note:** Candy, Flaherty, Levy and Ramis were all members of the Second City comedy troupe.

74 *Heavy Traffic* (1973) *½

U.S.; Rated X; 76 mins.; Premiered August 8, 1973; Ralph Bakshi.

Synopsis: A look at urban life through the eyes of a young cartoonist in New York City.

Notes: Lurid Ralph Bakshi film is technically well-done—combining live-action and animation—but not for every taste; Bakshi's second film, following 1972's *Fritz the Cat*; Produced by Steve Krantz and presented by Samuel Z. Arkoff (of American International Pictures).

Credits: Director—Ralph Bakshi; Screenplay by Ralph Bakshi; Music by Ray Shanklin and Ed Bogas.

Voices: Joseph Kaufmann (Michael), Beverly Hope Atkinson (Carole), Frank De

Kova (Angie), Terri Haven (Ida), Mary Dean Lauria (Molly), Jacqueline Mills (Rosalyn), Lillian Adams (Rosa), Jim Bates, Jamie Farr, Robert Easton, Charles Gordone, Michael Brandon, Morton Lewis, Bill Striglos, Jay Lawrence, Lee Weaver.

75 *Heidi's Song* (1982) *

U.S.; Rated G; 94 mins.; Released November 19, 1982; Premiered June 14, 1997 in New York; Hanna-Barbera.

Synopsis: Heidi, a young orphan living in the Swiss Alps with her grandpa, is taken away by her aunt to live with a rich family in Frankfurt.

Notes: Bland animated telling of the classic children's tale. For very young viewers only; Produced by Joseph Barbera and William Hanna (of *Yogi Bear* and *Flintstones* fame).

Credits: Director—Robert Taylor; Supervising Animators—Hal Ambro, Charlie Downs; Screenplay by Joseph Barbera, Jameson Brewer and Robert Taylor, based on the 1880 novel by Johanna Spyri; Music score by Hoyt S. Curtin; Songs by Sammy Cahn (*Journey Back to Oz*) and Burton Lane; **Note:** Composer Lane's (1912–97) best-known work is the musical *Finian's Rainbow* (1947).

Voices: Lorne Greene (Grandfather), Sammy Davis, Jr. (Head Ratte), Margery Gray (Heidi), Michael Bell (Willie), Peter Cullen (Gruffle), Roger DeWitt (Peter), Richard Erdman (Herr Sessman), Fritz Feld (Sebastian), Pamelyn Ferdin (Klara), Joan Gerber (Fräulein Rottenmeier), Virginia Gregg (Aunt Dete), Janet Waldo (Tinette), Frank Welker (Schoodle/Hootie), Mike Winslow (Mountain).

76 *Hercules* (1997) **

U.S.; Rated G; 92 mins.; Released June 27, 1997 (Video: February 1998, Walt Disney); Walt Disney.

Synopsis: In order to prove his heroism to his father (Zeus), Greek strongman Hercules must defeat Hades, the Lord of the Dead.

Notes: Disney returns to lighter fare, following *The Hunchback of Notre Dame* (1996), putting an enjoyable comic spin on the Greek myth while poking fun at hero worship and their own merchandising; Disney's 35th animated feature; Famed British caricaturist Gerald Scarfe served as production designer. Scarfe's best-known film work is the animation for *Pink Floyd—The Wall* (1982); Directors John Musker and Ron Clements were the directing team behind Disney's *The Little Mermaid* (1989) and *Aladdin* (1992); Produced by Musker, Clements and Alice Dewey.

Credits: Directors—John Musker, Ron Clements; Supervising Animators—Chris Bailey, Nancy Beiman, Andreas Deja, Ken Duncan, Eric Goldberg, Nik Ranieri, Ellen Woodbury; **Note:** Bailey directed the Oscar-nominated short *Runaway Brain* (1995); Screenplay by Ron Clements, John Musker, Bob Shaw, Donald McEnery and Irene Mecchi; Music by Alan Menken (his sixth Disney animated film score); Songs by Menken and David Zippel (Tony winner for *City of Angels*); Songs—"Go the Distance," "The Gospel Truth," "I Won't Say (I'm in Love)," "One Last Hope," "Zero to Hero" and "A Star Is Born."

Voices: Tate Donovan (Hercules), Josh Keaton (Young Hercules), Roger Bart (Young Hercules' singing voice), Danny DeVito (Phil), James Woods (Hades), Susan Egan (Meg), Bobcat Goldthwait (Pain), Matt Frewer (Panic), Rip Torn (Zeus), Samantha Eggar (Hera), Barbara Barrie (Alcmene), Hal Holbrook (Amphitryon), Paul Shaffer (Hermes), Amanda Plummer, Carole Shelley, Paddi Edwards (The Fates), Charlton Heston (Narrator), Patrick Pinney (Cyclops), Lillias White (Calliope), Vaneese Thomas (Clio), Cheryl Freeman (Melpomene), La Chanze (Terpsichore), Roz Ryan (Thalia), Corey Burton (Burnt Man), Jim Cummings (Nessus), Keith David (Apollo), Mary Kay Bergman (The Earthquake Lady), Kathleen Freeman (Heavyset Woman), Bug Hall, Kellen Hathaway (Little Boys), Wayne Knight (Demetrius), Aaron Michael Metchik (Ithicles); **Note:** Egan was Tony-nominated for playing Belle in the 1994 Broadway stage version of Disney's *Beauty and the Beast*.

Honors: Academy Award nomination—Song ("Go the Distance").

77 *Here Come the Littles* (1985) $\frac{1}{2}$

Luxembourg; Rated G; 76 mins.; DIC Enterprises.

Synopsis: The Littles—tiny people who live in house walls—help a 12-year-old boy who is forced to live with his mean uncle.

Notes: Dull kids film based on the popular children's books and Saturday morning TV series *The Littles* (1983–86); DIC, an international production company founded by Jean Chalopin, also turned its series *Heathcliff* and *Rainbow Brite* into features; Produced by Chalopin, Andy Heyward and Tetsuo Katayama; Released May, 1985.

Credits: Director—Bernard Deyries; Animation Directors—Tsukasa Tannai, Yoshinobu Michihata; Screenplay by Woody Kling, based on the novels by Jon Peterson; Music by Shuki Levy and Haim Saban.

Voices: Jimmy E. Keegan (Henry Bigg), Bettina Bush (Lucy Little), Donavan Freberg (Tom Little), Hal Smith (Uncle Augustus), Gregg Berger (William Little), Patricia Parris (Helen Little), Alvy Moore (Grandpa Little), Robert David Hall (Dinky Little), Mona Marshall (Mrs. Evans); **Note:** Freberg is the son of comedian Stan Freberg.

78 *Hey Good Lookin'* (1982) $\frac{1}{2}$

U.S.; Rated R; 77 mins.; Released October 1, 1982; Ralph Bakshi.

Synopsis: A look at street gang life in New York City during the 1950s as seen through the eyes of Vinnie, leader of The Stompers.

Notes: Crude, raunchy, adult feature from *Fritz the Cat* director Bakshi; For fans only; The film was released after a long delay (it was made in 1975 but shelved by Warner Bros. after it previewed badly); Produced by Bakshi.

Credits: Director—Ralph Bakshi; Screenplay by Ralph Bakshi; Music by John Madara and Ric Sandler.

Voices: Richard Romanus (Vinnie), David Proval (Crazy), Jesse Welles (Eva), Tina Bowman (Rozzie), Danny Wells, Bennie Massa, Gelsa Palao, Paul Roman, Larry Bishop, Tabi Cooper (Stompers), Juno Dawson (Waitress), Shirley Jo Finney (Chaplin), Martin Garner (Yonkel), Terry Haven (Alice), Allen Joseph (Max), Philip M. Thomas (Chaplin), Frank De Kova (Old Vinnie), Angelo Grisanti (Solly), Candy Candido (Sal), Ed Peck (Italian Man), Lillian Adams, Mary Dean Lauria (Italian Women), Donna Ponterotto (Gelsa), Toni Basil (The Lockers' staging and choreography).

79 *Hey There, It's Yogi Bear* (1964) * $\frac{1}{2}$

U.S.; Rated G; 89 mins.; Premiered June 1, 1964; Hanna-Barbera.

Synopsis: Yogi Bear and his little pal Boo-Boo leave Jellystone Park to find Yogi's girlfriend, Cindy Bear, who has been captured by Chizzling Brothers Circus.

Notes: Yogi Bear's feature debut is pleasant fare for kids; The first full-length animated feature from TV's Hanna-Barbera studio; Working title—*Whistle Your Way Back Home*; Yogi, the picnic basket-loving bear who debuted on *The Huckleberry Hound show* in 1958, starred in the popular *The Yogi Bear Show* (1961–63) and in several later series (1973–75/78–79/85–88/91–92); Produced by William Hanna and Joseph Barbera.

Credits: Directors—William Hanna, Joseph Barbera; Director of Animation—Charles A. Nichols; Screenplay by William Hanna, Joseph Barbera and Warren Foster; Music by Marty Paich; Songs by Ray Gilbert, Doug Goodwin and David Gates; Songs—"Ven-E, Ven-O, Ven-A" (sung by James Darren), "Like I Like You," "Wet Your Whistle," "St. Louie," "Ash Can Parade" and the title song.

Voices: Daws Butler (Yogi Bear), Julie Bennett (Cindy), Don Messick (Boo-Boo/Ranger Smith), Mel Blanc (Grifter), J. Pat O'Malley (Snively), Hal Smith (Corn Pone), Jean VanderPyl; **Note:** Charles Dawson "Daws" Butler (1917–88) was one of the cartoon world's leading voice artists (his characters include Yogi, Huckleberry Hound and Quick Draw McGraw).

Hoppity Goes to Town **see** *Mr. Bug Goes to Town.*

80 *Hugo the Hippo* (1976) *½

Hungarian-U.S.; Rated G; 90 mins.; Released June 1976; Brut/Hungarofilm Pannonia Filmstudio.

Synopsis: In ancient Zanzibar, a young boy tries to help a baby hippo and others of his species from being slaughtered by man.

Notes: Charming, nicely-animated children's fable; Hungarian title—*Hugo a vizilo*; Produced by Robert Halmi.

Credits: Director—William Feigenbaum; Animation Director—Jozsef Gemes; Screenplay by Tom Baum; Music by Burt Keyes; Songs by Robert Larimer; Songs—"It's Really True," "I Always Wanted to Make a Garden," "Somewhere You Can Call Home," "H-I-P-P-O-P-O-T-A-M-U-S," "You Said a Mouthful," "Best Day Ever Made," "Mr. M'Bow-Wow," "Wherever You Go, Hugo," "Harbor Chant" and "Zing Zang."

Voices: Burl Ives (Narrator), Robert Morley (The Sultan), Paul Lynde (Aban Khan), Jesse Emmet (Royal Magician), Ronnie Cox (Jorma), Len Maxwell (Judge), Percy Rodriguez (Jorma's Father), Marie Osmond, Jimmy Osmond (Vocalists), Tom Scott, Don Marshall, H.B. Barnum III, Marc Copage, Charles Walken, Lee Weaver, Richard Williams, Frank Welker, Ron Pinkard, Michael Rye, Marc Wright, Ellsworth Wright, Vincent Esposito, Court Benson, Peter Benson, Mona Tera, Bobby Eilbacher, Peter Fernandez, Allen Swift, Derek Power, Frederick O'Neal, Al Fann, Thomas Anderson, Jerome Ward, Shawn Campbell, Lisa Huggins, John McCoy, Alicia Fleer, Lisa Kohane, Bobby Dorn, Pat Bright, Robert Lawrence, Nancy Wible, Jerry Hausner.

81 *The Hunchback of Notre Dame* (1996) **½

U.S.; Rated G; 90 mins.; Released June 21, 1996 (Video: March 1997, Walt Disney); Walt Disney.

Synopsis: Quasimodo, a deformed, hunchbacked bellringer who lives atop Notre Dame's bell tower with his stone gargoyle friends, yearns to belong and to have the love of the Gypsy girl Esmerelda.

Notes: Disney's most adult-themed animated feature (its 34th) offers up a poignant musical version of the classic story, with lavish animation beautifully recreating 15th-century Paris; *Hunchback* has been filmed at least seven times since 1905, the standout being the 1939 version starring Charles Laughton; Gary Trousdale and Kirk Wise were the directing team behind *Beauty and the Beast* (1991); Produced by Don Hahn.

Credits: Directors—Gary Trousdale, Kirk Wise; Supervising Animators—James Baxter, Dave Burgess, Russ Edmonds, Will Finn, Tony Fucile, Ron Husband, David Pruiksma, Mike Surrey, Kathy Zielinski; Screenplay by Tab Murphy, Irene Mecchi, Bob Tzudiker, Noni White and Jonathan Roberts, based on the 1831 novel *Notre Dame de Paris* by Victor Hugo; Musical score by Alan Menken and Stephen Schwartz; Songs (8 in all) include "Hellfire," "Out There," "Someday" and "God Help the Outcasts."

Voices: Tom Hulce (Quasimodo), Demi Moore (Esmerelda), Heidi Mollenhauer (Esmerelda's singing voice), Kevin Kline (Phoebus), Tony Jay (Claude Frollo), Jason Alexander (Hugo), Charles Kimbrough (Victor), Mary Wickes/Jane Withers (Laverne), Paul Kandel (Clopin), David Ogden Stiers (Archdeacon), Mary Kay Bergman (Quasimodo's Mother), Corey Burton (Brutish Guard), Jim Cummings (Guards and Gypsies),

Bill Fagerbakke (Oafish Guard), Patrick Pinney (Guards and Gypsies), Gary Trousdale (The Old Heretic), Frank Welker (Baby Bird); **Notes:** Hulce was Oscar-nominated for playing Mozart in *Amadeus* (1984). The drawing of Moore's Esmerelda was also modeled after the actress. Veteran character actress Wickes died in October 1995 at 85, shortly before finishing her role (Withers completed it). Kimbrough plays Jim Dial on TV's *Murphy Brown*.

Honors: Academy Award nomination—Musical score.

82 *I Married a Strange Person* (1997) * ½

U.S.; Not Rated; 74 mins.; Premiered September 8, 1997 at the Toronto Film Festival; Bill Plympton.

Synopsis: A woman's new husband grows an extra brain lobe on the back of his neck which turns his fantasies into reality.

Notes: Not for young children; Plympton's second animated feature, following *The Tune* (1992); Includes the previously-released short *How to Make Love to a Woman*; Produced by Plympton.

Credits: Director—Bill Plympton; Written and animated by Bill Plympton; Music by Maureen McElheron.

Voices: J.B. Adams, Max Brandt, Chris Cooke, Tom Larson, Charis Michaelson, Ruth Ray, Toni Rossi, John A. Russo, Richard Spore, Etta Valeska.

Ichabod and Mr. Toad **see** *The Adventures of Ichabod and Mr. Toad.*

83 *The Incredible Mr. Limpet* (1964) * ½

U.S.; Not Rated; 102 mins.; Premiered March 28, 1964, at Weeki Wachee Springs, Florida—on the ocean floor, 20 feet below the water's surface; Warner Bros.

Synopsis: Henry Limpet, a meek, fish-loving clerk, miraculously turns into a fish and becomes a secret weapon for the navy during World War II.

Notes: Pleasant live-action family film with animated underwater sequences; Working titles—*Henry Limpet, Mister Limpet, Be Careful How You wish*; Produced by John C. Rose.

Credits: Director—Arthur Lubin; **Note:** Lubin (1901–95) is best known for directing five Abbott and Costello films (1941–42) and directing-producing TV's *Mr. Ed* (1961–65); Special Piscatorial Effects (animation)—Vladimir Tytla, Gerry Chiniquy, Hawley Pratt, Robert McKimson, Maurice Noble, Don Peters, John Dunn; Screenplay by Jameson Bewer and John C. Rose, based on the 1942 novel *Mr. Limpet* by Theodore Pratt; Music by Frank Perkins; Songs by Sammy Fain and Harold Adamson; Songs—"The Mr. Limpet March (Super Doodle Dandy)," "I Wish I Were a Fish," "Be Careful How You Wish," "Deep Rapture" and "Hail to Henry Limpet."

Cast/Voices: Don Knotts (Henry Limpet), Jack Weston (George Stickle), Carole Cook (Bessie Limpet), Andrew Duggan (Admiral Harlock), Larry Keating (Admiral Spewter), Charles Meredith (Admiral Fivestar), Oscar Beregi (Admiral Doemitz); Elizabeth MacRae (Ladyfish), Paul Frees (Crusty); **Note:** Knotts won five Emmys for playing Deputy Barney Fife (1960–65) on TV's *The Andy Griffith Show*.

84 *Invitation to the Dance* (1956) * ½

U.S.; Not Rated; 93 mins.; MGM.

Synopsis: Three tales interpreted entirely in dance—"Circus," "Ring Around the Rosy" and "Sinbad the Sailor" (anim./live-action).

Notes: The final "Sinbad" sequence, featuring Gene Kelly in animated surroundings, highlights this three-part dance film; Hanna-Barbera, who had done animation (featuring "Tom and Jerry") for two previous MGM musicals—*Anchors Aweigh* (1945) with Kelly and *Dangerous When Wet* (1953) with Esther Williams—animated the "Sinbad" sequence. Nearly 40 artists worked on the sequence, making 250,000 sketches; The film—Gene Kelly's first solo-directorial effort—took four years to produce, but flopped at the box office, signaling the end of the big Hollywood musical era; Produced by Arthur Freed.

Credits: Director—Gene Kelly; Cartoon Sequence—Joseph Barbera, William Hanna, Michael Lah; Written and choreographed by Gene Kelly; Music score by Jacques Ibert, Andre Previn, Roger Edens, based on the music of Nikolay Andreyevitch Rimsky-Korsakov.

Cast: Gene Kelly, Carol Haney, Cyd Charisse, David Kasday, Igor Youskevitch, Claire Sombert, David Paltenghi, Daphne Dale, Claude Bessy, Tommy Rall, Belita, Irving Davies, Diana Adams, Tamara Toumanova.

Honors: Award—West Berlin Film Festival (Grand Prize).

85 *James and the Giant Peach* (1996) **

U.S.; Rated PG; 80 mins.; Released April 12, 1996 (Video: October 1996, Walt Disney); Walt Disney/Allied Filmmakers.

Synopsis: A lonely English orphan, living with his wicked aunts, climbs into a magically enlarged peach and—with some giant insect companions—sets off on a fantastic journey across the ocean.

Notes: Visually-striking fantasy from the makers of *The Nightmare Before Christmas*, using the same stop-motion animation technique; Live-action scenes (35 mins) frame the animated adventure (45 mins); The film also uses paintings, computer graphics and conventional cel animation; Produced by Denise Di Novi and Tim Burton.

Credits: Director—Henry Selick; Animation Supervisor—Paul Berry; Screenplay by Karey Kirkpatrick, Jonathan Roberts (*The Lion King*) and Steve Bloom, based on the 1961 children's story by Roald Dahl; **Notes:** Famed British TV playwright Dennis Potter (*The Singing Detective*) wrote a draft of the script. Dahl (1916–90) also wrote the classic *Charlie and the Chocolate Factory* (1964); Music by Randy Newman (*Toy Story*); Original songs by Newman; Songs—"My Name Is James," "That's the Life," "Family," "Eating the Peach" (lyrics by Roald Dahl) and "Good News."

Cast: Joanna Lumley (Aunt Spiker), Miriam Margolyes (Aunt Sponge), Pete Postlethwaite (Old Man), Paul Terry (James); **Voices:** Simon Callow (Grasshopper), Richard Dreyfuss (Centipede), Jane Leeves (Ladybug), Miriam Margolyes (Glowworm), Susan Sarandon (Spider), David Thewlis (Earthworm); **Notes:** Lumley played Patsy on the TV series *Absolutely Fabulous*. Leeves plays Daphne Moon on TV's *Frasier* (1993–).

Honors: Academy Award nomination—Musical Score.

86 *Jetsons: The Movie* (1990) *

U.S.; Rated G; 82 mins.; Released July 6, 1990 (Video: November 1990, MCA/Universal); Hanna-Barbera.

Synopsis: George Jetson and family are transferred by his boss, Mr. Spacely, to a Spacely Sprocket plant in outer space.

Notes: Weak feature debut of the futuristic animated sitcom, benefiting from several computer-animated sequences; The original TV series, created by Hanna-Barbera following the success of their prehistoric sitcom *The Flintstones*, consisted of only 24 episodes (1962–63). Fifty-one more were later produced (1984–88); Cost of film—$12 million; Produced by William Hanna and Joseph Barbera.

Credits: Directors—William Hanna, Joseph Barbera; Supervising Director—Iwao Takamoto; Supervising Animation Director—Dave Michener; Screenplay by Dennis Marks; Music score by John Debney; Songs by Tim James, Steve McClintock, Steve Klempster, Mike Piccirillo, Carl Wurtz, Phil Colemand, George Tobin and Mark Mancina; Songs—"Jetsons Main Title" (by Hanna, Barbera and Hoyt Curtin), "Gotcha," "Maybe

Love, Maybe Not," "Staying Together," "First Time in Love," "With You All the Way," "I Always Thought I'd See You Again," "You and Me," "Home" and "We're the Jetsons (Jetsons' Rap)."

Voices: George O'Hanlon (George Jetson), Penny Singleton (Jane Jetson), Mel Blanc (Mr. Spacely), Tiffany (Judy Jetson), Patrick Zimmerman (Elroy Jetson), Don Messick (Astro), Jean VanderPyl (Rosie the Robot), Ronnie Schell (Rudy 2), Patti Deutsch (Lucy 2), Dana Hill (Teddy 2), Russi Taylor (Fergie Furbelow), Paul Kreppel (Apollo Blue), Rick Dees (Rocket Rick), Michael Bell, Brian Cummings, Rob Paulsen, Janet Waldo, Jim Ward, Jeff Bergman, Brad Garrett, Susan Silo, B.J. Ward, Frank Welker; **Notes:** Blanc's last voice role. The legendary Warner Bros. voice artist died July 10, 1989 at 81. O'Hanlon (who originated George Jetson) also does his last voice work here (he died in 1989). Waldo, Judy Jetson's original voice, again voiced Judy for this film, but the producers later replaced her voice with that of young pop singer Tiffany.

87 *Journey Back to Oz* (1974) *½
U.S.; Rated G; 90 mins.; Filmation.

Synopsis: Dorothy travels back to Oz where she meets old and new friends and finds that the magical land is threatened by another wicked witch, named Mombi.

Notes: Enjoyable animated sequel to *The Wizard of Oz* (1939). For kids mainly; Released after a long delay (it was filmed in 1964); Later reedited (with added live-action scenes featuring Bill Cosby and friends) and shown as a holiday TV special (December 1976); Produced by Norm Prescott and Lou Scheimer.

Credits: Director—Hal Sutherland; Animation Supervisor—Amby Paliwoda; Sequence Directors—Rudy Larriva, Don Towsley; Screenplay by Fred Ladd and Norm Prescott, based on the story by L. Frank Baum; Music and lyrics by James Van Heusen and Sammy Cahn; **Note:** Van Heusen (1913–90) and Cahn (1913–93) won 3 Best Song Oscars together (1957, '59, '63).

Voices: Liza Minnelli (Dorothy), Mickey Rooney (Scarecrow), Paul Lynde (Pumpkinhead), Danny Thomas (Tinman), Herschel Bernardi (Woodenhead), Milton Berle (Cowardly Lion), Margaret Hamilton (Aunt Em), Jack E. Leonard (The Signpost), Ethel Merman (Mombi), Rise Stevens (Glinda), Mel Blanc (Crow), Paul Ford (Uncle Henry), Dallas McKennon (Omby Amby), Larry Storch (Amos); **Notes:** Minnelli provides the voice of the same character her mother, the late Judy Garland, played in the 1939 film. Hamilton, of course, played the wicked witch in the original film.

88 *The Jungle Book* (1967) **½
U.S.; Rated G; 78 mins.; Premiered September 14, 1967 in Los Angeles; Released October 18, 1967 (Video: May 1991, Walt Disney); Walt Disney.

Synopsis: Mowgli, an orphaned Indian boy raised by wolves, learns about life and the true meaning of friendship from his jungle friends while eluding the man-hating tiger Shere Khan.

Notes: Disney's fun, tuneful animated version of the Kipling tale, with excellent voice characterizations; The last Disney animated feature produced in Walt Disney's lifetime (he died of cancer at age 65 on December 15, 1966). Director Wolfgang Reitherman (1909–85), who joined the Disney studio in 1933, succeeded Disney as head of the studio's animation department; A 3 1/2-year production; A box-office smash when first released (earning $11.5 million); Characters from the film were later revived in the Disney TV series *Tale Spin* (1990–94); Live-action versions of the story have also been filmed (1942, '94).

Highlights: Baloo's "Bare Necessities" musical number, and Mowgli's encounter with King Louis the orangutan.

Credits: Director—Wolfgang Reitherman; Directing Animators—Milt Kahl, Ollie Johnston, Frank Thomas, John Lounsbery; Screenplay by Larry Clemmons, Ralph Wright,

Ken Anderson and Vance Gerry, based loosely on the "Mowgli" stories (1893–95) by Rudyard Kipling; Music by George Bruns; Songs by Robert B. and Richard M. Sherman, Terry Gilkyson; Songs—"I Wanna Be Like You," "Kaa's Song," "My Own Home," "Colonel Hathi's March," "That's What Friends Are For" and "The Bare Necessities."

Voices: Phil Harris (Baloo the bear), Sebastian Cabot (Bagheera the panther), Louis Prima (King Louie of the Apes), George Sanders (Shere Khan the tiger), Sterling Holloway (Kaa the snake), J. Pat O'Malley (Colonel Hathi the elephant), Bruce Reitherman (Mowgli the Man Cub), Verna Felton, Clint Howard (Elephants), Chad Stuart, Lord Tim Hudson (Vultures), John Abbott, Ben Wright (Wolves), Darleen Carr (The Girl); **Notes:** Harris (1906–95) and Prima (1910–78) were both popular bandleaders of the '40s and '50s. Veteran English actor Sanders (1906–72), famous for playing suave, cynical characters, won an Oscar for his performance in 1950's *All About Eve.*

Honors: Academy Award nomination—Song ("The Bare Necessities" music and lyrics by Gilkyson).

89 *Lady and the Tramp* (1955) ***
U.S.; Rated G; 75 mins.; Premiered June 16, 1955 in New York; Released June 22, 1955 (Video: October 1987, Walt Disney); Walt Disney.

Synopsis: The adventures of Lady, a pampered cocker spaniel, and Tramp, a carefree mongrel from the wrong side of the tracks.

Notes: Classic canine tale from Disney Studios, filled with great music, action and romance. A beautifully animated film for all ages; Disney's first animated feature to be shot in wide-screen CinemaScope; More than 300 animators and artists worked on the film for three years (making some 300,000 drawings); The film, which cost $4 million to produce, was a huge box-office success (grossing over $25 million).

Highlights: Aunt Sarah's mischievous Siamese cats, the romantic "Belle Notte" scene outside Tony's restaurant, and Peg the Pekingese singing her torch song "He's a Tramp."

Credits: Directors—Hamilton Luske, Clyde Geronimi, Wilfred Jackson; Directing Animators—Milt Kahl, Franklin Thomas, Oliver Johnston, Jr., John Lounsbery, Wolfgang Reitherman, Eric Larson, Hal King, Les Clark; Screenplay by Erdman Penner, Joe Rinaldi, Ralph Wright and Donald Da Gradi, based on the short novel *Happy Dan, the Whistling Dog* by Ward Greene; Music by Oliver Wallace; Songs by Peggy Lee and Sonny Burke; Songs—"The Siamese Cat Song," "La-La-Lu," "Peace on Earth," "Belle Notte" and "He's a Tramp."

Voices: Barbara Luddy (Lady), Larry Roberts (Tramp), Peggy Lee (Darling/Peg/Si/Am), Bill Thompson (Jock/Bull/Dachsie), Bill Baucon (Trusty), Stan Freberg (Beaver), Verna Felton (Aunt Sarah), Alan Reed (Boris), George Givot (Tony), Dallas McKennon (Toughy/Professor), Lee Millar (Jim Dear), The Mellomen (dogs); **Note:** Lee, whose song hits include "Fever" and "Is That All There Is?," later sued Disney for royalties from video sales and was awarded (in March 1991) $3.83 million.

90 *The Land Before Time* (1988) **
U.S.; Rated G; 66 mins.; Released November 18, 1988; Sullivan Bluth.

Synopsis: An orphaned brontosaurus and four other young dinosaurs face many dangers on their journey to the vegetation-rich Great Valley.

Notes: Exciting, well-animated prehistoric tale aimed at young audiences; Don Bluth's third animated feature and the first production from his Sullivan Bluth Studios Ireland (which opened in Dublin in 1985); Although it opened on the same day as Disney's *Oliver and Company*, the film earned a respectable $47.9 million at the box office; Followed by four made-for-video sequels (1994, '95, '96, '97); Produced by Bluth, Gary Goldman and John Pomeroy; Executive Producers—George Lucas and Steven Spielberg.

Credits: Director—Don Bluth; Directing Animators—John Pomeroy, Linda Miller, Ralph Zondag, Dan Kuenster, Lorna Pomeroy, Dick Zondag; Screenplay by Stu Krieger, based on a story by Judy Freudberg and Tony Geiss (the screenwriters for Bluth's *An American Tail*); Music by James Horner, performed by The London Symphony Orchestra, Kings College School Choir, The Choristers of St. Paul's Cathedral and Ladies' Chorus; Song—"If We Hold On Together" (performed by Diana Ross) by Horner and Will Jennings.

Voices: Pat Hingle (Narrator/Rooter), Helen Shaver (Littlefoot's Mother), Gabriel Damon (Littlefoot), Bill Erwin (Grandfather), Candy Hutson (Cera), Burke Byrnes (Daddy Topps), Judith Barsi (Ducky), Will Ryan (Petrie).

91 *The Last Unicorn* (1982) * ½

U.S.; Rated G; 88 mins.; Released November 1982; Rankin-Bass.

Synopsis: A beautiful unicorn sets out to free her lost unicorn companions from an evil king.

Notes: Handsomely-animated fantasy tale for kids from the Rankin-Bass studio (*The Daydreamer*, *Mad Monster Party?*); Produced by Arthur Rankin, Jr., and Jules Bass, and presented by Lord Grade.

Credits: Directors—Arthur Rankin, Jr., Jules Bass; Animation Director—Katsuhisa Yamada; Screenplay by Peter S. Beagle (cowriter on Ralph Bakshi's *Lord of the Rings*), from his 1968 novel; Music and lyrics by Jimmy Webb; Songs performed by the music group America.

Voices: Mia Farrow (The Unicorn/Lady Amalthea), Alan Arkin (Schmendrick), Jeff Bridges (Prince Lir), Tammy Grimes (Molly Grue), Robert Klein (Butterfly), Angela Lansbury (Mommy Fortuna), Christopher Lee (King Haggard), Keenan Wynn (Capt. Cully), Paul Frees (Cat), René Auberjonois (Skull), Brother Theodore (Rukh), Jack Lester, Edward Peck, Don Messick, Nellie Bellflower, Kenneth Jennings.

92 *Light Years* (1988) *

French-U.S.; Rated PG; 79 mins; Released January 1988.

Synopsis: A young prince on the planet Gandahar must save his peaceful world from threatening mutants.

Notes: Unexceptional sci-fi tale, for fans only; American version (dubbed in English by American actors) of the French film *Gandahar*; The film is based on the drawings of Philippe Caza; René Laloux's third feature effort. He began developing it back in 1974, a year after the release of his first film, *Fantastic Planet*.

Credits: Director—Rene Laloux; Screenplay by famed science fiction writer Isaac Asimov; Original screenplay (fr.) by Raphael Cluzel, adapted by Rene Laloux from the novel *Robots Against Gandahar* by Jean-Pierre Andrevan; Music by Jack Maeby, Bob Jewett and Gabriel Yared.

Voices: Glenn Close (Ambisextra), Christopher Plummer (Metamorphis), Jennifer Grey (Airelle), John Shea (Sylvain), Penn Jillette (Chief of the Deformed), David Johansen (Shayol), Terrence Mann (The Collective Voice), Charles Busch, Bridget Fonda, Sheila McCarthy, Paul Shaffer, Teller, Earl Hyman, Earl Hammond, Alexander Marshall.

93 *The Lion King* (1994) **

U.S.; Rated G; 88 mins.; Released June 15, 1994, rereleased: November 1994 (Video: February 1995, Walt Disney); Walt Disney.

Synopsis: After his father is murdered by his villainous uncle, a young lion prince is forced into exile until he matures and can return to claim his rightful title as king.

Notes: Disney's first animated feature to be based on an original—if overly-familiar

—story (borrowing mostly from *Bambi* and *Hamlet*) tackles the themes of death, responsibility and growing up with music, humor and the usual top-notch animation; Disney's 32nd animated feature; 800 animators, artists and technicians spent three years on the film, making one million drawings; Original director George Scribner (*Oliver and Company*) was let go after the studio changed the film's direction away from his nonmusical concept; The film, which cost $45 million to produce, grossed $40.9 million in its first three days of release. It went on to become the highest-grossing film of 1994 (earning over $300 million in the U.S.) and Disney's all-time top-grosser; Spawned the Saturday morning TV series *Timon and Pumbaa* (1995–); An acclaimed stage version, directed by Julie Taymor and starring Samuel E. Wright (*The Little Mermaid*), opened on Broadway in November 1997 (it went on to win the 1998 Tony Award for best musical); Produced by Don Hahn (*Beauty and the Beast*).

Highlight: the opening "Circle of Life" sequence, and Timon and Pumbaa's song "Hakuna Matata" (which means "no worries").

Credits: Directors—Roger Allers, Rob Minkoff; Supervising Animators—Mark Henn, Ruben Aquino, Tony Fucile, Andreas Deja, Anthony DeRosa, Aaron Blaise, Tony Bancroft, Michael Surrey, James Baxter, Ellen Woodbury, Russ Edmunds, David Burgess, Alex Kupershmidt; Screenplay by Irene Mecchi, Jonathan Roberts and Linda Woolverton; Musical score by Hans Zimmer (*Rain Man*, *Driving Miss Daisy*); Music by Elton John, lyrics by Tim Rice; Songs—"Circle of Life," "I Just Can't Wait to be King," "Be Prepared," "Hakuna Matata" and "Can You Feel the Love Tonight?"

Voices: Matthew Broderick (Simba), Jonathan Taylor Thomas (Young Simba), James Earl Jones (Mufasa), Jeremy Irons (Scar), Rowan Atkinson (Zaza), Nathan Lane (Timon), Ernie Sabella (Pumbaa), Whoopi Goldberg (Shenzi), Cheech Marin (Banzai), Jim Cummings (Ed), Robert Guillaume (Rafiki), Madge Sinclair (Sarabi), Moira Kelly (Nala), Niketa Calame (Young Nala), Zoe Leader (Sarafina); **Notes:** Thomas plays Randy on TV's *Home Improvement* (1991–). British comedian Atkinson starred in TV's *Blackadder* and *Bean*. Lane has starred on Broadway (*Guys and Dolls*) and film (*The Birdcage*).

Honors: Academy Awards—Original Score and Song ("Can You Feel the Love Tonight?"), also nominated for Songs ("Circle of Life" and "Hakuna Matata"); Golden Globes—Best Film Musical/Comedy, Score, Song ("Can You Feel the Love Tonight?").

94 *The Little Mermaid* (1989) ***

U.S.; Rated G; 82 mins.; Released November 17, 1989 (Video: May 1990, Walt Disney); Walt Disney.

Synopsis: A young mermaid falls in love with a handsome prince and makes a deal with a sea witch in order to be with him in his human world.

Notes: Disney's most successful animated feature in years is a tuneful, superbly-animated version of the classic tale; The studio's 28th animated feature and its first animated fairy tale since 1959's *Sleeping Beauty*; The $23 million film earned over $80 million at the box office, more than any previous Disney animated film on first release; The first fully-animated feature to receive an Academy Award (it won two) since *Dumbo* (1941); Spawned a Saturday morning cartoon series (1992–95); Produced by John Musker and Howard Ashman.

Highlights: the showstopping reggae number "Under the Sea," and the final showdown with Ursula the sea witch.

Credits: Directors—John Musker, Ron Clements; Directing Animators—Mark Henn, Glen Keane, Duncan Marjoribanks, Ruben Aquino, Andreas Deja, Matthew O'Callaghan; Screenplay by John Musker and Ron Clements, based on the 1837 fairy tale by Hans Christian Andersen; Musical score by Alan Menken; Songs by Menken and coproducer Howard Ashman (the songwriting team behind the hit musical *Little Shop of Horrors*); Songs—"Part of Your World," "Under the Sea," "Poor Unfortunate Souls," "Les Poissons," "Fathoms Below," "Daughters of Triton" and "Kiss the Girl."

Voices: Jodi Benson (Ariel), Pat Carroll (Ursula), Kenneth Mars (Triton), Buddy Hackett (Scuttle), Samuel E. Wright (Sebastian), Christopher Daniel Barnes (Eric), René Auberjonois (Louis), Jason Marin (Flounder), Edie McClurg (Carlotta), Ben Wright (Grimsby), Will Ryan (Seahorse), Paddi Edwards (Flotsam/Jetsam); **Notes:** Tony nominee Samuel E. Wright played the grape in Fruit of the Loom ads and Dizzy Gillespie in the film *Bird* (1988). Barnes later played Greg Brady in *The Brady Bunch Movie* (1995) and its sequel. Ben Wright (1915–89) voiced Roger Radcliff in Disney's *101 Dalmatians* (1961).

Honors: Academy Awards—Original Score and Song ("Under the Sea"), also nominated for Song ("Kiss the Girl").

95 *Little Nemo: Adventures in Slumberland* (1992) * $\frac{1}{2}$

Japanese-U.S.; Rated G; 85 mins.; Released August 21, 1992 (Video: February 1993, Hemdale Home Video); Tokyo Movie Shinsha.

Synopsis: After being transported to Slumberland, a young boy sets out to rescue the king of the land who has been abducted to Nightmareland by a dark demon.

Notes: Engaging kids adventure based on the 1905 comic-strip *Little Nemo in Slumberland* by cartoonist/animation pioneer Winsor McCay, whose first cartoon short *Little Nemo* (1911) was also based on the strip; Produced by Yutaka Fujioka.

Credits: Directors—Masami Hata, William Hurtz; Animation Directors—Kazuhide Tomonoga, Nobuo Tomizawa; Screenplay by Chris Columbus (director of *Home Alone*) and Richard Outten, based on characters created by Winsor McCay; Story by French comic-book icon Jean Moebius Giraud and Yutaka Fujioka; Concept for Screen—Ray Bradbury; Music by Thomas Chase and Steve Rucker; Songs by Richard M. and Robert B. Sherman (of *Mary Poppins* fame); Title songs sung by Melissa Manchester.

Voices: Gabriel Damon (Nemo), Mickey Rooney (Flip), René Auberjonois (Prof. Genius), Danny Mann (Icarus), Laura Mooney (Princess Camille), Bernard Erhard (King Morpheus), William E. Martin (Nightmare King), Alan Oppenheimer (Oomp), Michael Bell (Oompy), Sidney Miller (Oompe), Neil Ross (Oompa), John Stephenson (Oompo), Jennifer Darling, Greg Burson, Sherry Lynn, Guy Christopher, Nancy Cartwright, Ellen Gerstell, Tress MacNeille, Michael McConnohie, Beau Weaver, Michael Gough, Kathleen Freeman, Michael Sheehan, June Foray, Gregg Berger, Bert Kramer, Bever-Leigh Banfield.

96 *The Looney, Looney, Looney Bugs Bunny Movie* (1981) * $\frac{1}{2}$

U.S.; Rated G; 80 mins.; Released November 20, 1981; Warner Bros.

Synopsis: A cartoon compilation divided into three parts—Yosemite Sam dealing with the Devil, Bugs Bunny outwitting gangsters Rocky and Mugsy, and an award show parody. Cartoons shown—*Knighty Knight Bugs* (Oscar-winner), *Sahara Hare*, *Roman Legion Hare*, *High Diving Hare*, *Hare Trimmed*, *Wild and Wooly Hare*, *Catty Cornered*, *Golden Yeggs*, *The Unmentionables*, *Three Little Bops* and *Show Biz Bugs*. See SHORTS.

Notes: Fine Warner Bros. compilation feature (the studio's second) with several outstanding cartoons (the 11 shown date from 1949 to 1963); Aka *Friz Freleng's Looney, Looney, Looney Bugs Bunny Movie*; The feature debut of famed Warner cartoon director Friz Freleng who, in 1980, was made head of the studio's revitalized animation division. He also directed-produced four Warner Bros. TV specials (1977–81); Features Bugs Bunny, Daffy Duck, Yosemite Sam, Porky Pig, Tweety, Sylvester, Rocky and Mugsy, and others; Produced by Freleng.

Credits: Director—Friz Freleng; Sequence Directors—David Detiege, Phil Monroe, Gerry Chiniquy; Screenplay by John Dunn, David Detiege and Friz Freleng; Music by Rob Walsh, Don McGinnis, Milt Franklyn, Bill Lava, Shorty Rogers and Carl Stalling.

Voices: Mel Blanc, June Foray, Frank Nelson, Frank Welker, Stan Freberg, Ralph James.

97 *The Lord of the Rings* (1978) $*\frac{1}{2}$
U.S.; Rated PG; 133 mins.; Ralph Bakshi.

Synopsis: In Middle-earth, a hobbit named Frodo embarks on a quest to destroy an all-powerful ring sought after by the Dark Lord Sauron.

Notes: Ralph Bakshi's ambitious adaption of the classic Tolkien saga suffers from excess length and overuse of the rotoscope process (tracing from live-action footage); Bakshi (of *Fritz the Cat* fame) had planned to tell the entire epic story in two films (*Lord* covers only a book-and-a-half of Tolkien's fantasy trilogy), but because of the poor response to this first film, the second was never produced; The film—Bakshi's fifth animated feature—took three years, $6 million, 164 artists and 250,000 drawings to produce; Tolkien has also been adapted in two Rankin-Bass TV productions, *The Hobbit* (1977) and *The Return of the King* (1980); Produced by Saul Zaentz (Oscar winner for 1975's *One Flew Over the Cuckoo's Nest*).

Credits: Director—Ralph Bakshi; Screenplay by Chris Conkling and Peter S. Beagle (*The Last Unicorn*), based on the books *The Fellowship of the Ring* and *The Two Towers* (from the trilogy "Lord of the Rings," 1954–55) by J(ohn) R(onald) R(euel) Tolkien (1892–1973); Music by Leonard Rosenman (*Barry Lyndon*).

Voices: Christopher Guard (Frodo), John Hurt (Aragorn), William Squire (Gandalf), Michael Scholes (Sam), Dominic Guard (Pippin), Simon Chandler (Merry), Norman Bird (Bilbo), Michael Graham-Cox (Boromir), Anthony Daniels (Legolas), David Buck (Gimli), Peter Wood Thorpe (Gollum), Fraser Kerr (Saruman), Phillip Stone (Theoden), Michael Deacon (Wormtongue), Andre Morell (Elrond), Alan Tilvern (Innkeeper), Annette Crosbie (Galadriel), John Westbrook (Treebeard).

98 *Mad Monster Party?* (1967) *
U.S.; Not Rated; 94 mins.; Premiered Mar. 8, 1967 in New York; Rankin-Bass (Videocraft International).

Synopsis: Frankenstein gathers together a group of famous monsters, including The Wolfman, Dracula and The Mummy, to announce his retirement.

Notes: Amusing Rankin-Bass production using Animagic (stop-motion photography of three-dimensional figures); Puppet design by Jack Davis; Produced by Arthur Rankin, Jr., and presented by Joseph E. Levine.

Credits: Director—Jules Bass; Screenplay by Len Korobkin, Harvey Kurtzman and Forrest J Ackerman, based on a story by Arthur Rankin, Jr.; Music and lyrics by Maury Laws and Jules Bass.

Voices: Boris Karloff (Baron von Frankenstein), Phyllis Diller (Frankenstein's Wife), Gale Garnett, Ethel Ennis, Allen Swift; **Note:** Karloff (1887–1969) played the monster (his star-making role) in the classic 1931 film *Frankenstein*. His most famous cartoon voice was that of the Grinch (and narrator) in the TV perennial *Dr. Seuss' How the Grinch Stole Christmas* (1966).

99 *The Magic Pony* (1977) $*\frac{1}{2}$
Russian-U.S.; Rated G; 80 mins.; Soyuzmult Film Studios.

Synopsis: A peasant boy befriends a pony with magical powers who leads him on a series of fabulous adventures.

Notes: Enjoyable fantasy tale for kids; American version of a Russian animated feature, *The Humpbacked Horse* (aka *The Magic Horse*) from Ivan Ivanov-Vano (1900–87), which was a remake of a film he made in 1947; Produced by C.B. Wismar.

Credits: Director—Ivan Ivanov-Vano; Animation by Lev Milchin; Story by E. Pomeschikov and P. Pozhkov, based on the Russian folk tale by Peter Yershov; English adaption by George Malko; Songs by Tom Ed Williams; Songs—"Ride a Magic Pony," "Lonely Child," "A Whale of a Way" and "On This Beautiful Day."

Voices: Jim Backus (King), Hans Conreid (Red-Haired Groom), Erin Moran (Zip the Pony), Johnny Whitaker (Ivan), Diana Alton, Robb Cigne, John Craig, Wayne Heffley, Jason Wingreen, Sandra Wirth; **Notes:** Backus was the voice of "Mr. Magoo." Moran and Whitaker were both TV child actors (on *Happy Days* and *Family Affair*, respectively).

100 *Make Mine Music* (1946) ** ½

U.S.; Not Rated; 75 mins.; Released August 15, 1946; Walt Disney.

Synopsis: Ten musical cartoon shorts—*The Martins and the Coys, Blue Bayou, All the Cats Join In, Without You, Casey at the Bat, Two Silhouettes, Peter and the Wolf, After You've Gone, Johnnie Fedora and Alice Bluebonnet* and *The Whale Who Wanted to Sing at the Met.* See SHORTS.

Notes: A variety of musical stories and interludes are superbly rendered by the Disney studio in this compilation feature; Walt Disney had originally planned to do Prokofieff's "Peter and the Wolf" as part of a *Fantasia* sequel, but because of that film's poor box-office performance the project was abandoned; The visual compliment to "Blue Bayou" was taken from a deleted *Fantasia* sequence visualizing Debussy's "Claire de Lune."

Highlights: the two Benny Goodman shorts, *Peter and the Wolf*, and the imaginative final sequence about an operatic whale named Willie.

Credits: Supervisor: Joe Grant; Sequence Directors—Jack Kinney, Samuel Armstrong, Clyde Geronimi, Hamilton Luske, Robert Cormack, Joshua Meador; Stories by Homer Brightman, Dick Huemer, Dick Kinney, John Walbridge, Tom Oreb, Dick Shaw, Eric Gurney, Sylvia Holland, T. Hee, Ed Penner, Dick Kelsey, Jim Bodrero, Roy Williams, Cap Palmer, Jesse Marsh and Erwin Graham; Musical Director—Charles Wolcott; Music Associates—Ken Darby, Olive Wallace, Edward Plumb; "Peter and the Wolf" by Serge Prokofieff; Songs by Ray Gilbert, Eliot Daniel, Allie Wrubel and Bobby Worth.

Voices/Music: The King's Men, The Ken Darby Chorus, The Benny Goodman Quartet and Orchestra, The Pied Pipers, Andy Russell, Jerry Colonna, Dinah Shore, Sterling Holloway, The Andrews Sisters, Nelson Eddy, Pinto Colvig, with the ballet dancing of Tania Riabouchinska and David Lichine.

Honors: Award—Cannes Film Festival winner (Animation).

101 *The Man Called Flintstone* (1966) * ½

U.S.; Rated G; 87 mins.; Premiered August 1, 1966 in Indianapolis, Indiana; Hanna-Barbera.

Synopsis: A James Bond spoof in which Fred Flintstone and Barney Rubble become international secret agents going after the "Green Goose" and his SMIRK agents.

Notes: Young viewers should enjoy this feature film debut of TV's prehistoric comedy *The Flintstones* (1960–66), which was the first animated prime-time series (made-for-TV); A live-action feature version of the series was produced in 1994 with John Goodman (as Fred); Produced by William Hanna and Joseph Barbera;

Credits: Directors—Joseph Barbera, William Hanna; Director of Animation—Charles A. Nichols; Screenplay by Harvey Bullock and Ray Allen; Music by Marty Paich and Ted Nichols; Songs by John McCarthy and Doug Goodwin; Songs—"Pensate Amore" (sung by Louis Prima), "Team Mates," "Spy Type Guy," "The Happy Sounds of Paree," "When I'm Grown Up," "Tickle Toddle" and the title song.

Voices: Alan Reed, Sr. (Fred), Mel Blanc (Barney), Jean VanderPyl (Wilma), Gerry Johnson (Betty), Don Messick, Janet Waldo, Paul Frees, Harvey Korman, John Stephenson, June Foray; **Note:** Character actor Reed (1907–77) started on radio in the '30s.

102 *The Man from Button Willow* (1965) *

U.S.; Rated G; 84 mins.; Eagle Films.

Synopsis: The adventures of Justin Eagle, America's first undercover agent in 1869, who must rescue a Senator kidnapped by mean speculators.

Notes: Minor western tale aimed at kids; The first film distributed through Dale Robertson's company, United Screen Artists; Produced by Phyllis Bounds Detiege.

Credits: Director—David Detiege; Screenplay by David Detiege; Music by George Stoll and Robert Van Eps; Songs by Phil Bounds, Dale Robertson, George Bruns and Mel Henke.

Voices: Dale Robertson (Justin Eagle), Edgar Buchanan (Sorry), Barbara Jean Wong (Stormy), Howard Keel, Herschel Bernardi, Ross Martin, Shepard Menken, Clarence Nash, Buck Buchanan, Cliff Edwards, Verna Felton, Pinto Colvig, Thurl Ravenscroft, John Hiestand, Edward Platt; **Notes:** Robertson and Buchanan (1903–79) appeared in many film and TV westerns from the '40s into the '60s.

103 *The Many Adventures of Winnie the Pooh* (1977) ***
U.S.; Rated G; 74 mins.; Released Mar. 3, 1977; Walt Disney.

Synopsis: Three "Winnie the Pooh" tales—*Winnie the Pooh and the Honey Tree*, *Winnie the Pooh and the Blustery Day* and *Winnie the Pooh and Tigger Too*. See SHORTS.

Notes: A collection of three excellent "Winnie the Pooh" featurettes (1966, '68, '74), with some new animation added; Disney's next "Pooh" feature was the made-for-video *Pooh's Grand Adventure: The Search for Christopher Robin* (1997); Produced by Wolfgang Reitherman.

Credits: Directors—Wolfgang Reitherman, John Lounsbery; Written by Larry Clemmons, Vance Gerry, Ken Anderson, Ted Berman, Ralph Wright, Xavier Atencio, Julius Svendsen and Eric Cleworth, based on the classic children's stories by A.A. Milne; Music and lyrics by Richard M. and Robert B. Sherman.

Voices: Sebastian Cabot (Narrator), Sterling Holloway (Winnie the Pooh), Paul Winchell (Tigger), John Fiedler (Piglet), Junius Matthews (Rabbit), Hal Smith (Owl), Ralph Wright (Eeyore), Bruce Reitherman/Jon Walmsley/Timothy Turner (Christopher Robin), Barbara Luddy (Kanga), Clint Howard/Dori Whitaker (Roo), Howard Morris (Gopher).

104 *Mary Poppins* (1964) ***
U.S.; Rated G; 139 mins.; Premiered August 29, 1964; Walt Disney.

Synopsis: In London in 1910, a magical nanny takes the two children in her charge on a series of exciting adventures.

Notes: Enchanting live-action Disney classic, with a memorable 20-minute sequence combining animation and live actors; Broadway star Julie Andrews made her screen debut with this film which, coupled with *The Sound of Music* the following year, would rocket her to movie stardom; An enormous box-office hit and one of the highest-grossing musicals of all time; Produced by Walt Disney and Bill Walsh.

Highlights: the delightful "Jolly Holiday" animation sequence, the "Feed the Birds" number (a favorite song of Walt Disney's), and the energetic dancing of the chimney sweeps on the rooftops of London.

Credits: Director—Robert Stevenson; Animation Director—Hamilton Luske; Screenplay by Bill Walsh and Don DaGradi, based on the classic 1934 book by P(amela) L. Travers (1899–1996); Music and lyrics by Richard M. and Robert B. Sherman; Music Supervisor/Arranger/Conductor—Irwin Kostal; Songs—"A Spoonful of Sugar," "Jolly Holiday," "Supercalifragilisticexpialidocious," "Chim Chim Cher-ee," "Step in Time," "Feed the Birds," "The Life I Lead," "The Perfect Nanny," "Sister Suffragette," "Stay Awake," "Fidelity Feduciary Bank" and "Let's Go Fly a Kite"; **Note:** The Sherman Brothers, sons of songwriter Al Sherman ("No, No, a Thousand Times, No"), have written songs for over 20 Disney films since 1961, including *The Jungle Book* (1967) and *The Aristocats* (1970).

Cast: Julie Andrews (Mary Poppins), Dick Van Dyke (Bert/Mr. Dawes, Sr.), David Tomlinson (Mr. Banks), Glynis Johns (Mrs. Banks), Ed Wynn (Uncle Albert), Hermione Baddeley (Ellen), Karen Dotrice (Jane), Matthew Garber (Michael), Arthur Treacher, Reginald Owen, Elsa Lanchester, Jane Darwell, Reta Shaw, Arthur Malet, James Logan, Don Barclay, Alma Lawton, Marjorie Eaton, Marjorie Bennett; **Notes:** Dotrice also starred in Disney's *The Three Lives of Thomasina* (1964). Veteran screen actress Darwell (*The Grapes of Wrath*) makes her last film appearance (at age 85) as the bird woman (she died in 1967).

Honors: Academy Awards—Actress (Julie Andrews), Original Score, Song ("Chim Chim Cher-ee"), Special Visual Effects and Film Editing, also nominated for Best Picture, Director, Screenplay, Cinematography, Art Direction, Sound, Score Adaption and Costume Design.

105 *Melody Time* (1948) **$\frac{1}{2}$
U.S.; Not Rated; 75 mins.; Released May 27, 1948; Walt Disney.

Synopsis: Seven musical cartoon shorts—*Once Upon a Wintertime*, *Bumble Boogie*, *Johnny Appleseed*, *Little Toot*, *Trees*, *Blame It on the Samba* and *Pecos Bill* (see SHORTS).

Notes: Disney's last musical compilation is an enjoyable mixed bag of shorts ranging from pleasant to outstanding; Includes live-action footage of Roy Rogers and friends (*Pecos Bill*) and organist Ethel Smith (*Blame It on the Samba*, which also stars Donald Duck and the parrot Joe Carioca).

Highlights: the dazzling visuals of *Blame It on the Samba* and *Bumble Boogie*, and the delightful tall tales *Johnny Appleseed* and *Pecos Bill*.

Credits: Supervisor: Ben Sharpsteen; Sequence Directors—Hamilton Luske, Jack Kinney, Wilfred Jackson, Clyde Geronimi; Directing Animators—Eric Larson, Ward Kimball, Milt Kahl, Oliver M. Johnston, Jr., John Lounsbery, Les Clark; Stories by Erdman Penner, Harry Reeves, Ken Anderson, Homer Brightman, Ted Sears, Joe Rinaldi, Winston Hibler, Art Scott, Bob Moore, Bill Cottrell, Jesse Marsh and John Walbridge; *Little Toot* by Hardie Gramatky; *Trees* (poem) by Joyce Kilmer; Musical Directors—Eliot Daniel, Ken Darby; Songs by Kim Gannon, Ray Gilbert, Allie Wrubel, Benny Benjamin, Walter Kent, Johnny Lange, Bobby Worth, George Weiss, Eliot Daniel and Ernesto Nazareth; Songs—"The Lord Is Good to Me," "The Apple Song," "The Pioneer Song," "Blue Shadows on the Trail" and the title tunes, including "Bumble Boogie" (from "Flight of the Bumble Bee" by Nikolay Rimsky-Korsakov, arranged by Jack Fina).

Cast: Ethel Smith, Roy Rogers (with his horse Trigger), Sons of the Pioneers, Bobby Driscoll, Luana Patten, Bob Nolan; Voices and music—Buddy Clark (Title song vocalist/host), Frances Langford, Freddy Martin's Orchestra with Jack Fina, Dennis Day, The Andrews Sisters, Fred Waring and His Pennsylvanians, Pinto Colvig, The Dinning Sisters; **Note:** Clark died in a plane crash in October 1949 (he was 37).

Mighty Mouse in The Great Space Chase **see** *The Great Space Chase.*

106 *Mr. Bug Goes to Town* (1941) **
U.S.; Not Rated; 77 mins.; Released December 4, 1941; Max Fleischer.

Synopsis: A big-city grasshopper named Hoppity, his girlfriend Honey Bee and their bug pals go in search of a new, safer place to live.

Notes: The Fleischers' second (following 1939's *Gulliver's Travels*) and last cartoon feature is a fun, well-animated tale, despite a rather weak storyline; Retitled *Hoppity Goes to Town*; The film—the first animated feature based on an original story—flopped when first released, leading to the end of the Fleischer Studio; The film's title is a play on Frank Capra's *Mr. Deeds Goes to Town* (1936); Produced by Max Fleischer.

Highlights: the film's opening sequence, and the exciting construction site scene.

Credits: Director—Dave Fleischer; Directors of Animation—Willard Bowsky, Myron Waldman, Thomas Johnson, David Tendlar, James Culhane, H.C. Ellison, Stan Quackenbush, Graham Place; Screenplay by Dan Gordon, Ted Pierce, Isadore Sparber, William Turner, Carl Mayer, Graham Place, Bob Wickersham and Cal Howard, from an original story by Dave Fleischer, Gordon, Pierce and Sparber; Music by Leigh Harline; Songs by Hoagy Carmichael, Frank Loesser (*Guy and Dolls*) and Sammy Timberg; Songs—"We're the Couple in the Castle," "I'll Dance at Your Wedding," "Boy Oh Boy," "Katy-Did, Katy-Didn't" and "Be My Little Baby Bumble Bee"; **Note:** Harline won two Oscars the year before for his work on Disney's *Pinocchio*.

Voices: Kenny Gardner, Gwen Williams, Jack Mercer, Ted Pierce, Carl Mayer, Stan Freed, Pauline Loth.

107 *Mondo Plympton* (1997) **
U.S.; Not Rated; 80 mins.; Released August 1997; Bill Plympton.

Synopsis: Shorts—*Your Face* (Oscar-nominee), *How to Kiss*, *25 Ways to Quit Smoking*, *Boomtown*, *Push Comes to Shove*, *Nose Hair* and *How to Make Love to a Woman* (see SHORTS).

Notes: Compilation film featuring the comic-surreal work of Bill Plympton; The shorts date from 1985 to 1995; The film also includes samples of Plympton's commercial work, and clips from *The Tune* (1992) and his first live-action feature *J. Lyle* (1994); Produced by Plympton.

Credits: Director—Bill Plympton; Animated by Bill Plympton; Written by Bill Plympton, Maureen McElheron and P. C. Vey; Music by Maureen McElheron and Timothy Clark.

Voices: Chris Hoffman, Daniel Kaufman, Ruth Maleczech, Valerie Vasilevski, Maureen McElheron, Bill Plympton.

108 *The Mouse and His Child* (1977) $\frac{1}{2}$
U.S.; Rated G; 83 mins.; Released November 18, 1977; Murakami-Wolf.

Synopsis: A wind-up toy mouse and child come to life and venture into the outside world, which proves dangerous when they fall into the clutches of Manny the rat.

Notes: Disappointing adaption of Russell Hoban's children's classic; Produced by Walt deFaria.

Credits: Directors—Fred Wolf, Chuck Swenson; Screenplay by Carol Mon Pere, based on the 1967 novel by Russell Hoban; Music by Roger Kellaway (Oscar nominee for 1976's *A Star Is Born*); Lyrics by Gene Lees.

Voices: Peter Ustinov (Manny), Alan Barzman (Mouse), Cloris Leachman (Euterpe), Andy Devine (Frog), Marcy Swenson (Mouse Child), Sally Kellerman (Seal), Joan Gerber (Elephant), Neville Brand (Iggy), Regis Cordic (Clock/Hawk), Bob Holt (Muskrat), Maitzi Morgan (Startling/Teller), Frank Nelson (Crow), Cliff Norton (Crow), Cliff Osmond (Serpentina), Iris Rainer (Paper People), Bob Ridgely (Jack in the Box), Charles Woolf (Bluejay/The Paper People), Mel Leven (Ralphie); **Notes:** Ustinov won Oscars for his performances in *Spartacus* (1960) and *Topkapi* (1964). Devine's last film role (he died in February 1977 at 71).

109 *My Little Pony: The Movie* (1986) $\frac{1}{2}$
U.S.; Rated G; 100 mins.; Released June 1986 (Video: October 1986, Vestron); Sunbow/Marvel/Hasbro.

Synopsis: Cute little ponies try to stop a family of evil witches from covering Ponyland with a purple lava-like substance called the Smooze.

Notes: Bland, syrupy kids film featuring the popular children's toy characters, who went on to star in their own TV series (1986–90); Marvel Productions (founded in 1980) also produced the *Transformers* series and feature (1986); Produced by Michael Joens, Joe Bacal and Tom Griffin.

Credits: Director—Michael Joens; Supervising Animators—Pierre DeCelles, Michael Fallows, Ray Lee; Screenplay by George Arthur Bloom; Music by Rob Walsh; Songs by Tommy Goodman and Barry Harman; Theme song by Spencer Michlin and Ford Kinder.

Voices: Danny DeVito (Grundle King), Madeline Kahn (Draggle), Tony Randall (The Moochik), Cloris Leachman (Hydia), Rhea Perlman (Reeka), Tammy Amerson (Megan), Jon Bauman (The Creature), Michael Bell (Grundle), Alice Playten (Baby Lickety Split/Bushwoolie #1), Charlie Adler (Spike/Woodland Creature), Sheryl Bernstein (Buttons/Woodland Creature/Bushwoolie), Susan Blu (Lofty/Grundle/Bushwoolie), Cathy Cavadini (North Star), Nancy Cartwright (Gusty/Bushwoolie #4), Peter Cullen (Grundle/Ahgg), Laura Dean (Sundance/Bushwoolie #2), Ellen Gerstell (Magic Star), Keri Houlihan (Molly), Katie Leigh (Fizzy/Baby Sunshine), Scott Menville (Danny), Laurel Page (Sweet Stuff), Sarah Partridge (Wind Whistler), Russie Taylor (Morning Glory/Rosedust/Bushwoolie/Skunk), Jill Wayne (Shady/Baby Lofty), Frank Welker (Bushwoolie #3/Grundle).

The Nightmare Before Christmas **see** *Tim Burton's The Nightmare Before Christmas.*

110 *Nine Lives of Fritz the Cat* (1974) *
U.S.; Rated R; 76 mins.; Released June 26, 1974; Steve Krantz.

Synopsis: The further adventures of the hipster alleycat, who escapes his nagging wife by getting stoned and fantasizing about his wilder former lives.

Notes: Second-rate sequel to Ralph Bakshi's 1972 cult favorite *Fritz the Cat;* Produced by Steve Krantz, and presented by Samuel Z. Arkoff.

Credits: Director—Robert Taylor; Screenplay by Robert Taylor, Fred Halliday and Eric Monte, based on Robert Crumb's underground comic-strip character; Music by Tom Scott and the L.A. Express.

Voices: Skip Hinnant (Fritz), Reva Rose (Fritz's Old Lady), Bob Holt, Pat Harrington, Jr., Robert Ridgely, Fred Smoot, "Sweet" Dick Whittington, Luke Walker, Peter Leeds, Louisa Moritz, Larry Moss, Joan Gerber, Jim Johnson, Jay Lawrence, Stanley Adams, Carole Androsky, Lynn Roman, Ralph James, Eric Monte, Glynn Turman, Ron Knight, Gloria Jones, Renny Rooker, Peter Hobbs, Buddy Arett, John Hancock, Chris Graham, Felton Perry, Anthony Mason, Serena Grant.

111 *The Nutcracker Prince* (1990) *
Canadian; Rated G; 75 mins.; Released November 21, 1990; Lacewood.

Synopsis: At a Christmas party, young Clara's uncle tells her the story of her Nutcracker Prince doll, which comes to life that night to do battle with the evil Mouseking.

Notes: Mildly entertaining animated version of the holiday classic; Produced by Kevin Gillis.

Credits: Director—Paul Schibli; Screenplay by Patricia Watson, based on the book *The Nutcracker and the Mouseking* by E.T.A. Hoffmann; Classic score by Peter Ilyich Tchaikovsky (from his 1892 ballet), performed by The London Symphony Orchestra; Original music by Victor Davies; Songs by Kevin Gillis and Jack Lenz; Songs—"Always Come Back to You (Love Theme from *The Nutcracker Prince*)" and "Save This Dance."

Voices: Kiefer Sutherland (Nutcracker Prince), Megan Follows (Clara), Mike MacDonald (Mouseking), Peter O'Toole (Pantaloon), Phyllis Diller (Mousequeen), Peter Boretski (Uncle Drosselmeier), Len Carlson, Marvin Goldhar, Lynne Gorman, Keith Hampshire, Elizabeth Hanna, George Merner, Stephanie Morgenstern, Christopher Owens, Susan

Roman, Theresa Sears, Diane Stapley, Mona Waserman, Noam Zylberman; **Note:** Follows is best known for playing Anne Shirley in the popular TV films *Anne of Green Gables* (1985) and *Anne of Avonlea* (1987).

112 *Of Stars and Men* (1961) **
U.S.; Not Rated; 53 mins.; Hubley Studio.

Synopsis: The story of human evolution—from the first micro-organisms to man's current place in the world and in the universe.

Notes: Educational-philosophical film, done with wit and style, from the studio of John and Faith Hubley, the husband-and-wife animation team who, since 1955, have produced many original, thought-provoking shorts—three of which have won Oscars; Produced by John and Faith Hubley.

Credits: Director—John Hubley; Animation Directors—William Littlejohn, Gary Mooney; Screenplay by Harlow Shapley, John and Faith Hubley, based on the book by Shapely; Music by Walter Trampler, and featuring works by Petzel, Gabrieli, Bach, Handel, Mozart and Beethoven.

Voices: Harlow Shapley (Commentator), Mark Hubley, Hamp Hubley (Children's Voices).

113 *Oliver and Company* (1988) *$\frac{1}{2}$
U.S.; Rated G; 72 mins.; Released November 18, 1988 (Video: September 1996, Walt Disney); Walt Disney.

Synopsis: In New York City, a kitten named Oliver joins up with a streetwise gang of dogs owned by Fagin, a man who trains dogs to steal.

Notes: Fun dog-and-cat takeoff on the Charles Dickens tale. Plenty of action and music, but no classic; Disney's 27th animated feature; More than 300 animators, artists and technicians worked for two-and-a-half years to produce the film (which consists of 119,275 hand-painted cels); Computers were used to assist in the animation of several scenes; The drawing of Dodger was based on the design of Tramp from *Lady and the Tramp*; Cost of film—$18 million; The film, which opened on the same day as Don Bluth's *Land Before Time*, earned $53.1 million at the box office (outgrossing the Bluth film by only about $5 million).

Credits: Director—George Scribner; Supervising Animators—Mike Gabriel, Glen Keane, Ruben A. Aquino, Hendel Butoy, Mark Henn, Doug Krohn; Screenplay by Jim Cox, Timothy J. Disney and James Mangold, inspired by Charles Dickens' *Oliver Twist*; Story by Vance Gerry, Mike Gabriel, Joe Ranft, Jim Mitchell, Chris Bailey, Kirk Wise, Dave Michener, Roger Allers, Gary Trousdale, Kevin Lima, Michael Cedeno, Pete Young and Leon Joosen; Music by J.A.C. Redford; Songs by Barry Mann, Howard Ashman, Dan Hartman, Charlie Midnight, Dean Pitchford, Tom Snow, Barry Manilow, Jack Feldman, Bruce Sussman, Rob Minkoff, Ron Rocha, Ruben Blades, Rocky Pedilla, Michael Eckhart and Jon St. James; Songs—"Once Upon a Time in New York City" (performed by Huey Lewis), "Why Should I Worry?," "Streets of Gold" (performed by Ruth Pointer), "Perfect Isn't Easy," "Good Company," "Buscando Guayaba" (performed by Blades) and "Fast Lane."

Voices: Joey Lawrence (Oliver), Billy Joel (Dodger), Cheech Marin (Tito), Roscoe Lee Browne (Francis), Richard Mulligan (Einstein), Sheryl Lee Ralph (Rita), Dom DeLuise (Fagin), Taurean Blacque (Roscoe), Robert Loggia (Sykes), Carl Weintraub (Desoto), Natalie Gregory (Jenny), William Glover (Winston), Bette Midler (Georgette).

114 *Oliver Twist* (1974) *
U.S.; Rated G; 75 mins.; Filmation.

Synopsis: An orphan boy in 19th-century London joins up with a gang of young thieves led by the villainous Fagin.

Notes: Animated musical version of the Dickens' tale; Later re-edited and shown as a TV special (Apr. 1981); Produced by Lou Scheimer and Norman Prescott.

Highlight: Based on the novel by Charles Dickens.

Credits: Director—Hal Sutherland; Music by George Blais.

Voices: Josh Albee (Oliver Twist), Les Tremayne (Fagin), Davey Jones (Artful Dodger), Lola Fisher (Nancy), Phil Clark, Cathleen Cordell, Michael Evans, Robert Holt, Larry D. Mann, Dallas McKennon, Billy Simpson, Larry Storch, Jane Webb, Helene Winston.

115 *Once Upon a Forest* (1993) *

U.S.; Rated G; 71 mins.; Released June 18, 1993 (Video: September 1993, FoxVideo); Hanna-Barbera/HTV Cymru-Wales.

Synopsis: After a chemical spill destroys their home, three forest creatures set off on a journey to find a herb that will save the life of their sick badger friend.

Notes: Preachy, slow-moving environmental fable for kids; Produced by David Kirschner (creator of *An American Tail*) and Jerry Mills.

Credits: Director—Charles Grosvenor; Animation Director—Dave Michener; Screenplay by Mark Young and Kelly Ward, based on characters and concept created by Rae Lambert; Music by James Horner; Songs by Horner, Will Jennings, Michael Tavera, Kelly Ward, Mark Young, Andrae Crouch and Sandra Crouch; Songs—"Please Wake Up," "He's Gone/He's Back" and "Once Upon a Time with Me."

Voices: Michael Crawford (Cornelius), Ben Vereen (Phineas), Ellen Blain (Abigail), Ben Gregory (Edgar), Paige Gosney (Russell), Elizabeth Moss (Michelle), Paul Eiding (Abigail's Father), Janet Waldo (Edgar's Mom), Susan Silo (Russell's Mom), Will Nipper (Willy), Charlie Adler (Waggs), Rickey Collins (Bosworth), Angel Harper (Bosworth's Mom), Don Reed (Marshbird), Robert David Hall (Truck Driver), Benjamin Smith (Russell's Brother), Haven Hartman (Russell's Sister); **Note:** Crawford won a Tony Award in 1988 for playing the title role in the hit musical *The Phantom of the Opera*.

116 *101 Dalmatians* (1961) ***

U.S.; Rated G; 79 mins.; Premiered in New York November 18, 1960; Released January 25, 1961 (Video: April 1992, Walt Disney); Walt Disney.

Synopsis: In London, two parent dogs named Pongo and Perdita fight to rescue their puppies, who have been stolen for their fur by the villainous Cruella DeVil.

Notes: Disney's charming, high-entertaining follow-up to *Sleeping Beauty* features a different animation style than previous Disney films, with backgrounds outlined in pen and ink rather than painted; The first Disney feature to use the time-saving Xerox method (developed by Ub Iwerks) of transferring drawings to cels; 300 artists worked on the $4 million production for 5 years; The film features 6,469,952 spots (which required 800 gallons of black paint); The dogs from the pound in *Lady and the Tramp* make a cameo appearance in a pet shop window, and in another scene the "Silly Symphony" short *Springtime* (1929) is shown on TV; A live-action version of the film was produced in 1996 with Glenn Close (as Cruella); Spawned a TV series in 1997.

Highlight: the climactic car chase with Cruella and her thugs.

Credits: Directors—Wolfgang Reitherman, Hamilton S. Luske, Clyde Geronimi; Directing Animators—Milt Kahl, Marc Davis, Ollie Johnston, Frank Thomas, John Lounsbery, Eric Larson; **Note:** Davis' last film. The Disney veteran (he joined the studio in 1935) moved on to help design many of Disney's famous theme park attractions, before retiring in 1978. Davis—animator of Snow White, Cinderella, Tinker Bell, Maleficent, Sleeping Beauty and others—cited the deliciously mean Cruella DeVil as his favorite creation;

Story by Bill Peet, based on the 1956 novel *The Hundred and One Dalmatians* by Dodie Smith (1896–1990); Music by George Bruns; Songs by Mel Leven and Franklyn Marks; Songs—"Cruella DeVil," "Dalmatian Plantation," "Remember When" and "Kanine Krunchies Kommercial" (sung by Lucille Bliss).

Voices: Rod Taylor (Pongo), J. Pat O'Malley (Jasper/other dogs), Betty Lou Gerson (Cruella/Miss Birdwell), Martha Wentworth (Nani/Goose/Cow), Ben Wright (Roger Radcliff), Cate Bauer (Perdita), Frederic Worlock (Horace/Inspector Craven), Lisa Davis (Anita), Tom Conway (Quizmaster/Collie), David Frankham (Sergent Tibs), Tudor Owen (Towser), George Pelling (Danny), Ramsay Hill (TV Announcer/Labrador), Queenie Leonard (Princess), Marjorie Bennett (Duchess), Micky Maga (Patch), Barbara Beaird (Rolly), Mimi Gibson (Lucky), Sandra Abbott (Penny), Thurl Ravenscroft (The Captain), Barbara Luddy (Rover), Paul Frees (Dirty Dawson), Lucille Bliss (TV commercial singer), Sylvia Marriott, Max Smith, Bob Stevens, Lisa Daniels, Dal McKennon, Rickie Sorensen, Basil Ruysdael; **Notes:** Taylor starred in such classic films as *The Time Machine* (1960) and *The Birds* (1963). Gerson started on radio in the '30s playing "Mary Marlin." Conway (1904–67) played the title role in "The Falcon" film series (1942–46), a role he took over from his brother, George Sanders (voice of Shere Khan in *The Jungle Book*).

117 *1001 Arabian Nights* (1959) * $\frac{1}{2}$
U.S.; Rated G; 75 mins.; UPA.

Synopsis: Mr. Magoo is a lamp dealer whose nephew, Aladdin, acquires a magic lamp wanted by the sinister Wazir.

Notes: The near-sighted Mr. Magoo made his feature debut in this amusing updating of the *Arabian Nights* tales; The first feature-length cartoon from the UPA (United Productions of America) studio; Produced by UPA founder Stephen Bosustow.

Credits: Director—Jack Kinney; **Note:** Disney veteran Kinney directed many of Goofy's best cartoons during the '40s; Director of Animation—Abe Levitow; Sequence Directors—Rudy Larriva, Gil Turner, Osmond Evans, Tom McDonald, Alan Zaslove; Screenplay by Czenzi Ormonde; Music by George Duning.

Voices: Jim Backus (Uncle Abdul Azziz Magoo), Kathryn Grant (Princess Yasminda), Dwayne Hickman (Aladdin), Hans Conried (The Wicked Wazir), Herschel Bernardi (The Jinni), Alan Reed (The Sultan), Daws Butler (Omar the Rug Maker), Clark Sisters (Three Maids from Damascus); **Notes:** Grant was the wife (1959–77) of Bing Crosby. Hickman played TV's *Dobie Gillis* (1959–63).

118 *The Pagemaster* (1994) * $\frac{1}{2}$
U.S.; Rated G; 75 mins.; Released November 1994 (Video: April 1995, FoxVideo). Turner Pictures/Twentieth Century Fox.

Synopsis: A timid 10-year-old boy takes refuge from a storm inside a library where a mysterious librarian sends him on a magical (and animated) journey into the world of books (*Dr. Jekyll & Mr. Hyde, Moby Dick, Treasure Island*, etc.).

Notes: Children's fantasy extolling the fun and importance of reading. Not bad, though the animation is only average; The animated story is framed by 17 minutes of live-action; The $34 million film—the brainchild of David Kirschner (*An American Tail, Hocus Pocus*)—began production in 1990; Produced by Kirschner and Paul Gertz.

Credits: Directors—Maurice Hunt (animation), Joe Johnston (live-action); **Note:** Hunt was a visual effects supervisor at Disney. Johnston, who directed 1989's *Honey, I Shrunk the Kids*, won an Oscar for Best Visual Effects for *Raiders of the Lost Ark* (1981); Supervising Animator—Bruce Smith; Animation Sequence Director—Glenn Chaika; Screenplay by David Casci, David Kirschner and Ernie Contreras; Story by Kirschner and Casci; Music by James Horner; Songs by Horner, Barry Mann, Cynthia Weil and Diane Warren; Songs—"Dream Away" and "Whatever You Imagine."

Cast: Macaulay Culkin (Richard Tyler), Christopher Lloyd (Mr. Dewey/The Pagemaster), Ed Begley, Jr. (Alan Tyler), Mel Harris (Claire Tyler), Canan J. Howell, Alexis Kirschner, Jessica Kirschner, Guy Mansker, Brandon McKay, Stephen Sheehan; **Voices:** Whoopi Goldberg (Fantasy), Patrick Stewart (Adventure), Frank Welker (Horror), Leonard Nimoy (Dr. Jekyll and Mr. Hyde), George Hearn (Captain Ahab), Jim Cummings (Long John Silver), Dorian Harewood (Jamaican Pirates), Ed Gilbert (George Merry), Dick Erdman, Fernando Escandon, Robert Piccardo (Pirates), Phil Hartman (Tom Morgan), B. J. Ward (Queen of Hearts).

119 *Panda and the Magic Serpent* (1961) * $\frac{1}{2}$
Japanese-U.S.; Not Rated; 76 mins.; Toei Doga.

Synopsis: A wizard in ancient China tries to separate a pair of lovers—Hsu Hsien, a mortal, and Pai Niang, a lovely immortal.
Notes: Pleasant fairy tale, the first feature from Japan's Toei Doga animation studio (formerly Nihon Doga, founded in 1947); Originally released in Japan in 1958 as *Hakujaden* (*The White Snake*).
Credits: Directors—Kazuhiko Okabe, Taiji Yabushita; **Note:** Yabushita (1903–86) also codirected *Alakazam the Great!* (*Saiyu-ki*) (1961). Screenplay by Taiji Yabushita and Shin Uehara, inspired by the Chinese fairy tale *Pai she chuan*; Music by Chuji Kinoshita.
Voices: Marvin Miller (Narrator).

120 *The Pebble and the Penguin* (1995) *
U.S.; Rated G; 74 mins.; Released April 11, 1995 (Video: August 1995, MGM/UA); Don Bluth Ireland/MGM.

Synopsis: Hubie the penguin has to beat out a rival in order to present his beloved with a pebble as part of the penguins' full moon mating ceremony.
Notes: So-so musical-adventure for kids, inspired by the real-life mating custom of the Adeli penguins; Don Bluth's last feature from his Ireland studios before joining Twentieth Century–Fox's new animation division; Working title—*The Penguin Story*; Produced by Russell Boland.
Credits: Directing Animators—John Pomeroy, Len Simon, Richard Bazley, Sylvia Hoefnagels, Ralf Palmer, John Hill, John Power; Screenplay by Rachel Koretsky and Steve Whitestone; Music by Barry Manilow, Bruce Sussman and Mark Watters; Songs include "Now and Forever."
Voices: Martin Short (Hubie), Annie Golden (Marina), Tim Curry (Drake), James Belushi (Rocko), Shani Wallis (Narrator), Scott Bullock (Chubby/Gentoo), Louise Vallance (Priscilla/Chinstrap), Pat Musick (Pola/Chinstrap), Angeline Ball (Gwynne/Chinstrap), Kendall Cunningham (Timmy), Alissa King (Petra), Michael Nunes (Beany), Neil Ross (Scrawny), Philip Clarke (King), B. J. Ward (Megellenic), Hamilton Camp (Megellenic), Will Ryan (Royal/Tika), Stanley Jones (McCallister).

121 *Peter Pan* (1953) ** $\frac{1}{2}$
U.S.; Rated G; 76 mins.; Released February 5, 1953 (Video: September 1990, Walt Disney); Walt Disney.

Synopsis: A magical flying boy named Peter Pan takes three London children into Neverland where they come up against the villainous pirate Captain Hook.
Notes: Disney's classic version of the popular children's tale is a magical, beautifully animated film for all ages; Walt Disney began planning the film as early as 1935 (he bought the film rights in 1939), but when war broke out it was temporarily shelved until 1949; Disney artists changed Tinker Bell from what was only a beam of light in the stage version into a curvaceous pixie (her figure was not based on Marilyn Monroe as rumored;

Margaret Kerry was the live-action model); The artists based many of their sketches on live-action footage featuring actor Hans Conried and dancer Roland Dupree; The Broadway musical version of the story opened the following year (with Mary Martin as Peter).

Highlights: the "You Can Fly" sequence in which Peter and children fly over London, and Peter's battles with Captain Hook.

Credits: Supervisor: Ben Sharpsteen; Directors—Hamilton Luske, Clyde Geronimi, Wilfred Jackson; Directing Animators—Milt Kahl, Frank Thomas, Wolfgang Reitherman, Ward Kimball, Ollie Johnston, Marc Davis, Eric Larson, John Lounsbery, Les Clark, Norm Ferguson; Screenplay by Ted Sears, Erdman Penner, Bill Peet, Winston Hibler, Joe Rinaldi, Milt Banta, Ralph Wright and Bill Cottrell, based on the 1904 children's play by Sir James M. Barrie (1860–1937); Musical score by Oliver Wallace; Songs by Wallace, Sammy Fain, Sammy Cahn, Frank Churchill, Erdman Penner, Winston Hibler and Ted Sears; Songs— "The Second Star to the Right," "You Can Fly," "A Pirate's Life," "Following the Leader (Tee Dum, Tee Dee)," "What Makes the Red Man Red?," "Your Mother and Mine" and "The Elegant Captain Hook."

Voices: Bobby Driscoll (Peter Pan), Kathryn Beaumont (Wendy), Hans Conried (Captain Hook/Mr. Darling), Bill Thompson (Mr. Smee), Heather Angel (Mrs. Darling), Paul Collins (Michael), Tommy Luske (John), Candy Candido (Indian Chief), Tom Conway (Narrator); **Notes:** Child star Driscoll (*Song of the South, Treasure Island*) appeared in only a few more films before his career faded (he died of a heart attack at 31 in 1968). Beaumont was the voice of Alice in Disney's *Alice in Wonderland* (1951). Character actor Conried (1917–82) is best known for playing Uncle Tonoose on TV's *Make Room for Daddy* (1958–64/70–71).

122 *Pete's Dragon* (1977) *½
U.S.; Rated G; 134 mins.; Premiered November 3, 1977; Walt Disney.

Synopsis: An orphaned boy in turn-of-the-century Maine leaves his foster family and goes on a journey with his pet dragon, whom no one else can see.

Notes: Average, overlong live-action family musical in which only Elliott the Dragon is animated. For kids only; 30 minutes were cut from the film for its 1984 reissue; Produced by Ron Miller and Jerome Courtland.

Credits: Director—Don Chaffey; **Note:** Chaffey's (1917–90) other film credits include *Jason and the Argonauts* (1963) and Disney's *The Three Lives of Thomasina* (1964); Animation Director—Don Bluth; Elliott created by Ken Anderson; Screenplay by Malcolm Marmorstein, based on a story by Seton I. Miller and S.S. Field; Musical Director—Irwin Kostal (*West Side Story, The Sound of Music*); Songs by Al Kasha and Joel Hirschhorn; Songs—"I Saw a Dragon," "It's Not Easy," "Every Little Piece," "The Happiest Home in These Hills," "Brazzle Dazzle Day," "Boo Boo Bopbopbop (I Love You Too)," "There's Room for Everyone," "Passamashloddy," "Bill of Sale" and "Candle on the Water."

Cast: Sean Marshall (Pete), Mickey Rooney (Lampie), Jim Dale (Dr. Terminus), Helen Reddy (Nora), Red Buttons (Hoagy), Shelley Winters (Lena Gogan), Jean Kean (Miss Taylor), Jim Backus (The Mayor), Charles Tyner, Gary Morgan, Jeff Conway, Cal Bartlett, Walter Barnes, Robert Easton, Roger Price, Robert Foulk, Ben Wrigley, Joe Ross, Al Checco, Henry Slate, Jack Collins; **Voice:** Charlie Callas (Elliott).

Honors: Academy Award nominations—Original Song Score/Adaption Score and Song ("Candle on the Water").

123 *The Phantom Tollbooth* (1969) **
U.S.; Rated G; 90 mins.; Premiered December 31, 1969 in San Francisco; MGM/Chuck Jones.

Synopsis: A young boy passes through a magical toll booth and enters the Kingdom of Wisdom where numbers and letters are at war with each other.

Notes: Unusual fantasy tale should entertain both kids and adults; Video title—*The Adventures of Milo in the Phantom Tollbooth*; Animated, with live-action scenes at the beginning and end; The first animated feature from both MGM Studios and cartoon director Chuck Jones (of Warner Bros. fame); Produced by Jones, Abe Levitow and Les Goldman.

Credits: Directors—Chuck Jones, Abe Levitow (animation), David Monahan (live-action); Animation Directors—Ben Washam, Hal Ambro, George Nicholas; **Note:** Washam was an animator for Chuck Jones at Warner Bros. (1942–63) before following him to MGM; Screenplay by Chuck Jones and Sam Rosen, based on the 1961 book by Norton Juster; Musical score by Dean Elliott; Songs by Lee Pockriss, Norman Gimbel and Paul Vance; Songs—"Milo's Song," "Time Is a Gift," "Word Market," "Numbers Are the Only Thing That Count," "Rhyme and Reason Reign," "Don't Say There's Nothing to Do in the Doldrums" and "Noise, Noise, Beautiful Noise."

Cast: Butch Patrick (Milo); **Voices:** Hans Conried, Mel Blanc, June Foray, Candy Candido, Les Tremayne, Daws Butler, Patti Gilbert, Shep Menken, Cliff Norton, Larry Thor; **Note:** Patrick played Eddie on TV's *The Munsters* (1964–66).

124 *Pinocchio* (1940) ***

U.S.; Rated G; 88 mins.; Premiered February 7, 1940 at New York's Central Theater; Released February 23, 1940 (Video: July 1985, Walt Disney); Walt Disney.

Synopsis: A lonely woodcutter wishes for a son of his very own, and gets one when the Blue Fairy brings his wooden boy puppet to life. But the puppet—aided by his conscience, Jiminy Cricket—must prove himself before he can become a real boy.

Notes: An undisputed Disney masterpiece. The studio's follow-up to their highly successful first feature *Snow White and the Seven Dwarfs* (1937) has everything—an involving story, wonderful songs, brilliant animation and memorable characters (particularly Jiminy Cricket, in his debut); 750 artists worked on the film for two years, making over 2 million drawings; Walt Disney, unhappy with the way the film was going, scrapped all the work (including animation) that was done during the first five months of production; Originally budgeted at $500,000, the film eventually cost $2.6 million; Renowned children's book illustrator Gustaf Tenggren contributed preliminary sketches to inspire the animators; Dancer Marge Belcher (later Marge Champion), who modeled for Snow White, also modeled for the Blue Fairy; Figaro the cat later appeared in his own cartoon series (1943–47); Entered in the Library of Congress National Film Registry in 1994.

Highlights: the clocks of Geppetto's workshop, the "I've Got No Strings" musical number, the Pleasure Island sequence (in which Lampwick is transformed into a donkey), and the terrifying chase with Monstro the whale.

Credits: Supervising Directors—Ben Sharpsteen, Hamilton Luske; Sequence Directors—Bill Roberts, Jack Kinney, Norman Ferguson, Wilfred Jackson, T. Hee; Animation Direction—Fred Moore, Milton Kahl, Ward Kimball, Eric Larson, Franklin Thomas, Vladimir Tytla, Arthur Babbitt, Woolie Reitherman; Screenplay by Ted Sears, Webb Smith, Joseph Sabo, Otto Englander, William Cottrell, Erdman Penner and Aurelius Battaglia, based on the 1880 story by Carlo Collodi (1826–90); Music and lyrics by Leigh Harline, Ned Washington and Paul J. Smith; Songs—"When You Wish Upon a Star," "Little Woodenhead," "Give a Little Whistle," "Turn on the Old Music Box," "(Hi Diddle De Dee) An Actor's Life for Me" and "I've Got No Strings"; **Note:** Lyricist Washington (1901–76) won his third Oscar in 1952 for the theme to *High Noon* ("Do Not Forsake Me, Oh My Darlin'").

Voices: Dickie Jones (Pinocchio), Cliff Edwards (Jiminy Cricket), Christian Rub (Geppetto), Evelyn Venable (The Blue Fairy), Walter Catlett (J. Worthington Foulfellow), Frankie Darro (Lampwick), Charles Judels (Stromboli/The Coachman), Don Brodie (Barker); **Notes:** Child actor Jones (b. 1927) later starred in TV's *Buffalo Bill, Jr.* (1955, syndicated). Edwards (1895–1971), a star of vaudeville, Broadway and film, started his career as "Ukulele Ike." Thirties actress Venable (1913–93) was the model for the torchbearer in the Columbia Pictures logo.

Honors: Academy Awards—Original Score and Song ("When You Wish Upon a Star" music by Harline, lyrics by Washington).

125 *Pinocchio and the Emperor of the Night* (1987) *
U.S.; Rated G; 88 mins.; Filmation.

Synopsis: Pinocchio, now a real boy, and a live wooden bug named Gee Willikers have a series of adventures.

Notes: Pale sequel to the classic story and Disney film; From Filmation, the studio that also produced the *Snow White* sequel, *Happily Ever After* (1990); Produced by Lou Scheimer.

Credits: Director—Hal Sutherland; Supervising Animators—John Celestri, Chuck Harvey, Kamoon Song; Screenplay by Robby London, Barry O'Brien and Dennis O'Flaherty, inspired by Carlo Collodi's classic tale; Music by Anthony Marinelli and Brian Banks; Songs by Barry Mann, Will Jennings, Steve Tyrell, Marinelli and Banks; Songs— "Love Is the Light Inside Your Heart," "You're a Star" (performed by King Creole and the Coconuts), "Do What Makes You Happy" and "Neon Cabaret."

Voices: Scott Grimes (Pinocchio), Don Knotts (Gee Willikers), Edward Asner (Scalawag), Tom Bosley (Geppetto), Lana Beeson (Twinkle), Linda Gary (Beatrice), James Earl Jones (Emperor of the Night), Jonathan Harris (Lieutenant Grumblebee), Ricky Lee Jones (Good Fairy), Frank Welker (Igor), William Windom (Puppetino); **Note:** Harris played Dr. Smith on TV's *Lost in Space* (1965–68).

126 *Pinocchio in Outer Space* (1964) *
Belgian-U.S.; Not rated; 71 mins.; Swallow/Belvision.

Synopsis: Pinocchio, a puppet once again, and his space friend Nurtle face many dangers on a magical trip to Mars and back.

Notes: Adequate kids adventure starring the famous wooden puppet; American version of a Belgian film, *Pinocchio dans l'espace*, from Ray Goossens (b. 1924), artistic director of Belgium's Belvision production company (founded in 1955); Produced by Norm Prescott and Fred Ladd; Opened January 1, 1964 in New York.

Credits: Director—Ray Goossens; Screenplay by Fred Laderman, based on an idea by Norm Prescott, inspired by Carlo Collodi's original story; Music by F. Leonard, H. Dobbelaere and E. Schurmann; Songs by Robert Sharp and Arthur Korb; Songs—"The Little Toy Shop," "Doin' the Impossible" and "Goody Good Morning."

Voices: Arnold Stang (Nurtle the Turtle), Peter Lazer (Pinocchio), Conrad Jameson, Cliff Owens, Mavis Mims, Kevin Kennedy, Minerva Pious, Jess Cain, Norman Rose.

127 *Pippi Longstocking* (1997) *
Canadian-German-Swedish; Rated G; 75 mins.; Released August 22, 1997 (Video: November 1997, Warner); Nelvana/Ab Svensk Filmindustri/IdunaFilm/Trickompany.

Synopsis: After her father disappears at sea, Pippi Longstocking is left home alone to deal with the town busybody and with two burglars looking to steal her father's coins.

Notes: Lackluster musical starring Astrid Lindgren's spunky redhead; A $10 million production; Produced by Waldemar Bergendahl, Hasmi Giakoumis, Merle-Anne Ridley and Michael Schaack.

Credits: Director—Clive Smith; **Note:** Smith's credits include Nelvana's first feature *Rock and Rule* (1983) and the short-lived TV series *Family Dog* (1993); Animation Directors—Robin Budd, Bill Giggie, Ute V. Munchow-Pohl, Edson Basarin; Screenplay by Catharina Stackelberg, based on the books (the first of which appeared in 1945) by Astrid Lindgren; Music by Anders Berglund; Songs by Berglund, Great Big Music and

Thinkmusic; Songs—"What Shall I Do Today," "Hey-Ho, I'm Pippi," "Recipe for Life," "Pluttifikation" and "A Bowler and a New Gold Tooth."

Voices: Melissa Altro (Pippi), Catherine O'Hara (Mrs. Prysselius), Gordon Pinsent (Capt. Longstocking), Dave Thomas (Thunder-Karlsson), Carol Pope (Teacher), Wayne Robson (Bloom), Chris Wiggins (Fridolf), Rick Jones (Kling), Phillip Williams (Klang/Ringmaster), Noah Reid (Tommy), Olivia Garratt (Annika), Judy Tate (Annika's singing voice), Richard Binsley (Mr. Nilsson/Dog), Karen Bernstein (Mrs. Settergren), Martin Lavut (Mr. Settergren), Mari Trainor (Mrs. Klang), Elva Mai Hoover (Mrs. Kling), Melleny Melody (Snake Lady), Howard Jerome (Adolph), Kyle Fairley, Zachary Spider, Brown Smith (Kids).

128 *The Plague Dogs* (1982) **

British-U.S.; Rated PG; 99 mins.; Released in the United States in 1984; Nepenthe Productions.

Synopsis: A pair of dogs escape from an experimental veterinary lab and are soon hunted by the lab doctors and nearby sheep owners.

Notes: Powerful, well-animated adventure tale with a strong statement about animal rights; Martin Rosen's second animated adaption of a Richard Adams novel, following 1978's *Watership Down*; Produced by Rosen.

Credits: Director—Martin Rosen; Directors of Animation—Tony Guy, Colin White; Screenplay by Martin Rosen, based on a novel by Richard Adams; Music by Patrick Gleeson.

Voices: John Hurt (Snitter), Christopher Benjamin (Rowf), James Bolam (The Tod), Nigel Hawthorne (Dr. Robert Boycott), Judy Geeson (Pekinese), Barbara Leigh-Hunt (Farmer's Wife), Warren Mitchell (Tyson/Wag), Bernard Hepton (Stephen Powell), Brian Stirner (Lab Assistant), Penelope Lee (Lynn Driver), Geoffrey Mathews (Farmer), John Bennett (Don), John Franklyn-Robbins (Williamson), Bill Maynard (Editor), Malcolm Terris (Robert), Phillip Locke, Brian Spink, Tony Church, Anthony Valentine, William Lucas (Civil Servants), Dandy Nichols (Phyllis), Rosemary Leach (Vera), Patrick Stewart (Major).

129 *Pocahontas* (1995) **

U.S.; Rated G; 81 mins.; Premiered in New York's Central Park, June 10, 1995; Released June 23, 1995 (Video: March 1996, Walt Disney); Walt Disney.

Synopsis: In 1607 the young Powhatan Indian maiden Pocahontas meets British Captain John Smith, but their ensuing romance is threatened by their clashing cultures.

Notes: Disney's fact-bending historical-musical romance—a kind of early–American *West Side Story*—benefits from gorgeous animation and a strong pro-nature message; Disney's 33rd animated feature, and the studio's first to be inspired by a real-life figure; The real Pocahontas (1595–1617) was only 12 in 1607 when she met the 29-year-old Smith. She later married another white settler (John Rolfe), moved to England and died of smallpox at 21; Supermodel Christy Turlington was used as a model (one of several) for Pocahontas; Produced by James Pentecost.

Credits: Directors—Mike Gabriel, Eric Goldberg; Supervising Animators—Glen Keane, John Pomeroy, Duncan Marjoribanks, Nik Ranieri, Ruben A. Aquino, Ken Duncan, Chris Buck, T. Daniel Hofstedt, Dave Pruiksma, Anthony DeRosa, Michael Cedeno; Screenplay by Carl Binder, Susannah Grant and Philip LaZebnik; Musical score by Alan Menken and Stephen Schwartz (*Godspell, Pippin*); Songs—"The Virginia Company," "Steady as the Beating Drum," "Just Around the Riverbend," "Mine, Mine, Mine," "Savages," "Listen with Your Heart" and "Colors of the Wind."

Voices: Irene Bedard (Pocahontas), Judy Kuhn (Pocahontas' singing voice), Mel Gibson (John Smith), David Ogden Stiers (Gov. Ratcliffe/Wiggins), Linda Hunt (Grandmother

Willow), Russell Means (Powhatan), Billy Connolly (Ben), Christian Bale (Thomas), Joe Baker (Lon), James Apaumut Fall (Kocoum), John Kassir (Meeko), Danny Mann (Percy), Michelle St. John (Nakoma), Gordon Tootoosis (Kekata), Frank Welker (Flit), Jim Cummings; **Note:** Gibson (*Braveheart*), not known for his vocal skills, does his own singing in the film. Stiers played Cogsworth the clock in Disney's *Beauty and the Beast* (1991).

Honors: Academy Awards—Musical Score and Song ("Colors of the Wind"); Golden Globes—Best Score, Song ("Colors of the Wind").

130 *Pound Puppies and the Legend of Big Paw* (1988) $\frac{1}{2}$
U.S.; Rated G; 76 mins.; Released March 1988; Atlantic/Kushner-Locke.

Synopsis: The Pound Puppies try to find a stolen magical bone which allows dogs and children to communicate with each other.

Notes: Boring limited-animation kids film tied in with the popular line of toys and TV series (1986–88); Produced by Donald Kushner and Peter Locke.

Credits: Director—Pierre DeCelles; Screenplay by Jim Carlson and Terrence McDonnell; Music by Richard Kosinski, Sam Winans and Bill Reichenbach; Songs by Ashley Hall, Stephanie Tyrell and Steve Tyrell.

Voices: George Rose (McNasty), B.J. Ward (Whopper), Ruth Buzzi (Nose Marie), Brennan Howard (Cooler), Cathy Cavadini (Collette), Nancy Cartwright (Bright Eyes), Greg Berg, Ryan Davis, Joe Deido, Ashley Hall, Janice Kawaye, Alwyn Kusher, Mark Vieha, Jasper Kushner, Robbie Lee, Tony Longo, Hal Rayle, Wayne Scherzer, Susan Silo, James Swodek, Frank Welker; **Note:** Actress/voice artist Cartwright is best known as the voice of Bart Simpson on TV's *The Simpsons* (1989–).

131 *The Princess and the Goblin* (1993) *
Welsh-Hungarian; Rated G; 82 mins.; Released in U.S. June 3, 1994 (Video: September 1994, Hemdale Home Video); Siriol Productions/Pannonia Film Company/S4C Wales-NHK Enterprises.

Synopsis: A sheltered princess and a miner's son team up to defeat a race of evil goblins who are threatening her kingdom.

Notes: Children's fantasy from Hungarian animator Jozsef Gemes (b. 1939); Hungarian title—*A Hercegno es a kobold*.

Credits: Director—Jozsef Gemes; Screenplay by Robin Lyons, based on a book by George MacDonald; Music by Istvan Lerch.

Voices: Joss Ackland (King), Claire Bloom (Great-Great-Grandmother), Sally Ann Marsh (Princess Irene), Rik Mayall (Prince Froglip), Peter Murray (Curdie), Peggy Mount (Queen), William Hootkins, Victor Spinetti.

132 *The Puppetoon Movie* (1987) **
U.S.; Not Rated; 80 mins.; Released June 12, 1987; Leibovit Productions.

Synopsis: A collection of nine "Puppetoon" shorts—*Hoola Boola*, *John Henry and the Inky Poo* (Oscar nominee), *Tubby the Tuba* (Oscar nominee), *Tulips Shall Grow* (Oscar nominee), *Jasper in a Jam*, *The Philips Broadcast of 1938*, *Sleeping Beauty*, *South Sea Sweethearts* and *Together in the Weather* (see SHORTS).

Notes: Great compilation celebrating the visual imagination of producer-director George Pal, who produced over 40 puppet cartoons in his acclaimed "Puppetoon" series (dating from the early '30s to 1947); The film includes appearances by Gumby, a Gremlin and the Pillsbury Doughboy.

Credits: Director—George Pal; Compiled, written and produced by Arnold Leibovit; Music by Buddy Baker.

Voices: Rex Ingram, Victor Jory.

133 *Race for Your Life, Charlie Brown* (1977) * ½
U.S.; Rated G; 75 mins.; Released August 1977; Lee Mendelson-Bill Melendez.

Synopsis: The Peanuts gang go to summer camp where they enter a raft race against a group of bullies.

Notes: Lesser "Peanuts" feature (their third) is still a fun adventure for kids; Followed by *Bon Voyage, Charlie Brown (and Don't Come Back!)* (1980); Produced by Mendelson and Melendez.

Credits: Director—Bill Melendez; Co-Director—Phil Roman; Screenplay by Charles M. Schulz, based on his comic-strip characters; Bluegrass musical score by Ed Bogas (*Fritz the Cat*); Songs by Bogas, Lee Mendelson, Erno Rapee and Lew Pollack; Songs—"The Greatest Leader," "Charmine" and the title song (sung by Larry Finlayson).

Voices: Duncan Watson, Greg Felton, Stuart Brotman, Gail Davis, Liam Martin, Kirk Jue, Jordan Warren, Jimmy Ahrens, Melanie Kohn, Tom Muller, Fred Van Amberg, Bill Melendez.

134 *Raggedy Ann and Andy* (1977) * ½
U.S.; Rated G; 85 mins.; Richard Williams.

Synopsis: The adventures of two rag dolls who come to life to rescue a French doll who has been kidnapped by a notorious pirate.

Notes: Ambitious, superbly-animated musical adaption of the classic children's stories, hampered by a weak storyline and forgettable songs; Richard Williams replaced original director Abe Levitow (*Gay Purr-ee*), who had become ill; Includes live-action scenes featuring the director's daughter; Produced over two years by a group of veteran animators at a cost of $4 million; The film—originally planned as a *Hallmark Hall of Fame* TV special—was financed by the Bobbs-Merrill Company (a subsidiary of International Telephone and Telegraph), which also backed two "Raggedy Ann and Andy" TV specials (1978, '79) from Chuck Jones; Oscar-winner Williams (*A Christmas Carol*) later directed the acclaimed animation for the 1988 hit *Who Framed Roger Rabbit*; The Fleischer Studio produced a special two-reel "Raggedy Ann and Andy" short back in 1941; Produced by Richard Horner.

Credits: Director—Richard Williams; Sequence Director—Gerald Potterton; Animators include Richard Williams, Grim Natwick, Art Babbitt, Emery Hawkins, Tissa David, Gerry Chiniquy and Hal Ambro; Screenplay by Patricia Thackray and Ray Wilk, based on characters created (in 1918) by Johnny Gruelle; Music and lyrics by Joe Raposo; Songs—"I Look and What Do I See!" "No Girl's Toy," "Rag Dolly," "Poor Babette," "A Miracle," "Ho-Yo," "Candy Hearts," "Song Blue," "The Mirage," "I Never Get Enough," "I Love You," "Looney Anthem," "It's Not Easy Being King," "Hooray for Me," "You're My Friend" and "Home"; **Note:** Raposo (1937–89) wrote over 1,000 songs ("Bein' Green," "C is for Cookie," etc.) for TV's *Sesame Street* (from 1969).

Cast/Voices: Claire Williams (Marcella); Didi Conn (Ann), Mark Baker (Andy), Fred Stuthman (Camel), Niki Flacks (Babette), George S. Irving (The Captain), Arnold Stang (Queasy), Joe Silver (The Greedy), Alan Sues (The Looney Knight), Marty Brill (King Koo Koo), Paul Dooley (Gazooks), Mason Adams (Grandpa), Allen Swift (Maxi-Fixit), Hetty Galen (Susie Pincushion), Sheldon Harnick (Barney Beanbag/Socko), Ardyth Kaiser (Topsy), Margery Gray, Lynne Stuart (The Twin Pennies); **Notes:** Conn starred in the film *You Light Up My Life* that same year. Harnick is a Tony-winning lyricist (*Fiddler on the Roof*).

135 *Rainbow Brite and the Star Stealer* (1985) ½
U.S.; Rated G; 97 mins.; Released November 1985 (Video: March 1986, Warner); DIC Enterprises.

Synopsis: Rainbow Brite—a little girl who brings rainbow colors and happiness to the world—and a boy named Krys try to stop the Dark Princess from stealing Spectra, the world's light source.

Notes: Blandly-animated feature starring the toy/cartoon characters created by Hallmark Properties; Produced by Jean Chalopin, Andy Heyward and Tetsuo Katayama.

Credits: Directors—Bernard Deyries, Kimio Yabuki; Screenplay by Howard R. Cohen; Story by Cohen and Jean Chalopin; Music by Shuki Levy and Haim Saban; Lyrics by Howard R. Cohen; Songs—"Brand New Day" and "Rainbow Brite and Me."

Voices: Bettina (Rainbow Brite), Patrick Fraley (Lurky/On-X/Buddy Blue/Dog Guard/Spectran/Slurthie/Glitterbot), Peter Cullen (Murky/Castle Monster/Glitterbot/Guard/Skydancer/Slurthie), Robbie Lee (Twin/Shy Violet/Indigo/La La Orange/Spectran/Sprites), Andre Stojka (Starlite/Wizard/Spectran), David Mendenhall (Krys), Rhonda Aldrich (The Princess/The Creature), Les Tremayne (Orin/Bombo/TV Announcer), Mona Marshall (Red Butler/Witch/Castle Creature/Spectran/Patty O'Green/Canary Yellow), Jonathan Harris (Count Blogg), Marissa Mendenhall (Stormy), Scott Menville (Brian), Charles Adler (Popo), David Workman (Sergeant Zombo).

136 *The Reluctant Dragon* (1941) ** ½
U.S.; Rated G; 72 mins.; Released June 20, 1941; Walt Disney.

Synopsis: Robert Benchley visits the Walt Disney Studio and sees firsthand how cartoons are made. Segments include "Casey Jr." (a demonstration of cartoon sound effects) and the cartoons—*Baby Weems*, *How to Ride a Horse* (with Goofy) and *The Reluctant Dragon* (see SHORTS).

Notes: Delightful behind-the-scenes documentary, highlighted by the excellent title cartoon; *Dragon*—Disney's first significant venture into live-action filming—also includes guest appearances by Bambi and Donald Duck (in his feature debut); The first 20 minutes of the film are in black-and-white; Later reedited and shown as *Behind the Scenes of Walt Disney Studios*.

Credits: Director—Alfred L. Werker (live-action); Cartoon Directors—Hamilton Luske, Jack Kinney, Jim Handley, Ford Beebe, Erwin Verity, Jasper Blystone; Screenplay by Ted Sears, Al Perkins, Larry Clemmons and Bill Cottrell, with additional dialogue by Robert Benchley and Harry Clork; *The Reluctant Dragon* by Erdman Penner and T. Hee, from the Kenneth Grahame story; *Baby Weems* by Joe Grant, Dick Huemer and John P. Miller; Musical score by Frank Churchill and Larry Morey.

Cast: Robert Benchley (Himself), Frances Gifford (Doris), Nana Bryant (Mrs. Benchley), Buddy Pepper (Humphrey, the guide), Florence Gill, Clarence Nash, Alan Ladd, John Dehner, Truman Woodworth, Hamilton MacFadden, Maurice Murphy, Jeffy Corey, Henry Hall, Frank Faylen, Lester Dorr, Gerald Mohr, Norm Ferguson, Ward Kimball, Jimmy Luske, the Walt Disney Studio staff, and Walt Disney (Himself); **Voices:** Barnett Parker (Dragon), Claud Allister (Sir Giles), Billy Lee (Boy), J. Donald Wilson (Narrator), Clarence Nash (Donald Duck), Pinto Colvig (Goofy), Leone LeDoux/Raymond Severn (Baby Weems), Ernie Alexander (John Weems), Linda Marwood (Mrs. John Weems), Art Gilmore (FDR), Edward Marr (Walter Winchell), Gerald Mohr ("Baby Weems" Narrator), John McLeish (Goofy Short Narrator), The Rhythmaires; **Notes:** Benchley (1889–1945) was a popular humorist/writer in the '30s and '40s. Ladd, who appears as a *Baby Weems* story man, became a star a year later in *This Gun for Hire*.

137 *The Rescuers* (1977) **
U.S.; Rate G; 77 mins.; Released June 22, 1977; Walt Disney.

Synopsis: Two mice from the Mouse Rescue Aid Society try to rescue a little orphan girl who has been kidnapped by the evil Madame Medusa.

Notes: The Disney Studio's 22nd animated feature—the best since Walt Disney's death—is a fun, imaginative children's adventure; A four-year production, which cost $6 million and required 330,000 drawings; Sequel—*The Rescuers Down Under* (1990); Produced by Wolfgang Reitherman.

Credits: Directors—Wolfgang Reitherman, John Lounsbery, Art Stevens; Directing Animators—Ollie Johnston, Frank Thomas, Milt Kahl, Don Bluth; **Note:** Disney veteran Kahl's last film before retiring (he joined the studio in 1934); Screenplay by Larry Clemmons, Ken Anderson, Vance Gerry, David Michener, Burny Mattinson, Frank Thomas, Fred Lucky, Ted Berman and Dick Sebast, based on the 1959 stories *The Rescuers* and *Miss Bianca* by Margery Sharp (1905–91); Music by Artie Butler; Songs by Carol Connors, Ayn Robbins and Sammy Fain; Songs (sung by Shelby Flint)—"The Journey," "Rescue Aid Society," "Tomorrow Is Another Day," and "Someone's Waiting for You"; **Note:** Connors and Robbins also cowrote the Oscar-nominated *Rocky* theme "Gonna Fly Now" (1976).

Voices: Bob Newhart (Bernard), Eva Gabor (Miss Bianca), Geraldine Page (Madame Medusa), Joe Flynn (Mr. Snoops), Jeanette Nolan (Ellie Mae), Pat Buttram (Luke), Jim Jordan (Orville the albatross), John McIntire (Rufus), Michelle Stacy (Penny), Bernard Fox (Chairman), Larry Clemmons (Gramps), James Macdonald (Evinrude), George Lindsey (Rabbit), Bill McMillan (TV Announcer), Dub Taylor (Digger), John Fiedler (Owl); **Notes:** Flynn's (*McHale's Navy*) last film role (he died in 1974). Jordan (1896–1988) is best known for playing "Fibber McGee" on radio's *Fibber McGee and Molly* (1935–57).

Honors: Academy Award nomination—Song ("Someone's Waiting for You" music by Fain, lyrics by Connors and Robbins).

138 *The Rescuers Down Under* (1990) **

U.S.; Rated G; 77 mins.; Released November 16, 1990 (Video: September 1991, Walt Disney); Walt Disney.

Synopsis: When a boy in Australia is kidnapped by an evil poacher, Bernard and Miss Bianca from the Mouse Rescue Aid Society are off to the rescue again.

Notes: Superb, computer-enhanced animation highlights this sequel (Disney's first to an animated feature) to 1977's *The Rescuers*; Four years in production; Released in theaters with the new "Mickey Mouse" short *The Prince and the Pauper*; Produced by Thomas Schumacher.

Credits: Directors—Mike Gabriel, Hendel Butoy; Supervising Animators—Glen Keane, Mark Henn, Russ Edmonds, David Cutler, Ruben A. Aquino, Nik Ranieri, Ed Gombert, Anthony De Rosa, Kathy Zielinski, Duncan Marjoribanks; Screenplay by Jim Cox, Karey Kirkpatrick, Byron Simpson and Joe Ranft, based on characters created by Margery Sharp; Music by Bruce Broughton; Songs—"Black Slacks" and "Waltzing Matilda."

Voices: Bob Newhart (Bernard), Eva Gabor (Miss Bianca), John Candy (Wilbur the albatross), George C. Scott (McLeach), Tristan Rogers (Jake), Adam Ryen (Cody), Wayne Robson (Frank), Frank Welker (Joanna), Ed Gilbert (François), Bernard Fox (Chairmouse/Doctor), Douglas Seale (Krebbs), Peter Firth (Red), Billy Barty (Baitmouse), Carla Meyer (Faloo/Mother), Russi Taylor (Nurse Mouse); **Note:** Newhart and Gabor reprise the roles they played in the original film.

139 *Robin Hood* (1973) *$\frac{1}{2}$

U.S.; Rated G; 83 mins.; Released November 8, 1973 (Video: December 1984, Walt Disney); Walt Disney.

Synopsis: A balladeer rooster tells the story of the legendary Sherwood Forest bandit, with the familiar cast of characters being played by animals.

Notes: Not one of Disney's best, but kids should enjoy this light animated version of the famous tale; Produced by Wolfgang Reitherman.

Credits: Director—Wolfgang Reitherman; Directing Animators—Milt Kahl, Ollie Johnston, Frank Thomas, John Lounsbery; Story by Larry Clemmons, based on character and story conceptions by Ken Anderson; Story Sequences—Eric Cleworth, Vance Gerry, Frank Thomas, Ken Anderson, Dave Michener and Julius Svendsen; Music by George Bruns; Songs by Roger Miller, Floyd Huddleston, Bruns and Johnny Mercer (four-time Oscar winner); Songs—"Oo-de-lally," "Not in Nottingham," "Whistle-Stop," "The Phony King of England" and "Love" (sung by Nancy Adams).

Voices: Brian Bedford (Robin Hood, a fox), Phil Harris (Little John, a bear), Monica Evans (Maid Marion, a vixen), Peter Ustinov (Prince John, a lion), Andy Devine (Friar Tuck, a badger), Terry Thomas (Sir Hiss, a snake), Roger Miller (Allen a Dale, a rooster), Carole Shelley (Lady Kluck, a chicken), Pat Buttram (Sheriff of Nottingham, a wolf), George Lindsey (Trigger, a vulture), Ken Curtis (Nutsy, a vulture); **Note:** Harris had also lent his voice to Disney's two previous films, *The Jungle Book* and *The Aristocats*. Miller (1936–92), who wrote and sang three of the film's songs, is best known for his hit "King of the Road" (1965).

Honors: Academy Award nomination—Song ("Love" music by Bruns, lyrics by Huddleston); Other award—National Board of Review Awards (Special Citation, 1973).

140 *Rock-A-Doodle* (1992) * ½
U.S.; Rated G; 74 mins.; Released April 3, 1992 (Video: August 1992, HBO); Sullivan Bluth.

Synopsis: To save his farm from flooding, a young boy travels into another world to find a singing rooster whose crow can make the sun rise again.

Notes: Don Bluth's fifth animated feature (following 1989's *All Dogs Go to Heaven*) is a structurally-ragged, but well-animated tale with some amusing Elvis Presley–style tunes; Includes live-action scenes (of about 7 minutes) of the boy's family and farm; Produced by Bluth, Gary Goldman and John Pomeroy.

Credits: Director—Don Bluth; Co-Directors—Dan Kuenster, Gary Goldman; Sequence Directors—Dick Zondag, Ralph Zondag; Directing Animators—John Pomeroy, Jeffrey J. Varab, Jean Morel, Linda Miller, T. Daniel Hofstedt, Ken Duncan, Lorna Pomeroy-Cook, Jeff Etter; Screenplay by David N. Weiss; Story by Weiss, Don Bluth, John Pomeroy, David Steinberg, T. J. Kuenster and Gary Goldman; Music score by Robert Folk; Original songs by T.J. Kuenster; Songs—"Sun Do Shine," "We Hate the Sun," "Come Back to You," "Bouncers' Theme Song," "Treasure Hunting Fever," "Kiss N' Coo," "The Owls Picnic," "Tweedle Te Dee," "Sink or Swim," "Back to the Country" and "Tyin' Your Shoes."

Cast/Voices: Glen Campbell (Chanticleer the rooster), Christopher Plummer (The Duke, an owl), Toby Scott Ganger (Edmond), Ellen Greene (Goldie), Eddie Deezen (Snipes the magpie), Sandy Duncan (Peepers the mouse), Phil Harris (Narrator/Patou the dog), Charles Nelson Reilly (Hunch), Kathryn Holcomb (Mother), Stan Ivar (Dad), Christian Hoff (Scott), Jason Marin (Mark), Will Ryan (Stuey the pig), Sorrell Booke (Pinky), Dee Wallace (Mother), Louise Chamis (Minnie Rabbit), Bob Galaco (Radio Announcer), Jake Steinfeld (Farmyard Bully/Max the Bouncer).

141 *Rock and Rule* (1983) * ½
U.S.; Rated PG; 85 mins.; Nelvana.

Synopsis: Angel, a punk rock singer in post-apocalyptic New York, is kidnapped by the villainous Mok, who wants her voice for evil purposes.

Notes: So-so musical-fantasy helped by good animation and a fine rock soundtrack; The first full-length feature film from Nelvana, the Canadian animation studio which later produced the three *Care Bears* features; The film cost $8.9 million to produce; Produced by Patrick Loubert and Michael Hirsh.

Credits: Director—Clive A. Smith; Screenplay by Peter Sauder and John Halfpenny; Story by Sauder and Patrick Loubert; Music by Patrick Cullen; Songs performed by Debbie Harry, Lou Reed, Cheap Trick, Earth Wind and Fire, and Iggy Pop; Songs—"Angel's Song," "Invocation Song," "Send Love Through," "Pain and Suffering," "My Name Is Mok," "Born to Raise Hell," "I'm the Man," "Ohm Sweet Ohm," "Dance, Dance, Dance" and "Hot Dogs and Sushi."

Voices: Don Francks (Mok), Paul Le Mat (Omar), Susan Roman (Angel), Sam Langevin (Mok's Computer), Dan Hennessey (Dizzy), Greg Duffell (Stretch/Zip), Chris Wiggins (Toad), Brent Titcomb (Sleazy), Donny Burns (Quadhole/1st Radio Announcer), Martin Lavut (Mylar/2nd Radio Announcer), Catherine Gallant (Cindy), Keith Hampshire (Other Computers), Melleny Brown (Carnegie Hall Groupie), Anna Bourque (Edna), Nick Nichols (Borderguard), John Halfpenny (Uncle Mikey), Maurice LaMarche (Sailor), Catherine O'Hara (Aunt Edith).

142 *Rover Dangerfield* (1991) *½
U.S.; Rated G; 74 mins.; Released August 1991; Hyperion.

Synopsis: A city-slicker dog from Las Vegas is abandoned in the country by the boyfriend of his showgirl owner and has to adjust to life down on the farm.

Notes: Likeable animated musical-comedy starring comedian Rodney Dangerfield in canine form; Produced by Willard Carroll and Thomas L. Wilhite (producers of *The Brave Little Toaster*), and executive produced by Dangerfield.

Highlight: the computer-animated opening.

Credits: Directors—Jim George, Bob Seeley; Sequence Directors—Steve Moore, Matthew O'Callaghan, Bruce Smith, Dick Sebast, Frans Vischer, Skip Jones; Screenplay by Rodney Dangerfield; Story by Dangerfield and Harold Ramis, from an idea by Dangerfield; Music by David Newman; Songs by Rodney Dangerfield and Billy Tragesser; Songs—"It's a Dog's Life," "Somewhere There's a Party," "I'd Give Up a Bone for You," "I'm in Love with the Dog Next Door," "I'd Never Do It on a Christmas Tree" and "I Found a Four-Leaf Clover When I Met Rover."

Voices: Rodney Dangerfield (Rover), Susan Boyd (Daisy), Ronnie Schell (Eddie), Ned Luke (Raffles), Shawn Southwick (Connie), Dana Hill (Danny), Sal Landi (Rocky), Tom Williams (Coyote/Rooster), Chris Collins (Big Boss/Coyote/Sparky/Wolf/Horse), Robert Bergen (Gangster/Farm Voice), Paxton Whitehead (Count), Ron Taylor (Mugsy), Bert Kramer (Max), Eddie Barth (Champ), Ralph Monaco (Truck Driver), Tress MacNeille (Queenie/Chorus Girls/Hen/Chickens/Turkey), Michael Sheehan (Jose/Sheep), Lara Cody (Gigi/Chorus Girl/Sheep), Ron Taylor (Bruno), Owen Bush, Ken White, Gregg Berger, Heidi Banks, Dennis Blair, Don Stuart, Robert Pine, Danny Mann, Bernard Erhard, Burton Sharp, Louise Chamis, Bill Farmer, Barbara Goodson, Patricia Parris, Ross Taylor.

143 *Saludos Amigos* (1943) **
U.S.; Rated G; 43 mins.; Released February 6, 1943; Walt Disney.

Synopsis: Donald Duck and a parrot named Joe Carioca star in this salute South America, featuring four animated sequences—*Lake Titicaca*, *Pedro*, *El Gaucho Goofy* and *Aquarela do Brasil* (Watercolor of Brazil). See SHORTS.

Notes: Enjoyable, segmented Disney travelogue promoting America's Good Neighbor Policy of the '40s; The animated sequences are linked by live-action footage (16 mm) taken during a goodwill tour Walt Disney and crew made in August 1941 of Argentina, Peru, Chile and Brazil, sponsored by the State Department; Followed by the similar, but more fully-developed *The Three Caballeros* (1945).

Credits: Supervisor: Norman Ferguson; Sequence Directors—Bill Roberts, Hamilton Luske, Jack Kinney, Wilfred Jackson; Story by Homer Brightman, Ralph Wright, Roy

Williams, Dick Huemer, Harry Reeves and Joe Grant; Musical Director—Charles Wolcott; Music by Edward H. Plumb and Paul J. Smith; Songs include "Brazil" (by Ary Barroso and S. K. Russell) and the title song (by Wolcott and Ned Washington).

Voices: Fred Shields (Narrator), Clarence Nash (Donald Duck), Jose Oliveira (Joe Carioca).

Honors: Academy Award nominations—Musical Score, Song ("Saludos Amigos") and Sound (C. O. Slyfield).

144 *Santa and the Three Bears* (1970) *
U.S.; Rated G; 63 mins.; A R and S Film Enterprises.

Synopsis: A kindly park ranger impersonates Santa Claus for two bear cubs who put off hibernating to experience the joy of Christmas.

Notes: Animated holiday tale for children; The film opens with live-action scenes of a grandfather telling the story to his grandchildren; Later reedited and shown on TV as a holiday special; Produced by Tony Benedict.

Credits: Director—Tony Benedict; Supervising Animator—Bill Hutten; Screenplay by Tony Benedict; Music and lyrics by Doug Goodwin, Tony Benedict and Joe Leahy; Songs (sung by Joyce Taylor)—"The Wonder of Christmastime," "Wintertime," "World of Toy People" and "Sleepytime Song."

Cast/Voices: Hal Smith (Grandfather), Beth Goldfarb (Beth), Brian Hobbs (Brian); Hal Smith (Mr. Ranger/Santa Claus), Jean VanderPyl (Nana), Annette Ferra (Nikomi), Bobby Riha (Chinook); **Note:** Smith (1916–94) played Otis the town drunk on TV's *The Andy Griffith Show* (1960–67). VanderPyl is best known as the voice of Wilma Flintstone on TV's *The Flintstones*.

145 *The Secret of NIMH* (1982) ** ½
U.S.; Rated G; 82 mins.; Released July 2, 1982; Don Bluth Productions.

Synopsis: A widowed mouse, seeking help for her family, comes upon a group of super-intelligent rats who have escaped from an experimental laboratory (NIMH, The National Institute of Mental Health).

Notes: Fabulous adventure tale featuring some of the most dazzling, detailed non–Disney animation in years; The first feature film from Don Bluth and his team of animators who had defected from the Disney Studio in 1979 to form their own production company (their first effort was an animated sequence for the 1980 Olivia Newton-John film *Xanadu*). A staff of about 55 people worked on the film for two-and-a-half years, making approximately 150,000 drawings and 1,000 background paintings; The film was a critical success when first released but did not perform well at the box office, due in part to a bad marketing campaign; Produced by Bluth, Gary Goldman and John Pomeroy.

Credits: Director—Don Bluth; Directing Animators—John Pomeroy, Gary Goldman; Screenplay by Don Bluth, John Pomeroy, Gary Goldman and Will Finn, based on the Newbery Award–winning children's book *Mrs. Frisby and the Rats of NIMH* by Robert C. O'Brien; Music by Jerry Goldsmith (*Planet of the Apes*, *Chinatown*), performed by the National Philharmonic Orchestra of London.

Voices: Elizabeth Hartman (Mrs. Brisby), Derek Jacobi (Nicodemus), Dom DeLuise (Jeremy the crow), Arthur Malet (Mr. Ages), Hermione Baddeley (The Shrew), John Carradine (Great Owl), Peter Strauss (Justin), Paul Shenar (Jennar), Tom Hattan (Farmer Fitzgibbons), Shannen Doherty (Teresa), Wil Wheaton (Martin), Jodi Hicks (Cynthia), Ian Fried (Timmy), Lucille Bliss, Aldo Ray; **Notes:** Jacobi played the title role in the acclaimed TV miniseries *I, Claudius* (1976). Doherty later went on to star (1990–94) in the hit TV series *Beverly Hills, 90210*.

146 *The Secret of the Sword* (1985)
U.S.; Rated G; 87 mins.; Released May 17, 1985; Filmation.

Synopsis: In the land of Etheria, He-Man must free his twin sister She-Ra, Princess of Power, from evil ruler Hordak and teach her the powers of the sword.

Notes: Poorly-produced feature film based on the Saturday morning TV series *He-Man and the Masters of the Universe* (1983, synd.) and *She-Ra: Princess of Power* (1985, synd.) and the line of Mattel toys; Working title—*Princess of Power*; Produced by Arthur Nadel.

Credits: Directors—Bill Reed, Gwen Wetzler, Ed Friedman, Lou Kachivas, Marsh Lamore; Screenplay by Larry Ditillo and Bob Forward; Music by Shuki Levy, Haim Saban and Erika Lane; Song—"I Have the Power" (performed by Erika Scheimer and Noam Kaniel) by Scheimer, Levy and Saban.

Voices: John Erwin (Adam/He-Man), Melendy Britt (Adora/She-Ra), George DiCenzo (Hordak), Alan Oppenheimer, Erik Gunden, Linda Gary, Erika Scheimer.

147 *Shame of the Jungle* (1979) $\frac{1}{2}$
French-Belgian-U.S.; Rated R; 73 mins.; Released in U.S. September 14, 1979.

Synopsis: A takeoff on Tarzan films which follows the adventures of jungle man Shame, who sets out to rescue his kidnapped female companion, June.

Notes: Low-grade spoof, of interest only for some of the voices; American version of a 1975 film, *La Honte de la Jungle* (85m), by Belgian animator Picha (b. Jean-Paul Walravens, 1942); Aka *Jungle Burger*.

Credits: Directors—Picha, Boris Szulzinger; Screenplay by Picha and Pierre Bartier; Dialogue by Michael O'Donoghue and Anne Beatts (writers for TV's *Saturday Night Live*); Original characters by Picha; Music by Teddy Lasry and Mark Moulins.

Voices: Johnny Weissmuller, Jr. (Shame), John Belushi (Perfect Master), Bob Perry (Narrator), Christopher Guest (Chief M'Bulu/Short/Police Voice/Nurse), Andrew Duncan (Siamese Twin), Brian Doyle-Murray (Siamese Twin), Bill Murray (Speaker), Pat Bright (Queen Bazonga), Emily Prager (June), Guy Sorel (Prof. Cedric Addlepate), Judy Graubart (Steffanie Starlet), Adolph Caesar (Brutish); **Notes:** Weissmuller, Jr., is the son of the famed screen Tarzan of the '30s and '40s. Belushi, Murray, Guest, and Doyle-Murray are all former cast members of *Saturday Night Live*.

148 *shinbone alley* (1971) *$\frac{1}{2}$
U.S.; Rated G; 84 mins.; Released April 1971; A Fine Arts Film.

Synopsis: The adventures of poet archy the cockroach and free-spirited mehitabel the alley cat.

Notes: Lightly entertaining animated version of the Broadway musical; Produced by Preston M. Fleet.

Credits: Director—John D. Wilson; Screenplay by Joe Darion, based on the 1957 musical by Darion and Mel Brooks, from the *archy and mehitabel* stories (1916–30) by Don Marquis and drawings of George Herriman (creator of "Krazy Kat"); Music by George Kleinsinger; Lyrics by Joe Darion; Songs—"I Am Only a Poor Humble Cockroach," "Blow Wind Out of the North," "Cheerio My Deario (Toujours Gai)," "Ah, the Theater, the Theater," "What Do We Care If We're Down and Out?," "The Moth Song," "Lullaby for Mehitabel's Kittens," "The Shinbone Alley Song," "The Lightning Bug Song," "Here Pretty Pretty Pussy," "Ladybugs of the Evening," "Archy's Philosophies," "They Don't Have It Here," "Romeo and Juliet" and "Come to Meeoww."

Voices: Eddie Bracken (archy), Carol Channing (mehitabel), John Carradine (tyrone t tattersall), Alan Reed, Sr. (big bill), Hal Smith, Sal Delano, Ken Sansom, Joan Gerber, Byron Kae, The Jackie Ward Singers; **Notes:** Channing (*Hello, Dolly*) and Bracken (*Hail *the Conquering Hero*) play the roles that Eartha Kitt and Bracken originated on Broadway. Reed is best known as the voice of Fred Flintstone on TV's *The Flintstones.*

149 *The Singing Princess* (1967) *½
Italian; Not Rated; 76 mins.

Synopsis: A cruel sheik, with the help of an evil sorcerer, schemes to marry the lovely Princess Zeila to gain her kingdom, but a court minstrel, who really loves her, gets in his way.

Notes: Italian fairy tale from Anton Gino Domeneghini (1897–1966), a former advertising artist who worked on the film for seven years; The film opened in Rome in December 1949 as *La rosa di Bagdad.* The English version, *Rose of Bagdad*, was released in Great Britain in 1952; Produced by Domeneghini.

Credits: Director—Anton Gino Domeneghini; English dialogue and lyrics by Nina and Tony Maguire; Music by Riccardo Pick Mangiagalli; Songs—"Song for the Bee," "Sunset Prayer" and "The Flower Song."

Voices: Julie Andrews (Princess Zeila), Howard Marion-Crawford (Narrator).

150 *Sleeping Beauty* (1959) ***
U.S.; Rated G; 75 mins.; Released January 29, 1959 (Video: October 1986, Walt Disney); Walt Disney.

Synopsis: A beautiful princess, cursed at birth by an evil sorceress to prick her finger on a spinning wheel and die before her 16th birthday, is hidden away by three good fairies until she meets a handsome prince.

Notes: Disney's most expensive animated feature (at that time, costing $6 million)—while not as emotionally engaging as earlier efforts—is a lavish and visually-dazzling production, photographed in widescreen Technirama 70; A six-year production (the film was first planned back in 1950); The flat, angular style of the artwork (designed by background artist Eyvind Earle) was based on 15th-century French manuscripts and tapestries; Future animator-director Don Bluth joined the Disney Studio in 1956 as an assistant animator on this film (he left the studio a year-and-a-half later but returned in 1971); A box-office failure (one of Disney's biggest) when first released; Disney's last animated fairy tale until 1989's *The Little Mermaid.*

Highlights: the opening "Hail the Princess Aurora" scene, and the brilliantly-animated climactic battle between the prince and the evil Maleficent in dragon form.

Credits: Supervising Director—Clyde Geronimi; Sequence Directors—Eric Larson, Wolfgang Reitherman, Les Clark; Directing Animators—Milt Kahl, Frank Thomas, Marc Davis, Ollie Johnston, John Lounsbery; Story by Erdman Penner, based on the Charles Perrault version (1697) of the classic fairy tale; Music score by George Bruns, adapted from the 1890 Tchaikovsky ballet; Songs by Bruns, Erdman Penner, Tom Adair, Sammy Fain, Winston Hibler, Jack Lawrence and Ted Sears; Songs—"Once Upon a Dream," "One Gift," "I Wonder," "Hail the Princess Aurora," "The Skump Song" and "The Sleeping Beauty Song."

Voices: Mary Costa (Princess Aurora), Bill Shirley (Prince Phillip), Eleanor Audley (Maleficent), Verna Felton (Flora), Barbara Luddy (Merryweather), Barbara Jo Allen (Fauna), Taylor Holmes (King Stefan), Bill Thompson (King Hubert), Bill Amsbery, Candy Candido, Pinto Colvig (Maleficent's Goons), Dal McKennon (Owl), Marvin Miller (Narrator); **Notes:** Shirley (1921–89) later dubbed Jeremy Brett's singing voice in *My Fair Lady* (1964). Audley (1905–91) also voiced the wicked stepmother in *Cinderella* (1950).

Honors: Academy Award nomination—Musical score.

Slip Slide Adventures **see** *The Water Babies.*

151 *The Smurfs and the Magic Flute* (1984) *
Belgian-French; Rated G; 74 mins.; Released August, 1984; Fine Performance Pictures/Studios Belvision.

Synopsis: The Smurfs search for a magical flute which, when played, causes people to dance uncontrollably.

Notes: The Smurfs' feature film debut is cute, inoffensive fare for kids; The popular little blue characters, created in 1957 by Belgian artist Pierre "Peyo" Culliford, were already comic-strip/cartoon stars in Europe (where they're known as "Schtroumpfs") before they appeared in their Emmy-winning Saturday morning TV series (1981–90) in the U.S.; Original Belgian title—*V'la les Schtroumpfs*; Produced by Jose Dutillieu.

Credits: Director—John Rust; Supervising Animator—Eddie Lateste; Screenplay by John Rust, based on characters created by Pierre Culliford; Music by Michel Legrand (*Yentl*).

Voices: Cam Clarke, Grant Gottschall, Patty Foley, Mike Reynolds, Ted Lehman, Bill Capizzi, Ron Gans, X. Phifer, Dudley Knight, John Rust, Richard Miller, David Page, Durga McBroom, Michael Sorich, Robert Axelrod.

152 *Snoopy, Come Home* (1972) **
U.S.; Rated G; 70 mins.; Released August 16, 1972; Lee Mendelson-Bill Melendez.

Synopsis: Snoopy leaves home to visit his former owner—a young girl in the hospital—and is haunted by "No Dogs Allowed" wherever he goes.

Notes: Entertaining "Peanuts" tale for all ages starring Charlie Brown's famous beagle; This second "Peanuts" film introduced Snoopy's yellow-feathered bird friend Woodstock; Followed by *Race for Your Life, Charlie Brown* (1977); Produced by Mendelson and Melendez.

Credits: Director—Bill Melendez; Screenplay by Charles M. Schulz, based on his comic-strip characters; Music and lyrics by Richard M. and Robert B. Sherman (of *Mary Poppins* fame); Songs—title song, "Best of Buddies," "Gettin' It Together," "Lila's Tune," "Fun on the Beach," "Changes," "Partners" and "No Dogs Allowed."

Voices: Chad Webber (Charlie Brown), David Carey (Schroeder), Robin Kohn (Lucy), Stephen Shea (Linus), Johanna Baer (Lila), Hilary Momberger (Sally), Chris De Faria (Patty), Linda Ercoli (Marcy), Linda Mendelson (Frieda), Bill Melendez (Snoopy).

153 *The Snow Queen* (1960) *½
Russian-U.S.; Not Rated; 70 mins.; Soyuzmultfilm.

Synopsis: A young girl named Gerda searches for her beloved friend Kay, who is being held captive by the evil Snow Queen.

Notes: Well-animated telling of the famous fairy tale; American version of a 1957 Russian feature by Armenian animator Lev Atamanov (1905–81), with 15 minutes of live-action footage featuring Art Linkletter and friends; Famed cartoon director Dave Fleischer acted as technical supervisor on the film; Produced by Robert Faber.

Credits: Directors—Lev Atamanov, Phil Patton (American version); Animation and screenplay by Soyuzmultfilm Productions; Based on the 1844 fairy tale by Hans Christian Andersen; Prologue and adaption by Alan Lipscott and Bob Fisher; Music by Frank Skinner; Songs by Diane Lampert and Richard Loring; Songs—title song, "The Jolly Robbers" and "Do It While You're Young."

Cast/Voices: Art Linkletter, Tammy Marihugh, Jennie Lynn, Billy Booth, Rickey Busch; Sandra Dee (Gerda), Tommy Kirk (Kay), Patty McCormack (Angel), Louise Arthur (Snow Queen), Paul Frees (Ol' Dreamy/The Raven), June Foray (Court Raven), Joyce Terry (Princess), Richard Beals (Prince), Lillian Buyeff (Granny); **Note:** Voice artist/announcer Frees (1920–86) is best known as the voice of Boris Badenov on TV's *Rocky and His Friends/The Bullwinkle Show* (1959–63).

154 *Snow White and the Seven Dwarfs* (1937) ***

U.S.; Rated G; 83 mins.; Premiered December 21, 1937 at the Carthay Circle Theater in Los Angeles; Released February 4, 1938 (Video: October 1994, Walt Disney); Walt Disney.

Synopsis: An evil, jealous queen schemes to kill her beautiful stepdaughter Snow White, who the Magic Mirror claims is the fairest of them all. After being abandoned in the woods, Snow White finds refuge with seven friendly dwarfs.

Notes: The first full-length animated feature film and perhaps the most beloved of all of Disney's animated classics. A charming (and at times frightening) tale, with first-rate animation and some of the most memorable songs ever written; The film took three years, 750 artists and 2 million drawings to complete, costing Disney $1.6 million in production alone (it was originally budgeted at $250,000). The expensive film, referred to as "Disney's Folly" by some Hollywood moguls before its release, was an enormous box-office success, earning over $8 million, which made it Hollywood's highest-grossing film at that time. (It has since earned more than $400 million after eight rereleases, making it one of the highest-grossing cartoon films ever.); Several scenes were cut at the last minute, including one which showed the dwarfs enjoying soup; Dancer Marjorie Belcher (later known as Marge Champion) was the model for Snow White; *Snow White* was one of the first 25 films entered (in 1989) in the Library of Congress National Film Registry.

Highlights: Snow White's flight through the forest, the queen's transformation into an old hag, and her tempting of Snow White with the poison apple.

Credits: Supervising Director—David Hand; Sequence Directors—Perce Pearce, Larry Morey, William Cottrell, Wilfred Jackson, Ben Sharpsteen; Supervising Animators—Hamilton Luske, Vladimir Tytla, Fred Moore, Norman Ferguson, with 24 animators; **Note:** Fleischer Studio veteran Grim Natwick (creator of Betty Boop) was the chief animator of Snow White; Screenplay by Ted Sears, Otto Englander, Earl Hurd, Dorothy Ann Blank, Richard Creedon, Dick Richard, Merrill De Maris and Webb Smith, based on the Brothers Grimm fairy tale; Music by Frank Churchill, Leigh Harline and Paul Smith; Songs by Churchill and Larry Morey; Songs—"I'm Wishing," "One Song," "With a Smile and a Song," "Whistle While You Work," "Dig, Dig, Dig," "Heigh-Ho," "Bluddle-Uddle-Um-Dum," "Isn't This a Silly Song?" and "Some Day My Prince Will Come"; **Note:** Harline (1907–69) worked at Disney from 1932 to 1941, winning two Oscars for *Pinocchio* (1940).

Voices: Adriana Caselotti (Snow White), Harry Stockwell (Prince Charming), Lucille La Verne (The Queen), Moroni Olsen (Magic Mirror), Billy Gilbert (Sneezy), Pinto Colvig (Sleepy/Grumpy), Otis Harlan (Happy), Scotty Mattraw (Bashful), Roy Atwell (Doc), Stuart Buchanan (Humbert/The Queen's Huntsman), Marion Darlington (Bird sounds and warbling), The Fraunfelder Family (Yodeling); **Notes:** Caselotti (1916–97) was 18 years old, the daughter of a vocal coach, when she was hired by Disney in 1934 (she would be paid only $970 for her memorable work). Colvig was also the voice of Goofy.

Honors: Academy Award—Walt Disney received a Special Award (one large Oscar with seven small replicas), also nominated for Score; Other awards and citations—Venice Film Festival (Great Art Trophy, 1938), New York Film Critics Award (Special Award, 1938), *New York Times* (Best Film of the Year, 1938).

155 *So Dear to My Heart* (1949) **

U.S.; Not Rated; 84 mins.; Released January 19, 1949; Walt Disney.

Synopsis: In 1903 a young farm boy tries to tame a black lamb so that he can enter it in the County Fair competition.

Notes: Charming, nostalgic live-action Disney film featuring four animated sequences; Disney's second live-action film (single story) with animated episodes, following 1946's *Song of the South*.

Credits: Director—Harold Schuster; Animation Director—Hamilton Luske; Animators—Eric Larson, Milt Kahl, John Lounsbery, Les Clark, Hal King, Don Lusk, Marvin Woodward; Screenplay by John Tucker Battle, based on the 1947 novel by Sterling North (who later wrote the children's classic *Rascal*); Adaption by Maurice Rapf and Ted Sears; Cartoon Story Treatment—Marc Davis, Ken Anderson, William Peed; Musical score by Paul Smith; Songs by Larry Morey, Eliot Daniel, Don Raye, Gene DePaul, Irving Taylor, Ticker Freeman, Bob Wells and Mel Torme; Songs—title song, "It's What You Do with What You Got," "Stick-to-it-tivity," "County Fair" and "Lavender Blue."

Cast: Burl Ives (Uncle Hiram), Beulah Bondi (Granny), Bobby Driscoll (Jeremiah), Luana Patten (Tildy), Harry Carey, Raymond Bond, Walter Soderling, Matt Willis, Spelman B. Collins; **Voices:** John Beal, Ken Carson, Bob Stanton, The Rhythmaires; **Notes:** Popular folk balladeer Ives (1909–95), who made his film debut in 1946, also proved to be a fine dramatic actor (*Cat on a Hot Tin Roof*). Driscoll and Patten also starred together in Disney's *Song of the South* and *Melody Time*.

Honors: Academy Award—Special Award to Bobby Driscoll (Outstanding Juvenile Actor of 1949), also nominated for Song ("Lavender Blue" music by Daniel, lyrics by Morey).

156 *Song of the South* (1946) **½

U.S.; Rated G; 94 mins.; Released November 2, 1946; Walt Disney.

Synopsis: An elderly former slave on an old Southern plantation delights the local children, including a would-be runaway, with his enchanting tales of Br'er Rabbit.

Notes: Delightful live-action Disney classic featuring three fully-animated sequences (Uncle Remus's tales) and some innovative blending of live action and animation; The film was pulled from circulation during the 1960s when Disney Studios feared its racial characterizations might prove offensive to audiences (it was finally rereleased in 1972); The film's live-action scenes were photographed by Gregg Toland (1904–48), whose credits include *Citizen Kane* (1941) and *The Best Years of Our Lives* (1946).

Highlights: the superb animated sequences with Br'er Rabbit, Br'er Fox and Br'er Bear, and the "Zip-A-Dee Doo Dah" number.

Credits: Directors—Harve Foster (live-action), Wilfred Jackson (animation); Directing Animators—Milt Kahl, Eric Larson, Oliver M. Johnston, Jr., Les Clark, Marc Davis, John Lounsbery; Screenplay by Dalton Reymond, Morton Grant and Maurice Rapf, from an original story by Reymond; Animated episodes based on the "Uncle Remus" stories (1880–83) by Atlanta newspaperman Joel Chandler Harris (1848–1908); Music by Daniele Amfitheatrof, Paul J. Smith and Charles Wolcott; Songs by Wolcott, Allie Wrubel, Ray Gilbert, Foster Carling, Robert McGimsey, Sam Coslow, Arthur Johnston, Eliot Daniel, Hy Heath, Johnny Lange, Sunny Skylar and Ticker Freeman; Songs—title song, "How Do You Do?," "Uncle Remus Said," "Sooner or Later," "Everybody's Got a Laughing Place," "Zip-A-Dee Doo Dah," "Let the Rain Pour Down" and "Who Wants to Live Like That?".

Cast: Ruth Warrick (Sally), James Baskett (Uncle Remus), Bobby Driscoll (Johnny), Luana Patten (Ginny), Lucille Watson (Grandmother), Hattie McDaniel (Aunt Tempy), Glenn Leedy (Toby), Eric Rolf (John), George Nokes, Gene Holland (The Faver Boys), Mary Field (Mrs. Faver), Anita Brown (Maid); **Voices:** James Baskett (Br'er Fox), Nicodemus Stewart (Br'er Bear), Johnny Lee (Br'er Rabbit); **Note:** Baskett (1904–48) played lawyer Gabby Gibson on radio's *Amos 'n' Andy Show*.

Honors: Academy Awards—Song ("Zip-A-Dee Doo Dah" music by Wrubel, lyrics by Gilbert) and a Special Award to James Basket for his heartwarming portrayal of Uncle Remus, also nominated for Musical Score.

157 *Space Jam* (1996) *

U.S.; Rated PG; 87 mins.; Released November 15, 1996 (Video: March 1997, Warner); Warner Bros.

Synopsis: Basketball star Michael Jordan is recruited by the Looney Tunes cartoon characters to play on their team in a high-stakes game against the otherworldly Monstars.

Notes: Mediocre mix of live action and animation aimed at young audiences. Jordan makes his film debut alongside Bugs Bunny, Daffy Duck, Porky Pig and the rest of the classic Looney Tunes stable; The film—which cost a whopping $90 million to produce—was a box-office hit, earning $200 million; Animation Producers—Ron Tippe, Jerry Rees, Steven Paul Leiva; Produced by Ivan Reitman (*Heavy Metal*).

Credits: Directors—Joe Pytka (live action), Bruce W. Smith, Tony Cervone (animation); **Note:** Pytka also directed the 1992 Nike Hare Jordan ads that inspired the film; Supervising Animators—Neil Boyle, Uli Meyer, Rob Stevenhagen, Chuck Gammage, Jeff Siergey, Jim Kammerud, Dave Spafford, Bruce Woodside; Screenplay by Leo Benvenuti and Steve Rudnick, Timothy Harris and Herschel Weingrad; Music by James Newton Howard; Songs include R. Kelly's "I Believe I Can Fly," Steve Miller's "Fly Like an Eagle" (performed by Seal) and the Quad City DJ's "Space Jam."

Cast: Michael Jordan (Himself), Wayne Knight (Stan Podolak), Theresa Randle (Juanita Jordan), Manner "Mooky" Washington (Jeffrey Jordan), Eric Gordon (Marcus Jordan), Penny Bae Bridges (Jasmine Jordan), Brandon Hammond (Young Michael Jordan), Thom Barry (James Jordan), Charles Barkley, Muggsy Bogues, Shawn Bradley, Patrick Ewing, Larry Johnson, Larry Bird, Bill Murray, Ahmad Rashad, Del Harris, Vlade Divac, Cedric Ceballos, Jim Rome, Paul Westphal, Danny Ainge; **Voices:** Billy West (Bugs Bunny/Elmer Fudd), Dee Bradley Baker (Daffy Duck/Tasmanian Devil/Bull), Danny DeVito (Swackhammer), Bob Bergen (Bert/Herbie/Marvin Martian/Porky Pig/Tweety), Bill Farmer (Sylvester/Yosemite Sam/Foghorn Leghorn), June Foray (Granny), Maurice LaMarche (Pepe Le Pew), Kath Soucie (Lola Bunny), Jocelyn Blue, Charity James, June Melby, Catherine Reitman, Colleen Wainwright (Nerdlucks), Dorian Harewood, Joey Camen, T. K. Carter, M. Darnell Suttles, Steve Kehela (Monstars), Frank W. Welker (Charles the Dog).

158 *Starchaser: The Legend of Orin* (1985) * ½
U.S.; Rated PG; 101 mins.; Released May 1985 (Video: May 1986, Paramount); Coleman—Rosenblatt.

Synopsis: A heroic boy named Orin sets out with his magic sword to free his people from a race of robots ruled by a tyrant named Zygon.

Notes: Better-than-average sci-fi tale, released theatrically in 3-D (the first animated feature to use that process) and wide-screen; Produced by Hahn.

Credits: Directors—Steven Hahn, John Sparey; Animation Directors—Mitch Rochon, Jang-Gil Kim; Screenplay by Jeffrey Scott (grandson of Three Stooges leader Moe Howard); Music by Andrew Belling, performed by The New World Philharmonic.

Voices: Joe Colligan (Orin), Carmen Argenziano (Dagg), Noelle North (Elan/Aviana), Anthony DeLongis (Zygon), Les Tremayne (Arthur), Tyke Caravelli (Silica), Ken Sansom (Magreb), John Moschitta, Jr. (Auctioneer/Z. Gork), Mickey Morton (Minemaster), Herb Vigran (Pung/Hopps), Dennis Alwood (Shooter), Mona Marshall (Kallie), Tina Romanus (Aunt Bella), Ryan MacDonald, John Garwood, Joseph Dellasorte, Philip Clarke, Mike Winslow, Thomas H. Watkins, Daryl T. Bartley.

Streetfight **see** *Coonskin*.

159 *The Swan Princess* (1994) **
U.S.; Rated G; 89 mins.; Released November 1994 (Video: August 1995, Turner); Rich Animation.

Synopsis: Prince Derek searches for his bride-to-be, Princess Odette, who has been transformed into a swan by Rothbart, an evil enchanter.

Notes: Charming, Disney-esque fairy tale with a modern PC sensibility; The first feature from Rich Animation Studios, which was founded by former Disney director Richard Rich (*The Black Cauldron*); Cost of film—$35 million; Made-for-video sequel—*The Swan Princess: Escape from Castle Mountain* (1997), from the same makers; Produced by Rich and Jared F. Brown.

Credits: Director—Richard Rich; Animation Director—Steven E. Gordon; Supervising Animators—Chrystal S. Klabunde, Steven E. Gordon, Bruce Woodside, Rick Farmiloe, Donnachada Daly, Michel Gagne; Screenplay by Brian Nissen; Story by Richard Rich and Nissen, based loosely on the story of *Swan Lake*; Music by Lex de Azevedo; Songs by de Azevedo and David Zippel; Songs—"Far Longer Than Forever," "Eternity," "This Is My Idea," "Practice, Practice, Practice," "No Fear," "No More Mr. Nice Guy" and "Princesses on Parade."

Voices: Michelle Nicastro (Princess Odette), Liz Callaway (Odette's singing voice), Howard McGillin (Prince Derek), Jack Palance (Rothbart), John Cleese (Jean-Bob), Steven Wright (Speed), Steve Vinovich (Puffin), Mark Harelik (Lord Rogers), James Arrington (Chamberlain), Davis Gaines (Chamberlain's singing voice), Joel McKinnon Miller (Bromley), Dakin Matthews (King William), Sandy Duncan (Queen Uberta), Adam Wylie (Young Derek), Adrian Zahiri (Young Odette), Tom Alan Robbins (Musician), Bess Hopper (Hag), Brian Nissen (Narrator); **Note:** Rothbart does a few one-arm push-ups in one scene as Palance did when he accepted his Oscar at the 1992 Academy Awards.

160 *The Sword in the Stone* (1963) ******
    U.S.; Rated G; 80 mins.; Premiered August 9, 1963 in New York; Released December 25, 1963 (Video: March 1986, Walt Disney); Walt Disney.

Synopsis: The story of how a young squire named Wart, under the guidance of Merlin the Magician, became King of England.

Notes: Disney's version of the Arthurian legend, while not one of the studio's classics, is an enjoyable family film; Disney first bought the film rights to the T. H. White novel back in 1939.

Highlight: the wizards' duel between Merlin and the tricky Mad Madame Mim.

Credits: Director—Wolfgang Reitherman; Directing Animators—Frank Thomas, Ollie Johnston, Milt Kahl, John Lounsbery; Screenplay by Bill Peet, based on the 1938 novel *The Once and Future King* by T. H. White; Music score by George Bruns; Songs by Richard M. and Robert B. Sherman; Songs—"That's What Makes the World Go 'Round," "A Most Befuddling Thing," "Higitus Figitus," "Mad Madame Mim," "Blue Oak Tree" and "The Legend of the Sword in the Stone" (sung by Fred Darian).

Voices: Rickie Sorensen (Wart), Sebastian Cabot (Sir Ector), Karl Swenson (Merlin), Junius Matthews (Archimedes), Martha Wentworth (Madame Mim/Granny Squirrel), Norman Alden (Kay), Barbara Jo Allen (Skullery Maid), Alan Napier (Sir Pelinor), Ginny Tyler (Little Girl Squirrel), The Mellomen, Richard Reitherman, Robert Reitherman; **Note:** Cabot (1918–77) played Mr. French on TV's *Family Affair* (1966–71) and narrated Disney's "Winnie the Pooh" series.

Honors: Academy Award nomination—Music Score.

The Thief and the Cobbler **see** *Arabian Knight.*

161 *The Three Caballeros* (1945) ****$\frac{1}{2}$**
    U.S.; Rated G; 71 mins.; Released February 3, 1945; Walt Disney.

Synopsis: Donald Duck and his friends Joe Carioca (a Brazillian parrot) and Panchito (a Mexican rooster) celebrate Latin America with a collection of shorts and musical numbers. Segments include "Baia," "Le Pinata" and the cartoon stories—*Pablo, the Cold-Blooded Penguin* and *The Flying Gauchito* (see SHORTS).

Notes: Disney's second Good Neighbor salute to Latin America (following 1943's *Saludos Amigos*) is a lively mix of dazzling animation and great Latin music; Disney Studios' first significant attempt at combining live action and animation; The silly Aracuan Bird also appears (he later shows up in the *Blame It on the Samba* sequence from 1948's *Melody Time*); Live-action scenes were filmed in Patzcuaro, Veracruz and Acapulco.

Highlight: the "Os Quindins de Yaya" number, and the performance of the title song by Donald and friends.

Credits: Supervisor: Norman Ferguson; Sequence Directors—Clyde Geronimi, Jack Kinney, Bill Roberts; Animation Directors—Ward Kimball, Eric Larson, Fred Moore, John Lounsbery, Les Clark, Milton Kahl; Live-action Director—Harold Young; Story by Homer Brightman, Ernest Terrazas, Ted Sears, Bill Peed, Ralph Wright, Elmer Plummer, Roy Williams, William Cottrell, Del Connell and James Bodrero; Music by Charles Wolcott, Paul J. Smith and Edward Plumb; Musical numbers by Manuel Esperon, Ary Barroso, Agustin Lara and Wolcott; Lyrics by Ray Gilbert; Songs—title song, "Baia," "Os Quindins de Yaya" (performed by Aurora Miranda), "You Belong to My Heart" (performed by Dora Luz), "Pandeiro and Flute," Pregoes Carioca," "Lilonga" and "Mexico" (performed by Carlos Ramirez).

Cast/Voices: Aurora Miranda, Carmen Molina, Dora Luz, Nestor Amaral, Almirante, Trio Calaveras, Ascencio Del Rio Trio, Padua Hills Players; Clarence Nash (Donald Duck), Joaquin Garay (Panchito), Jose Oliveira (Joe Carioca), Sterling Holloway, Frank Graham, Fred Shields (Narrators).

Honors: Academy Award nominations—Musical Score and Sound (C. O. Slyfield).

Thumbelina **see** *Hans Christian Andersen's Thumbelina.*

162 *Tim Burton's The Nightmare Before Christmas* (1993) **

U.S.; Rated PG; 76 mins.; Released October 15, 1993 (Video: September 1994, Touchstone); Burton/Dinovi.

Synopsis: A bored Jack Skellington—Pumpkin King and ruler of Halloweentown—discovers Christmas and plots to make it his own.

Notes: Macabre musical fantasy from the mind of Tim Burton, featuring dazzling stop-motion animation and art design, but hurt by shaky storytelling and mostly forgettable songs; A staff of 120 (including 13 animators) worked on the $22 million production for more than two years, finishing about one minute of stop-motion footage a week; Burton (director of *Beetlejuice* and *Batman*) originally proposed the story to Disney in 1981 as a TV special (at the time, Burton was an apprentice animator at the studio); Burton's last stop-motion effort was the 1982 short *Vincent*; Director Henry Selick's previous work included channel-ID spots for MTV Music Television; Burton and Selick teamed again for 1996's *James and the Giant Peach*; Produced by Burton and Denise Dinovi.

Credits: Director—Henry Selick; Animation Supervisor—Eric Leighton; Visual Effects Supervisor—Pete Kozachik; Screenplay by Caroline Thompson (*Edward Scissorhands*), adapted by Michael McDowell, based on a story and characters created by Tim Burton; Music, lyrics and score by Danny Elfman (*Batman, The Simpsons*); Songs include "This Is Halloween," "Jack's Lament," "What's This?," "Oogie Boogie's Song" and "Kidnap the Sandy Claus."

Voices: Chris Sarandon (Jack Skellington), Danny Elfman (Jack's singing voice/Barrel), Catherine O'Hara (Sally/Shock), William Hickey (Evil Scientist), Ken Page (Oogie Boogie), Glenn Shadix (Mayor), Ed Ivory (Santa), Paul Reubens (Lock); **Note:** Reubens, better known as Pee-Wee Herman, starred in Tim Burton's feature directing debut *Pee-Wee's Big Adventure* (1985).

Honors: Academy Award nomination—Visual Effects (Pete Kozachik, Eric Leighton, Ariel Velasco Shaw, Gordon Baker).

163 *Tom and Jerry: The Movie* (1993) *

U.S.; Rated G; 84 mins.; Released July 30, 1993 (Video: Family Home Entertainment); A Film Roman Production/Turner Entertainment.

Synopsis: When a wrecking ball destroys their home, Tom and Jerry are forced onto the streets where they befriend a young runaway in trouble.

Notes: The violent, nonspeaking cat-and-mouse team from the popular MGM shorts of the '40s become talking buddies in this bland musical adventure; Tom and Jerry's previous feature appearances were in the live-action musicals *Anchors Aweigh* (1945) and *Dangerous When Wet* (1953); Joseph Barbera, co-creator/director (with William Hanna) of the "Tom and Jerry" cartoon series (1940–58), acted as creative consultant on the film; Produced by Phil Roman.

Credits: Director—Phil Roman; **Note:** Roman has won five Emmy Awards (1984–97) for his work on "Garfield" specials and on the series *The Simpsons*; Screenplay by Dennis Marks; Musical score by Henry Mancini; Songs by Mancini and Leslie Bricusse.

Voices: Richard Kind (Tom), Dana Hill (Jerry), Anndi McAfee (Robyn Starling), Charlotte Rae (Aunt Figg), Tony Jay (Mr. Lickboot), Henry Gibson (Dr. Applecheek), Rip Taylor (Captain Kiddie), Howard Morris (Squawk), Edmund Gilbert (Puggsy/Daddy Starling), David Lander (Frankie da Flea), Michael Bell (Ferdinand/Straycatcher), Sydney Lassick (Straycatcher), Raymond McLeod (Alleycat/Bulldog), Mitchell D. Moore, Scott Wojahn (Alleycats), Tino Insana (Patrolman), Don Messick (Droopy), B. J. Ward, Greg Burson.

164 *Toy Story* (1995) **$\frac{1}{2}$

U.S.; Rated G; 81 mins.; Released November 22, 1995 (Video: October 1996, Walt Disney); Walt Disney/Pixar.

Synopsis: A little boy's toy cowboy becomes jealous of his owner's new favorite, a Space Ranger action figure, but the two must work together when they fall into the hands of a mean neighbor kid.

Notes: Imaginative, strikingly-animated tale, the first feature film to be produced entirely with computer animation; One of the highest-grossing films of 1995; The film—started in 1991—was produced at a cost $30 million by Pixar Animation Studios (a computer graphics company) in association with Disney; The film features many classic children's toys, including Mr. Potato Head, Etch-A-Sketch, Barrel of Monkeys, Green Army Men and Slinky Dog; Produced by Ralph Guggenheim and Bonnie Arnold.

Credits: Director—John Lasseter; **Note:** Lasseter, a former Disney animator, joined Pixar in 1986 and won an Oscar for the computer-animated short *Tin Toy* (1988); Supervising Animator—Peter Docter; Screenplay by Joss Whedon, Andrew Stanton, Joel Cohen and Alec Sokolow, based on the story by John Lasseter, Stanton, Peter Docter and Joe Ranft; Musical score by Randy Newman; Songs written and performed by Newman; Songs—"You've Got a Friend in Me," "Strange Things" and "I Will Go Sailing No More."

Voices: Tom Hanks (Woody), Tim Allen (Buzz Lightyear), Don Rickles (Mr. Potato Head), Jim Varney (Slinky Dog), Wallace Shawn (Rex), John Ratzenberger (Hamm), Annie Potts (Bo Peep), John Morris (Andy), Erik Von Detten (Sid), Laurie Metcalf (Mrs. Davis), R. Lee Ermey (Sergeant), Sarah Freeman (Hannah), Penn Jillette (TV Announcer); **Notes:** Metcalf won three Emmys for playing Jackie on TV's *Roseanne* (1988–97). Ermey played the drill sergeant in *Full Metal Jacket* (1987).

Honors: Academy Award—Special Achievement Award (John Lasseter), also nominated for Screenplay, Musical Score and Song ("You've Got a Friend in Me").

165 *The Transformers: The Movie* (1986).

U.S.; Rated PG; 86 mins.; Released by August 8, 1986; Sunbow/Marvel Entertainment/Toei Animation Company.

Synopsis: The good Autobots fight to win back their home planet from the Decepticons, who are aided by the evil forces of Unicron.

Notes: Loud, violent sci-fi fare based on the popular Hasbro toys and TV series (syndicated, 1984); Produced by Joe Bacal and Tom Griffin.

Credits: Director—Nelson Shin; Animated by the Toei Animation Company; Screenplay by Ron Friedman and Flint Dille; Music score by Vince DiCola.

Voices: Orson Welles (Unicron), Eric Idle (Wreck Gar), Robert Stack (Ultra Magnus), Leonard Nimoy (Galvatron), Judd Nelson (Hot Rod/Rodimus Prime), Lionel Stander (Kup), Scatman Crothers (Jazz), Casey Kasem (Cliffjumper), Don Messick (Gears), Susan Blu (Arcee), Peter Cullen (Prime/Ironside), John Moschitta (Blurr), Norm Alden (Kranix), Jack Angel (Astrotrain), Michael Bell (Prowl/Scrapper/Swoop/Junkion), Gregg Berger (Grimlock), Arthur Burghardt (Devastator), Corey Burton (Spike/Brown/Shockwave), Roger C. Carmel (Cyclonus/Quintesson Leader), Rege Cordic (Quintesson Judge), Bud Davis (Dirge), Walker Edmiston (Inferno), Paul Eiding (Perceptor), Ed Gilbert (Blitzwing), Dan Gilvean (Bumblebee), Buster Jones (Blaster), Stan Jones (Scourge), Chris Latta (Starscream), David Mendenhall (Daniel), Hal Rayle (Shrapnel), Clive Revill (Kickback), Neil Ross (Bonecrusher/Hook/Springer/Slag), Frank Welker (Soundwave/Megatron/Rumble/Frenzy/Wheelie/Junkion); **Notes:** One of Welles's last film roles (he died in October 1985). Idle is a member of the British comedy troupe Monty Python.

166 *Treasure Island* (1972) *
U.S.; Rated G; 75 mins.; Filmation.

Synopsis: Young Jim Hawkins and a mouse named Hiccup travel the high seas in search of buried treasure.

Notes: Animated telling of the classic adventure story; Later shown as a TV special (in April 1980); Produced by Lou Scheimer and Norman Prescott.

Highlight: Based on the story by Robert Louis Stevenson.

Credits: Director—Hal Sutherland; Music by George Blais; Songs—"Fifteen Men on a Dead Man's Chest," "Find the Boy/Find the Mouse and We Find the Map" and "Proper Punishment."

Voices: Richard Dawson (Long John Silver), Larry Storch (Captain Flint), Davy Jones (Jim Hawkins), Larry D. Mann (Squire Trelawney), Jane Webb (Mother), Dal McKennon (Parrot).

167 *A Troll in Central Park* (1994) *½
U.S.; Rated G; 76 mins.; Don Bluth.

Synopsis: A good troll with a magical green thumb is banished to New York City and makes his home—and some new friends—in Central Park.

Notes: Okay children's fantasy from Don Bluth; Produced by Bluth, Goldman and John Pomeroy.

Credits: Directors—Don Bluth, Gary Goldman; Supervising Directing Animator—John Pomeroy; Directing Animators—Ralf Palmer, John Hill, Len Simon, Piet Derycker, Jean Morel, T. Daniel Hofstedt, Cathy Jones, Jeff Varab; Screenplay by Stu Krieger, from a story by Don Bluth, Gary Goldman, John Pomeroy, T. J. Kuenster and Krieger; Music by Robert Folk; Songs by Folk and Norman Gimbel, Barry Mann and Cynthia Weil; Songs—"Queen of Mean," "Welcome to My World," "Absolutely Green" and "Friends Like Us."

Voices: Dom DeLuise (Stanley), Cloris Leachman (Queen Gnorga), Jonathan Pryce (Alan), Hayley Mills (Hilary), Charles Nelson Reilly (Llort), Phillip Glasser (Gus), Tawny Sunshine Glover (Rosie), Neil Ross (Generic Pansy), Pat Musik (Pansy), Will Ryan (Boss).

168 *The Tune* (1992) **

U.S.; Not Rated; 70 mins.; Released September 1992; Bill Plympton.

Synopsis: A songwriter suffers writer's block when he is given 47 minutes to compose a hit song, but finds inspiration after he takes a wrong turn into the strange town of Flooby Nooby.

Notes: Funny, offbeat musical comedy, the first feature film from animator Bill Plympton (b. 1946), whose delightfully twisted work has been a favorite of animation festivals and featured on MTV and in the limited-release compilation film *Mondo Plympton* (1997); The film—notable as the first animated feature drawn entirely by one person—required approximately 30,000 pencil-and-watercolor drawings; *The Tune* includes two previously-released shorts, *The Wiseman* and *Push Comes to Shove*; Plympton's second animated feature, *I Married a Strange Person*, was released in 1997; Produced by Plympton.

Highlight: the gruesomely-funny "Lovesick Hotel."

Credits: Director—Bill Plympton; Animated by Bill Plympton; Screenplay by Bill Plympton, P. C. Vey and Maureen McElheron; Songs by Maureen McElheron; Songs—"My Love for You," "Flooby Nooby," "Isn't It Good Again," "Dig My Do," "Home," "The Wiseone" (instrumental), "Lovesick Hotel," "No Nose Blues," "Dance All Day," "Love Is My Bottom Line" and "Be My Only Love."

Voices: Daniel Neiden (Del), Maureen McElheron (Didi), Marty Nelson (Mayor/Mr. Mega/Mrs. Mega), Chris Hoffman (The Wiseone/Surfer/Tango Dancer/Note), Emily Bindiger (Dot), Jimmy Ceribella (Cabbie), Ned Reynolds (Houndog), Jeff Knight (Bellhop), Jennifer Senka (Surfer/Note).

169 *Twice Upon a Time* (1983) *$\frac{1}{2}$

U.S.; Rated PG; 75 mins.; Korty Films/Lucasfilm Ltd.

Synopsis: Two unlikely heroes try to prevent the evil leaders of the Murkworks from covering the world with nightmares.

Notes: Bizarre, funny fantasy film using a new cut-out style of animation called Lumage; The film—executive produced by George Lucas—received only a limited theatrical release; Produced by Bill Couturie.

Credits: Directors—John Korty, Charles Swenson; **Note:** Korty won an Emmy for directing the acclaimed TV film *The Autobiography of Miss Jane Pittman* (1974); Animation Directors—Brian Narelle, Carl Willat, Henry Selick; Screenplay by John Korty, Charles Swenson, Suella Kennedy and Bill Couturie, from a story by Korty, Couturie and Kennedy; Music by Dawn Atkinson and Ken Melville; Songs—"Life Is but a Dream," "Out on My Own," "Heartbreak Town," "Champagne Time" and the title song.

Voices: Lorenzo Music (Ralph), Judith Kahan Kampmann (Fairy Godmother), Marshall Efron (Synonamess Botch), James Cranna (Rod Rescueman/Scuzzbopper), Julie Payne (Flora Fauna), Hamilton Camp (Greensleeves), Paul Frees (Narrator/Chief of State/Judges and Bailliff); **Note:** Music was the voice of Carleton the doorman on TV's *Rhoda* (which he also coproduced) and later provided Garfield the cat's distinctive cartoon voice.

170 *Victory Through Air Power* (1943) **

U.S.; Not Rated; 65 mins.; Released July 17, 1943; Walt Disney.

Synopsis: Documentary study of aviation and the strategic bombing theories of Major Alexander de Seversky.

Notes: Fascinating World War II propaganda feature from Walt Disney Studios; The film, which is part live action, cost $788,000 to produce; Later reedited and shown as *History of Aviation*.

Credits: Supervising Director—David Hand; Sequence Directors—Clyde Geronimi, Jack Kinney, James Algar; Live-action Director—H. C. Potter (director of the zany 1941 film *Hellzapoppin*); Screenplay by T. Hee, Erdman Penner, William Cottrell, Jim Bodrero, George Stallings and Jose Rodriquez, based on the 1942 book by Major Alexander P. de Seversky; Story Direction—Perce Pearce; Music score by Edward H. Plumb, Paul J. Smith and Oliver G. Wallace.

Cast: Alexander P. de Seversky; Voice—Art Baker (Narrator).

Honors: Academy Award nomination—Score.

171 *The Wacky World of Mother Goose* (1967) $*\frac{1}{2}$
U.S.; Not Rated; 82 mins.; Rankin-Bass.

Synopsis: Mother Goose and her fairy tale friends try to keep the wicked Count Warptwist from taking over Fairyland.

Notes: Fun adventure for kids featuring some of their favorite fairy tale characters; Produced by Arthur Rankin, Jr.

Credits: Director—Jules Bass; Story by Romeo Muller, based on characters from Charles Perrault's *Mother Goose Tales*; Music and lyrics by Jules Bass and George Wilkins.

Voices: Margaret Rutherford (Mother Goose).

172 *Wallace and Gromit: The Best of Aardman Animation* (1996) $**\frac{1}{2}$
British; Not Rated; 75 mins.; Released May 1996; Aardman Animations.

Synopsis: A collection of clay-animated commercials (for British Heat Electric), music videos (Nina Simone's "My Baby Just Cares for Me") and shorts (*A Close Shave, Creature Comforts, Wat's Pig, Pib and Pog*) (see SHORTS).

Notes: Entertaining compilation from Britain's Aardman Animation studio, highlighted by Park's Oscar-winning "Wallace and Gromit" adventure *A Close Shave* (1995).

Credits: Directors—Nick Park, Peter Lord, David Sproxton, Richard Goleszowski, Peter Peake; Voices—Peter Sallis, Anne Reid.

173 *The Water Babies* (1978) *
British-Polish; Rated G; 92 mins.; Ariadne/Studio Miniatur Filmowych.

Synopsis: In London in 1850, a young chimney sweep jumps into a pond and meets an assortment of underwater characters.

Notes: Fanciful, but uninspired, combination of live action and animation (underwater scenes); Aka *Slip Slide Adventures*; Cost of film—$2 million; The last directorial effort from British actor-director Lionel Jeffries (*The Railway Children*); Produced by Peter Shaw.

Credits: Director—Lionel Jeffries; Animation Directors—Tony Cuthbert, Jack Stokes, Miroslaw Kijowicz; Screenplay by Michael Robson, based on the 1863 novel by Charles Kingsley (1819–75); Music by Phil Coulter; Songs by Coulter and Bill Martin.

Cast: James Mason (Grimes), Billie Whitelaw (Mrs. Doasyouwouldbedoneby), Bernard Cribbins (Masterman), Joan Greenwood (Lady Harriet), David Tomlinson (Sir John), Tommy Pender (Tom), Samantha Gates (Ellie), Paul Luty (Sladd); **Voices:** Jon Pertwee, Olive Gregg, Lance Percival, David Jason, Cass Allan, Liz Proud, Una Stubbs.

174 *Watership Down* (1978) $**\frac{1}{2}$
British; Rated PG; 92 mins.; Released October 1978; A Nepenthe Production.

Synopsis: Serious fable about a family of rabbits who face many perils in their search for a new and safer place to live.

Notes: Beautifully-animated allegory based on the Richard Adams bestseller; The film—Martin Rosen's first animated feature—cost $4.8 million and took three years to

produce; Rosen adapted another Adams story, *The Plague Dogs*, in 1982; Rosen replaced original director John Hubley (of UPA and Hubley Studio fame); Produced by Rosen.
Highlight: Zero Mostel's funny vocal performance as the sea gull Kahaar.
Credits: Director—Martin Rosen; Animation Supervisor—Philip Duncan; Director of Animation—Tony Guy; Supervising Animators—Arthur Humberstone, George Jackson; Screenplay by Martin Rosen, based on the 1972 novel by Richard Adams; Music score by Angela Morley and Malcolm Williamson; Song—"Bright Eyes" by Mike Batt, and sung by Art Garfunkel.
Voices: Michael Hordern (Narrator), John Hurt (Hazel), Ralph Richardson (Chief Rabbit), Zero Mostel (Kehaar), Richard Briers (Fiver), Denholm Elliott (Cowslip), Michael Graham-Cox (Bigwig), Hannah Gordon (Hyzenthlay), Harry Andrews (Gen. Woundwort), Joss Ackland (Black Rabbit), John Bennett (Capt. Holly), Simon Cadell (Blackberry), Roy Kinnear (Pipkin), Richard O'Callaghan (Dandelion), Terence Rigby (Silver), Mary Maddox (Clover), Lyn Farleigh (Cat), Nigel Hawthorne (Campion), Clifton Jones (Blackavar), Michelle Price (Lucy), Derek Griffiths (Vervain); **Note:** British actor Hurt played Caligula in the TV miniseries *I, Claudius* (1976) and John Merrick in *The Elephant Man* (1980). Mostel's last film role. The three-time Tony-winning star of Broadway (*Fiddler on the Roof*) and film (*The Producers*) died in September 1977.

175 *We're Back! A Dinosaur's Story* (1993) $*\frac{1}{2}$
U.S.; Rated G; 78 mins.; Released November, 1993 (Video: April 1994, MCA/Universal); Amblimation.

Synopsis: With the aid of a kindly scientist, four dinosaurs are given intelligence and allowed to travel to modern-day New York City where they befriend two lonely children.
Notes: Kid-friendly dinosaur tale presented by Steven Spielberg, whose more "biting" dino flick, *Jurassic Park*, was released earlier that year; A box-office disappointment (earning only $8.7 million); Produced by Stephen Hickner.
Credits: Directors—Dick Zondag, Ralph Zondag, Phil Nibbelink, Simon Wells; Supervising Animators—Jeffrey J. Varab, Bibo Bergeron, Kristof Serrand, Rob Stevenhagen, Thierry Schiel, Sahin Ersoz, Borge Ring; **Note:** Ring directed the Oscar-winning short *Anna & Bella* (1984); Screenplay by John Patrick Shanley (*Moonstruck*), based on the book by Hudson Talbott; Music by James Horner; Song—"Roll Back the Rock (To the Dawn of Time)" by Horner and Thomas Dolby.
Voices: John Goodman (Rex), Blaze Berdahl (Buster), Rhea Perlman (Mother Bird), Jay Leno (Vorb), Rene LeVant (Woog), Felicity Kendall (Elsa), Charles Fleischer (Dweeb), Walter Cronkite (Capt. Neweyes), Joey Shea (Louie), Julia Child (Dr. Bleeb), Kenneth Mars (Prof. Screweyes), Yeardley Smith (Cecilia), Martin Short (Stubbs the Clown); **Notes:** Smith provides the voice of Lisa Simpson on TV's *The Simpsons*. Fleischer is the voice of Roger Rabbit.

176 *When the Wind Blows* (1988) **
British; Rated PG; 80 mins.; Released in U.S. March 1988; Meltdown (British Screen/Film Four International/TVC London/Penguin Books).

Synopsis: An old English couple living in the coutry faithfully follow the government's instructions in preparing for an impending nuclear holocaust.
Notes: Dark, thoughtful British feature in which old, simpler memories of war are confronted by the horrifying modern reality; Originally shown in England in 1986; Produced by John Coates.
Credits: Director—Jimmy T. Murakami; Screenplay by Raymond Briggs (*The Snowman*), from his bestselling 1982 book (and 1983 play); Musical score by Roger Waters; Songs by Waters, David Bowie, Erdal Kizilcay, Genesis, Paul Hardcastle, Hugh Cornwell, Glenn Tilbrook and Chris Difford; Songs—title song (performed by Bowie), "Towers of

Faith," "Folded Flags," "The Brazilian" (performed by Genesis), "The Shuffle," "Facts and Figures" and "What Have They Done" (performed by Squeeze).

Voices: Peggy Ashcroft (Hilda Bloggs), John Mills (Jim Bloggs), Robin Houston (Announcer).

Honors: Award—Getz World Peace Prize (Chicago Film Festival, 1987).

177 *Who Framed Roger Rabbit* (1988) ***

U.S.; Rated PG; 103 mins.; Released June 24, 1988; Amblin Entertainment/Touchstone Pictures.

Synopsis: In Hollywood in 1947, cartoon star Roger Rabbit is framed for the murder of a movie tycoon and—with the help of a down-and-out private eye—tries to find the real murderer.

Notes: An innovative, highly-entertaining feature which convincingly places animated characters in a live-action world; Produced by the companies of Steven Spielberg and Walt Disney, the film took eight years and $50.6 million to complete and required the work of 700 creative artists and craftsmen; Cameos are made by such veteran cartoon stars (many of whom have never appeared together on film before) as Bugs Bunny, Mickey Mouse, Betty Boop, Droopy, Tweetie, Dumbo, Yosemite Sam, and Daffy and Donald Duck (playing dueling pianos); The biggest box office hit of 1988, earning more than $300 million worldwide; The film spawned a series of "Roger Rabbit" shorts (see *Tummy Trouble* [1989]); Produced by Robert Watts and Frank Marshall.

Highlights: the opening "Roger Rabbit" cartoon, the Ink and Paint Club sequence (with Daffy, Donald and Jessica Rabbit performing), the car chase with Benny the Cab, and the final showdown with Judge Doom.

Credits: Director—Robert Zemeckis; Director of Animation—Richard Williams; Supervising Animators—Andreas Deja, Russell Hall, Phil Nibbelink, Simon Wells; **Notes:** Zemeckis is the director of such film hits as *Back to the Future* (1985) and *Forrest Gump* (1994); Williams won an Oscar for the short *A Christmas Carol* (1972) and an Emmy for the TV special *Ziggy's Gift* (1982); Screenplay by Jeffrey Price and Peter C. Seaman, based on the book *Who Censored Roger Rabbit?* by Gary K. Wolf; Music by Alan Silvestri; Includes the song "Why Don't You Do Right?" sung by Jessica Rabbit.

Cast: Bob Hoskins (Eddie Valiant), Christopher Lloyd (Judge Doom), Joanna Cassidy (Dolores), Stubby Kaye (Marvin Acme), Alan Tilvern (R. K. Maroon), Richard Le Parmentier (Lt. Santino), Joel Silver (Raoul, the director); **Voices:** Charles Fleischer (Roger Rabbit/Benny the Cab/Greasy/Psycho), Lou Hirsch (Baby Herman), Kathleen Turner (Jessica Rabbit, uncredited), Amy Irving (Jessica's singing voice), Mel Blanc (Bugs Bunny/Daffy Duck/Porky Pig/Tweetie/Sylvester), Mae Questel (Betty Boop), Tony Anselmo (Donald Duck), David Lander (Weasel), June Foray (Lena Hyena/Wheezy), Wayne Allwine (Mickey Mouse), Joe Alaskey (Yosemite Sam), Mary T. Radford (Hippo), Tony Pope (Goofy/Wolf), Pat Buttram (Bullet #1), Jim Cummings (Bullet #2), Jim Gallant (Bullet #3), Richard Williams (Droopy), Russi Taylor (Birds/Minnie Mouse), Cherry Davis (Woody Woodpecker), Fred Newman (Stupid), Les Perkins (Toad), Peter Westy (Pinocchio); **Note:** Voice veterans Blanc and Questel provided their classic characters' original voices.

Honors: Academy Awards—Film Editing (Arthur Schmidt), Sound Effects Editing (Charles L. Campbell, Louis L. Edemann), Visual Effects (Ken Ralston, Richard Williams, Edward Jones, George Gibbs) and a Special Achievement Award to Richard Williams; also nominated for Art Direction, Cinematography and Sound.

178 *Will Vinton's Festival of Claymation* (1987) **

U.S.; Not Rated; 90 mins.; Released Febuary, 1987; Will Vinton Productions.

Synopsis: A collection of Claymation works from Will Vinton Productions, includ-

ing commercials, film clips (*The Adventures of Mark Twain*), music videos (John Fogerty's "Vanz Kant Danz") and shorts (*The Creation, Dinosaur, The Great Cognito*) (see SHORTS).
Notes: Good Vinton compilation, hosted by a pair of dinosaur film critics.
Credit: Director—Will Vinton.

179 *Wizards* (1977) $\frac{1}{2}$

U.S.; Rated PG; 81 mins.; Ralph Bakshi.

Synopsis: Post-apocalyptic tale about two battling wizards, Avatar and Blackwolf, and the conflict between technology and nature.

Notes: Ralph Bakshi's fourth film is a sloppy mixture of film techniques: animation, live action, still drawings (by artist Michael Ploog) and rotoscoping (tracing from live-action footage). A poor precursor to Bakshi's more elaborate fantasy *Lord of the Rings* (1978); Produced by Bakshi.

Credits: Director—Ralph Bakshi; Sequence Animator—Irwin Spence; Screenplay by Ralph Bakshi; Music by Andrew Belling.

Voices: Bob Holt (Avatar), Steve Gravers (Blackwolf), Jesse Welles (Elinore), Richard Romanus (Weehawk), James Connell (President), David Proval (Peace), Mark Hamill (Sean), Barbara Sloane (Fairy), Angelo Grisanti (Frog), Hyman Wien (Priest), Christopher Tayback (Peewhittle), Peter Hobbs (General), Tina Bowman (Prostitute).

180 *Yellow Submarine* (1968) ** $\frac{1}{2}$

British; Rated G; 85 mins.; Premiered July 17, 1968, at the Pavilion in London, and in Los Angeles on November 12, 1968 (Video: September 1987, MGM/UA); Apple Film/King Features.

Synopsis: The Beatles try to save the happy kingdom of Pepperland from the Blue Meanies—haters of color and music.

Notes: Delightful psychedelic fantasy nicely blends surreal, colorful animation with great Beatles music; The first British animated feature since 1954's *Animal Farm*, and the third Beatles feature, following their live-action efforts *A Hard Day's Night* (1964) and *Help!* (1965). The "Fab Four" had little involvement in the film's production, but do make a brief appearance at the end singing "All Together Now"; Animated by London's TVC studio (co-founded by George Dunning in 1957); Dianne Jackson (director of the acclaimed 1982 short *The Snowman*) was an animator on the film; Produced by King Features (Al Brodax) and Apple Films (formed by the Beatles in February 1968). Brodax also produced the Saturday morning cartoon series *The Beatles* (1965–69).

Highlight: the "Lucy in the Sky with Diamonds" sequence.

Credits: Director—George Dunning; **Note:** Dunning (1920–79) was a veteran of the National Film Board of Canada and (briefly) UPA studios; Animation Directors—Bob Balser, Jack Stokes; Animation designed by German artist Heinz Edelmann, based on psychedelic designs by Peter Max; Screenplay by Lee Minoff, Al Brodax, Erich Segal (author of *Love Story*) and Jack Mendelsohn, from an original story by Minoff; Inspired by the 1966 song by John Lennon and Paul McCartney; Musical direction/original film music by George Martin; Songs by John Lennon, Paul McCartney and George Harrison; Songs—"Yellow Submarine," "All You Need Is Love," "Hey Bulldog" (cut from U.S. version), "When I'm Sixty-Four," "Nowhere Man," "Lucy in the Sky with Diamonds," "Sgt. Pepper's Lonely Hearts Club Band," "A Day in the Life," "Eleanor Rigby" and "All Together Now"; **Note:** The film's soundtrack, released in January 1969, also included the songs "It's All Too Much" and "Only a Northern Song."

Cast/Voices: John Lennon, Paul McCartney, George Harrison, Ringo Starr; John Clive (John), Geoffrey Hughes (Paul), Peter Batten (George), Paul Angelus (Ringo/Chief Blue Meanie), Dick Emery (Lord Mayor/Nowhere Man/Max), Lance Percival (Old Man); **Note:** Percival was the voice of Paul and Ringo for the *Beatles* cartoon TV series.

PART 2: Features with Animated Sequences

The following is a list of live-action features which include shorter sequences of animation. The animator or studio responsible is given in parentheses. This list does not include the stop-motion "effects" animation of Willis O'Brien (*King Kong*) and Ray Harryhausen (*The 7th Voyage of Sinbad, Jason and the Argonauts*).

181 *Alice in Wonderland* (1933)
All-star Paramount version of the Lewis Carroll tale. Walrus-Carpenter scene (Harman-Ising).

182 *Anchors Aweigh* (1945)
MGM musical starring Gene Kelly and Frank Sinatra. Kelly dances with Jerry the Mouse (Hanna-Barbera). The most famous non–Disney mix of animation and live action.

183 *And Now for Something Completely Different* (1971)
Debut feature from the British comedy troupe Monty Python. Cut-out animation sequences (Terry Gilliam).

184 *Batman Forever* (1995)
Main titles (Chris Hummel).

185 *Better Off Dead* (1985)
Comedy starring John Cusack. Title sequence (Bill Kopp). Clay-animated cheeseburger sequence (Jimmy Picker).

186 *The Big Broadcast of 1938* (1938)
"Rippling Rhythm" sequence (Warner Bros. studio).

187 *Cannonball Run II* (1984)
Animation sequence (Ralph Bakshi).

188 *The Charge of the Light Brigade* (1968)
Titles and other sequences (Richard Williams).

189 *Creepshow* (1982)
Stephen King horror anthology. Animation (Rick Catizone).

190 *Creepshow 2* (1987)
  Animation (Rick Catizone).

191 *Curse of the Pink Panther* (1983)
  Eighth entry in the series. Main titles (Arthur Leonardi, Marvel Productions Ltd.).

192 *Dangerous When Wet* (1953)
  Esther Williams swims with Tom & Jerry (Hanna-Barbera).

193 *Destination Moon* (1950)
  Sci-fi feature, produced by George Pal. Guest appearance by Woody Woodpecker in a training film (Walter Lantz).

194 *Flicks* (1987)
  Cartoon segment (Kirk Henderson).

195 *The Four-Poster* (1952)
  Film of Jan de Hartog play, starring Rex Harrison and Lilli Palmer. Titles and seven linking sequences (UPA—John Hubley).

196 *A Funny Thing Happened on the Way to the Forum* (1966)
  Film version of the Broadway show, starring Zero Mostel. Title sequence (Richard Williams).

197 *Funnyman* (1971)
  Animation sequences (John Korty).

198 *The Girl Next Door* (1953)
  Musical starring Dan Dailey and June Haver. Linking sequences (UPA).

199 *Grease* (1978)
  1950s musical starring John Travolta and Olivia Newton-John. Opening title sequence (John Wilson).

200 *Gremlins 2: The New Batch* (1990)
  Sequel to the 1984 horror comedy. Closing credits (Chuck Jones).

201 *Hi Diddle Diddle* (1943)
  Opening and ending (Warner Bros. studio).

202 *Holiday in Mexico* (1946)
  Musical starring Walter Pidgeon and Jane Powell. Opening (Hanna-Barbera).

203 *Hollywood Party* (1934)
  Color appearance by Mickey Mouse in a scene with Jimmy Durante (Walt Disney). Mickey's feature film debut.

204 *The King of Jazz* (1930)
Four-minute opening sequence (Walter Lantz). The first animation made in two-color Technicolor.

205 *The Lady Eve* (1941)
Preston Sturges comedy starring Henry Fonda and Barbara Stanwyck. Title sequence (Warner Bros. studio).

206 *Love Thy Neighbor* (1940)
Comedy starring Jack Benny and Fred Allen. Title sequence (Warner Bros. studio).

207 *Monty Python and the Holy Grail* (1974)
Second Python film pokes fun at the Arthurian legend. Cut-out animation sequences (Terry Gilliam).

208 *Monty Python's Life of Brian* (1979)
Biblical comedy from the British troupe. Cut-out animated opening (Terry Gilliam).

209 *Monty Python's The Meaning of Life* (1983)
Cut-out animation sequences (Terry Gilliam).

210 *Mrs. Doubtfire* (1993)
Animation sequence (Chuck Jones).

211 *My Dream Is Yours* (1949)
Musical-comedy starring Doris Day and Jack Carson. Bugs Bunny dream sequence (Friz Freleng).

212 *National Lampoon's Christmas Vacation* (1989)
Opening title sequence (Kroyer Films).

213 *One Crazy Summer* (1986)
Titles (Savage Steve Holland, Bill Kopp).

214 *The Parent Trap* (1961)
Disney comedy starring Hayley Mills. Puppet-animated titles (Bill Justice, T. Hee, Xavier Atencio).

215 *Pink Floyd—The Wall* (1982)
Animated sequence (Gerald Scarfe).

216 *The Pink Panther* (1964)
Classic comedy with Peter Sellers as the bumbling Inspector Clouseau. Title sequence (DePatie-Freleng).

217 *The Pink Panther Strikes Again* (1976)
Title sequence (Richard Williams).

218 *The Return of the Pink Panther* (1974)
Opening titles (Richard Williams).

219 *Return to Oz* (1985)
Sequel to the classic 1939 film. Claymation rock creatures (Will Vinton). Vinton was Oscar nominated (with Ian Wingrove, Zoran Perisic and Michael Lloyd) in the Visual Effects category.

220 *Ruthless People* (1986)
Comedy starring Danny DeVito and Bette Midler. Animation sequence (Sally Cruikshank).

221 *A Shot in the Dark* (1964)
Sequel to *The Pink Panther*, starring Peter Sellers as Inspector Clouseau. Title sequence (DePatie-Freleng).

222 *She Married a Cop* (1939)
Paddy Pig sequence (Warner Bros. studio).

223 *Sioux City Sue* (1946)
Gene Autry film, with animated sequences (Walter Lantz).

224 *Son of the Pink Panther* (1993)
Main titles, combining live action and animation (Kroyer Films).

225 *Song of Norway* (1970)
Musical biography of Edvard Grieg. Animation (Jack Kinney).

226 *Stay Tuned* (1992)
Animated Sequence (Chuck Jones).

227 *Steppenwolf* (1974)
Screen adaptation of the Herman Hesse novel. Animation (Jaroslav Bradac).

228 *Think Dirty/Every Home Should Have One* (1970)
British comedy starring Marty Feldman. Animation (Richard Williams).

229 *Tom Thumb* (1958)
George Pal fairy tale featuring puppet-animated toys (Gene Warren, Wah Chang).

230 *Twilight Zone—The Movie* (1983)
Feature adaptation of the classic 1959–1964 TV series. Sequence (on TV) from "It's a Good Life" segment (Sally Cruikshank). Cruikshank directed the acclaimed short *Quasi at the Quackadero* (1975).

231 *Two Guys from Texas* (1948)
Musical starring Dennis Morgan and Jack Carson. Bugs Bunny dream sequence (Friz Freleng).

232 *Variety Girl* (1947)

Star-laden black-and-white film featuring the color Puppetoon segment: "Romeow and Julicat" (George Pal). Pal's last Puppetoon short.

233 *A Very Brady Sequel* (1996)

Sequel to *The Brady Bunch Movie* (1995), based on the '70s sitcom. Tim Matheson's hallucination (Bob Kurtz).

234 *When's Your Birthday?* (1937)

Black-and-white comedy starring Joe E. Brown, with color opening sequence (Bob Clampett).

235 *The Wonderful World of the Brothers Grimm* (1962)

George Pal production featuring puppet-animated elves/dragon (Project Unlimited).

236 *The World According to Garp* (1982)

Film of the John Irving novel starring Robin Williams. Sequence in which the young Garp's drawing comes to life (John Canemaker).

237 *Xanadu* (1980)

Olivia Newton-John musical. Two-minute "Don't Walk Away" sequence (Don Bluth).

238 *Ziegfeld Follies* (1946)

Puppet-animated opening sequence (Lou Bunin). Bunin is best known for his 1950 film version of *Alice in Wonderland*.

PART 3: Animated Shorts

Academy Award winners and nominees, besides being identified as such, are denoted AA and †. All winners and nominees are for Best Animated Short unless otherwise noted. All shorts are color theatrical releases unless denoted "b&w" for black-and-white. Those made before Disney's *Steamboat Willie* (1928) are silent releases (with the exception of Max Fleischer's experimental "Song Cartune" series). Each short is approximately six to eight minutes in length, unless otherwise noted.

239 *The Abominable Snow Rabbit* (May 20, 1961)
Dir: Chuck Jones; Warner Bros.; Looney Tunes: Bugs Bunny, Daffy Duck.

240 *Ace in the Hole* (June 22, 1942)
Dir: Alex Lovy; Walter Lantz. Woody Woodpecker; Woody goes joyriding in a military plane; Lovy's first "Woody Woodpecker" cartoon.

241 *Acrobatty Bunny* (June 29, 1946)
Dir: Robert McKimson; Warner Bros.; Looney Tunes: Bugs Bunny; Bugs tangles with a circus lion; McKimson's first "Bugs Bunny" cartoon; Voices—Mel Blanc.

242 *Adam* (1991) †
Producer-Director: Peter Lord; Aardman Animations. Oscar nominee; Clay-animated retelling of the Book of Genesis; Written and animated by Aardman co-founder Lord (b. 1953).

243 *Admission Free* (June 10, 1932; b&w)
Dir: Dave Fleischer; Max Fleischer. Talkartoon, with Betty Boop.

244 *The Adventures of an* ✶ (1956)
Dir: John Hubley; Storyboard Inc. The first short John and Faith Hubley produced together. The renowned animating team formed Storyboard Inc. in 1955, following John's stint at UPA.

245 *The Adventures of the Road Runner* (June 1962; 26 mins)
Dir: Chuck Jones; Warner Bros.; Road Runner–Coyote, with Ralph Phillips; The Road Runner–Coyote chase is watched on TV by two boys; Special featurette, originally made for TV as a pilot for a proposed "Road Runner" series; Released in theaters with the feature *Lad: A Dog*; Includes footage from the shorts *From A to Z-Z-Z-Z* (1954) and *To Beep or Not to Beep* (1963); Co-Directors—Maurice Noble, Tom Ray; Music and song "Out on the

Desert" by Milt Franklyn; Voices—Mel Blanc (Coyote), Dick Beals (Ralph), Nancy Wible, Richard Tufeld.

Aesop's Fables (series) **see** *The Cat and the Canary* (1921)

246 *African Diary* (April 20, 1945)
Dir: Jack Kinney; Walt Disney. Goofy; Diary entries relate Goofy's African safari, which is cut short by an angry rhino; Voice—Pinto Colvig (Goofy).

247 *After You've Gone* (August 15, 1946; 3 mins)
Dir: Jack Kinney; Walt Disney; The Benny Goodman Quartet (clarinetist Goodman, drummer Cozy Cole, bassist Sid Weiss, pianist Teddy Wilson) performs the music in this superbly-animated short; Part of the feature *Make Mine Music*; Rereleased with another Disney-Goodman short *All the Cats Join In* (as *Two for the Record*) April 23, 1954.

248 *A-Haunting We Will Go* (May 13, 1949)
Dir: Seymour Kneitel; Paramount/Famous; Noveltoon, with Casper the Friendly Ghost (in his third appearance).

249 *Ain't She Tweet* (June 21, 1952)
Dir: Friz Freleng; Warner Bros.; Looney Tune: Tweety, Sylvester.

250 *Ain't That Ducky* (May 19, 1945)
Dir: Friz Freleng; Warner Bros.; Looney Tune: Daffy Duck; A hunter (a caricature of actor Victor Moore) goes after Daffy; Moore, himself, actually provided the hunter's voice; Voices—Mel Blanc.

251 *Ain't We Got Fun* (April 17, 1937)
Dir: Tex Avery; Warner Bros.; Merrie Melodie.

252 *Aladdin and His Wonderful Lamp* (August 10, 1934)
Producer-Director: Ub Iwerks; ComiColor.

253 *Aladdin and His Wonderful Lamp* (April 7, 1939)
Dir: Dave Fleischer; Max Fleischer; Popeye the Sailor, Olive Oyl, Bluto; Special two-reeler (twice the length of a normal short); The Fleischers' third and last "Popeye" two-reeler.

254 *A-Lad-In His Lamp* (October 23, 1948)
Dir: Robert McKimson; Warner Bros.; Looney Tune: Bugs Bunny; Arabian Nights spoof; Voices—Mel Blanc (Bugs), Jim Backus (Genie).

255 *Ali Baba* (January 30, 1936)
Producer-Director: Ub Iwerks; ComiColor.

256 *Ali Baba Bunny* (February 9, 1957)
Dir: Chuck Jones; Warner Bros.; Merrie Melodie: Bugs Bunny, Daffy Duck; Bugs and a very greedy Daffy tunnel into an Arabian cave filled with treasure; Voices—Mel Blanc.

257 *Alias St. Nick* (November 16, 1935)
Dir: Rudolf Ising; MGM; Happy Harmony.

Alice Comedies (series) **see** *Alice's Day at Sea* (1924)

258 *Alice's Day at Sea* (March 1, 1924; b&w)
Producer-Director: Walt Disney; Alice Comedy; The first short in the silent series, following a 1923 pilot film, *Alice's Wonderland*, which was Disney's last effort in his "Laugh-o-Gram" series. The "Alice Comedies" (aka "Alice in Cartoonland") combined live action and animation by placing a real young girl in a cartoon setting where she would interact with animated characters. Fifty-six were produced (1924–27), leading to Disney's next series, "Oswald the Lucky Rabbit" (1927–28), and then some mouse named Mickey; Cast—Virginia Davis (Alice); Note: Margie Gay took over the role of Alice in 1925. The role was also played briefly by Dawn O'Day (1925) and Lois Hardwick (1927).

259 *All A-Bir-r-r-d* (June 24, 1950)
Dir: Friz Freleng; Warner Bros.; Looney Tune: Tweety, Sylvester.

260 *All Fowled Up* (February 19, 1955)
Dir: Robert McKimson; Warner Bros.; Looney Tune: Foghorn Leghorn, Henery Hawk; Little chicken hawk Henery has his eye on Foghorn; Voices—Mel Blanc.

261 *All Nothing (Tout-rien)* (1980) †
Prod-Dir: Frédéric Back; Société Radio Canada; Oscar nominee.

262 *All Out for "V"* (August 7, 1942) †
Dir: Mannie Davis; Terrytoons; Terrytoon; Oscar nominee (Terrytoons' first).

263 *All the Cats Join In* (August 15, 1946; 4 mins)
Dir: Jack Kinney; Walt Disney; Teenagers gather at the local malt shop in this great Disney short animated to the swinging music of Benny Goodman and his orchestra; Part of the feature *Make Mine Music*; Rereleased with another Disney-Goodman short *After You've Gone* (as *Two for the Record*) April 23, 1954.

264 *All This and Rabbit Stew* (September 13, 1941)
Dir: Tex Avery; Warner Bros.; Merrie Melodie: Bugs Bunny; Bugs is pursued by a black hunter; Avery's fourth and last "Bugs Bunny" short; Voices—Mel Blanc.

265 *Alley to Bali* (March 15, 1954)
Dir: Don Patterson; Walter Lantz; Woody Woodpecker; Aka *Bali Ho*.

266 *All's Fair at the Fair* (August 26, 1938)
Dir: Dave Fleischer; Max Fleischer; Color Classic; A small-town couple visit the New York's World's Fair.

267 *Aloha Hooey* (January 30, 1942)
Dir: Tex Avery; Warner Bros.; Merrie Melodie; One of Avery's last WB shorts.

268 *Along Came Daffy* (June 4, 1947)
 Dir: Friz Freleng; Warner Bros.; Looney Tune: Daffy Duck, Yosemite Sam; Cookbook salesman Daffy visits the cabin of two starving brothers (Sam in a dual role); Voices—Mel Blanc.

269 *Alpine Climbers* (July 25, 1936)
 Dir: David Hand; Walt Disney; Mickey Mouse, Donald Duck, Pluto; While climbing in the Swiss Alps, Mickey finds an eagle's nest, Donald chases a mountain goat, and Pluto is rescued by a St. Bernard; Voices—Walt Disney (Mickey), Clarence Nash (Donald).

270 *Always Kickin'* (January 26, 1939)
 Dir: Dave Fleischer; Max Fleischer; Color Classic.

271 *Amoozin' But Confoozin'* (March 3, 1944)
 Dir: Sid Marcus; Columbia/Screen Gems. Lil' Abner; The first of five "Lil' Abner" cartoons (1944); The short-lived series was based on the popular comic strip (which debuted in 1934) by Al Capp (1909–79).

Amos 'n' Andy (series) **see** *The Rasslin' Match* (1934)

272 *And to Think I Saw It on Mulberry Street* (1944) †
 Prod-Dir: George Pal. Puppetoon; Oscar nominee; Based on the 1937 children's story by Dr. Seuss.

Andy Panda (series) **see** *Life Begins for Andy Panda* (1939)

Animated Antics (series) **see** *The Dandy Lion* (1940)

273 *Animated Grouch Chasers* (March 1915; b&w)
 Producer-Director: Raoul Barre; Debut of the early silent cartoon series "Animated Grouch Chasers," the first from the Raoul Barre Studio (for the Edison Company). Live actors introduced the animated "Grouch Chaser" segments by opening the pages of a comic album. Stories featured such characters as Kid Kelly, Hercules Hicks and Silas Bunkum. Over ten were produced (1915).

274 *Anna & Bella* (1984) **AA**
 Dir: Borge Ring; Netherlands; Oscar-winner; Charming, sentimental tale about the memories a photo album brings to two elderly sisters; Danish animator Ring (b. 1921) also directed the Oscar-nominated *Oh, My Darling* (1978); Produced by Cilia Van Dijk.

275 *Another Froggy Evening* (January, 1995)
 Dir: Chuck Jones; Warner Bros./Chuck Jones Film Prods. Michigan J. Frog; Sequel to Jones' classic *One Froggy Evening* (1955); Produced by Jones and Linda Jones Clough; Voice—Jeff McCarthy (Michigan J. Frog).

The Ant and the Aardvark (series) **see** *Never Bug an Ant* (1966)

276 *Ant Pasted* (May 9, 1953)
 Dir: Friz Freleng; Warner Bros.; Looney Tune: Elmer Fudd; Elmer wages war with an army of ants; Voice—Arthur Q. Bryan (Elmer).

277 *Any Bonds Today?* [aka *Leon Schlesinger Presents Bugs Bunny*] (1942)
Dir: Bob Clampett; Warner Bros.; War bond trailer featuring Bugs Bunny (with Porky Pig and Elmer Fudd) singing "Any Bonds Today?" written by Irving Berlin.

278 *Any Rags* (January 2, 1932; b&w)
Dir: Dave Fleischer; Max Fleischer; Talkartoon, with Betty Boop and Bimbo; Ragman Bimbo sings the title song (1902, written by Thomas S. Allen) while making his rounds; Voice—Mae Questel (Betty).

279 *Apes of Wrath* (April 18, 1959)
Dir: Friz Freleng; Warner Bros.; Merrie Melodie: Bugs Bunny.

280 *Apple Andy* (May 20, 1946)
Dir: Dick Lundy; Walter Lantz; Andy Panda.

281 *Aquamania* (December 29, 1961) †
Dir: Wolfgang Reitherman; Walt Disney; Goofy; Oscar nominee; Goofy and his son accidentally take part in a water skiing race; Voice—Pinto Colvig (Goofy).

282 *Aquarela do Brasil* (*Watercolor of Brazil*) (February 6, 1943)
Dir: Wilfred Jackson; Walt Disney; Donald Duck is introduced to Latin rhythms by parrot Joe Carioca (voiced by Jose Oliveira); Part of the feature *Saludos Amigos*; Rereleased June 24, 1955; Songs—"Brazil" by Ary Barroso and S. K. Russell (sung by Aloysio Oliveira), "Tico Tico No Fuba (samba)" by Zequinha de Abreu; Voice—Clarence Nash (Donald).

283 *Arctic Antics* (June 5, 1930; b&w)
Dir: Ub Iwerks; Walt Disney; Silly Symphony.

284 *The Arctic Giant* (February 27, 1942)
Dir: Dave Fleischer; Max Fleischer; Superman.

285 *The Aristo Cat* (June 19, 1943)
Dir: Chuck Jones; Warner Bros.; Merrie Melodie: Hubie and Bertie (debut); The two Brooklyn-accented mice (created by Jones) outwit a pampered pussycat; Hubie and Bertie appeared in six shorts (1943–51); Voices—Mel Blanc.

286 *The Army Mascot* (May 22, 1942)
Dir: Clyde Geronimi; Walt Disney; Pluto.

287 *The Art of Self-Defense* (December 26, 1941)
Dir: Jack Kinney; Walt Disney; Goofy.

288 *The Art of Skiing* (November 14, 1941)
Dir: Jack Kinney; Walt Disney; Goofy; Goofy demonstrates skiing techniques in this classic short.

Astronut (series) **see** *Brother from Outer Space* (1964)

289 *The Athlete* (August 29, 1932; b&w)
Dir: Walter Lantz, William Nolan; Walter Lantz; Pooch the Pup (debut); Lantz's cute little pup was the first non–Oswald the Rabbit cartoon character to emerge from his studio. Pooch starred in 14 shorts (1932–33).

290 *The Autograph Hound* (September 1, 1939)
Dir: Jack King; Walt Disney; Donald Duck; Donald tries to get the autographs of such Hollywood stars as Greta Garbo, Mickey Rooney, Sonja Henie, and Shirley Temple; Voice—Clarence Nash (Donald).

291 *Automania 2000* (1963) †
Dir: John Halas, Joy Batchelor; Halas-Batchelor; Oscar nominee; Satirical short on motorization from Britain's Halas and Batchelor Studio (*Animal Farm*).

292 *Autumn* (February 13, 1930; b&w)
Dir: Ub Iwerks; Walt Disney; Silly Symphony.

293 *Aviation Vacation* (August 2, 1941)
Dir: Tex Avery; Warner Bros.; Merrie Melodie; A round-the-world sightseeing tour by plane.

294 *The Awful Orphan* (January 29, 1949)
Dir: Chuck Jones; Warner Bros.; Merrie Melodie: Porky Pig, Charlie Dog; Charlie wants Porky to be his new master; Voices—Mel Blanc.

Babbit and Catstello (series) **see** *A Tale of Two Kitties* (1942)

295 *Babes in the Woods* (November 19, 1932)
Dir: Burt Gillett; Walt Disney; Silly Symphony; An army of elves come to the rescue of two children being held captive by a witch in this retelling of "Hansel and Gretel."

296 *Baby Bottleneck* (March 16, 1946)
Dir: Bob Clampett; Warner Bros.; Looney Tune: Porky Pig, Daffy Duck; The baby boom is on and Porky and Daffy get into the baby-delivery business; Voices—Mel Blanc.

Baby Face Mouse (series) **see** *Cheese Nappers* (1938)

Baby Huey (series) **see** *One Quack Mind* (1951)

297 *Baby Wants a Bottleship* (July 3, 1942; b&w)
Dir: Dave Fleischer; Max Fleischer; Popeye the Sailor; The last Fleischer produced "Popeye" short (the series would continue at Famous Studios until 1957); Voice—Jack Mercer (Popeye).

298 *Baby Weems* (June 20, 1941)
Walt Disney; The story of a miraculous baby with a genius IQ is presented in a series of drawings; An early Disney experiment with the limited, simpler animation style later employed at the UPA studio; Part of the feature *The Reluctant Dragon*; Written by Joe Grant, Dick Huemer and John P. Miller; Voices—Leone LeDoux/Raymond Severn (Baby

Weems), Ernie Alexander (John Weems), Linda Marwood (Mrs. Weems), Edward Marr (Walter Winchell), Art Gilmore (FDR), Gerald Mohr (Narrator).

299 *Bacall to Arms* (August 3, 1946)
Dir: Bob Clampett; Warner Bros.; Merrie Melodie; In a movie theater, a girl-crazy wolf watches *To Have...To Have...To Have* (a spoof of 1944's *To Have and Have Not* starring Humphrey Bogart and Lauren Bacall); Voices—Mel Blanc.

300 *Back Alley Oproar* (March 27, 1948)
Dir: Friz Freleng; Warner Bros.; Merrie Melodie: Sylvester, Elmer Fudd; Sylvester sings on the backyard fence, disturbing Elmer's sleep; Color remake of 1941's *Notes to You* (with Porky Pig); Voices—Mel Blanc (Sylvester), Arthur Q. Bryan (Elmer).

301 *Backwoods Bunny* (June 13, 1959)
Dir: Robert McKimson; Warner Bros.; Merrie Melodie: Bugs Bunny; Bugs tangles with two hillbilly buzzards (voiced by Daws Butler); Voice—Mel Blanc (Bugs).

302 *Bad Luck Blackie* (January 22, 1949)
Dir: Tex Avery; MGM; A black cat brings bad luck to a bullying bulldog.

303 *Baggage Buster* (April 18, 1941)
Dir: Jack Kinney; Walt Disney; Goofy; Goofy, a baggage handler at a train station, comes in contact with a magician's trunk.

304 *Balance* (1989) AA
Dir: Christoph and Wolfgang Lauenstein; Lauenstein Prod; Oscar winner; Puppet-animated short from the twin Lauenstein brothers.

305 *Balloonland* (September 30, 1935)
Producer-Director: Ub Iwerks; ComiColor; The happy residents of Balloonland do battle with the evil Pincushion Man in this imaginative short; Aka *The Pincushion Man*.

306 *Ballot Box Bunny* (October 6, 1951)
Dir: Friz Freleng; Warner Bros.; Merrie Melodie: Bugs Bunny, Yosemite Sam; Political spoof with Bugs campaigning against Sam; Voices—Mel Blanc.

307 *Bambi Meets Godzilla* (1969; 1 min; b&w)
Producer-Director: Marv Newland; The little deer is squawshed by the monster's foot. Cult cartoon, the first from animator Newland (b. 1947).

308 *The Band Concert* (February 23, 1935)
Dir: Wilfred Jackson; Walt Disney; Mickey Mouse, Donald Duck; One of the all-time greatest Disney shorts has Mickey the conductor of an orchestra playing a rousing rendition of Rossini's "William Tell Overture" during a tornado; The first "Mickey Mouse" cartoon in color (Technicolor); Voice—Clarence Nash (Donald Duck).

309 *The Band Master* (December 1947)
Dir: Dick Lundy; Walter Lantz; Andy Panda.

310 *Banty Raids* (June 29, 1963)
   Dir: Robert McKimson; Warner Bros.; Merrie Melodie: Foghorn Leghorn (in his last short).

311 *The Barber of Seville* (April 10, 1944)
   Dir: James Culhane; Walter Lantz; Woody Woodpecker; At Tony Figaro's Seville Barbershop, Woody gives customers a shave and a haircut while singing "Largo el Factotum" (from Rossini's opera *Barber of Seville*); This outstanding short was Culhane's first and best "Woody Woodpecker" cartoon (he would direct nine).

Barney Bear (series) **see** *The Bear That Couldn't Sleep* (1939)

Barney Google (series) **see** *Tetched in the Head* (1935)

312 *The Barnyard Broadcast* (October 19, 1931; b&w)
   Dir: Burt Gillett; Walt Disney; Mickey Mouse, Minnie Mouse, Pluto; Cats wreak havoc during Mickey's radio show; Voice—Walt Disney (Mickey).

313 *Baseball Bugs* (February 2, 1946)
   Dir: Friz Freleng; Warner Bros.; Looney Tune: Bugs Bunny; Fine baseball spoof has Bugs taking on the thuggish Gas House Gorillas all by himself; Voices—Mel Blanc.

314 *The Bashful Buzzard* (September 5, 1945)
   Dir: Bob Clampett; Warner Bros.; Looney Tune: Beaky Buzzard (in his second appearance); Voice—Kent Rogers (Beaky).

315 *Bathing Buddies* (July 1, 1946)
   Dir: Dick Lundy; Walter Lantz; Woody Woodpecker, Wally Walrus; Tenant Woody tears apart Wally's apartment building to retrieve a dime he dropped down the bathtub drain; Voice—Ben Hardaway (Woody).

316 *Batty Baseball* (April 22, 1944)
   Dir: Tex Avery; MGM; Wacky baseball spoof.

317 *Be Human* (November 20, 1936; b&w)
   Dir: Dave Fleischer; Max Fleischer; Betty Boop, Grampy; A brutal farmer gets some of his own medicine from Prof. Grampy's Animal Aid Society; Voice—Mae Questel (Betty).

318 *Beach Picnic* (June 9, 1939)
   Dir: Clyde Geronimi; Walt Disney; Donald Duck, Pluto; Geronimi's directorial debut. Clyde "Gerry" Geronimi (1901–89), a former Bray Studio animator and later one of Disney's leading feature directors (*Cinderella*, *Lady and the Tramp*, etc.), would direct 23 shorts (1939–57), including the Oscar-winning *Lend a Paw* (1941).

319 *The Bead Game* (1977; 5 mins) †
   Producer-Director: Ishu Patel; National Film Board of Canada; Oscar nominee; Anti-war short—animated using thousands of colored beads—from India-born animator Patel; Music by J.P. Ghosh.

Beaky Buzzard (series) **see** *Bugs Bunny Gets the Boid* (1942)

Beans (series) **see** *I Haven't Got a Hat* (1935)

320 *Beanstalk Bunny* (February 12, 1955)
Dir: Chuck Jones; Warner Bros.; Merrie Melodie: Bugs Bunny, Daffy Duck, Elmer Fudd; Elmer plays the giant in this takeoff on "Jack and the Beanstalk"; Voices—Mel Blanc, Arthur Q. Bryan (Elmer).

321 *The Bear and the Bean* (January 31, 1948)
Dir: Michael Lah, Preston Blair; MGM; Barney Bear.

322 *The Bear and the Hare* (June 26, 1948)
Dir: Michael Lah, Preston Blair; MGM; Barney Bear.

323 *Bear Feat* (December 10, 1949)
Dir: Chuck Jones; Warner Bros.; Looney Tune: The Three Bears; The bear family rehearse their circus act; Voices—Billy Bletcher (Papa), Bea Benaderet (Mama), Stan Freberg (Junior).

324 *A Bear for Punishment* (October 20, 1951)
Dir: Chuck Jones; Warner Bros.; Merrie Melodie: The Three Bears; Mama and Junior Bear prepare an elaborate celebration for Father's Day in this hilarious short (the last in the series); Jones has called Mama's tap dance (animated by Ken Harris) "one of the finest pieces of animation ever done any place"; Voices—Billy Bletcher (Papa), Bea Benaderet (Mama), Stan Freberg (Junior).

325 *The Bear That Couldn't Sleep* (June 10, 1939)
Dir: Rudolf Ising; MGM; Barney Bear; Barney's debut short. The sleepy-eyed, Wallace Beery–like bear—one of MGM's first cartoon stars—appeared in 26 shorts (1939–54). Ising (of Harman-Ising) directed the series until he left MGM in 1943; Voice—Billy Bletcher (Barney).

326 *The Bear That Wasn't* (December 31, 1967)
Dir: Chuck Jones; MGM; One of Jones' last MGM shorts, based on a book by Frank Tashlin.

327 *The Bears and the Bees* (July 9, 1932; b&w)
Dir: Wilfred Jackson; Walt Disney; Silly Symphony.

328 *The Bear's Tale* (April 13, 1940)
Dir: Tex Avery; Warner Bros.; Merrie Melodie; The story of "Goldilocks and the Three Bears" with Red Riding Hood and the Wolf joining in; Voices—Mel Blanc, Tex Avery (Papa Bear).

The Beary Family (series) **see** *Fowled-Up Birthday* (1962)

329 *Bedtime for Sniffles* (November 23, 1940)
Dir: Chuck Jones; Warner Bros.; Merrie Melodie: Sniffles; Sniffles the mouse waits for Santa Claus to arrive in this charming short; Voice—Bernice Hansen (Sniffles).

330 *The Bee-Deviled Bruin* (May 14, 1949)
Dir: Chuck Jones; Warner Bros.; Merrie Melodie: The Three Bears; Papa Bear (Henry) attempts to get honey from a beehive—with help from Junior; Voices—Billy Bletcher (Papa), Bea Benaderet (Mama), Stan Freberg (Junior).

331 *Beep Beep* (May 24, 1952)
Dir: Chuck Jones; Warner Bros.; Merrie Melodie: Road Runner, Coyote; The second "Road Runner-Coyote" cartoon, following 1949's *Fast and Furry-Ous.*

332 *Beep Prepared* (November 11, 1961) †
Dir: Chuck Jones; Warner Bros.; Merrie Melodie: Road Runner, Coyote; Oscar nominee.

333 *Believe It or Else* (June 25, 1939)
Dir: Tex Avery; Warner Bros.; Merrie Melodie: Egghead; Parody of "Ripley's Believe It or Not"; Voice—Cliff Nazarro (Egghead).

334 *Ben and Me* (November 11, 1953; 20 mins) †
Dir: Hamilton Luske; Walt Disney; Oscar nominee (for Best Two-Reel Short); A Philadelphia church mouse named Amos becomes a very helpful assistant to Benjamin Franklin. Charming featurette based on the 1939 story by author-illustrator Robert Lawson (1892–1957); Voices—Sterling Holloway (Amos), Charles Ruggles (Ben), Hans Conried (Thomas Jefferson).

Betty Boop (series) **see** *Dizzy Dishes* (1930)

335 *Betty Boop and Grampy* (August 16, 1935; b&w)
Dir: Dave Fleischer; Max Fleischer; Betty Boop, Grampy (debut); Betty is invited to a party at the home of her inventor friend, Grampy. Fun, tuneful short, highlighted by the rousing "Hold That Tiger" finale; The spry, bearded old inventor, Grampy, would appear in some ten Fleischer shorts; Voice—Mae Questel (Betty).

336 *Betty Boop and Little Jimmy* (March 27, 1936; b&w)
Dir: Dave Fleischer; Max Fleischer; Betty Boop; Betty costars with "Little Jimmy," from the comic strip by James Swinnerton (1875–1974). The character (created in 1905) had appeared earlier in silent shorts from Hearst's International Film Service; Betty sings "Keep Your Girlish Figure"; Voice—Mae Questel (Betty).

337 *Betty Boop and the Little King* (January 31, 1936; b&w)
Dir: Dave Fleischer; Max Fleischer; Betty Boop, with The Little King; Otto Soglow's comic strip "King" was the star of his own Van Beuren series (1933–34).

338 *Betty Boop, Bizzy Bee* (August 19, 1932; b&w)
Dir: Dave Fleischer; Max Fleischer; Betty Boop, Bimbo, Koko the Clown; Betty is a busy lunchwagon cook.

339 *Betty Boop, with Henry, the Funniest Living American* (November 22, 1935; b&w)
Dir: Dave Fleischer; Max Fleischer; Betty Boop; Betty costars with "Henry" from the comic strip by Carl Anderson (1865–1948).

340 *Betty Boop's Bamboo Isle* (September 23, 1932; b&w)
Dir: Dave Fleischer; Max Fleischer; Betty Boop, Bimbo, with the music of The Royal Samoans (with Miri); Includes Betty's provocative hoola dance; Voice—Mae Questel (Betty).

341 *Betty Boop's Big Boss* (June 2, 1933; b&w)
Dir: Dave Fleischer; Max Fleischer; Betty Boop; Betty's new boss gets fresh; Betty sings "You'd Be Surprised" (1919, written by Irving Berlin); Score includes music from Paramount's 1932 feature *Love Me Tonight* (including "Mimi," which becomes "Betty"); Voice—Mae Questel (Betty).

342 *Betty Boop's Crazy Inventions* (January 27, 1933; b&w)
Dir: Dave Fleischer; Max Fleischer; Betty Boop, Bimbo, Koko the Clown.

343 *Betty Boop's Halloween Party* (November 3, 1933; b&w)
Dir: Dave Fleischer; Max Fleischer; Betty Boop; Betty sings "Here We Are" (1929, written by Harry Warren and Gus Kahn).

344 *Betty Boop's May Party* (May 12, 1933; b&w)
Dir: Dave Fleischer; Max Fleischer; Betty Boop, Bimbo, Koko the Clown.

345 *Betty Boop's Museum* (December 16, 1932; b&w)
Dir: Dave Fleischer; Max Fleischer; Betty Boop, Koko the Clown.

346 *Betty Boop's Rise to Fame* (May 18, 1934; b&w)
Dir: Dave Fleischer; Max Fleischer; Betty Boop, with a special appearance by Max Fleischer (being interviewed by a reporter); Includes footage from three earlier "Betty Boop" shorts (*Stopping the Show*, *Betty Boop's Bamboo Isle*, *The Old Man of the Mountain*); Voice—Mae Questel (Betty).

347 *Betty Boop's Ups and Downs* (October 14, 1932; b&w)
Dir: Dave Fleischer; Max Fleischer; Betty Boop.

348 *Betty Co-Ed* (August 1, 1931; b&w)
Dir: Dave Fleischer; Max Fleischer; Screen Song, with Rudy Vallee; Tuneful college spoof.

349 *Betty in Blunderland* (April 6, 1934; b&w)
Dir: Dave Fleischer; Max Fleischer; Betty Boop; Betty goes through the looking glass in this Lewis Carroll takeoff; Voice—Mae Questel (Betty).

350 *Bewitched Bunny* (July 24, 1954)
Dir: Chuck Jones; Warner Bros.; Looney Tune: Bugs Bunny; Bugs rescues Hansel and Gretel from Witch Hazel (voiced by June Foray); Voices—Mel Blanc.

351 *The Big Bad Wolf* (April 14, 1934)
Dir: Burt Gillett; Walt Disney; Silly Symphony, with the Big Bad Wolf, the Three Little Pigs, Little Red Riding Hood and Grandma; Followup to Disney's popular *Three Little Pigs* (1933) includes that short's hit song "Who's Afraid of the Big Bad Wolf?"

352 *Big Heel-Watha* (October 21, 1944)
Dir: Tex Avery; MGM; Screwy Squirrel, The Showgirl (Minnie Hot-Cha); A tubby Indian goes squirrel hunting; Includes many wartime gags (rationing, blackouts, etc.); Voice—Bill Thompson (Heel-Watha).

353 *The Big Snit* (1985; 9 mins) †
Dir: Richard Condie; National Film Board of Canada; Oscar nominee; A quarreling couple play Scrabble as nuclear annihilation looms. Hilariously bizarre; Memorable dialogue—"Stop shakin' yer eyes"; Written and animated by Condie; Music by Patrick Godfrey; Produced by Condie and Michael Scott; Voices—Jay Brazeau, Ida Osler, Randy Woods, Bill Guest.

354 *The Big Snooze* (October 5, 1946)
Dir: Bob Clampett; Warner Bros.; Looney Tune: Bugs Bunny, Elmer Fudd; Bugs turns Elmer's peaceful dream into a nightmare in this wonderfully chaotic short; Clampett's last Warner Bros. cartoon. He would go on to create the Emmy-winning TV puppet show *Time for Beany* (1950–55), which later became the cartoon TV series *Beany and Cecil* (1962–67); Voices—Mel Blanc (Bugs); Arthur Q. Bryan (Elmer).

355 *The Big Story* (1994; 2 mins; b&w) †
Producer-Directors: Tim Watts, David Stoten; Spitting Image Prod; Oscar nominee; Impressionist Frank Gorshin voices *three* Kirk Douglases in this stop-motion short about tough-talking newspapermen.

356 *Billion Dollar Limited* (January 9, 1942)
Dir: Dave Fleischer; Max Fleischer; Superman.

357 *Billy Boy* (May 8, 1954)
Dir: Tex Avery; MGM; A little billy goat's eating habits become too much for an easygoing farmer (well-voiced by Daws Butler).

358 *Bimbo's Initiation* (July 24, 1931; b&w)
Dir: Dave Fleischer; Max Fleischer; Talkartoon, with Bimbo, Betty Boop (in an early appearance); The nightmarish initiation into a mysterious club ("Wanna be a member? Wanna be a member?") places Bimbo into one harrowing predicament after another. A surreal Fleischer classic.

359 *The Bird Store* (January 16, 1932; b&w)
Dir: Wilfred Jackson; Walt Disney; Silly Symphony; Birds of all varieties sing in their cages and fight off a feline intruder.

360 *Birds Anonymous* (August 10, 1957) AA
Dir: Friz Freleng; Warner Bros.; Merrie Melodie: Sylvester, Tweety; Oscar winner; Great Freleng short has Sylvester trying to quit his bird habit; Voices—Mel Blanc.

361 *Birds in the Spring* (March 11, 1933)
Dir: David Hand; Walt Disney; Silly Symphony.

362 *Birds of a Feather* (February 10, 1931; b&w)
Dir: Burt Gillett; Walt Disney; Silly Symphony.

363 *Birdy and the Beast* (August 19, 1944)
　　Dir: Bob Clampett; Warner Bros.; Merrie Melodie: Tweety; In his second cartoon appearance (following 1942's *A Tale of Two Kitties*), Tweety violently fends off a hungry cat; Voices—Mel Blanc.

364 *Birth of a Notion* (April 12, 1947)
　　Dir: Robert McKimson; Warner Bros.; Looney Tune: Daffy Duck; Daffy finds a home for the winter, unaware that its Peter Lorre–like owner is looking for a duck's wishbone; Voices—Mel Blanc.

365 *Blackfly* (1991; 5 mins) †
　　Dir: Christopher Hinton; National Film Board of Canada; Oscar nominee; A surveyor in Ontario is overcome by blackflies; Title song written and performed by Canadian folk singer Wade Hemsworth; Animated by Hinton; Produced by Douglas Macdonald, Barrie McLean and William Pettigrew.

Blackie the Lamb (series) **see** *No Mutton for Nuttin'* (1943)

366 *Blame It on the Samba* (May 27, 1948)
　　Dir: Clyde Geronimi; Walt Disney; Donald Duck and parrot Joe Carioca dance to the rhythm of the samba as organist Ethel Smith (best known for her hit "Tico-Tico") plays. A superbly animated short combining live action and animation; The silly Aracuan Bird from *The Three Caballeros* (1945) also appears; Part of the feature *Melody Time*; The Dinning Sisters sing the title song (by Ernesto Nazareth and Ray Gilbert); Rereleased April 1, 1955.

367 *Blindscape* (1993) †
　　Producer-Director: Stephen Palmer; National Film and Television School; Oscar nominee.

368 *Blitz Wolf* (August 22, 1942) †
　　Dir: Tex Avery; MGM; Oscar nominee; The Three Little Pigs fight an all-out war with the Big Bad Wolf in this side-splitting lampoon of Adolf Hitler; Avery's first MGM cartoon, following his six-year stint at Warner Bros. Avery did his best work at MGM, directing cartoons noted for their fast pace, great timing and exaggerated comic style, and creating such characters as Droopy, The Wolf and the Showgirl, George and Junior, and Screwy Squirrel. He would direct 67 MGM shorts (1942–57), including the classics *Red Hot Riding Hood* (1943), *Swing Shift Cinderella* (1945), *King-Size Canary* (1947) and *Magical Maestro* (1952). Avery also worked briefly for Walter Lantz (1954–55) (see *I'm Cold*).

369 *Blow Me Down* (October 27, 1933; b&w)
　　Dir: Dave Fleischer; Max Fleischer; Popeye the Sailor.

370 *The Blow Out* (April 4, 1936; b&w)
　　Dir: Tex Avery; Warner Bros.; Looney Tune: Porky Pig (in his first starring appearance).

371 *Blue Bayou* (August 15, 1946; 4 mins)
　　Dir: Samuel Armstrong; Walt Disney; Beautiful animation—originally from a deleted

Fantasia sequence visualizing Debussy's "Claire de Lune"—is the highlight of this Disney short; Part of the feature *Make Mine Music*; Sung by the Ken Darby Chorus.

372 *The Blue Danube* (October 28, 1939)
Dir: Hugh Harman; MGM; Lovely cartoon visualizing the Strauss melody; The singing water sprite is rotoscoped (traced from live action).

The Blue Racer (series) **see** *Hiss and Hers* (1972)

373 *Boat Builders* (February 25, 1938)
Dir: Ben Sharpsteen; Walt Disney; Mickey Mouse, Donald Duck, Goofy.

Bobby Bumps (series) **see** *Bobby Bumps' Adventures* (1915)

374 *Bobby Bumps' Adventures* (1915; b&w)
Dir: Earl Hurd; Bray Studios; Bobby Bumps; Debut short in the early silent series (the second produced by the Bray Studios) about a little boy and his bulldog friend Fido. Bobby starred in some 60 shorts (1915–25); Hurd (1880–1940), Bobby's creator, was the man who developed the revolutionary cel process (patented, December 1914) of animating, which allowed action to be drawn on a clear celluloid sheet over a background scene, thus eliminating the need to redraw an entire picture for each frame.

375 *Bob's Birthday* (1993; 12 mins) AA
Dir: Alison Snowden, David Fine; Channel Four/National Film Board of Canada; Oscar winner; Comedy about a dentist facing a midlife crisis; Spawned the TV series *Bob and Margaret* (1998–); Written by Snowden and Fine (*George and Rosemary*); Animated by Snowden, Fine and Janet Perlman (*The Tender Tale of Cinderella Penguin*); Music by Patrick Godfrey; Voices—Andy Hamilton, Harry Enfield, Alison Snowden, Andrew MacLachlan, Tessa Wojiczak, Sally Grace; Produced by Snowden, Fine and David Verrall.

376 *The Bodyguard* (July 22, 1944)
Dir: William Hanna, Joseph Barbera; MGM; Tom and Jerry, Spike.

377 *Bone Trouble* (June 28, 1940)
Dir: Jack Kinney; Walt Disney; Pluto; Pluto takes another dog's bone and gets chased into a carnival's House of Mirrors; Kinney's directorial debut. Former animator Kinney (1909–92) directed 52 Disney shorts (1940–56), specializing in Goofy (see *Goofy's Glider*). He directed the Oscar-winning *Der Fuehrer's Face* (1943).

378 *Bongo* (September 27, 1947; 32 mins)
Dir: Jack Kinney; Walt Disney; A little circus bear leaves the big top for a free and relaxing life in the forest. Pleasant songs; Part of the feature *Fun and Fancy Free*; Based on a story by Sinclair Lewis; Songs—"Lazy Countryside," "Too Good to Be True" and "Say It with a Slap" by Bobby Worth, Eliot Daniel and Buddy Kaye; Voice—Dinah Shore (Narrator/Singer); Rereleased January 20, 1971.

379 *Boo Moon* (January 1, 1954)
Dir: Seymour Kneitel; Paramount/Famous; Casper the Friendly Ghost; Originally released in 3–D. Famous Studio's second (and last) 3–D short, following *Popeye, the Ace of Space* (1953).

380 *The Boob Weekly* (May 8, 1916; b&w)
Dir: Rube Goldberg; Raoul Barre; The Boob Weekly (debut); Early silent series of newsreel spoofs written and directed by cartoonist Rube Goldberg (1883–1970); Animated by George (Vernon) Stallings.

381 *The Boogie Woogie Bugle Boy of Company B* (September 1, 1941) †
Producer-Director: Walter Lantz; Oscar nominee.

382 *Book Revue* (January 5, 1946)
Dir: Bob Clampett; Warner Bros.; Looney Tune: Daffy Duck; Late at night in a quiet bookshop the book covers come to life.

383 *Boomtown* (1985)
Bill Plympton; The Android Sisters sing about U.S. defense spending; Plympton's first animated short; Title song by Jules Feiffer; Voices—Ruth Maleczech, Valeria Vasilevski (The Android Sisters); Produced by Connie D'Antuono.

384 *Boop-Oop-A-Doop* (January 16, 1932; b&w)
Dir: Dave Fleischer; Max Fleischer; Talkartoon, with Betty Boop, Bimbo, Koko the Clown; Betty—a tight rope walker in a circus—is harassed by her lecherous boss; Betty sings "Don't Take My Boop-Oop-A-Doop Away" (by Samuel Lerner and Sammy Timberg); Voice—Mae Questel (Betty).

Bosko (series) **see** *Sinkin' in the Bathtub* (1930)

385 *Bosko in Dutch* (March 22, 1933; b&w)
Dir: Friz Freleng, uncredited; Warner Bros.; Looney Tune: Bosko, Honey, Goopy Geer; Freleng's directorial debut. Isadore "Friz" Freleng (1906–95), a former Disney animator who joined Warner's cartoon studio at its inception under producer-directors Hugh Harman and Rudolf Ising, would become one of the studio's leading directors, creating (or cocreating) such characters as Porky Pig, Yosemite Sam, and Speedy Gonzales. He directed some 250 WB shorts (1933–38, 40–64), including four Oscar winners— *Tweetie Pie* (1947), *Speedy Gonzales* (1955), *Birds Anonymous* (1957) and *Knighty Knight Bugs* (1958).

386 *Bosko's Mechanical Man* (September 27, 1933; b&w)
Dir: Hugh Harman; Warner Bros.; Looney Tune: Bosko; The last Warner Bros. cartoon produced by Harman-Ising (the "Bosko" series continued at MGM into 1938).

387 *The Boss is Always Right* (January 15, 1960)
Dir: Seymour Kneitel; Paramount; Jeepers and Creepers (debut); The Abbott and Costello–like dog team (who would later evolve into "Swifty and Shorty") appeared in four shorts (1960); Voices—Eddie Lawrence (Swifty/Shorty).

388 *A Bout with a Trout* (October 10, 1947)
Dir: Isadore Sparber; Paramount/Famous; Little Lulu learns why it is wrong to play hooky from school via a "Swingin' on a Star" dream sequence.

389 *Bowery Bugs* (June 4, 1949)
Dir: Arthur Davis; Warner Bros.; Merrie Melodie: Bugs Bunny; Davis' only "Bugs Bunny" short as director.

390 *The Bowling Alley Cat* (July 18, 1942)
Dir: William Hanna, Joseph Barbera; MGM; Tom and Jerry; Classic "T & J" short finds the pair battling it out in a deserted bowling alley.

391 *The Box* (1967) AA
Prod: Fred Wolf; Murakami-Wolf Films; Oscar winner.

392 *Box-Office Bunny* (November 1990)
Dir: Darrell Van Citters; Warner Bros.; Looney Tune: Bugs Bunny, Elmer Fudd, Daffy Duck; The first theatrical "Bugs Bunny" short since 1964's *False Hare*; Released in theaters with the feature *Reversal of Fortune*; Voices—Jeff Bergman; Produced by Kathleen Helppie-Shipley.

393 *Boyhood Daze* (April 20, 1957)
Dir: Chuck Jones; Warner Bros.; Merrie Melodie: Ralph Phillips; Daydreamer Ralph is sent to his room in this enjoyable followup to *From A to Z-Z-Z-Z* (1954); Voice—Dick Beals (Ralph).

394 *The Brave Engineer* (March 3, 1950)
Dir: Jack Kinney; Walt Disney; Jerry Colonna narrates the famous tale of engineer Casey Jones; Based on the "Ballad of Casey Jones" by T. Lawrence Seibert and Eddie Newton; Sung by The King's Men.

395 *The Brave Little Tailor* (September 23, 1938) †
Dir: Burt Gillett; Walt Disney; Mickey Mouse, Minnie Mouse; Oscar nominee; Mickey is ordered by the king to kill a menacing giant after boasting he had killed seven (flies, that is). Classic "Mickey" short; The giant was animated by Vladimir "Bill" Tytla (1904–68), famed animator of the dwarfs (*Snow White*), Stromboli (*Pinocchio*) and the devil Chernabog (*Fantasia*); Voice—Walt Disney (Mickey).

396 *Bravo, Mr. Strauss* (February 26, 1943)
Producer-Director: George Pal; Puppetoon; When the Nazi-like Screwball Army (last seen in the Oscar-nominated *Tulips Shall Grow*) invades the Vienna Woods, a statue of Johann Strauss (with his violin) comes to life and leads them into the Danube River.

397 *Broken Toys* (December 14, 1935)
Dir: Ben Sharpsteen; Walt Disney; Silly Symphony; A sailor doll repairs other unwanted toys left at a dump site.

398 *Brother Brat* (July 15, 1944)
Dir: Frank Tashlin; Warner Bros.; Looney Tune: Porky Pig; Porky babysits a rather violent baby in this funny wartime short; Voices—Mel Blanc.

399 *Brother from Outer Space* (March, 1964)
Dir: Connie Rasinski; Terrytoons; Astronut; The first of 18 shorts (1964–71) starring the little space alien (and his sidekick Oscar Mild); Later shorts were featured first on TV's *The Astronut Show* (1965, synd.); Voices—Dayton Allen (Astronut), Bob McFadden (Oscar).

400 *Brotherly Love* (March 6, 1936; b&w)
Dir: Dave Fleischer; Max Fleischer; Popeye the Sailor, Olive Oyl.

401 *Buccaneer Bunny* (May 8, 1948)
Dir: Friz Freleng; Warner Bros.; Looney Tune: Bugs Bunny, Yosemite Sam; Pirate Sam chases Bugs on board his ship; Bugs and Sam's second teaming, following 1945's *Hare Trigger*; Voices—Mel Blanc.

402 *Buckaroo Bugs* (August 26, 1944)
Dir: Bob Clampett; Warner Bros.; Looney Tune: Bugs Bunny; Bugs heckles a stupid cowboy named Red Hot Ryder; Voices—Mel Blanc.

Buddy (series) **see** *Buddy's Day Out* (1933)

403 *Buddy's Bearcats* (June 23, 1934; b&w)
Dir: Jack King; Warner Bros.; Looney Tune: Buddy; Baseball short with Buddy's team playing the Battling Bruisers; King's directorial debut. The former Disney animator directed 20 WB shorts (1934–36) before returning to Disney, where he would launch the "Donald Duck" series (see *Modern Inventions*); Voice—Jack Carr (Buddy).

404 *Buddy's Day Out* (September 9, 1933; b&w)
Dir: Tom Palmer; Warner Bros.; Looney Tune: Buddy; The first of 23 shorts (1933–35) starring Buddy, a bland replacement for Warner's first cartoon star, Bosko; The first WB cartoon made without producer-directors Hugh Harman and Rudolf Ising (who took Bosko with them to MGM); Voice—Jack Carr (Buddy).

405 *The Bug Parade* (October 11, 1941)
Dir: Tex Avery; Warner Bros.; Merrie Melodie; Gag-reel focusing on the insect world.

Bugs Bunny (series) **see** *A Wild Hare* (1940)

406 *Bugs Bunny and the Three Bears* (February 26, 1944)
Dir: Chuck Jones; Warner Bros.; Merrie Melodie: Bugs Bunny, The Three Bears (debut); Bugs is lured to the home of the Three Bears; The disfunctional bear family would later appear in four very funny shorts of their own (1948–51), see *What's Bruin', Bruin?*; Voices—Mel Blanc (Bugs/Papa Bear), Bea Benaderet (Mama Bear), Stan Freberg (Junior Bear).

407 *Bugs Bunny Gets the Boid* (July 11, 1942)
Dir: Bob Clampett; Warner Bros.; Merrie Melodie: Bugs Bunny, Beaky Buzzard (debut); Bugs outsmarts a dimwitted, Mortimer Snerd–like buzzard; Beaky appeared in four shorts (1942–50); Voices—Mel Blanc (Bugs), Kent Rogers (Beaky).

408 *Bugs Bunny Nips the Nips* (April 22, 1944)
Dir: Friz Freleng; Warner Bros.; Merrie Melodie: Bugs Bunny; Wartime short finds Bugs stranded on an island inhabited by Japanese troops; Rarely shown on TV due to the Japanese stereotypes; Voices—Mel Blanc.

409 *Bugs Bunny Rides Again* (June 12, 1948)
Dir: Friz Freleng; Warner Bros.; Merrie Melodie: Bugs Bunny, Yosemite Sam; Western spoof; Voices—Mel Blanc.

410 *Bugs in Love* (October 1, 1932; b&w)
Dir: Burt Gillett; Walt Disney; Silly Symphony; Two romancing ladybugs are threatened by a hungry crow.

411 *Building a Building* (January 7, 1933; b&w) †
Dir: David Hand; Walt Disney; Mickey Mouse; Oscar nominee.

412 *The Bulleteers* (March 26, 1942)
Dir: Dave Fleischer; Max Fleischer; Superman.

413 *Bully for Bugs* (August 8, 1953)
Dir: Chuck Jones; Warner Bros.; Looney Tune: Bugs Bunny; Bugs fights a ferocious bull in this classic Jones short; Highlight—Bugs' final, Rube Goldberg-esque assault on the bull; Voices—Mel Blanc.

414 *Bumble Boogie* (May 27, 1948; 3 mins)
Dir: Jack Kinney; Walt Disney; Terrific animation (of a bee menaced by piano keys) illustrates this jazzy takeoff on Rimsky-Korsakov's "Flight of the Bumblebee," performed by Freddy Martin's Orchestra with Jack Fina on piano; Part of the feature *Melody Time*; Rereleased with *Trees* (as *Contrasts in Rhythm*) March 11, 1955; Note: Martin (1907–83) was known as the "Concerto King" during the Big-Band era for his popular adaptions of classical music.

415 *Bunny Hugged* (March 10, 1951)
Dir: Chuck Jones; Warner Bros.; Merrie Melodie: Bugs Bunny; Good wrestling spoof with Bugs taking on "The Crusher"; Voices—Mel Blanc.

416 *The Busy Beavers* (June 22, 1931; b&w)
Dir: Wilfred Jackson; Walt Disney; Silly Symphony; Beavers construct a dam to a musical beat.

417 *Butterscotch and Soda* (July 6, 1948)
Dir: Bill Tytla; Paramount/Famous; Noveltoon, with Little Audrey; The first cartoon appearance of Little Audrey, the little girl (and comic book character) whom Famous acquired after losing the rights to "Little Lulu." Audrey appeared in 15 shorts (1948–58); Voice—Mae Questel (Little Audrey); Note: Questel was also the voice of Betty Boop, Olive Oyl, Little Lulu, and others.

Buzzy the Crow (series) **see** *Stupidstitious Cat* (1947)

418 *Caballero Droopy* (September 27, 1952)
Dir: Dick Lundy; MGM; Droopy; The first "Droopy" not directed by Tex Avery and the MGM debut of former Disney and Lantz director Lundy, who would helm a new series of "Barney Bear" shorts (10, 1952–54) for the studio.

419 *The Cactus Kid* (April 11, 1930; b&w)
Producer-Director: Walt Disney; Mickey Mouse, Minnie Mouse, Pegleg Pete.

420 *The Cagey Canary* (November 22, 1941)
Dir: Tex Avery, Bob Clampett; Warner Bros.; Merrie Melodie; Cat vs. canary; Clampett finished the film following Avery's departure from the studio.

421 *The Calico Dragon* (March 30, 1935) †
Dir: Rudolf Ising; MGM; Happy Harmony; Oscar nominee (MGM's first).

422 *Canhead* (1996) †
Producer-Director: Timothy Hittle; Oscar nominee; Clay animated short.

423 *Canine Caddy* (May 30, 1941)
Dir: Clyde Geronimi; Walt Disney; Mickey Mouse, Pluto.

424 *Canine Casanova* (July 27, 1945)
Dir: Charles Nichols; Walt Disney; Pluto, Fifi; Pluto rescues Fifi from the dog pound.

425 *Canine Patrol* (December 7, 1945)
Dir: Charles Nichols; Walt Disney; Pluto; Pluto encounters a baby turtle on the beach.

426 *Canned Feud* (February 3, 1951)
Dir: Friz Freleng; Warner Bros.; Looney Tune: Sylvester; Superior Freleng short deals with Sylvester's frantic attempts to obtain a can opener; Voices — Mel Blanc.

427 *Canvas Back Duck* (December 25, 1953)
Dir: Jack Hannah; Walt Disney; Donald Duck, Huey, Dewey and Louie; Donald fights in a boxing match against "Pee Wee" Pete; Voice — Clarence Nash (Donald).

The Captain and the Kids (series) **see** *Cleaning House* (1938)

428 *The Captain Is Examined for Insurance* (January 8, 1917; b&w)
Producer-Director: Gregory La Cava; International Film Service; The Katzenjammer Kids; First short in the early silent series based on Rudolph Dirks' (1877–1968) popular comic strip about a turn-of-the-century German family, with the Captain, Mamma, the Inspector, and the boys Hans and Fritz. Over 30 shorts were produced (1917–18) by William Randolph Hearst's International Film Service before the series ended due to the anti–German sentiment that existed during World War I; La Cava (1892–1952) was a former cartoonist who later had success in live-action features (he directed the '30s film classics *My Man Godfrey* and *Stage Door*); MGM revived the series (with sound) in 1938 under the title "The Captain and the Kids."

429 *The Captain's Christmas* (December 17, 1938)
Dir: Friz Freleng; MGM; The Captain and the Kids.

430 *Cartoons Ain't Human* (September 3, 1943; b&w)
Dir: Seymour Kneitel; Paramount/Famous; Popeye the Sailor; Famous Studios' last black-and-white cartoon.

431 *The Car of Tomorrow* (September 22, 1951)
Dir: Tex Avery; MGM; A preview of new car models; Best bit — a car with a glass bottom, enabling one to look down and see the pedestrians they've hit.

432 *Carrotblanca* (August 25, 1995)
Dir: Douglas McCarthy; Warner Bros.; Bugs Bunny, Daffy Duck, Yosemite Sam, Tweety, Pepe Le Pew, Sylvester, Foghorn Leghorn; *Casablanca* spoof; Shown in theaters

with *The Amazing Panda Adventure*; Voices—Jeff Bergman (Bugs), Joe Alaskey (Daffy/ Sylvester), Maurice LaMarche (Sam), Greg Burson (Pepe/Foghorn), Bob Bergen (Tweety), Tress MacNeille (Penelope); Written and produced by Timothy Cahill and Julie McNally.

433 *A Car-Tune Portrait* (June 26, 1937)
Dir: Dave Fleischer; Max Fleischer; Color Classic.

434 *Casanova Cat* (January 6, 1951)
Dir: William Hanna, Joseph Barbera; MGM; Tom and Jerry.

435 *The Case of the Stuttering Pig* (October 30, 1937; b&w)
Dir: Frank Tashlin; Warner Bros.; Looney Tune: Porky Pig, Petunia Pig; Horror spoof involving the reading of a will on a stormy night. Eerily filmed; Voices—Mel Blanc.

436 *Casey at the Bat* (August 15, 1946)
Dir: Clyde Geronimi; Walt Disney; Jerry Colonna narrates this amusing tale about the legendary Mudville slugger; Based on the 1888 poem by Ernest Lawrence Thayer; Part of the feature *Make Mine Music*; Rereleased July 16, 1954; Sequel—*Casey Bats Again* (1954); Note: Comedian Colonna (1904–86) later voiced the March Hare in Disney's *Alice in Wonderland* (1951).

437 *Casey Bats Again* (June 18, 1954)
Dir: Jack Kinney; Walt Disney; Sequel to *Casey at the Bat* (1946) has Casey's nine daughters forming their own baseball team; Voice—Jerry Colonna.

Casper the Friendly Ghost (series) **see** *The Friendly Ghost* (1945)

438 *Casper's Spree Under the Sea* (October 13, 1950)
Dir: Bill Tytla; Paramount/Famous; Casper the Friendly Ghost; The first "official" Casper short, following three earlier appearances in the "Noveltoon" series (1945–49); Tytla's only "Casper" short (and one of the last Paramount shorts from the former Disney great).

The Cat (series) **see** *Topcat* (1960)

439 *The Cat and the Canary* (May 13, 1921; b&w)
Producer-Directors: Paul Terry; Fables Studio; Aesop's Fables; The first short in the long-running series of cartoon fables produced by Paul Terry (later of Terrytoons fame) for Fables Studio. Over 340 silent "Fables" were produced (1921–29), then continued by Van Beuren with sound (1928–33), see *Dinner Time*.

440 *The Cat Came Back* (1988) †
Dir: Cordell Barker; National Film Board of Canada; Oscar nominee; Funny short details a man's desperate attempts to get rid of a troublesome cat; Written and animated by Barker; Music by John McCulloch; Voice—Richard Condie; Produced by Barker, Richard Condie and Ches Yetman.

441 *The Cat Concerto* (April 26, 1947) AA
Dir: William Hanna, Joseph Barbera; MGM; Tom and Jerry; Oscar winner; Concert pianist Tom fights with Jerry during a performance. One of the series' best.

442 *Cat Feud* (December 20, 1958)
Dir: Chuck Jones; Warner Bros.; Merrie Melodie: Marc Antony (dog), Pussyfoot (kitten).

443 *Cat Fishin'* (February 22, 1947)
Dir: William Hanna, Joseph Barbera; MGM; Tom and Jerry, Spike; Tom goes fishing, using Jerry as bait.

444 *Cat Happy* (September 1950)
Dir: Connie Rasinski; Terrytoons; Little Roquefort (debut); Terrytoons' cat-and-mouse team—Little Roquefort (mouse) and Percy (cat)—appeared in 19 shorts (1950–55); Voices—Tom Morrison.

445 *The Cat That Hated People* (November 20, 1948)
Dir: Tex Avery; MGM; A cat, tired of being mistreated by people, takes a rocket to the moon; Wild.

446 *The Cat's Meow* (January 25, 1957)
Dir: Tex Avery; MGM; CinemaScope remake of 1950's *Ventriloquist Cat.*

447 *Cat-Tails for Two* (August 29, 1953)
Dir: Robert McKimson; Warner Bros.; Merrie Melodie: Speedy Gonzales (in his first cartoon appearance); For Speedy's official debut see *Speedy Gonzales* (1955).

448 *Catty Cornered* (October 31, 1953)
Dir: Friz Freleng; Warner Bros.; Merrie Melodie: Tweety, Sylvester.

449 *Caviar* (February 23, 1930)
Dir: Paul Terry, Frank Moser; Terrytoons; Terrytoon; The first cartoon released by the Terrytoons studio, formed in 1929 by Paul Terry following his association with "Aesop's Fables." Over 330 shorts (not featuring a major character) were produced in the long-running series (1930–66).

450 *Ceiling Hero* (August 24, 1940)
Dir: Tex Avery; Warner Bros.; Merrie Melodie; Gag-filled look at aviation.

451 *Cellbound* (November 25, 1955)
Dir: Tex Avery, Michael Lah; MGM; A prisoner escapes from jail by hiding in a TV set, which was bought by the warden for his wife; One of Avery's last-released shorts.

452 *The Chain Gang* (October 1930; b&w)
Dir: Burt Gillett; Walt Disney; Mickey Mouse, Pegleg Pete, Pluto (debut); Mickey escapes from a chain gang; The first cartoon appearance of Mickey's ever-curious canine companion, Pluto (who debuts here as one of the bloodhounds tracking Mickey). Pluto, who remained truer to his animal nature than other Disney stars (he never spoke), would go from supporting player to starring in his own series (from 1937). Pluto appeared in 104 shorts (1930–53, '83, '90); Voice—Walt Disney (Mickey).

453 *Charade* (1984) AA
Dir: Jon Minnis; Sheridan College Prod; Oscar winner; Canadian short about a funny game of charades; Written, animated and voiced by Minnis.

454 *Chariots of Fur* (December 21, 1994)
Dir: Chuck Jones; Warner Bros./Chuck Jones Film Prods; Road Runner, Coyote; The first theatrical "Road Runner–Coyote" short since 1966 and the first effort from Chuck Jones Film Productions, which Jones formed in 1993 with his daughter Linda Jones Clough to produce new cartoons in the classic Warner Bros. tradition; Other new titles include *Another Froggy Evening* (1995) and *Superior Duck* (1995); Released in theaters with the feature *Richie Rich*; Note: The Jones team won an Emmy in 1996 for an animated production of *Peter and the Wolf.*

Charlie Dog (series) **see** *Little Orphan Airedale* (1947)

455 *The Charm Bracelet* (September 1, 1939; b&w)
Columbia/Screen Gems; Phantasy, with Scrappy; The first short in Columbia's "Phantasies" series (56 shorts, 1939–47), which featured a variety of characters and stories.

456 *Cheese Nappers* (July 4, 1938; b&w)
Dir: Alex Lovy; Walter Lantz; Baby Face Mouse (debut); The little mouse would star in 5 shorts (1938).

457 *Chess-Nuts* (May 13, 1932; b&w)
Dir: Dave Fleischer; Max Fleischer; Talkartoon, with Bimbo, Betty Boop; A chess board king kidnaps Betty; Voice—Mae Questel (Betty).

458 *Chicken à la King* (April 16, 1937)
Dir: Dave Fleischer; Max Fleischer; Color Classic.

459 *The Chicken from Outer Space* (1995) †
Dir: John R. Dilworth; Cartoons, Inc/Cartoon Network Prod; Oscar nominee.

460 *Chicken Little* (December 17, 1943)
Dir: Clyde Geronimi; Walt Disney. Wartime Disney short about a fox who uses psychology to ensnare a group of chickens.

461 *Chilly Willy* (December 21, 1953)
Dir: Paul J. Smith; Walter Lantz; Chilly Willy; The first of 49 shorts (1953–72) starring the little penguin, followed the next year by Tex Avery's superior *I'm Cold*, which really launched the series.

462 *The China Shop* (January 13, 1934)
Dir: Wilfred Jackson; Walt Disney; Silly Symphony; China figurines come to life in the after hours.

463 *Chip an' Dale* (November 28, 1947) †
Dir: Jack Hannah; Walt Disney; Donald Duck, Chip n' Dale (in their third short); Oscar nominee; Donald cuts down the chipmunks' home for firewood; The first of 16 Donald–Chip 'n' Dale teamings (1947–56); Voice—Clarence Nash (Donald).

Chip 'n' Dale (series) **see** *Private Pluto* (1943)

464 *Chips Ahoy* (February 24, 1956)
Dir: Jack Kinney; Walt Disney; Donald Duck, Chip 'n' Dale; The chipmunks take

Donald's model boat out on the water; Kinney's last Disney short, and Donald's last teaming with Chip 'n' Dale; Voice—Clarence Nash (Donald).

465 *A Christmas Carol* (1972; 21 mins) AA
Producer-Director: Richard Williams; Oscar winner; Miserly Scrooge learns the meaning of Christmas in this handsomely-drawn adaption of the 1843 novella by Charles Dickens; Originally an ABC TV special (it aired December 21, 1971); Other cartoon versions of the holiday classic include *Mickey's Christmas Carol* (1983) and the UPA TV special *Mr. Magoo's Christmas Carol* (1962); Master Animator—Ken Harris; Music by Tristram Cary; Voices—Sir Michael Redgrave (Narrator), Alastair Sim (Scrooge), Melvyn Hayes (Bob Cratchit), Joan Sims (Mrs. Cratchit), Alexander Williams (Tiny Tim), Michael Hordern (Marley's Ghost), Paul Whitsun-Jones (Ragpicker/Fezziwig), David Tate (Scrooge's Nephew/Charity Man), Diana Quick (Christmas Past), Felix Felton (Christmas Present), Annie West (Christmas Yet to Come), Mary Ellen Ray (Mrs. Dilber); Note: Sim (1900–76) had previously played Scrooge in the acclaimed 1951 live-action feature version; Executive Producer—Chuck Jones.

466 *Christmas Comes but Once a Year* (December 4, 1936)
Dir: Dave Fleischer; Max Fleischer; Color Classic, with Grampy; Inventor Grampy cheers up a group of unhappy orphans on Christmas day by crafting toys out of a variety of household objects.

467 *Christmas Cracker* (1963; 9 mins) †
Dir: Gerald Potterton, Jeff Hale, Norman McLaren, Grant Munro; National Film Board of Canada; Oscar nominee; Three animated film pieces on a Christmas theme; Produced by Tom Daly.

468 *Christopher Crumpet* (June 25, 1953) †
Dir: Robert Cannon; UPA; Jolly Frolics (last in the series); Oscar nominee; Followed by *Christopher Crumpet's Playmate* (1955).

469 *Christopher Crumpet's Playmate* (September 8, 1955)
Dir: Robert Cannon; UPA; Sequel to *Christopher Crumpet* (1953).

470 *The Chump Champ* (November 4, 1950)
Dir: Tex Avery; MGM; Droopy, Spike; Droopy and Spike compete in various sporting events, including swimming, baseball and skeet shooting.

471 *Cinderella Meets Fella* (July 23, 1938)
Dir: Tex Avery; Warner Bros.; Merrie Melodie: Egghead; Zany Cinderella spoof; Voice—Cliff Nazarro (Egghead).

472 *The Circus Comes to Clown* (December 26, 1947)
Dir: Isadore Sparber; Paramount/Famous; Screen Song; The first "Screen Song" from Famous Studios, which produced 38 of them (1947–51). The "follow the bouncing ball" series originated at Fleischers'.

Claude Cat (series) **see** *Mouse Wreckers* (1949)

Claude Cat and Frisky Puppy (series) **see** *Two's a Crowd* (1950)

473 *Claws for Alarm* (May 22, 1954)
Dir: Chuck Jones; Warner Bros.; Merrie Melodie: Porky Pig, Sylvester; Porky and Sylvester spend the night at a haunted hotel. As in Jones' *Scaredy Cat* (1948), Porky is oblivious to the dangers Sylvester sees all around them; Voices—Mel Blanc.

474 *Clay (or the Origin of the Species)* (1964) †
Producer-Director: Eliot Noyes, Jr.; Harvard University; Oscar nominee; Clay-animated chronicle of evolution; The first effort from then 22-year-old Noyes.

475 *Cleaning House* (February 19, 1938; b&w)
Dir: Robert Allen; MGM; The Captain and the Kids (series debut); Short-lived series (15 shorts, 1938–39) based on Rudolph Dirks' "Katzenjammer Kids" comic-strip, which had appeared earlier in silent cartoons (1917–18) from the Hearst studio; Warner Bros. director Friz Freleng was lured to MGM to work on this series (frustrated creatively, he quickly returned to WB in 1939); Voice—Billy Bletcher (Captain).

Clint Clobber (series) **see** *Clint Clobber's Cat* (1957)

476 *Clint Clobber's Cat* (July, 1957)
Dir: Connie Rasinski; Terrytoons; Clint Clobber; The first of seven shorts (1957–59) starring gruff apartment super DeWitt Clinton Clobber.

477 *Clock Cleaners* (October 15, 1937)
Dir: Ben Sharpsteen; Walt Disney; Mickey Mouse, Donald Duck, Goofy; Delightful Disney classic has the trio cleaning a clock atop a high building.

478 *The Clock Watcher* (January 26, 1945)
Dir: Jack King; Walt Disney; Donald Duck; Donald is a giftwrapper in a department store; Voice—Clarence Nash (Donald).

479 *A Close Shave* (November 16, 1995; 30 mins) AA
Dir: Nick Park; Aardman Animations; Wallace and Gromit; Oscar winner; The third "W & G" short finds the pair involved with a lovely wool shop owner and her sheep-stealing dog. Delightful; Produced on a tighter schedule than Park's previous shorts (18 months) and on a larger budget (twice the amount of his last short); Premiered at the 1995 London Film Festival; Written by Park and Bob Baker; Music by Julian Nott; Voices—Peter Sallis (Wallace), Anne Reid (Wendolene Ramsbottom); Produced by Michael Rose and Carla Shelley.

480 *Closed Mondays* (1974) AA
Producer-Directors: Will Vinton, Bob Gardiner; Lighthouse Prods; Oscar winner; Claymation short about a drunk who stumbles into an art gallery where the paintings come to life; Vinton's first clay-animated short.

481 *Club Sandwich* (January 25, 1931; b&w)
Dir: Paul Terry, Frank Moser; Terrytoons; Farmer Al Falfa (sound debut); Paul Terry brought back his white-bearded farmer, who first appeared in silent shorts (from 1916), in a new sound series (44 shorts, 1931–37) for Terrytoons; Aka *Dancing Mice*.

482 *Coal Black and De Sebben Dwarfs* (January 16, 1943)
Dir: Bob Clampett; Warner Bros.; Merrie Melodie; Jazzy, sexy, all-black version of

Snow White tells the story of So White and her Prince Chawmin'. One of the all-time great Warner Bros. cartoons; Rarely shown on TV because of its racial characterizations; Voices—Vivian Dandridge (So White), Ruby Dandridge (Mammy), Zoot Wilson (Prince Chawmin'); Note: Vivian and Ruby are the sister and mother (respectively) of film star Dorothy Dandridge.

483 *Cobweb Hotel* (May 15, 1936)
Dir: Dave Fleischer; Max Fleischer; Color Classic; A spider invites honeymooning flies into his sinister hotel.

484 *Cock o' the Walk* (November 30, 1935)
Dir: Ben Sharpsteen; Walt Disney; Silly Symphony; Classic short featuring terrific send-ups of lavish Hollywood dance numbers.

485 *Cockaboody* (1972)
Dir: John Hubley; Hubley Studio.

486 *Cock-a-Doodle Dog* (February 10, 1951)
Dir: Tex Avery; MGM; Spike; An irritating rooster drives Spike crazy with its crowing.

Colonel Heeza Liar (series) **see** *Colonel Heeza Liar in Africa* (1914)

487 *Colonel Heeza Liar in Africa* (January 14, 1914; b&w)
Producer-Director: John R. Bray; Colonel Heeza Liar; Debut short in the early cartoon series (Bray's first) about a bald, pint-sized army colonel and teller of tall tales. The character, created by Bray, was inspired by both Baron Münchausen and Teddy Roosevelt (whose own adventures in Africa were well known). The Colonel appeared in some 60 silent shorts (1914–24); Bray's second cartoon, following *The Dachshund and the Sausage* (1913); Walter Lantz was an animator on this series (from 1921).

Color Classics (series) **see** *Poor Cinderella* (1934)

Color Rhapsodies (series) **see** *Holiday Land* (1934)

488 *Comicalamities* (April 1, 1928; b&w)
Producer-Director: Pat Sullivan; Felix the Cat; One of Felix's best shorts has the famous feline cleverly taking the cartoon's drawing into his own hands; Animated by Otto Messmer.

ComiColor (series) **see** *Jack and the Beanstalk* (1933)

489 *Confidence* (July 31, 1933; b&w)
Dir: Walter Lantz, William C. Nolan; Walter Lantz; Oswald the Rabbit; Morale-boosting short in which the ghost of the Depression encircles the world and Oswald looks to President Roosevelt to cure the country's woes; Part live action.

490 *Conrad the Sailor* (February 28, 1942)
Dir: Chuck Jones; Warner Bros.; Merrie Melodie: Daffy Duck, Conrad Cat.

491 *The Coo Coo Nut Grove* (November 28, 1936)
Dir: Friz Freleng; Warner Bros.; Merrie Melodie; Caricatures of such Hollywood stars as Katherine Hepburn, Mae West, Harpo Marx, and Edward G. Robinson highlight this enjoyable short.

492 *The Cookie Carnival* (May 25, 1935)
Dir: Ben Sharpsteen; Walt Disney; Silly Symphony; A lovely young cookie is elected queen of Cookie Land; Voice—Pinto Colvig.

493 *Cool Cat* (October 14, 1967)
Dir: Alex Lovy; Warner Bros.; Looney Tune: Cool Cat (debut); The hipster tiger, Cool Cat (one of Warner Bros.' last cartoon characters) appeared in six shorts (1967–69); Voices—Larry Storch (Cool Cat), The Clingers (theme singers); Note: Storch played Corp. Agarn on TV's *F-Troop* (1965–67).

494 *A Corny Concerto* (September 18, 1943)
Dir: Bob Clampett; Warner Bros.; Merrie Melodie: Bugs Bunny, Porky Pig, Elmer Fudd; Wonderful spoof of Disney's *Fantasia* featuring two Strauss waltzes—"A Tale of the Vienna Woods" and "The Blue Danube"; Elmer introduces the segments; Musical direction by Carl Stalling; Voice—Arthur Q. Bryan (Elmer).

495 *The Counterfeit Cat* (December 24, 1949)
Dir: Tex Avery; MGM; Spike; In order to get closer to a canary, a cat poses as a dog (by borrowing the top of a real dog's head!).

496 *The Country Cousin* (October 31, 1936) AA
Dir: David Hand; Walt Disney; Silly Symphony; Oscar winner; A country mouse visits his cousin in the big city.

497 *The Cow* (1989; 10 mins) †
Producer-Director: Alexander Petrov; The "Pilot" Co-op Animated Film Studio with VPTO Videofilm; Oscar nominee.

498 *A Cowboy Needs a Horse* (November 6, 1956)
Dir: Bill Justice; Walt Disney; A boy dreams that he's a heroic cowboy in this charming short; Title song by Paul Mason Howard and Billy Mills.

499 *Crac* (1981) AA
Producer-Directors: Frédéric Back; Société Radio–Canada; Oscar winner; French Canadian history comes alive through an old rocker housed in a museum of modern art. Excellent short from illustrator Back (b. 1924), who joined the animation unit of Société Radio–Canada in 1968. His other films include *The Man Who Planted Trees* (1987) and *The Mighty River* (1993); Music by Normand Roger.

500 *Cracked Quack* (July 5, 1952)
Dir: Friz Freleng; Warner Bros.; Merrie Melodie: Daffy Duck, Porky Pig; Daffy decides to stay at Porky's house rather than fly south for the winter; Voices—Mel Blanc.

501 *The Crackpot Quail* (February 15, 1941)
Dir: Tex Avery; Warner Bros.; Merrie Melodie; A dumb dog goes quail hunting in this funny Avery short.

502 *Crazy Cruise* (March 14, 1942)
Dir: Tex Avery, Bob Clampett; Warner Bros.; Merrie Melodie: Bugs Bunny (cameo); Travelogue spoof; Avery's last WB short (it was completed by Clampett).

503 *Crazy for Daisy* (March 24, 1950)
Dir: Jack Hannah; Walt Disney; Donald Duck, Chip 'n' Dale, Daisy Duck; Includes reused animation (of a band concert, children playing) from *Casey at the Bat* (1946) and cameos by Goofy, Mickey and Minnie Mouse.

504 *Crazy House* (September 23, 1940)
Producer-Director: Walter Lantz; Andy Panda; Car trouble forces Andy and his Pop to spend the night in a bizarre funhouse.

505 *Crazy Mixed-Up Pup* (February 14, 1955) †
Dir: Tex Avery; Walter Lantz; Oscar nominee; A man and his dog are run over by a car and after receiving medical attention (a confused paramedic mixes up the dog and people plasma) they begin to reverse roles. Hilarious Avery classic, the best of the four shorts he made at the Lantz studio (1954–55); The husband-and-wife team, Maggie and Sam, would appear in three more shorts (1956–57); Voices — Daws Butler (Sam), Grace Stafford (Maggie).

506 *Crazy Town* (March 25, 1932; b&w)
Dir: Dave Fleischer; Max Fleischer; Talkartoon, with Betty Boop, Bimbo.

507 *Crazy with the Heat* (August 1, 1947)
Dir: Bob Carlson; Walt Disney; Donald Duck, Goofy; Donald and Goofy's car conks out in the desert; Voices — Clarence Nash (Donald), Pinto Colvig (Goofy).

508 *The Creation* (1981) †
Producer-Director: Will Vinton; Oscar nominee; Claymation short narrated by James Earl Jones.

509 *Creature Comforts* (1990; 5 mins) AA
Producer-Director: Nick Park; Aardman Animations; Oscar winner; Zoo animals are interviewed about their living conditions. Hilarious clay-animated short — part of Aardman's "Lip Sync" series — from Park, director of the acclaimed "Wallace & Gromit" series; Won the Special Jury Prize at the 1991 Annecy Festival (France); Park's *A Grand Day Out* was Oscar-nominated that same year.

510 *The Critic* (1963; 4 mins) AA
Dir: Ernest Pintoff; Pintoff-Crossbow Prods; Oscar winner; Hilarious short written and voiced by Mel Brooks, whose offscreen narrator comments on the abstract images he sees; Animator Pintoff (*Flebus, The Violinist*) went on to direct live-action features (from 1965).

511 *Cross-Country Detours* (March 16, 1940)
Dir: Tex Avery; Warner Bros.; Merrie Melodie; Travelogue spoof.

512 *Crowing Pains* (July 12, 1947)
Dir: Robert McKimson; Warner Bros.; Looney Tune: Foghorn Leghorn (in his second cartoon appearance), Sylvester, Henery Hawk.

513 *The Crunch Bird* (1971) AA
Prod: Ted Petok; Maxwell-Petok-Petrovich Prods; Oscar winner.

Cubby the Bear (series) **see** *Opening Night* (1933)

514 *The Cuckoo Clock* (June 10, 1950)
Dir: Tex Avery; MGM; A cat tries to kill a crazy cuckoo. One of Avery's best.

515 *Cue Ball Cat* (November 25, 1950)
Dir: William Hanna, Joseph Barbera; MGM; Tom and Jerry.

516 *Cured Duck* (October 26, 1945)
Dir: Jack King; Walt Disney; Donald Duck, Daisy Duck; Donald tries to cure his bad temper; Voice—Clarence Nash (Donald).

517 *Curtain Razor* (May 21, 1949)
Dir: Friz Freleng; Warner Bros.; Looney Tune: Porky Pig; Talent scout Porky auditions a variety of acts; Voices—Mel Blanc.

518 *The Dachshund and the Sausage* (June 12, 1913; b&w)
Producer-Director: John R. Bray; Aka *The Artist's Dream*; A drawing of a dog comes to life after the artist (Bray) leaves the room; The first animated short from cartoonist/illustrator John R(andolph) Bray (1879–1978), who would go on to produce, through his studio, the animated series "Colonel Heeza Liar," "Dinky Doodle," among others. He also pioneered the use of printed backgrounds which saved the work of redrawing them.

519 *Daffy Dilly* (October 21, 1948)
Dir: Chuck Jones; Warner Bros.; Merrie Melodie: Daffy Duck.

520 *The Daffy Doc* (November 26, 1938; b&w)
Dir: Bob Clampett; Warner Bros.; Looney Tune: Daffy Duck, Porky Pig; Daffy needs a patient to operate on and finds one when Porky walks by the hospital. Prime example of early Daffy, when the duck was at his daffiest; Voices—Mel Blanc.

521 *Daffy Doodles* (April 16, 1946)
Dir: Robert McKimson; Warner Bros.; Looney Tune: Daffy Duck, Porky Pig; Daffy is a serial mustache-painter (he paints mustaches on ads and people's faces) and Porky is the cop out to catch him; The directorial debut of McKimson (1910–77), a Warner animator since 1932. He would direct 175 WB shorts (1946–69), creating Foghorn Leghorn, the Tasmanian Devil and such cartoon classics as *Walky Talky Hawky* (1946) and *Gorilla My Dreams* (1948); Voices—Mel Blanc.

Daffy Duck (series) **see** *Porky's Duck Hunt* (1937)

522 *Daffy Duck and Egghead* (January 1, 1938)
Dir: Tex Avery; Warner Bros.; Merrie Melodie: Daffy Duck, Egghead; Daffy makes his second, very looney appearance (following 1937's *Porky's Duck Hunt*) taunting hunter Egghead (who would later evolve into Elmer Fudd); Daffy sings the Looney Tunes signature theme "The Merry-Go-Round Broke Down" (written by Dave Franklin and Cliff Friend); Voices—Mel Blanc (Daffy), Cliff Nazaro (Egghead).

523 *Daffy Duck and the Dinosaur* (April 22, 1939)
Dir: Chuck Jones; Warner Bros.; Merrie Melodie: Daffy Duck; Daffy is hunted by a Jack Benny–like caveman and his dinosaur; Voices—Mel Blanc.

524 *Daffy Duck Hunt* (March 26, 1949)
Dir: Robert McKimson; Warner Bros.; Looney Tune: Daffy Duck, Porky Pig.

525 *Daffy Duck in Hollywood* (December 3, 1938)
Dir: Tex Avery; Warner Bros.; Merrie Melodie: Daffy Duck; Daffy wreaks havoc in a movie studio; Voices—Mel Blanc.

526 *Daffy Duck Slept Here* (March 6, 1948)
Dir: Robert McKimson; Warner Bros.; Merrie Melodie: Daffy Duck, Porky Pig; Porky is forced to share a hotel room with Daffy; Voices—Mel Blanc.

527 *The Daffy Duckeroo* (October 24, 1942; b&w)
Dir: Norman McCabe; Warner Bros.; Looney Tune: Daffy Duck; Daffy tangles with an Indian squaw's jealous boyfriend. One of McCabe's best; Voices—Mel Blanc.

528 *Daffy the Commando* (November 28, 1943)
Dir: Friz Freleng; Warner Bros.; Looney Tune: Daffy Duck; Good wartime short has Daffy invading a Nazi foxhole and includes a closing appearance by Hitler himself; Voices—Mel Blanc.

529 *Daffy's Southern Exposure* (May 2, 1942; b&w)
Dir: Norman McCabe; Warner Bros.; Looney Tune: Daffy Duck; Daffy, wracked with hunger during a cold winter, comes to the home of a wolf (who's also quite hungry); Voices—Mel Blanc.

Daisy Duck (series) **see** *Don Donald* (1937)

530 *The Dance Contest* (November 23, 1934; b&w)
Dir: Dave Fleischer; Max Fleischer; Popeye the Sailor, Olive Oyl, Bluto, Wimpy; Popeye outdances Bluto in a contest judged by Wimpy; Voices—Jack Mercer (Popeye), Mae Questel (Olive).

531 *Dance of the Hours* (November 13, 1940; 12 mins)
Dir: T. Hee, Norm Ferguson; Walt Disney; Hilarious ballet parody featuring dancing ostriches, hippos, elephants and alligators, set to Amilcare Ponchielli's (1834–86) ballet from his 1876 opera *La Gioconda*; The pas de deux between Hyacinth Hippo and Ben Ali Gator is a classic; Part of the feature *Fantasia*; Animation Supervisor—Norm Ferguson; Leopold Stokowski conducts the Philadelphia Orchestra.

532 *Dancing on the Moon* (July 12, 1935)
Dir: Dave Fleischer; Max Fleischer; Color Classic; Honeymooning couples take a trip to the moon for a night of dancing and romance; Title song by Charlie Tobias and Murray Mencher.

533 *The Dandy Lion* (September 20, 1940)
Dir: Dave Fleischer; Max Fleischer; Animated Antics (series debut); One of the last

series from the Fleischer Studios, "Animated Antics" served as a tryout for various characters (some from the Fleischers' 1939 feature *Gulliver's Travels*). Twelve were produced (1940–41).

534 *Dangerous Dan McFoo* (July 15, 1939)
Dir: Tex Avery; Warner Bros.; Merrie Melodie; Funny western parody; Voice—Arthur Q. Bryan (Dan).

535 *Daredevil Droopy* (March 31, 1951)
Dir: Tex Avery; MGM; Droopy, Spike; Droopy and Spike compete for a job as a circus daredevil; Voice—Bill Thompson (Droopy).

536 *A Date with Duke* (October 31, 1947)
Producer-Director: George Pal; Puppetoon; Duke Ellington performs his "Perfume Suite" with the aid of puppet-animated perfume bottles; Part live action.

537 *A Day at the Zoo* (March 11, 1939)
Dir: Tex Avery; Warner Bros.; Merrie Melodie: Egghead; Gag-filled short spotlighting various zoo animals.

538 *Dedalo* (*Daedalus*) (1976) †
Producer-Director: Manfredo Manfredi; Oscar nominee; Also an award winner at the Ottawa Festival, 1976.

539 *Deduce, You Say* (September 29, 1956)
Dir: Chuck Jones; Warner Bros.; Looney Tune: Daffy Duck, Porky Pig; Daffy is Dorlock Homes and Porky is Watkins in this clever parody; Voices—Mel Blanc.

540 *Deputy Droopy* (October 28, 1955)
Dir: Tex Avery, Michael Lah; MGM; Droopy; Two inept thieves try to "quietly" rob a jail safe guarded by Droopy; Very funny; One of Avery's last MGM shorts (Lah would take over the "Droopy" series).

541 *Der Fuehrer's Face* (January 1, 1943) AA
Dir: Jack Kinney; Walt Disney; Donald Duck; Oscar winner; Donald's nightmare has him working for the Nazis. Great, rarely-shown wartime short commissioned by the U.S. Treasury Department; Working title—*Donald Duck in Nutzi Land*; Hit title song by Oliver Wallace (*Dumbo*); Voice—Clarence Nash (Donald).

542 *Designs on Jerry* (September 2, 1955)
Dir: William Hanna, Joseph Barbera; MGM; Tom and Jerry; Tom plans an elaborate mousetrap for Jerry.

543 *Destruction, Inc.* (December 25, 1942)
Dir: Isadore Sparber; Paramount/Famous; Superman; A ring of saboteurs threaten the Metropolis Munition Plant; Voices—Bud Collyer (Superman), Joan Alexander (Lois Lane).

544 *Detouring America* (August 26, 1939) †
Dir: Tex Avery; Warner Bros.; Merrie Melodie; Oscar nominee; Comical tour of the U.S.

545 *Devil May Hare* (June 19, 1954)
Dir: Robert McKimson; Warner Bros.; Looney Tune: Bugs Bunny, Tasmanian Devil (debut); McKimson's whirly, growling Tasmanian Devil appeared in five shorts (1954–64), four of which co-starred Bugs.

546 *Dig That Dog* (April 12, 1954)
Dir: Ray Patterson; Walter Lantz.

Dinky Doodle (series) **see** *The Magic Lamp* (1924)

Dinky Duck (series) **see** *The Orphan Duck* (1939)

547 *Dinner Time* (December 17, 1928–copyright date; b&w)
Dir: Paul Terry; Van Beuren; Aesop's Fables; The first sound "Fable" and the first short produced by Van Beuren, which took over Terry's Fables Studio. In 1929, Terry left Van Beuren to form Terrytoons and "Fables" continued under John Foster, Mannie Davis and Harry Bailey. One hundred sound "Fables" were produced (1928–33).

548 *Dinosaur* (1980; 13 mins)
Producer-Director: Will Vinton; A boy's class project comes to life via Claymation dinosaurs; Animated by Barry Bruce, Don Merkt, Matt Wuerker and Joan C. Gratz (Oscar winner for 1992's *Mona Lisa Descending a Staircase*); Written by Susan Shadburne; Voice—Michele Mariana.

549 *Dippy Diplomat* (August 27, 1945)
Dir: James Culhane; Walter Lantz; Woody Woodpecker, Wally Walrus; Woody ruins a barbecue Wally is preparing for an ambassador (by the name of Ivan Awfulitch); Voice—Ben Hardaway (Woody).

550 *The Discontented Canary* (September 1, 1934)
Dir: Rudolf Ising; MGM; Happy Harmony; Debut of the "Happy Harmonies" series (30 shorts, 1934–38), which was MGM's first, produced in association with Hugh Harman and Rudolf Ising (the team who also launched Warner Bros.' cartoon studio with their "Looney Tunes" and "Merrie Melodies"). "Harmonies" was a series of musical fantasies and fables similar to Disney's "Silly Symphonies."

551 *Dixieland Droopy* (December 4, 1954)
Dir: Tex Avery; MGM; Droopy; Highly-entertaining Avery short stars Droopy as John Pettybone, a little pooch with a love for Dixieland music; Voice—Bill Thompson (Droopy).

552 *The Dizzy Acrobat* (May 31, 1943) †
Dir: Alex Lovy; Walter Lantz; Woody Woodpecker; Oscar nominee.

553 *Dizzy Dishes* (August 9, 1930; b&w)
Dir: Dave Fleischer; Max Fleischer; Talkartoon, with Bimbo, Betty Boop (debut, unbilled); The very first cartoon appearance of Betty Boop (although at this early stage she is unnamed—and half-dog!). Betty, probably the sexiest cartoon star of all time (only Tex Avery's Showgirl and Jessica Rabbit come close), was created by animator Grim Natwick (1890–1990) and partly modeled after actress-singer Helen Kane (who later sued). Betty's short skirt and sexy-but-sweet personality helped her become the Fleischers'

number one star. However, much of her appeal was lost when the Production Code in 1934 forced the studio to lengthen her skirt and stifle her sexiness. Betty appeared in 106 shorts (1930–39) and was voiced for most of the series by Mae Questel (1908–98).

554 *Dizzy Red Riding Hood* (December 12, 1931)
Dir: Dave Fleischer; Max Fleischer; Talkartoon, with Betty Boop, Bimbo; Classic Fleischer short starring Betty as a very sexy Red; Voice—Mae Questel (Betty).

Doc (series) **see** *Mouse Trapped* (1959)

555 *Doctor De Soto* (1984) †
Dir: Michael Sporn; Michael Sporn Animation, Inc; Oscar nominee; Based on a story by William Steig; Produced by Sporn and Morton Schindel.

556 *Dr. Ha Ha Ha* (February 1966)
Dir: Ralph Bakshi; Terrytoons; James Hound (debut); Based on the popular James Bond film character, canine secret agent James Hound appeared in 17 shorts (1966–67); Bakshi's second theatrical Terrytoons series, following "Sad Cat"; Voice—Dayton Allen (James Hound).

557 *Dr. Jekyll and Mr. Mouse* (June 14, 1947) †
Dir: William Hanna, Joseph Barbera; MGM; Tom and Jerry; Oscar nominee.

558 *Dog, Cat and Canary* (January 5, 1945) †
Dir: Howard Swift; Columbia/Screen Gems; Color Rhapsody, with Flippy (debut); Oscar nominee; The yellow canary Flippy (and his cat nemisis, Flop) appeared in five shorts (1945–47).

559 *Dog Trouble* (April 18, 1942)
Dir: William Hanna, Joseph Barbera; MGM; Tom and Jerry, Spike and Tyke, Mammy; Spike and Tyke's debut. The father-and-son dog duo appeared in 20 "T & J" shorts (1942–57) and in two of their own (1957).

560 *The Dogfather* (June 27, 1974)
DePatie-Freleng; The Dogfather; The first in a series of 17 shorts (1974–76) parodying the 1972 gangster film *The Godfather*; Voices—Bob Holt (The Dogfather), Daws Butler (Louie/Pugg).

561 *Doggone Tired* (July 30, 1949)
Dir: Tex Avery; MGM; A rabbit tries to keep a hunting dog awake all night so that he will be too tired for the next morning's hunt.

562 *The Dognapper* (November 17, 1934; b&w)
Dir: David Hand; Walt Disney; Mickey Mouse, Donald Duck; Police officers Mickey and Donald track down dognapper Pegleg Pete; Voices—Walt Disney (Mickey), Clarence Nash (Donald).

563 *Don Donald* (January 9, 1937)
Dir: Ben Sharpsteen; Walt Disney; Donald Duck, Daisy Duck (debut); Donald takes

Daisy joyriding through Mexico; The first cartoon appearance of Donald's girlfriend Daisy, who would appear with him in over ten shorts; Voice—Clarence Nash (Donald).

564 *Donald and the Wheel* (June 21, 1961; 17 mins)
Dir: Hamilton Luske; Walt Disney; Donald Duck (in one of his last shorts); A look at the history of the wheel and its many modern uses; Voices—Clarence Nash (Donald), The Mellomen (featuring Thurl Ravenscroft); Note: Ravenscroft was later the voice of Kelloggs' Tony the Tiger.

Donald Duck (series) **see** *The Wise Little Hen* (1934)

565 *Donald in Mathmagic Land* (June 26, 1959; 27 min) †
Dir: Hamilton Luske; Walt Disney; Donald Duck; Oscar nominee (for Best Documentary Short); Donald guides the viewer through a mysterious land filled with mathematical fun in this educational Disney featurette; Voice—Clarence Nash (Donald), Paul Frees (Narrator).

566 *Donald's Cousin Gus* (May 19, 1939)
Dir: Jack King; Walt Disney; Donald Duck; Donald is visited by his cousin, Gus Goose; Voice—Clarence Nash (Donald).

567 *Donald's Crime* (June 29, 1945) †
Dir: Jack King; Walt Disney; Donald Duck, Huey, Dewey and Louie, Daisy Duck; Oscar nominee; Donald is haunted by guilt after he takes money from his nephews' piggy bank; Voice—Clarence Nash (Donald).

568 *Donald's Dilemma* (July 11, 1947)
Dir: Jack King; Walt Disney; Donald Duck, Daisy Duck; A hit on the head turns Donald into a great crooner; Donald sings "When You Wish Upon a Star"; Voice—Clarence Nash (Donald).

569 *Donald's Double Trouble* (June 28, 1946)
Dir: Jack King; Walt Disney; Donald Duck, Daisy Duck; Donald pays a well-spoken, good-tempered look-alike to help him win back Daisy; Voice—Clarence Nash (Donald).

570 *Donald's Dream Voice* (May 21, 1948)
Dir: Jack King; Walt Disney; Donald Duck, Daisy Duck; Donald improves his voice with voice pills; Voice—Clarence Nash (Donald).

571 *Donald's Lucky Day* (January 13, 1939)
Dir: Jack King; Walt Disney; Donald Duck; Delivery boy Donald is unknowingly given a bomb to deliver—and on Friday the 13th!; Voice—Clarence Nash (Donald).

572 *Donald's Nephews* (April 15, 1938)
Dir: Jack King; Walt Disney; Donald Duck, Huey, Dewey and Louie (in their debut); Donald is paid a visit by his three mischievous nephews; Huey, Dewey and Louie would costar with Donald in over 20 shorts, later teaming with Uncle Scrooge McDuck in *Scrooge McDuck and Money* (1967) and the *DuckTales* TV series (1987–92); Voice—Clarence Nash (Donald).

573 *Donald's Off Day* (December 8, 1944)
    Dir: Jack Hannah; Walt Disney; Donald Duck, Huey, Dewey and Louie; The boys trick Donald into thinking he's dying; The directorial debut of animator-writer Hannah, who would direct 63 Disney shorts (1944–56), specializing in Donald Duck, Chip 'n' Dale and Humphrey Bear. He then moved on to the Walter Lantz studio (23 shorts, 1959–63); Voice—Clarence Nash (Donald Duck).

574 *Donald's Snow Fight* (April 10, 1942)
    Dir: Jack King; Walt Disney; Donald Duck, Huey, Dewey and Louie; A snowball war breaks out between Donald and his nephews; Voice—Clarence Nash (Donald).

575 *Don't Give Up the Sheep* (January 3, 1953)
    Dir: Chuck Jones; Warner Bros.; Looney Tune: Ralph Wolf and Sam Sheepdog (in their debut); The sheep stealer and sheep protector who, later on, would punch in for work together, appeared in seven shorts (1953–63); Voices—Mel Blanc.

576 *Don't Look Now* (November 7, 1936)
    Dir: Tex Avery; Warner Bros.; Merrie Melodie; A cupid and a devil tamper with the romance of two bears; Voice—Tommy Bond (Devil); Note: Bond played Butch (1932–40) in the "Our Gang" series.

577 *The Doonesbury Special* (1977) †
    Dir: John and Faith Hubley; Hubley Studios; Oscar nominee; This animated adaption of the Garry Trudeau comic strip was John Hubley's last film (he died February 21, 1977 at 62); Aired as a TV special, November 27, 1977; Written and produced by Trudeau and John and Faith Hubley; Voices—Richard Cox (Zonker Harris), Barbara Harris (Joanie Caucus), David Grant (Mike), Charles Levin (Mark Slackmeyer/Ralphie), Richard Bruno (B. D.), Rebecca Nelson, Rev. William Sloane Coffin, Jr., Jack Gilford, Mark Baker, Eric Elice, Ben Haley, Jr., Will Jordan, Linda Baer, Eric Jaffe, Michelle Browne, Thomas Baxton, Lenny Jackson, Patrice Leftwich, Jimmy Thudpacker.

578 *The Dot and the Line* (December 31, 1965) AA
    Dir: Chuck Jones; MGM; Oscar winner; A line and a squiggle vie for the love of a dot; Robert Morley narrates this unusual tale by Norton Juster; Jones' feature *The Phantom Tollbooth* (1969) was also based on a Juster story.

579 *Double Dribble* (December 20, 1946)
    Dir: Jack Hannah; Walt Disney; Goofy.

580 *Dough for the Do-Do* (September 2, 1949)
    Warner Bros.; Merrie Melodie: Porky Pig; Color remake of Bob Clampett's classic *Porky in Wackyland* (1938) using much of Clampett's original animation; Friz Freleng provided the new animation; Voices—Mel Blanc.

581 *The Dover Boys* (September 10, 1942)
    Dir: Chuck Jones; Warner Bros.; Merrie Melodie; The three Dover boys (Tom, Dick, and Larry) must rescue Dainty Dora Standpipe from the clutches of dastardly Dan Backslide in this sidesplitting spoof of gay '90s melodramas. A Jones classic; The short employed a new "smear"-style of animation, which speeds up the comic action; Animated by future UPA director Robert Cannon (*Gerald McBoing-Boing*); Voices—Mel Blanc.

582 *Downhearted Duckling* (November 13, 1954)
Dir: William Hanna, Joseph Barbera; MGM; Tom and Jerry.

583 *Draftee Daffy* (January 27, 1945)
Dir: Bob Clampett; Warner Bros.; Looney Tune: Daffy Duck; Daffy takes desperate measures to avoid "the little man from the draft board" in this fast and frantic wartime short; Voices—Mel Blanc.

584 *The Drag* (1965; 8 mins) †
Dir: Carlos Marchiori; National Film Board of Canada; Oscar nominee; Aka *L'Homme-cheminee*; A man discusses his smoking habit on a psychiatrist's couch; Produced by Wolf Koenig and Robert Verrall.

585 *Dragalong Droopy* (February 20, 1954)
Dir: Tex Avery; MGM; Droopy; Sheep herder Droopy battles a cattle rancher; Memorable dialogue—"Moo moo! Bah bah!"

586 *Dragon Around* (July 16, 1954)
Dir: Jack Hannah; Walt Disney; Donald Duck, Chip 'n' Dale; The chipmunks battle Donald's dragon-like earthmover; Voice—Clarence Nash (Donald).

587 *Dream Doll* (1979; 13 mins) †
Dir: Bob Godfrey, Zlatko Grgic; Bob Godfrey Films/Zagreb Films/Halas and Batchelor; Oscar nominee; British short about a man in love with an inflatable doll, from Godfrey (*Great*) and Croation animator Grgic (1931–88); Written by Stephen Penn; Music by John Hyde.

588 *A Dream Walking* (September 28, 1934; b&w)
Dir: Dave Fleischer; Max Fleischer; Popeye the Sailor, Olive Oyl, Bluto, Wimpy; Classic "Popeye" short has him looking after Olive during her late-night sleepwalk along high building ledges and construction girders; Theme music—"Did You Ever See a Dream Walking?" by Mack Gordon and Harry Revel (from the 1933 film *Sitting Pretty*); Voices—Jack Mercer (Popeye), Mae Questel (Olive).

589 *Dripalong Daffy* (November 17, 1951)
Dir: Chuck Jones; Warner Bros.; Merrie Melodie: Daffy Duck, Porky Pig; Daffy shoots it out with a wanted criminal (Nasty Canasta) in this wonderful western spoof; Voices—Mel Blanc.

590 *Droopy's Double Trouble* (November 17, 1951)
Dir: Tex Avery; MGM; Droopy, Spike; Droopy's strong twin brother Drippy helps him guard an estate from moocher Spike; Voices—Bill Thompson (Droopy/Drippy).

591 *Droopy's Good Deed* (May 5, 1951)
Dir: Tex Avery; MGM; Droopy, Spike; Droopy and Spike compete for the title of "Best Scout"; Voice—Bill Thompson (Droopy).

592 *Duck Amuck* (February 28, 1953)
Dir: Chuck Jones; Warner Bros.; Merrie Melodie: Daffy Duck, with a guest appear-

ance by Bugs Bunny; Daffy is tormented by an off-camera artist in this all-time Jones classic which cleverly parodies the cartoon form itself; Remade as *Rabbit Rampage* (1955), with Bugs in the lead; Voices—Mel Blanc.

593 *Duck Dodgers in the 24 1/2th Century* (July 25, 1953)
    Dir: Chuck Jones; Warner Bros.; Merrie Melodie: Daffy Duck, Porky Pig, Marvin Martian; Duck Dodgers (Daffy) is sent on a dangerous mission to Planet X. Excellent parody of space serials with fabulous futuristic backgrounds by layout man Maurice Noble; Jones made a sequel—*Duck Dodgers and the Return of the 24 1/2th Century* (1980)—which was intended for theatrical release, but was shown instead as part of the 1981 TV special *Daffy Duck's Thanks-for-Giving Special*; Voices—Mel Blanc.

594 *Duck Pimples* (August 10, 1945)
    Dir: Jack Kinney; Disney; Donald Duck; Donald's imagination gets the better of him when he listens to a scary radio program; Voice—Clarence Nash (Donald).

595 *Duck! Rabbit! Duck!* (October 3, 1953)
    Dir: Chuck Jones; Warner Bros.; Merrie Melodie: Bugs Bunny, Daffy Duck, Elmer Fudd; The trio's third cartoon together is another debate on exactly what season it is—Duck? Rabbit? Baseball?; Voices—Mel Blanc, Arthur Q. Bryan (Elmer).

596 *Duck Soup to Nuts* (May 27, 1944)
    Dir: Friz Freleng; Warner Bros.; Looney Tune: Daffy Duck, Porky Pig; Porky hunts Daffy in this first-rate Freleng short; Voices—Mel Blanc.

597 *The Ducksters* (September 2, 1950)
    Dir: Chuck Jones; Warner Bros.; Looney Tune: Daffy Duck, Porky Pig; Daffy is the sadistic host of a radio quiz game with Porky the unfortunate contestant in this wickedly funny short; Voices—Mel Blanc.

598 *The Ducktators* (August 1, 1942; b&w)
    Dir: Norman McCabe; Warner Bros.; Looney Tune; Wartime short featuring web-footed caricatures of Hitler, Mussolini and Hirohito; Voices—Mel Blanc.

599 *Dumb-Hounded* (March 20, 1943)
    Dir: Tex Avery; MGM; Droopy (debut), The Wolf; Bloodhound Droopy trails an escaped convict; Droopy, the deadpan little basset hound, was based on the Wallace Wimple character from radio's *Fibber McGee and Molly*. He became MGM's biggest cartoon star next to Tom and Jerry, appearing in 24 shorts (17 directed by Avery), 1943–58; Droopy was voiced most often by Bill Thompson (who also voiced Wimple).

600 *The Duxorcist* (November 20, 1987)
    Dir: Greg Ford, Terry Lennon; Warner Bros.; Looney Tune: Daffy Duck; Daffy's first theatrical short since 1968's *See Ya Later, Gladiator*; Later included in the feature *Daffy Duck's Quackbusters* (1988); Voices—Mel Blanc, B. J. Ward.

601 *The Early Bird Dood It* (August 29, 1942)
    Dir: Tex Avery; MGM.

602 *The Early Worm Gets the Bird* (January 13, 1940)
Dir: Tex Avery; Warner Bros.; Merrie Melodie.

603 *Easter Yeggs* (June 28, 1947)
Dir: Robert McKimson; Warner Bros.; Looney Tune: Bugs Bunny, Elmer Fudd; Bugs takes the Easter Bunny's place and delivers the eggs (or, as Bugs calls them, "the technicolor hen fruit") himself in this funny short; Voices—Mel Blanc (Bugs), Arthur Q. Bryan (Elmer).

604 *Educated Fish* (October 29, 1937) †
Dir: Dave Fleischer; Max Fleischer; Color Classic; Oscar nominee.

605 *Education for Death* (January 15, 1943)
Dir: Clyde Geronimi; Walt Disney; Wartime propaganda short about Nazi indoctrination of German youth.

Egghead (series) **see** *Egghead Rides Again* (1937)

606 *Egghead Rides Again* (July 17, 1937)
Dir: Tex Avery; Warner Bros.; Merrie Melodie: Egghead (debut); Cowboy wannabe Egghead tries out for a job at a western ranch; The Joe Penner–like little character, Egghead, would appear in 12 shorts (1937–39) before evolving into Elmer Fudd in 1940 (*Elmer's Candid Camera*); Voice—Cliff Nazarro (Egghead).

607 *Eggs* (1971)
Dir: John Hubley; Hubley Studios; The struggle of Death and the Goddess of Fertility for control of mankind's future; Music by Quincy Jones.

608 *Eggs Don't Bounce* (December 24, 1943)
Dir: Isadore Sparber; Paramount/Famous; Little Lulu (debut); The first of 26 shorts (1943–48) starring Marjorie H. Buell's mischievous comic-strip character Little Lulu (of *Saturday Evening Post* fame). The series was replaced by "Little Audrey" in 1948 after Paramount lost the rights to "Lulu"; Lulu's hit theme song was written by Fred Wise, Sidney Lippman and Buddy Kaye; Voice—Mae Questel (Lulu).

609 *8 Ball Bunny* (July 8, 1950)
Dir: Chuck Jones; Warner Bros.; Looney Tune: Bugs Bunny; Bugs helps a little penguin get back to the South Pole; Voices—Mel Blanc.

610 *El Gaucho Goofy* (February 6, 1943)
Dir: Jack Kinney; Walt Disney; Goofy; Goofy learns the ways of the Argentine cowboy and about life out on the pampas; Narrated by Fred Shields, with backgrounds inspired by painter F. Molina Campos; Part of the feature *Saludos Amigos*; Rereleased June 10, 1955.

611 *El Terrible Toreador* (1929; b&w)
Producer-Director: Walt Disney; Silly Symphony (second in the series); Early sound short about a brave bullfighter; Score includes music from Bizet's *Carmen*.

612 *Electric Earthquake* (May 15, 1942)
Dir: Dave Fleischer; Max Fleischer; Superman.

613 *An Elephant Never Forgets* (January 2, 1935)
Dir: Dave Fleischer; Max Fleischer; Color Classic.

614 *Eleventh Hour* (November 20, 1942)
Dir: Dan Gordon; Paramount/Famous; Superman.

615 *Elmer Elephant* (March 28, 1936)
Dir: Wilfred Jackson; Walt Disney; Silly Symphony; Young Elmer, teased by the other animals at Tillie Tiger's birthday party, returns to save the day.

Elmer Fudd (series) **see** *Elmer's Candid Camera* (1940)

616 *Elmer's Candid Camera* (March 2, 1940)
Dir: Chuck Jones; Warner Bros.; Merrie Melodie: Bugs Bunny, Elmer Fudd; Elmer's first "official" short (having evolved from the character Egghead) and an early one for Bugs (who is still in his formative years here). For Bugs' official debut see *A Wild Hare* (1940); Elmer, the bald, dim-witted little man—most often seen as a hunter looking for "wabbits"—would appear in some 60 shorts (1940–62); Voices—Mel Blanc (Bugs), Arthur Q. Bryan (Elmer); Note: Bryan (1899–1959) was a veteran radio performer, best known for playing Doc Gamble on *Fibber McGee and Molly.*

617 *Elmer's Pet Rabbit* (January 4, 1941)
Dir: Chuck Jones; Warner Bros.; Merrie Melodie: Bugs Bunny, Elmer Fudd; Bugs (with a different voice) makes his significant cartoon appearance in this short; Voices— Mel Blanc, Arthur Q. Bryan.

618 *The Emperor's New Clothes* (April 30, 1953)
Dir: Ted Parmelee; UPA; Jolly Frolics.

619 *The Enchanted Square* (May 9, 1947)
Dir: Seymour Kneitel; Paramount/Famous; Noveltoon, with Raggedy Ann; The third (and last) short starring Johnny Gruelle's "Raggedy Ann."

620 *the end* (1995) †
Dir: Chris Landreth; Alias/Wavefront Prod; Oscar nominee; Computer-animated short; Written and animated by Landreth; WAC (World Animation Celebration) Award winner; Produced by Landreth and Robin Bargar.

621 *Ersatz (The Substitute)* (1961; 9 mins) AA
Dir: Dusan Vukotic; Zagreb Film; Oscar winner; The first foreign animated film to win an Academy Award; Animated by Vukotic (b. 1927); Written by Rudolf Sremec; Music by Tomislav Simovic.

622 *Every Child (Chaque enfant)* (1979) AA
Dir: Eugene Fedorenko; National Film Board of Canada; Oscar winner; Canadian entry in a series of short films produced for the United Nations Organization to celebrate the International Year of the Child; Animated by Fedorenko; Voices—Les Mimes electriques, Patrice Arbour, Bernard Carez; Produced by Derek Lamb.

623 *Evolution* (1971; 10 mins) †
Dir: Michael Mills; National Film Board of Canada; Oscar nominee; Entertaining short from British animator Mills about how life evolved on Earth; Written and animated by Mills; Music by Doug Randle; Produced by Mills and Robert Verrall.

624 *The Eyes Have It* (March 30, 1945)
Dir: Jack Hannah; Walt Disney; Donald Duck, Pluto; Donald hypnotizes Pluto; Voice—Clarence Nash (Donald).

Fables (series) **see** *The Little Lost Sheep* (1939)

625 *Fair Weather Friends* (November 18, 1946)
Dir: James Culhane; Walter Lantz; Woody Woodpecker; Culhane's last short for Lantz.

626 *Falling Hare* (October 30, 1943)
Dir: Bob Clampett; Warner Bros.; Merrie Melodie: Bugs Bunny; Bugs fights a pesky airplane gremlin in this fine wartime short; Voices—Mel Blanc.

627 *False Hare* (July 16, 1964)
Dir: Robert McKimson; Warner Bros.; Looney Tune: Bugs Bunny; The last theatrical "Bugs Bunny" cartoon until 1990's *Box-Office Bunny*; Voices—Mel Blanc.

628 *The Family That Dwelt Apart* (1973) †
Dir: Yvon Mallette; National Film Board of Canada; Oscar nominee; The "benefits" of progress come to a family's idyllic island home; Narrated by E.B. White (*Charlotte's Web*), and based on a story of his published in *New Yorker* magazine; Music by Eldon Rathburn; Produced by Mallette and Robert Verrall.

629 *Famous Fred* (1997; 25 mins) †
Dir: Joanna Quinn; TVC-London/Channel 4/S4C; Oscar nominee; Musical short about a rock star cat, based on a book by Posy Simmonds; A grand prize winner at the 1997 Annecy Animation Festiva; Voices—Lenny Henry, Tom Courtenay.

630 *Fantasmagorie* (August 17, 1908; 2 mins; b&w)
Dir: Emil Cohl; Gaumont; A drawing of a clown comes to life in this inventive early short; The first French animated film and the first effort by pioneer animator Cohl; Cohl (1857–1938), a former caricaturist and photographer, came to the U.S. in 1912 and directed the series "The Newlyweds" (he returned to France in 1914). By the early '20s he had made over 250 films (possibly over 300), but would die broke and forgotten; Produced at the Gaumont Studio in Paris.

631 *Farm of Tomorrow* (September 18, 1954)
Dir: Tex Avery; MGM; Followup to Avery's *House of Tomorrow* (1949) looks at possible new farming innovations.

Farmer Al Falfa (series) **see** *Farmer Al Falfa's Catastrophe* (1916)

632 *Farmer Al Falfa's Catastrophe* (February 3, 1916; b&w)
Producer-Director: Paul Terry; Farmer Al Falfa (debut); Paul Terry created this early

series about a bald, bearded old farmer and his barnyard adventures while working at the Bray Studio. The long-lasting character would appear in numerous silent shorts (of his own and in Terry's "Aesop's Fables" series) and in 44 sound shorts (for Terrytoons, 1931–37), see *Club Sandwich*.

633 *Farmyard Symphony* (October 14, 1938)
Dir: Jack Cutting; Walt Disney; Silly Symphony; Musical short with chickens, pigs, etc. performing selections from Verdi, Wagner and others.

634 *Fast and Furry-ous* (September 16, 1949)
Dir: Chuck Jones; Warner Bros.; Looney Tune: Road Runner, Coyote (series debut); The first cartoon in the "Road Runner–Coyote" chase series—one of the most popular cartoon series of all time. Created by Jones and his longtime writer Michael Maltese, the series followed the persistent Coyote's many unsuccessful attempts to catch the elusive Road Runner (whose vocabulary consisted only of "Beep! Beep!"). Jones directed the first 25 shorts of this series (39 shorts, 1949–66). A new "Road Runner" short, *Chariots of Fur*, was produced in 1994.

635 *Fastest with the Mostest* (January 19, 1960)
Dir: Chuck Jones; Warner Bros.; Looney Tune: Road Runner, Coyote.

636 *The Fatal Note* (September 29, 1933; b&w)
Dir: James Tyer, George Stallings; Van Beuren; The Little King (debut); The first of 10 shorts (1933–34) starring the nonspeaking comic strip character created by Otto E. Soglow (1900–75). The Little King would later reappear (with a voice) in the Fleischer short *Betty Boop and the Little King* (1936).

637 *Father Noah's Ark* (April 8, 1933)
Dir: Wilfred Jackson; Walt Disney; Silly Symphony; Superbly-animated Disney short; Disney retold the story in 1959 with the stop-motion animated *Noah's Ark*.

638 *A Feather in His Hare* (February 7, 1948)
Dir: Chuck Jones; Warner Bros.; Looney Tune: Bugs Bunny; Bugs is hunted by an Indian; Voices—Mel Blanc.

639 *Feed the Kitty* (February 2, 1952)
Dir: Chuck Jones; Warner Bros.; Merrie Melodie: Marc Antony and Pussyfoot (series debut); Heartwarming tale about the friendship between a large bulldog (Marc Antony) and a cute little kitten (Pussyfoot). Among Jones' best; The dog-and-kitty team would appear in four shorts (1952–58); Voice—Bea Benaderet.

640 *Feline Follies* (November 9, 1919; b&w)
Producer-Director: Pat Sullivan; Felix the Cat (debut); One of the most popular cartoon stars of the silent era, this black, pointy-eared cat—created and animated by Otto Messmer (1892–1983)—appeared in over 150 shorts (1919–31). His popularity declined with the advent of sound and the debut of Mickey Mouse. The series was initially produced for the Paramount Screen Magazine (newsreel series); Felix later appeared in several sound cartoons (1936, Van Beuren), a TV series (1960, syndicated) and his own feature (1989).

641 *Feline Frame-Up* (February 13, 1954)
Dir: Chuck Jones; Warner Bros.; Looney Tune: Marc Antony (dog), Pussyfoot (kit-

ten), Claude Cat; Claude gets Marc Antony kicked out of the house. One of Jones' funniest; Voices—Mel Blanc.

642 *Felix in Hollywood* (July 15, 1923; b&w)
Producer-Director: Pat Sullivan; Felix the Cat; Animated by Otto Messmer.

Felix the Cat (series) **see** *Feline Follies* (1919)

643 *Ferdinand the Bull* (November 25, 1938) AA
Dir: Dick Rickard; Walt Disney; Oscar winner; The story of a bull who would rather sit and smell the roses than take part in a bullfight; Based on the bestselling children's book *The Story of Ferdinand* (1936) by Munro Leaf (1905–76) and illustrator Robert Lawson (*Ben and Me*); The first in a long series of Disney cartoon specials, which replaced the "Silly Symphony" series; Voices are provided by animator Milt Kahl (Young Ferdinand) and Walt Disney (Ferdinand's Mother).

644 *A Feud There Was* (September 24, 1938)
Dir: Tex Avery; Warner Bros.; Merrie Melodie: Egghead; Egghead tries to make peace between two feuding hillbilly families; Voice—Cliff Nazarro (Egghead).

645 *Fiddlesticks* (August 16, 1930)
Producer-Director: Ub Iwerks; Flip the Frog (debut); The first short from the studio of former Disney animator Iwerks and one of the first cartoons to be produced with the two-color process called Cinecolor; Flip appeared in 37 shorts (1930–33). His features would become more humanized after the first few shorts at the urging of producer Pat Powers.

646 *Field and Scream* (April 30, 1955)
Dir: Tex Avery; MGM; A comical guide to fishing and hunting.

647 *5th Column Mouse* (March 6, 1943)
Dir: Friz Freleng; Warner Bros.; Merrie Melodie; Excellent wartime short about a group of mice who unite in true military fashion against a sinister cat.

Figaro (series) **see** *Figaro and Cleo* (1943)

648 *Figaro and Cleo* (October 15, 1943)
Dir: Jack Kinney; Walt Disney; Figaro, Cleo; The mischievous little black cat, Figaro, gets into all kinds of trouble trying to catch goldfish Cleo; Figaro, who debuted with Cleo in the feature *Pinocchio* (1940), would appear in three shorts of his own (1943–47) and three with Pluto (1944–49). Minnie Mouse often appeared as his owner.

649 *Fine Feathered Frenzy* (October 25, 1954)
Dir: Don Patterson; Walter Lantz; Woody Woodpecker; Woody answers an ad from a "Gorgeous Gal" seeking matrimony; Voice—Grace Stafford (Woody).

650 *Fine Feathered Friend* (October 10, 1942)
Dir: William Hanna, Joseph Barbera; MGM; Tom and Jerry.

651 *The Fire Fighters* (August 6, 1930; b&w)
Dir: Burt Gillett; Walt Disney; Mickey Mouse, Minnie Mouse; Fire chief Mickey rescues Minnie from a burning building; Voice—Walt Disney (Mickey).

652 *The First Bad Man* (September 30, 1955)
Dir: Tex Avery; MGM; Humorous look at prehistoric Texas and how an outlaw named Dinosaur Dan forced the creation of the first jail.

653 *Fish Fry* (June 19, 1944) †
Dir: James Culhane; Walter Lantz; Andy Panda; Oscar nominee; A cat tries to snatch Andy's cute—and violent—pet goldfish.

654 *Fit to be Tied* (July 26, 1952)
Dir: William Hanna, Joseph Barbera; MGM; Tom and Jerry, Spike; Spike (the dog) comes to Jerry's rescue whenever the mouse rings a bell—that is, until a new leash law is passed.

655 *The 500 Hats of Bartholomew Cubbins* (April 30, 1943) †
Producer-Director: George Pal; Puppetoon; Oscar nominee; Based on the 1938 children's story by Dr. Seuss.

656 *The Flea Circus* (November 6, 1954)
Dir: Tex Avery; MGM; Music and love in a French flea circus; Voice—Bill Thompson (François).

657 *Flebus* (August 1957)
Dir: Ernest Pintoff; Terrytoons; Arty, UPA-style graphic design highlights this offbeat Pintoff short (his only for Terrytoons); Pintoff (b. 1931), a talented veteran of UPA (where he worked on TV's *The Gerald McBoing-Boing Show*), went on to produce his own shorts (*The Violinist, The Critic*, etc.) and in 1965 directed the first of seven (1965–81) live-action features (*Harvey Middleman, Fireman*); Filmed in CinemaScope.

Flip the Frog (series) **see** *Fiddlesticks* (1930)

Flippy (series) **see** *Dog, Cat and Canary* (1945)

658 *Flowers and Trees* (July 30, 1932) AA
Dir: Burt Gillett; Walt Disney; Silly Symphony; Oscar winner; Imaginative, beautifully animated short about two trees in love; The first animated short to win an Academy Award and the first cartoon made in Technicolor (all subsequent "Silly Symphonies" were also made in Technicolor). Disney would have exclusive rights to the three-color Technicolor process for the next three years; Premiered at Grauman's Chinese Theater in Hollywood (with the feature *Strange Interlude*).

659 *The Fly* (1980) AA
Dir: Ferenc Rofusz; Pannonia Film; Oscar winner; The life and death of a fly, as seen from the fly's point-of-view; Aka *La Mouche* and *A Legy*; Written by Rofusz.

660 *Flying Cat* (January 12, 1952)
Dir: William Hanna, Joseph Barbera; MGM; Tom and Jerry; Tom uses a makeshift pair of wings to reach Jerry and a canary high in a birdhouse.

661 *The Flying Gauchito* (February 3, 1945)
Dir: Jack Kinney; Walt Disney; A boy befriends a flying donkey; Part of the feature *The Three Caballeros*; Rereleased July 15, 1955.

662 *The Flying Mouse* (July 14, 1934)
Dir: David Hand; Walt Disney; Silly Symphony; A young mouse yearns to fly like the birds, but after a magic fairy gives him wings he learns the importance of being himself.

Foghorn Leghorn (series) **see** *Walky Talky Hawky* (1946)

663 *The Foghorn Leghorn* (October 9, 1948)
Dir: Robert McKimson; Warner Bros.; Merrie Melodie: Foghorn Leghorn, Henery Hawk; Chicken hawk Henery is determined to eat a chicken; One of the film's animators is Pete Burness, who would join UPA in 1950 to direct the "Mr. Magoo" series; Voices—Mel Blanc.

Foofle (series) **see** *Foofle's Train Ride* (1959)

664 *Foofle's Train Ride* (May, 1959)
Dir: Dave Tendlar; Terrytoons; Foofle (debut); First in a short-lived series (3 shorts, 1959–60).

665 *Football Now and Then* (October 2, 1953)
Dir: Jack Kinney; Walt Disney; A modern football team plays against a team of old-timers in this sequel of sorts to Kinney's Oscar-nominated *How to Play Football* (1944).

666 *For Scent-imental Reasons* (November 12, 1949) AA
Dir: Chuck Jones; Warner Bros.; Looney Tune: Pepe Le Pew; Oscar winner (Warner Bros.' second); In a perfume shop, Pepe mistakes a cat for a lovely female skunk; Two Jones shorts won Oscars that year (the other was for the documentary *So Much for So Little*); Voices—Mel Blanc.

667 *For Whom the Bulls Toil* (May 9, 1953)
Dir: Jack Kinney; Walt Disney; Goofy; Goofy is mistaken for a matador; Features trumpet playing by Rafael Mendez; Voice—Pinto Colvig (Goofy).

668 *Forward March Hare* (February 4, 1953)
Dir: Chuck Jones; Warner Bros.; Looney Tune: Bugs Bunny; Bugs is drafted into the army; Voices—Mel Blanc.

669 *Fowled-Up Birthday* (March 27, 1962)
Dir: Jack Hannah; Walter Lantz; The Beary Family (debut); The first of 28 shorts (1962–72) in the series—a take off on TV's *The Life of Riley*—starring Charlie Beary and his family; Voices—Paul Frees (Charlie/Junior), Grace Stafford (Bessie/Suzy); Note: Stafford (wife of Lantz) was also the voice of Woody Woodpecker.

Fox and the Crow (series) **see** *The Fox and the Grapes* (1941)

670 *The Fox and the Grapes* (December 5, 1941)
Dir: Frank Tashlin; Columbia/Screen Gems; Color Rhapsody, with the Fox and the

Crow (in their debut); Created by famed Warner Bros. director Tashlin, the hungry Fox and the slick, black Crow became two of Columbia's biggest cartoon stars, appearing together in 24 shorts (1941–50). UPA produced three of them (1948–50) after Columbia's cartoon studio closed.

Foxy (series) **see** *Lady Play Your Mandolin* (1931)

Fractured Fables (series) **see** *My Daddy the Astronaught* (1967)

671 *A Fractured Leghorn* (September 16, 1950)
Dir: Robert McKimson; Warner Bros.; Merrie Melodie: Foghorn Leghorn; One of Foghorn's funniest shorts has him competing for a worm with a cat who wants it for fishing; Voices—Mel Blanc.

672 *Fraidy Cat* (January 17, 1942)
Dir: William Hanna, Joseph Barbera; MGM; Tom and Jerry.

673 *Frank Film* (1973; 9 mins) AA
Producer-Directors: Frank and Caroline Mouris; Oscar winner; The Mouris' acclaimed debut short; Entered in the Library of Congress National Film Registry in 1996.

674 *Frankenstein's Cat* (November 27, 1942)
Dir: Mannie Davis; Terrytoons; Super Mouse (aka Mighty Mouse, in his second appearance, following *The Mouse of Tomorrow*).

675 *Freewayphobia* (February 13, 1965)
Dir: Les Clark; Walt Disney; Goofy (in one of his last shorts); Instructional Disney short, subtitled "The Art of Driving the Super Highway"; Voice—Pinto Colvig (Goofy).

676 *Freight Fright* (March, 1965)
Dir: Connie Rasinski; Terrytoons; Possible Possum (debut); This late-entry Terrytoon series, a spinoff of TV's *Deputy Dawg* (1960, synd.), featured guitar-strumming Possible Possum and his friends in the southern town of Happy Hollow; 18 shorts were released theatrically (1965–71); Voices—Lionel Wilson (Possible Possum/Billy Bear/Owlawishus Owl/Macon Mouse).

677 *Fresh Fish* (November 4, 1939)
Dir: Tex Avery; Warner Bros.; Merrie Melodie; Comical look at marine life.

678 *Fresh Hare* (August 22, 1942)
Dir: Friz Freleng; Warner Bros.; Merrie Melodie: Bugs Bunny, Elmer Fudd; Bugs is chased by a dim-witted Mountie (Elmer); Voices—Mel Blanc (Bugs), Arthur Q. Bryan (Elmer).

679 *The Friendly Ghost* (November 16, 1945)
Dir: Isadore Sparber; Paramount/Famous; Noveltoon, with Casper the Friendly Ghost (debut); The first cartoon appearance of Casper, the lonely little ghost who unintentionally scares off those he tries to befriend. Cocreated by producer-animator Joseph Oriolo (1913–85), Casper went on to become one of Famous Studios' most popular—if repeti-

tious—characters, appearing in 54 shorts (1945–59), as well as his own Harvey comic book series. He later starred in a computer-generated live-action feature (1995); Cowritten by Otto Messmer (of "Felix the Cat" fame); Narrated by Frank Gallop.

680 *The Frog, the Dog and the Devil* (1986) †
Dir: Bob Stenhouse; New Zealand National Film Unit; Oscar nominee; Unusual, strikingly animated short, New Zealand's first international award winner.

681 *From A to Z-Z-Z-Z* (October 16, 1954) †
Dir: Chuck Jones; Warner Bros.; Looney Tune: Ralph Phillips (debut); Oscar nominee; Young daydreamer Ralph Phillips fantasizes during class. One of Jones' best; Ralph also appeared in *Boyhood Daze* (1957) and *The Adventures of the Road Runner* (1962); Voices—Dick Beals (Ralph), Bea Benaderet (Teacher).

682 *From Hare to Heir* (September 3, 1960)
Dir: Friz Freleng; Warner Bros.; Merrie Melodie: Bugs Bunny, Yosemite Sam.

683 *Fuddy Duddy Buddy* (October 18, 1951)
Dir: John Hubley; UPA; Mr. Magoo; Hubley's last "Magoo" short (of three) and one of the series' best; Voice—Jim Backus (Mr. Magoo).

684 *Funny Face* (December 24, 1932; b&w)
Producer-Director: Ub Iwerks; Flip the Frog; Flip decides to get a new face from Dr. Skinnum to impress his girlfriend.

685 *Funny Little Bunnies* (March 24, 1934)
Dir: Wilfred Jackson; Walt Disney; Silly Symphony; Bunnies paint eggs and prepare Easter baskets in the magical land where the rainbow ends.

686 *The Further Adventures of Uncle Sam: Part Two* (1970) †
Dir: Bob Mitchell, Dale Case; Haboush Company; Oscar nominee.

Gabby (series) **see** *King for a Day* (1940)

687 *Gadmouse the Apprentice Good Fairy* (January 1965)
Dir: Ralph Bakshi; Terrytoons; Sad Cat (debut); Bakshi, who joined Terrytoons in 1956, made his directorial debut with this series (13 shorts, 1965–68)—one of the studio's last—about a backwoods cat and his friends; Voices—Bob McFadden (Sad Cat/Impresario/Letimore/Fenimore).

688 *Gagarin* (1995; 3 mins) †
Producer-Director: Alexij Kharitidi; Second Frog Animation Group Prod; Oscar nominee; Humorous Russian short about a little bug who takes a ride in a shuttlecock.

689 *Gallopin' Gaucho* (1929; b&w)
Producer-Director: Walt Disney; Mickey Mouse, Minnie Mouse; The second "Mickey Mouse" cartoon produced; Originally made in 1928 as a silent short, then released a year later with sound (see *Plane Crazy* and *Steamboat Willie*); Voices—Walt Disney (Mickey), Marcellite Garner (Minnie).

690 *The Game (Igra)* (1963; 11 mins) †
Prod: Dusan Vukotic; Zagreb Film; Oscar nominee; Vukotic's *Ersatz (The Substitute)* won an Oscar in 1961; Aka *Surogat*; Written and animated by Vukotic; Music by Tomis-lav Simovic.

691 *A Gander at Mother Goose* (May 25, 1940)
Dir: Tex Avery; Warner Bros.; Merrie Melodie; A comical look at nursery rhymes.

692 *Gandy the Goose* (March 4, 1938; b&w)
Dir: John Foster; Terrytoons; Gandy Goose; The first of 49 shorts (1938–55) starring the Ed Wynn–like goose, who would in later shorts be paired with the cat Sourpuss; Aka *Gandy's Adventures*; Voice—Arthur Kay (Gandy).

693 *Garden Gopher* (September 30, 1950)
Dir: Tex Avery; MGM; Spike.

694 *Gaston Is Here* (May, 1957)
Dir: Connie Rasinski; Terrytoons; Gaston Le Crayon (debut); The first of five shorts (1957–59) starring the French artist whose paintings come to life.

Gaston Le Crayon (series) **see** *Gaston Is Here* (1957)

695 *Gee Whiz-z-z* (May 5, 1956)
Dir: Chuck Jones; Warner Bros.; Looney Tune: Road Runner, Coyote; One of the series' best.

George and Junior (series) **see** *Henpecked Hoboes* (1946)

696 *George and Rosemary* (1987) †
Dir: Alison Snowden, David Fine; National Film Board of Canada; Oscar nominee; An aging, heavyset bachelor yearns for the love of the woman who lives across the street. Funny, charming short; Written and animated by Snowden and Fine; Music by Patrick Godfrey; Voices—Cec Linder (Narrator), Doris Malcolm, Marty Myers, Alexander Wel-don; Produced by Eunice Macaulay.

697 *Georgie and the Dragon* (September 27, 1951)
Dir: Robert Cannon; UPA; Jolly Frolics; The story of a Scottish boy and his pet dragon.

698 *Gerald McBoing-Boing* (January 25, 1951) AA
Dir: Robert Cannon; UPA; Jolly Frolics; Oscar winner; Delightful short, written by children's author Theodor "Dr. Seuss" Geisel (1904–91), about a boy who speaks only in sound effects. UPA's most celebrated cartoon short and one of the best examples (along with *Rooty Toot Toot* and *The Tell-Tale Heart*) of that studio's modern, stylized approach to animation; The first UPA short to win an Academy Award; Gerald would appear in four shorts (1951–56) and in his own TV series *The Gerald McBoing-Boing Show* (1956–57); Entered in the Library of Congress National Film Registry in 1995; Designed by William Hurtz; Animators—Bill Melendez (later of "Peanuts" fame), Rudy Larriva, Pat Matthews, Willis Pyle, Frank Smith; Story adapted by Phil Eastman and Bill Scott (later the cocre-ator/voice of TV's "Bullwinkle"); Narrated by Marvin Miller (of TV's *The Millionaire*).

699 *Gerald McBoing-Boing on the Planet Moo* (February 9, 1956) †
Dir: Robert Cannon; UPA; Gerald McBoing-Boing (last in the series); Oscar nominee.

700 *Gerald McBoing-Boing's Symphony* (July 15, 1953)
Dir: Robert Cannon; UPA; Jolly Frolics, with Gerald McBoing-Boing (in his second short); Gerald fills in for a radio orchestra.

701 *Geri's Game* (November 25, 1997; 4 mins) AA
Dir: Jan Pinkava; Pixar; Oscar winner; Computer-animated short in which an old man plays a game of chess with himself; The short—Pixar's first since 1989—uses a new advanced technology to enhance the animation of skin and cloth; Produced by Karen Dufilho.

702 *Gertie the Dinosaur* (September 15, 1914—copyright date; b&w; 5 mins)
Producer-Director: Winsor McCay; Charming pencil-sketched animated film from famed cartoonist/animation pioneer McCay (*Little Nemo*). The film—which took six months and 10,000 drawings to produce—was McCay's most successful short and the first true example of what the animated film could do; Aka *Gertie the Trained Dinosaur*; The film was first shown as part of a stage act in which McCay (as a sort of dinosaur tamer) and Gertie appeared to interact. McCay then reedited it (adding a prologue featuring himself) for theatrical release later that year; Entered in the Library of Congress National Film Registry in 1991; Premiered February 8, 1914, at the Palace Theater in Chicago.

703 *Giantland* (November 25, 1933; b&w)
Dir: Burt Gillett; Walt Disney; Mickey Mouse; Mickey stars in this version of "Jack and the Beanstalk," a precursor to 1947's *Mickey and the Beanstalk*; Voice—Walt Disney (Mickey).

704 *Giddyap* (July 27, 1950)
Dir: Art Babbitt; UPA; Jolly Frolics; Directorial debut of former Disney animator Babbitt (1907–92). He directed only three UPA shorts (1950–51).

705 *The Goddess of Spring* (November 3, 1934)
Dir: Wilfred Jackson; Walt Disney; Silly Symphony; The Devil kidnaps the Goddess of Spring and makes her queen of his fiery kingdom below the earth. Superbly fantasy, performed in operatic style.

Go-Go Toons (series) **see** *The Space Squid* (1967)

706 *Gold Diggers of '49* (January 6, 1936; b&w)
Dir: Tex Avery; Warner Bros.; Looney Tune: Porky Pig (in his second short), Beans; The first short from famed director and master of the gag cartoon, Fred "Tex" Avery (1908–80), who joined Warner Bros. in 1935 after working for a time with Walter Lantz. At Warners he would help create Daffy Duck (*Porky's Duck Hunt*) and Bugs Bunny (*A Wild Hare*), directing 61 shorts (1936–42) before moving on to his greatest period at MGM (see *Blitz Wolf*); Voice—Joe Dougherty (Porky).

707 *The Golden Touch* (March 22, 1935)
Producer-Director: Walt Disney; Silly Symphony; King Midas is granted his wish— that everything he touches will turn to gold.

708 *Golden Yeggs* (August 5, 1950)
Dir: Friz Freleng; Warner Bros.; Merrie Melodie: Daffy Duck, Porky Pig, Rocky the gangster.

709 *Goldilocks and the Three Bears* (May 14, 1934; b&w)
Dir: Walter Lantz, William C. Nolan; Walter Lantz; Oswald the Rabbit.

710 *Goldimouse and the Three Cats* (March 15, 1960)
Dir: Friz Freleng; Warner Bros.; Looney Tune: Sylvester, Junior.

711 *Goliath II* (January 21, 1960; 15 mins) †
Dir: Wolfgang Reitherman; Walt Disney; Oscar nominee; A little elephant proves his might when the rest of his herd is scared off by a mouse; Directing Animator—John Lounsbery; Story by Bill Peet; Music by George Bruns; Narrated by Sterling Holloway.

712 *Gonzales Tamales* (November 30, 1957)
Dir: Friz Freleng; Warner Bros.; Merrie Melodie: Speedy Gonzales, Sylvester; Better-than-average "Speedy" short; Voices—Mel Blanc.

713 *Goodbye My Lady Love* (June, 1924; b&w)
Dir: Dave Fleischer; Max Fleischer; Song Cartune (with sound); One of the first shorts in Max Fleischer's groundbreaking sing-along cartoon series (other titles released in June, 1924—*Mother Pin a Rose on Me* and *Come Take a Trip in My Airship*); Years before Disney's *Steamboat Willie* (1928), Fleischer experimented with synchronized sound in this series, using the Phonofilm process developed by Dr. Lee DeForest. The cartoons were built around hit songs which audiences were invited to sing by "following the Bouncing Ball" (a white ball that pointed out the lyrics). Fleischer continued that concept in his first sound series "Screen Songs" (1929–38). Some 35 "Song Cartunes" were produced (1924–27).

Goodrich Dirt (series) **see** *Goodrich Dirt at the Seashore* (1917)

714 *Goodrich Dirt at the Seashore* (September 3, 1917; b&w)
Dir: Wallace A. Carlson; Bray; Goodrich Dirt; Debut of the silent series starring Carlson's hapless hobo. The first of 21 shorts (1917–19).

715 *Good Scouts* (July 8, 1938) †
Dir: Jack King; Walt Disney; Donald Duck, Huey, Dewey and Louie; Oscar nominee.

716 *A Good Time for a Dime* (May 9, 1941)
Dir: Dick Lundy; Walt Disney; Donald Duck.

717 *Good Will to Men* (December 23, 1955) †
Dir: William Hanna, Joseph Barbera; MGM; Oscar nominee; Remake of Hugh Harman's *Peace on Earth* (1939).

Goofy (series) **see** *Mickey's Revue* (1932)

718 *Goofy and Wilbur* (March 17, 1939)
    Dir: Dick Huemer; Walt Disney; Goofy; Goofy and his grasshopper pal Wilbur go fishing (with Wilbur acting as bait); Goofy's first cartoon of his own, after seven years as a supporting player; Voice—George Johnson (Goofy).

719 *The Goofy Gophers* (January 25, 1947)
    Dir: Art Davis; Warner Bros.; Looney Tune: Goofy Gophers (debut), Bugs Bunny (cameo); The gophers outwit a dog who is guarding a vegetable garden; Created by Bob Clampett before he left Warner Bros., the two courteous, well-spoken gophers (later nicknamed "Mac and Tosh") appeared in nine shorts (1947–65); Voices—Mel Blanc, Stan Freberg.

720 *Goofy's Freeway Trouble* (September 22, 1965)
    Dir: Les Clark; Walt Disney; Goofy; Goofy demonstrates bad driving habits in his last theatrical short (until 1983's *Mickey's Christmas Carol*); Narrated by Paul Frees.

721 *Goofy's Glider* (November 22, 1940)
    Dir: Jack Kinney; Walt Disney; Goofy; Goofy consults a manual to help him get his glider airborne; Kinney's first "Goofy" cartoon. He would direct the Goof's best shorts (39 in all, 1940–53), including the Oscar-nominated *How to Play to Football* (1944).

722 *Goonland* (October 21, 1938; b&w)
    Dir: Dave Fleischer; Max Fleischer; Popeye the Sailor; Popeye rescues his Pappy who was being held prisoner on the island of the Goons; Voice—Jack Mercer (Popeye).

723 *Goopy Geer* (April 16, 1932; b&w)
    Dir: uncredited; Warner Bros.; Merrie Melodie: Goopy Geer (debut); Goopy, a dog entertainer, performs at a nightclub; Goopy would appear in two more musical shorts that year.

724 *Gorilla My Dreams* (January 3, 1948)
    Dir: Robert McKimson; Warner Bros.; Looney Tune: Bugs Bunny; Bugs washes up on the shore of an island inhabited by gorillas in this hilarious short; Bugs sings "Trade Winds"; Voices—Mel Blanc.

725 *The Gorilla Mystery* (October 1, 1930; b&w)
    Dir: Burt Gillett; Walt Disney; Mickey Mouse, Minnie Mouse; Mickey must save Minnie from a ferocious gorilla; Voices—Walt Disney (Mickey), Marcellite Garner (Minnie).

Grampy (series) **see** *Betty Boop and Grampy* (1935)

726 *Grampy's Indoor Outing* (October 16, 1936; b&w)
    Dir: Dave Fleischer; Max Fleischer; Betty Boop, Grampy; Inventor Grampy brightens up a rainy day by turning his apartment into a playground for Betty's nephew. Great 3–D effects; Voice—Mae Questel (Betty).

727 *A Grand Day Out* (1990; 23 mins) †
    Dir: Nick Park; National Film & Television School; Wallace and Gromit (debut);

Oscar nominee; Wallace's love for cheese takes the pair on a trip to the moon. The first in a delightful series of clay-animated shorts featuring inventor/cheese-lover Wallace and his silent (mouthless, in fact), resourceful dog Gromit; Animated by Park (b. 1958), who joined Aardman Animations in 1985 and became one of the studio's brightest stars. His credits include TV commercials for the British Heat Electric Co.; Park, who worked on the film for six years, won the Oscar that year for another short, *Creature Comforts*; Winner of the 1990 BAFTA Award for Best Animated Short; Followed by *The Wrong Trousers* (1993) and *A Close Shave* (1995); Written by Park and Steve Rushton; Music by Julian Nott; Voice — Peter Sallis (Wallace); Produced by Rob Copeland.

728 *Grandfather's Clock* (June 29, 1934; b&w)
Dir: Burt Gillett, Jim Tyer; Van Beuren; Toddle Tales (series debut); This shortlived Van Beuren series (three shorts, 1934), the first from former Disney director Gillett (*Three Little Pigs*), combined live-action children and animated animals.

729 *Grasshoppers (Cavallete)* (1990) †
Producer-Director: Bruno Bozzetto; Oscar nominee; The long history of man's conflict with his fellow man is chronicled in this wickedly funny short from Italian animator Bozzetto (*Allegro Non Troppo*).

730 *The Grasshopper and the Ants* (February 10, 1934)
Dir: Wilfred Jackson; Walt Disney; Silly Symphony; The grasshopper's catchy song "The World Owes Me a Livin'" (by Leigh Harline and Larry Morey) highlights this Disney version of the fable; Voice — Pinto Colvig (Grasshopper).

731 *Great* (1975; 30 mins) AA
Dir: Bob Godfrey; Grantstern Ltd; Oscar winner; Splendid animated tribute to Victorian engineer Isambard Kingdom Brunel, designer of the Great Western railway and steamship lines; British animator Godfrey (b. 1922) also directed the Oscar-nominated *Kama Sutra Rides Again* (1971).

732 *The Great Cognito* (1982) †
Producer-Director: Will Vinton; Oscar nominee; Claymation short starring a nightclub impressionist whose features change to match the personalities in his World War II monologue; Written by Susan Shadburne.

733 *The Great De Gaulle Stone Operation* (December 21, 1965)
Dir: Friz Freleng, Gerry Chiniquy; DePatie-Freleng; The Inspector (debut); Based on the bumbling Inspector Clouseau character played by Peter Sellers in the film *The Pink Panther* (1964); The Inspector appeared in 34 shorts (1965–69); Voices — Pat Harrington, Jr. (The Inspector/Sgt. Deudeux).

734 *The Great Piggy Bank Robbery* (July 20, 1946)
Dir: Bob Clampett; Warner Bros.; Looney Tune: Daffy Duck, Porky Pig (cameo); Daffy dreams he is Duck Twacy and comes up against a sinister group of villains in this wild Clampett classic; One of Clampett's last WB shorts; Voices — Mel Blanc.

735 *A Greek Tragedy* (1986) AA
Linda Van Tulden, Willem Thijssen; CineTe pvba; Oscar winner.

736 *Greedy for Tweety* (September 28, 1957)
Dir: Friz Freleng; Warner Bros.; Looney Tune: Sylvester, Tweety.

737 *Greedy Humpty Dumpty* (July 10, 1936)
Dir: Dave Fleischer; Max Fleischer; Color Classic; Greedy for the gold he believes is in the sun, King Humpty Dumpty orders his subjects to build his wall higher and higher.

738 *Greetings Bait* (May 15, 1943) †
Dir: Friz Freleng; Warner Bros.; Merrie Melodie; Oscar nominee; A man goes fishing, using a Jerry Colonna–like worm as bait; Sequel to 1941's *The Wacky Worm*.

739 *Grin and Bear It* (August 13, 1954)
Dir: Jack Hannah; Walt Disney; Donald Duck, Humphrey Bear, The Ranger (J. Audubon Woodlore) (debut); Park bear Humphrey tries to mooch a little food from visitor Donald; The Ranger appeared in five shorts (1954–56); Voices—Clarence Nash (Donald), Bill Thompson (Ranger).

740 *A Gruesome Twosome* (June 9, 1945)
Dir: Bob Clampett; Warner Bros.; Merrie Melodie: Tweety; Tweety fights off two goofy cats in this outrageous short; Tweety's third and last solo appearance before teaming with Sylvester the cat; Voices—Mel Blanc.

741 *Gulliver Mickey* (May 19, 1934; b&w)
Dir: Burt Gillett; Walt Disney; Mickey Mouse, Pluto; Mickey plays the shipwrecked sailor; Voice—Walt Disney (Mickey).

742 *Gypsy Life* (August 3, 1945) †
Dir: Connie Rasinski; Terrytoons; Mighty Mouse; Oscar-nominee.

743 *Hair-Raising Hare* (May 25, 1946)
Dir: Chuck Jones; Warner Bros.; Looney Tune: Bugs Bunny; Bugs outwits an evil Peter Lorre-like scientist and his hairy, orange monster. Hilarious; Followed by the similar *Water, Water Every Hare* (1952); Voices—Mel Blanc.

744 *Half-Pint Pygmy* (August 17, 1948)
Dir: Tex Avery; MGM; George and Junior (last in the series).

Ham and Hattie (series) **see** *Trees and Jamaica Daddy* (1958)

745 *A Ham in a Role* (December 13, 1949)
Dir: Robert McKimson; Warner Bros.; Looney Tune: Goofy Gophers; The gophers heckle a Shakespeare-spouting dog; Voices—Mel Blanc, Stan Freberg.

746 *Hamateur Night* (January 28, 1939)
Dir: Tex Avery; Warner Bros.; Merrie Melodie: Egghead; Various acts perform on Amateur Night; The laughing hippo in the audience is voiced by director Avery; Voice—Cliff Nazarro (Egghead).

747 *Happy Go Nutty* (June 24, 1944)
    Dir: Tex Avery; MGM; Screwy Squirrel, Meathead (dog); Screwy escapes from a mental institution and it is up to "nut catcher" Meathead to bring him back.

Happy Harmonies (series) **see** *The Discontented Canary* (1934)

Happy Hooligan (series) **see** *He Tries the Movies Again* (1916)

748 *The Hardship of Miles Standish* (April 27, 1940)
    Dir: Friz Freleng; Warner Bros.; Merrie Melodie: Elmer Fudd; John Alden (Elmer) protects the lovely Priscilla from a hoard of indians; Voice—Arthur Q. Bryan (Elmer).

749 *The Hare-Brained Hypnotist* (October 31, 1942)
    Dir: Friz Freleng; Warner Bros.; Merrie Melodie: Bugs Bunny, Elmer Fudd; Elmer tries to catch Bugs using hypnosis; Voices—Mel Blanc (Bugs), Arthur Q. Bryan (Elmer).

750 *Hare Brush* (May 7, 1955)
    Dir: Friz Freleng; Warner Bros.; Looney Tune: Bugs Bunny, Elmer Fudd; Elmer is a millionaire who thinks he is a rabbit; Voices—Mel Blanc, Arthur Q. Bryan.

751 *Hare Conditioned* (August 11, 1945)
    Dir: Chuck Jones; Warner Bros.; Looney Tune: Bugs Bunny; Bugs is chased through a department store; Voices—Mel Blanc.

752 *Hare Do* (January 15, 1949)
    Dir: Friz Freleng; Warner Bros.; Merrie Melodie: Bugs Bunny, Elmer Fudd.

753 *Hare Force* (July 22, 1944)
    Dir: Friz Freleng; Warner Bros.; Merrie Melodie: Bugs Bunny; A dog tries to keep Bugs from sharing his warm fire on a cold winter night; Voices—Mel Blanc.

754 *A Hare Grows in Manhattan* (May 22, 1947)
    Dir: Friz Freleng; Warner Bros.; Merrie Melodie: Bugs Bunny; Bugs is bullied by some neighborhood dogs; Voices—Mel Blanc.

755 *Hare Lift* (December 20, 1952)
    Dir: Friz Freleng; Warner Bros.; Looney Tune: Bugs Bunny Yosemite Sam; Bank robber Sam hijacks a plane, mistaking Bugs for the pilot; Voices—Mel Blanc.

756 *Hare Remover* (March 23, 1946)
    Dir: Frank Tashlin; Warner Bros.; Merrie Melodie: Bugs Bunny, Elmer Fudd; Elmer is a scientist who tests his evil formula on Bugs; Tashlin's last WB short. He would leave animation to write and direct live-action features (including eight Jerry Lewis comedies, 1955–64); Voices—Mel Blanc, Arthur Q. Bryan (Elmer).

757 *Hare Ribbin'* (June 24, 1944)
    Dir: Bob Clampett; Warner Bros.; Merrie Melodie: Bugs Bunny; A dog (who talks like Bert Gordon's "Mad Russian" radio character) chases Bugs under the water, where most of this cartoon takes place; Voice—Mel Blanc.

758 *Hare Tonic* (November 10, 1945)
Dir: Chuck Jones; Warner Bros.; Looney Tune: Bugs Bunny, Elmer Fudd; Elmer brings Bugs home for a rabbit dinner in this hilarious short; Voices—Mel Blanc, Arthur Q. Bryan (Elmer).

759 *Hare Trigger* (May 5, 1945)
Dir: Friz Freleng; Warner Bros.; Merrie Melodie: Bugs Bunny, Yosemite Sam; The first cartoon appearance of Yosemite Sam. Created by Freleng—who was looking for a new character to star opposite Bugs Bunny—the hot-headed, loud-mouthed little cowboy appeared in 31 shorts (1945–64); Voices—Mel Blanc.

760 *Hare Trimmed* (June 20, 1953)
Dir: Friz Freleng; Warner Bros.; Merrie Melodie: Bugs Bunny, Yosemite Sam, Granny.

761 *Hare-Um Scare-Um* (August 12, 1939)
Dir: Ben Hardaway, Cal Dalton; Warner Bros.; Merrie Melodie: Bugs Bunny; Bugs (in his second appearance, following 1938's *Porky's Hare Hunt*) is still in his formative stage here. For his official debut see *A Wild Hare* (1940).

762 *Hare We Go* (January 6, 1951)
Dir: Robert McKimson; Warner Bros.; Merrie Melodie: Bugs Bunny; Bugs accompanies Christopher Columbus on his voyage to the New World; Voices—Mel Blanc.

763 *Haredevil Hare* (July 24, 1948)
Dir: Chuck Jones; Warner Bros.; Looney Tune: Bugs Bunny, Marvin Martian (debut); Bugs lands on the moon where a Martian is preparing to blow up the Earth; Marvin, the pint-sized, nasal-voiced Martian in the Roman brush-helmet, would appear in five shorts (1948–63); Voices—Mel Blanc.

764 *Hareway to the Stars* (March 29, 1958)
Dir: Chuck Jones; Warner Bros.; Looney Tune: Bugs Bunny, Marvin Martian.

765 *Harlem Wednesday* (1958)
Dir: John Hubley; Storyboard Inc; Music by Benny Carter.

Hashimoto (series) **see** *Hashimoto San* (1959)

766 *Hashimoto San* (September 6, 1959)
Dir: Bob Kuwahara, Dave Tendlar; Terrytoons; Hashimoto (debut); The first of 14 shorts (1959–63) starring the judo-trained, Japanese mouse Hashimoto. The shorts were later shown on TV's *The Hector Heathcote Show* (1963–65) and *The Astronut Show* (1965, synd.); Voices—John Myhers.

767 *The Hat* (1964)
Dir: John Hubley; Storyboard Inc; Soldiers guarding opposite sides of a border argue over a fallen hat; Music/Voices—Dizzy Gillespie, Dudley Moore.

768 *Hatch Up Your Troubles* (May 14, 1949) †
Dir: William Hanna, Joseph Barbera; MGM; Tom and Jerry; Oscar nominee.

769 *The Haunted House* (1929; b&w)
Producer-Director: Walt Disney; Mickey Mouse; Mickey comes upon a spooky old house inhabited by living skeletons, who go into a dance (a reprise of *The Skeleton Dance*).

770 *The Haunted Mouse* (February 15, 1941; b&w)
Dir: Tex Avery; Warner Bros.; Looney Tune; A cat is taunted by a ghost mouse; The first WB short credited to writer Michael Maltese (1908–81), who joined the studio in 1937. Maltese is best known for his later collaboration with Chuck Jones on many of the director's greatest shorts (*One Froggy Evening, What's Opera, Doc?*). He also cocreated (with Jones) the "Road Runner–Coyote" series.

771 *Have You Got Any Castles?* (June 25, 1938)
Dir: Frank Tashlin; Warner Bros.; Merrie Melodie; Book and magazine covers come to life in this terrific Tashlin short.

772 *Hawaiian Holiday* (September 24, 1937)
Dir: Ben Sharpsteen; Walt Disney; Mickey Mouse, Donald Duck, Goofy, Pluto, Minnie Mouse; Goofy's attempts at surfing highlight this all-star Disney short.

773 *Hawks and Doves* (December 18, 1968)
Dir: Hawley Pratt; DePatie-Freleng; Roland and Rattfink (series debut); The first of 17 shorts (1968–71) pitting dashing good-guy Roland against the villainous Rattfink; Voices—Leonard Weinrib.

774 *He Tries the Movies Again* (October 9, 1916; b&w)
Producer-Director: Gregory La Cava; International Film Service; Happy Hooligan (debut); Early silent series adapting the comic strip by Frederick Burr Opper (1857–1937). Over 50 shorts were produced (1916–21); After William Randolph Hearst closed his I.F.S. studio in 1918, he financed the series' continued production at a new studio.

775 *The Headless Horseman* (October 1, 1934)
Producer-Director: Ub Iwerks; ComiColor.

776 *Heaven Scent* (March 31, 1956)
Dir: Chuck Jones; Warner Bros.; Merrie Melodie: Pepe Le Pew.

777 *Heavenly Puss* (July 9, 1949)
Dir: William Hanna, Joseph Barbera; MGM; Tom and Jerry; After his death, Tom finds he will not be able to get into Heaven—and avoid the flames of Hell—unless he can persuade Jerry to sign a Certificate of Forgiveness within one hour. First-rate "T & J" short.

Heckle and Jeckle (series) **see** *The Talking Magpies* (1946)

778 *The Heckling Hare* (July 5, 1941)
Dir: Tex Avery; Warner Bros.; Merrie Melodie: Bugs Bunny; Hilarious Avery short pits Bugs against a very stupid dog; The film's ending was changed against Avery's wishes (originally Bugs and the dog, after their long fall from the cliff, fall through a hole in another cliff), leading to his departure from the studio; Voice—Mel Blanc (Bugs), Tex Avery (Willoughby, the dog).

Hector Heathcote (series) **see** *The Minute and a Half Man* (1959)

779 *Heir Conditioned* (November 26, 1955)
Dir: Friz Freleng; Warner Bros.; Looney Tune: Sylvester, Elmer Fudd; Sylvester inherits $3 million and receives a lesson in the importance of investing; An educational short, sponsored by the Sloane Foundation; Voices—Mel Blanc, Arthur Q. Bryan (Elmer).

780 *Hell Bent for Election* (1944)
Dir: Chuck Jones; UPA; Stylishly-animated campaign short for F.D.R.'s reelection; The first full-length short from UPA (United Productions of America), formed in 1943; Warner Bros. director Jones lent his talent free of charge; Produced by Stephen Bosustow.

781 *Hello, Aloha* (February 29, 1952)
Dir: Jack Kinney; Walt Disney; Goofy, with the music of Harry Owens and his Orchestra; An overworked Goofy finds relaxation in Hawaii—until the natives throw him into a live volcano; Voice—Pinto Colvig (Goofy).

Henery Hawk (series) **see** *The Squawkin' Hawk* (1942)

782 *Henpecked Hoboes* (October 26, 1946)
Dir: Tex Avery; MGM; George and Junior (series debut); The first of four Avery shorts (1946–48) starring the two bears—one a short wise-guy, the other a big dumb lug—based on characters in John Steinbeck's *Of Mice and Men*; Voices—Frank Graham (George), Tex Avery (Junior).

783 *The Hep Cat* (October 3, 1942)
Dir: Bob Clampett; Warner Bros.; Looney Tune; A dog chases a girl-crazy cat in this great Clampett short; The first color "Looney Tune"; Voices—Mel Blanc.

784 *Herb Alpert and the Tijuana Brass Double Feature* (1966) AA
Dir: John Hubley; Hubley Studios; I Feel Special series; Oscar winner (the Hubleys' third).

785 *Herman the CAToonist* (May 15, 1953)
Dir: I. Sparber; Paramount/Famous; Herman and Katnip.

786 *Herr Meets Hare* (January 13, 1945)
Dir: Friz Freleng; Warner Bros.; Merrie Melodie: Bugs Bunny; Bugs comes upon Nazi officer Hermann Goering hunting in the Black Forest; Bugs' appearance as Wagnerian maiden Brunhilde would be repeated for the classic *What's Opera, Doc?* (1957); Voices—Mel Blanc.

787 *Hiawatha's Rabbit Hunt* (June 7, 1941) †
Dir: Friz Freleng; Warner Bros.; Merrie Melodie: Bugs Bunny; Oscar nominee; Bugs heckles little Indian Hiawatha; Freleng's *Rhapsody in Rivets* was also Oscar-nominated that year; Voices—Mel Blanc.

788 *The Hick Chick* (June 15, 1946)
Dir: Tex Avery; MGM; A dopey country chicken (similar to Red Skelton's "Clem Kaddidlehopper" character) loses his girlfriend to a big-city rival.

789 *Hic-Up Pup* (April 17, 1954)
Dir: William Hanna, Joseph Barbera; MGM; Tom and Jerry, with Spike and Tyke.

790 *High Diving Hare* (April 30, 1949)
Dir: Friz Freleng; Warner Bros.; Looney Tune: Bugs Bunny, Yosemite Sam.

791 *High Note* (December 3, 1960) †
Dir: Chuck Jones; Warner Bros.; Looney Tune; Oscar nominee; Fine Jones short about a drunken note on a sheet of music.

792 *The Hill Farm* (1989; 18 mins) †
Producer-Director: Mark Baker; National Film and Television School; Oscar nominee; Written and animated by Baker; Music by Julian Nott.

793 *Hillbilly Hare* (August 12, 1950)
Dir: Robert McKimson; Warner Bros.; Merrie Melodie: Bugs Bunny; Bugs outwits two gun-toting hillbillies by leading them through a violent square dance. One of the director's best; Voices—Mel Blanc.

Hippety Hopper (series) **see** *Hop, Look and Listen* (1948)

794 *Hiss and Hers* (July 3, 1972)
DePatie-Freleng; The Blue Racer (debut); The blue snake—and his elusive prey, the Japanese Beetle—appeared in 15 shorts (1972–74); Voices—Larry D. Mann (Blue Racer), Tom Holland (Japanese Beetle).

795 *History of the World in Three Minutes Flat* (1980) †
Producer-Director: Michael Mills; Oscar nominee.

796 *The Hockey Champ* (April 28, 1939)
Dir: Jack King; Walt Disney; Donald Duck, Huey, Dewey and Louie; Donald challenges the boys to a hockey game; Voice—Clarence Nash (Donald).

797 *Hockey Homicide* (September 21, 1945)
Dir: Jack Kinney; Walt Disney; Goofy; Classic sports spoof.

798 *Hold the Lion, Please* (June 13, 1942)
Dir: Chuck Jones; Warner Bros.; Merrie Melodie: Bugs Bunny; A dopey lion sets out to prove he is "king of the jungle" by catching a rabbit; Voices—Mel Blanc.

799 *Hold That Pose* (November 3, 1950)
Dir: Jack Kinney; Walt Disney; Goofy; Goofy takes a stab at nature photography—until a bear proves an unwilling subject.

800 *The Hole* (1962) AA
Dir: John Hubley; Storyboard Inc; Oscar winner (the Hubleys' second); Two underground construction workers debate about the fate of the Earth; Voices—Dizzy Gillespie, George Matthews.

801 *The Hole Idea* (April 16, 1955)
Dir: Robert McKimson; Warner Bros.; Looney Tune; A crook steals samples of a great scientific invention—the portable hole.

802 *Holiday Highlights* (October 12, 1940)
Dir: Tex Avery; Warner Bros.; Merrie Melodie; Humorous look at the holidays.

803 *Holiday Land* (November 9, 1934) †
Columbia/Screen Gems; Color Rhapsody (series debut), with Scrappy; Oscar nominee (Columbia's first); The first color cartoon (filmed in two-color Technicolor) from Columbia/Screen Gems; 120 "Color Rhapsodies"—Columbia's version of Disney's "Silly Symphonies"—were produced (1934–49).

804 *Hollywood Daffy* (June 22, 1946)
Dir: Friz Freleng; Warner Bros.; Merrie Melodie: Daffy Duck; Daffy tries to get into a movie studio; Voices—Mel Blanc.

805 *Hollywood Steps Out* (May 24, 1941)
Dir: Tex Avery; Warner Bros.; Merrie Melodie; A Hollywood party provides the setting for wonderful cartoon caricatures of such celebrities as Clark Gable, Greta Garbo, Peter Lorre and Groucho Marx.

806 *Homesteader Droopy* (July 10, 1954)
Dir: Tex Avery; MGM; Droopy.

Honey Halfwitch (series) **see** *Poor Little Witch Girl* (1965)

807 *Honeymoon Hotel* (February 17, 1934)
Dir: Earl Duvall; Warner Bros.; Merrie Melodie; A bug couple go on their honeymoon; The first Warner Bros. cartoon in color (filmed in the early two-color process Cinecolor). All "Merrie Melodies" would be in color from 1936 on (the "Looney Tunes" series wouldn't switch to color until 1942).

808 *The Honey-Mousers* (December 8, 1956)
Dir: Robert McKimson; Warner Bros.; Looney Tune; Cartoon takeoff on TV's *The Honeymooners*; Followed by two sequels (1957, '60); Voices—Mel Blanc (Ralph Crumden), Daws Butler (Ned Morton), June Foray (Alice/Trixie).

809 *Honey's Money* (September 1, 1962)
Dir: Friz Freleng; Warner Bros.; Merrie Melodie: Yosemite Sam; Rare solo outing for Sam has him marrying a rich widow with a very large young son; Voices—Mel Blanc (Sam), June Foray (Widow), Billy Booth (Wentworth).

810 *Hooked Bear* (April 27, 1956)
Dir: Jack Hannah; Walt Disney; Humphrey Bear; The first official "Humphrey Bear" cartoon, following five supporting appearances with Donald Duck.

811 *Hoola Boola* (June 27, 1941)
Producer-Director: George Pal; Puppetoon.

Hoot Kloot (series) **see** *Kloot's Kounty* (1973)

812 *Hop, Look and Listen* (April 17, 1948)
   Dir: Robert McKimson; Warner Bros.; Looney Tune: Sylvester, Hippety Hopper (debut); Hippety, the kangaroo always mistaken by Sylvester to be a giant mouse, appeared in 12 shorts (1948–64); Voices—Mel Blanc.

813 *Horton Hatches the Egg* (April 11, 1942)
   Dir: Bob Clampett; Warner Bros.; Merrie Melodie; Delightful cartoon version of the 1940 children's story by Dr. Seuss (Theodor Geisel) about the elephant who is "faithful, one hundred percent."

814 *Hot and Cold* (August 14, 1933; b&w)
   Dir: Walter Lantz, William C. Nolan; Walter Lantz; Pooch the Pup; Musical short featuring the song "Turn on the Heat" (from the 1929 film *Sunny Side Up*).

815 *The Hot Spell* (July 10, 1936; b&w)
   Dir: Mannie Davis, George Gordon; Terrytoons; Farmer Al Falfa, with Puddy the Pup (debut); Puddy appeared in 11 shorts (1936–38).

816 *Hound Hunters* (April 12, 1947)
   Dir: Tex Avery; MGM; George and Junior.

817 *Housecleaning Blues* (January 15, 1937; b&w)
   Dir: Dave Fleischer; Max Fleischer; Betty Boop, Grampy; It is the morning after a party and Betty needs help from Grampy in cleaning up the mess in her house; Voice—Mae Questel (Betty).

818 *House-Hunting Mice* (October 7, 1948)
   Dir: Chuck Jones; Warner Bros.; Merrie Melodie: Hubie and Bertie.

819 *House of Tomorrow* (June 11, 1949)
   Dir: Tex Avery; MGM; Humorous look at the home of the future.

820 *The House That Jack Built (La Maison de Jean-Jacques)* (1967) †
   Dir: Ron Tunis; National Film Board of Canada; Oscar nominee; A man builds his suburban dream home, but is not satisfied; Animated by Tunis; Written by Don Arioli; Voices—Don Arioli, Les Nirenberg, Ben Lennick; Produced by Wolf Koenig and Jim Mackay.

821 *How Now McBoing-Boing* (September 9, 1954)
   Dir: Robert Cannon; UPA; Gerald McBoing-Boing (in his third short).

822 *How the Elephant Got His Trunk* (October 4, 1925; b&w)
   Dir: Walter Lantz; Bray; Un-Natural History (series debut); 16 shorts (1925–27) were produced in this silent series of phony fables, which was one of the last cartoon series from the Bray Studios (it closed in 1927). The series, created by Lantz (who would open his own studio in 1929), featured child actors performing with animated animals. Anita Louise (then billed as Anita Fremalt) was one of the actors.

823 *How to Avoid Friendship* (1964) †
Prod: William L. Snyder; Rembrandt Films; Self-Help series; Oscar nominee.

824 *How to be a Sailor* (January 28, 1944)
Dir: Jack Kinney; Walt Disney; Goofy; Narrated by John McLeish.

825 *How to Dance* (July 11, 1953)
Dir: Jack Kinney; Walt Disney; Goofy.

826 *How to Fish* (December 4, 1942)
Dir: Jack Kinney; Walt Disney; Goofy; Narrated by John McLeish.

827 *How to Kiss* (1989)
Producer-Director: Bill Plympton; Humorous instructional short on the art of the kiss. The nine styles demonstrated include: "The Heavy Make-Up Kiss," "The Nibble Kiss" and "The Big Passionate Kiss"; Written and animated by Plympton; Music by Maureen McElheron; Narrated by Chris Hoffman.

828 *How to Make Love to a Woman* (1995; 5 mins)
Producer-Director: Bill Plympton; Plympton short demonstrating 11 steps to better lovemaking; Included in the feature *I Married a Strange Person* (1997).

829 *How to Play Baseball* (September 4, 1942)
Dir: Jack Kinney; Walt Disney; Goofy.

830 *How to Play Football* (September 15, 1944) †
Dir: Jack Kinney; Walt Disney; Goofy; Oscar nominee; Fast and funny sports send-up. One of the best in Kinney's series of Goofy "How to's."

831 *How to Play Golf* (March 10, 1944)
Dir: Jack Kinney; Walt Disney; Goofy; Goofy's golf demonstration is interrupted by an angry bull.

832 *How to Ride a Horse* (June 20, 1941)
Dir: Jack Kinney; Walt Disney; Goofy; One of the earliest Goofy "How to's"; Part of the feature *The Reluctant Dragon*; Narrated by John McLeish; Rereleased February 24, 1950.

833 *How to Swim* (October 23, 1942)
Dir: Jack Kinney; Walt Disney; Goofy; Narrated by John McLeish.

834 *How War Came* (1941) †
Dir: Paul Fennell; Cartoon Films Ltd/Columbia; This Changing World series; Oscar nominee.

835 *How's Crops?* (March 23, 1934; b&w)
Dir: George Stallings; Van Beuren; Cubby the Bear; Aka *Brownie's Victory Garden*; Better-than-average "Cubby" short has him running a farm from beneath the ground.

Hubie and Bertie (series) **see** *The Aristo Cat* (1943)

Huey, Dewey and Louie (series) **see** *Donald's Nephews* (1938)

836 *Humorous Phases of Funny Faces* (1906; b&w)
    Producer-Director: James Stuart Blackton; A hand draws a series of faces which move and change on their own (a man rolls his eyes and blows smoke, etc.); The first American animated film (arguably the first ever), produced by pioneering director-animator Blackton (1875–1941). His followup, the live-action *The Haunted Hotel* (1907), was also well-received for its stop-motion effects. Blackton quit animation in 1909, but his work led the way for fellow pioneers Emil Cohl (*Fantasmagorie*), John R. Bray (*The Dachshund and the Sausage*) and, most notably, Winsor McCay (*Little Nemo, Gertie the Dinosaur*); Released by Vitagraph (which Blackton cofounded in 1897).

Humphrey Bear (series) **see** *Rugged Bear* (1953)

837 *Hunger (La faim)* (1974; 11 mins) †
    Dir: Peter Foldes; National Film Board of Canada; Oscar nominee; Satirical short contrasting hunger and gluttony, from Hungarian-born painter-animator Foldes (1924–77); Music by Pierre F. Brault; Produced by Foldes and René Jodoin.

838 *Hunger Strife* (October 5, 1960)
    Dir: Jack Hannah; Walter Lantz; Ranger Willoughby tries to keep the bears in line at Peachstone National Park; Reminiscent of the Hannah-directed Disney short *Grin and Bear It* (1954), from which Willoughby's character derived. For his next short he would become Inspector Willoughby (see *Rough and Tumbleweed*).

839 *Hunky and Spunky* (June 24, 1938) †
    Dir: Dave Fleischer; Max Fleischer; Color Classic; Oscar nominee; The donkey stars of this short appeared in several more "Color Classics," including *Snubbed by a Snob* (1940).

840 *The Hunting Season* (August 19, 1935)
    Dir: Burt Gillett, Tom Palmer; Van Beuren; Rainbow Parade, with Molly Moo Cow (debut); One of Van Beuren's last series characters, Molly would appear in five "Rainbow Parades" (1935–36).

841 *A Hunting We Will Go* (April 29, 1932; b&w)
    Dir: Dave Fleischer; Max Fleischer; Talkartoon, with Betty Boop, Bimbo, Koko the Clown.

842 *Hyde and Go Tweet* (May 14, 1960)
    Dir: Friz Freleng; Warner Bros.; Merrie Melodie: Tweety, Sylvester. Tweety turns into a hideous monster after drinking Dr. Jekyll's potion; Voices—Mel Blanc.

843 *Hypnotic Hick* (September 26, 1953)
    Dir: Don Patterson; Walter Lantz; Woody Woodpecker; The Lantz studio's only cartoon released in 3–D.

844 *The Hypo-Chondri-Cat* (April 15, 1950)
Dir: Chuck Jones; Warner Bros.; Merrie Melodie: Hubie and Bertie, Claude Cat.

845 *Hypothese Beta* (1967) †
Prod: Jean-Charles Meunier; Films Orzeaux; Oscar nominee.

846 *I Eats My Spinach* (November 17, 1933; b&w)
Dir: Dave Fleischer; Max Fleischer; Popeye the Sailor.

847 *I Gopher You* (January 30, 1954)
Dir: Friz Freleng; Warner Bros.; Merrie Melodie: Goofy Gophers; The gophers follow their stolen vegetables to a food-processing factory; Voices—Mel Blanc, Stan Freberg.

848 *I Haven't Got a Hat* (March 9, 1935)
Dir: Friz Freleng; Warner Bros.; Merrie Melodie: Porky Pig (debut), Beans (debut), Ham and Ex (pups); "Our Gang" homage with animal students performing in a school musical. Porky Pig makes his very first appearance in this amusing short; Porky, with his famous stutter and signature closing line "Th-Th-Th-That's all, folks!" became Warner's first major cartoon star, appearing in 155 shorts (1935–65). At first he was voiced by actor Joe Dougherty (who really stuttered), then by Mel Blanc (from 1937); Beans the cat appeared in nine shorts (1935–36).

849 *I Heard* (September 1, 1933; b&w)
Dir: Dave Fleischer; Max Fleischer; Betty Boop, with Bimbo and the music of Don Redman and his Orchestra; Workers at the Never Mine take lunch at Betty Boop's Tavern; Voice—Mae Questel (Betty).

850 *I Like Babies and Infinks* (September 18, 1937; b&w)
Dir: Dave Fleischer; Max Fleischer; Popeye the Sailor, Olive Oyl, Bluto, Swee Pea; Popeye and Bluto compete to stop Swee Pea from crying; Voices—Jack Mercer (Popeye), Mae Questel (Olive).

851 *I Love to Singa* (July 18, 1936)
Dir: Tex Avery; Warner Bros.; Merrie Melodie; A young owl yearns to sing jazz.

852 *I Only Have Eyes for You* (March 6, 1937)
Dir: Tex Avery; Warner Bros.; Merrie Melodie.

853 *I Taw a Putty Tat* (April 2, 1948)
Dir: Friz Freleng; Warner Bros.; Merrie Melodie: Tweety, Sylvester; The pair's second short together and one of their funniest; A partial remake of 1943's *Puss 'N' Booty*; Voices—Mel Blanc.

854 *I Wanna Be a Sailor* (September 25, 1937)
Dir: Tex Avery; Warner Bros.; Merrie Melodie.

855 *I Yam What I Yam* (September 29, 1933; b&w)

Dir: Dave Fleischer; Max Fleischer; Popeye the Sailor; The first official "Popeye" cartoon, following his debut in the "Betty Boop" short *Popeye the Sailor* (1933).

856 *Icarus Montgolfier Wright* (1962) †
Producer-Director: Jules Engel; Format Films; Oscar nominee; The directorial debut of Engel (a veteran of Disney and UPA studios), who founded Format Films in 1956; Based on a Ray Bradbury story.

857 *I'd Love to Take Orders from You* (May 18, 1936)
Dir: Tex Avery; Warner Bros.; Merrie Melodie.

858 *I'll Be Glad When You're Dead You Rascal You* (November 25, 1932; b&w)
Dir: Dave Fleischer; Max Fleischer; Betty Boop, Bimbo, Koko the Clown; The music of Louis Armstrong, who plays and sings the title song, highlights this short.

859 *I'm Cold* (December 20, 1954)
Dir: Tex Avery; Walter Lantz; Chilly Willy; A cold little penguin (Chilly) outwits a dog (voiced by Daws Butler) who is guarding a fur warehouse. Superior follow-up to Chilly's debut short *Chilly Willy* (1953); Cartoon great Avery, who had been brought to the Lantz studio (from MGM) to improve the bland penguin character, would direct one more "Chilly" short, the Oscar-nominated *The Legend of Rock-a-Bye Point* (1955); Aka *Some Like It Not*.

860 *I'm Mad* (March, 1994)
Dir: Rich Arons, Dave Marshall, Audu Paden; Warner Bros./Amblin Ent; Animaniacs; The theatrical debut of TV's *Animaniacs* (1993–); Released in theaters with *Hans Christian Andersen's Thumbelina*; Voices—Jess Harnell (Wakko Warner), Tress MacNeille (Dot Warner), Rob Paulsen (Yakko Warner/Dr. Scratchansniff).

861 *Imagination* (October 29, 1943) †
Dir: Bob Wickersham; Columbia/Screen Gems; Color Rhapsody; Oscar nominee.

862 *The Impatient Patient* (September 5, 1942; b&w)
Dir: Norman McCabe; Warner Bros.; Looney Tune: Daffy Duck; Delivery boy Daffy visits the creepy residence of a Dr. Jerkyl; Voices—Mel Blanc.

863 *The Impractical Joker* (June 18, 1937; b&w)
Dir: Dave Fleischer; Max Fleischer; Betty Boop, Grampy.

864 *In Dutch* (May 10, 1946)
Dir: Charles Nichols; Walt Disney; Pluto, Fifi (his girlfriend); Exiled from a Dutch village, Pluto redeems himself when the dike springs a leak.

865 *In My Merry Oldsmobile* (1930; b&w)
Dir: Dave Fleischer; Max Fleischer; Advertising short for Oldsmobile.

866 *In the Bag* (July 27, 1956)
Dir: Jack Hannah; Walt Disney; Humphrey Bear (last in the series), The Ranger; The

park ranger tricks Humphrey and the other bears into picking up litter by setting their work to music; Smokey the Bear has a cameo; Hannah's last Disney short; Filmed in CinemaScope; Voice—Bill Thompson (Ranger).

867 *Injun Trouble* (May 21, 1938; b&w)
Dir: Bob Clampett; Warner Bros.; Looney Tune: Porky Pig; A fearsome Injun Joe attacks Porky's wagon train; Color remake—*Wagon Heels* (1945); Voices—Mel Blanc.

Inki (series) **see** *The Little Lion Hunter* (1939)

868 *Inki and the Lion* (July 19, 1941)
Dir: Chuck Jones; Warner Bros.; Merrie Melodie: Inki; Jungle boy Inki (in his second short) tangles with a mysterious minah bird and an angry lion. The minah bird's theme music is Mendelssohn's "Hebrides [aka Fingal's Cave]" overture.

869 *Inki and the Minah Bird* (November 13, 1943)
Dir: Chuck Jones; Warner Bros.; Merrie Melodie: Inki. Jones' third Inki–lion–minah bird adventure; animated by Robert Cannon and James "Shamus" Culhane (who would soon move on to the Walter Lantz studio and direct some of Woody Woodpecker's best shorts).

870 *Inki at the Circus* (June 21, 1947)
Dir: Chuck Jones; Warner Bros.; Merrie Melodie: Inki.

Inkwell Imps (series) **see** *Koko Makes 'Em Laugh* (1927)

The Inspector (series) **see** *The Great De Gaulle Stone Operation* (1965)

Inspector Willoughby (series) **see** *Rough and Tumbleweed* (1961)

871 *Introducing Krazy Kat and Ignatz Mouse* (February 18, 1916; b&w)
International Film Service; Krazy Kat; The first cartoon starring George Herriman's comic-strip feline (and his supporting characters). Herriman (1881–1944) supervised the series and William Randolph Hearst, who syndicated the strip in his newspaper, produced it through his International Film Service company. Over 130 silent shorts were produced (1916–29) by Hearst, Bray and others, followed by a series of sound shorts (1929–40) from Columbia/Screen Gems (see *Ratskin*).

872 *The Invasion of the Bunny Snatchers* (1992)
Dir: Greg Ford, Terry Lennon; Warner Bros.; Bugs Bunny; Voices—Jeff Bergman; Produced by Bill Exter.

873 *The Invisible Mouse* (September 27, 1947)
Dir: William Hanna, Joseph Barbera; MGM; Tom and Jerry.

874 *Is It Always Right to Be Right?* (1970) AA
Dir: Lee Mishkin; Stephen Bosustow Prods; Oscar winner; Narrated by Orson Welles; produced by Nick Bosustow (son of former UPA head Stephen Bosustow).

875 *Is My Palm Red?* (February 17, 1933; b&w)
Dir: Dave Fleischer; Max Fleischer; Betty Boop, Bimbo; Betty visits palm reader Bimbo; Voice—Mae Questel (Betty).

876 *The Isle of Pingo-Pongo* (May 28, 1938)
Dir: Tex Avery; Warner Bros.; Merrie Melodie; Travelogue spoof.

877 *An Itch in Time* (December 4, 1943)
Dir: Bob Clampett; Warner Bros.; Merrie Melodie: Elmer Fudd; A hungry flea sets his sights on Elmer's dog; Voice—Arthur Q. Bryan (Elmer).

878 *It's Got Me Again* (May 14, 1932; b&w) †
Dir: Rudolf Ising; Warner Bros.; Merrie Melodie; Oscar nominee (Warner Bros.' first); Musical short pitting mice against cat.

879 *It's So Nice to Have a Wolf Around the House* (1979; 11 mins) †
Producer-Director: Paul Fierlinger; AR&T Prods for Learning Corporation of America; Oscar nominee.

880 *It's the Natural Thing to Do* (July 30, 1939; b&w)
Dir: Dave Fleischer; Max Fleischer; Popeye the Sailor, Olive Oyl, Bluto; Popeye and Bluto agree to give up fighting—for a little while; Voices—Jack Mercer, Mac Questel.

881 *It's Tough to Be a Bird* (December 10, 1969; 21 mins) AA
Dir: Ward Kimball; Walt Disney; Oscar winner; Funny look at birds' relations with man through the ages, presented using quick cuts, live action and cut-out animation. Voices—Richard Bakalyan (Narrator), Ruth Buzzi (Soprano).

882 *Jack and Old Mac* (July 18, 1956)
Dir: Bill Justice; Walt Disney; Two jazzy musical segments—"The House That Jack Built" and "Old McDonald Had a Band"; Music by George Bruns.

883 *Jack and the Beanstalk* (November 21, 1931; b&w)
Dir: Dave Fleischer; Max Fleischer; Talkartoon, with Betty Boop.

884 *Jack and the Beanstalk* (November 30, 1933)
Producer-Director: Ub Iwerks; ComiColor (series debut); Iwerks' "ComiColor" series of animated fables used the early two-color process called Cinecolor; 25 were produced (1933–36); Unlike Iwerks' first two series ("Flip the Frog" and "Willie Whopper"), which were MGM releases, the "ComiColors" were distributed independently by Pat Powers' Celebrity Productions.

885 *Jack Frost* (December 24, 1934)
Producer-Director: Ub Iwerks; ComiColor; Jack Frost rescues a little runaway bear from the clutches of Old Man Winter.

886 *Jack Wabbit and the Beanstalk* (June 12, 1943)
Dir: Friz Freleng; Warner Bros.; Merrie Melodie: Bugs Bunny.

James Hound (series) **see** *Dr. Ha Ha Ha* (1966)

887 *The Janitor* (1993; 4 mins) †
Producer-Director: Vanessa Schwartz; The National Film Board of Canada; Oscar

nominee; God's janitor claims responsibility for biblical events; Designed and animated by Schwartz; Written by Chris Many; Voice—Geoffrey Lewis.

888 *Japoteurs* (September 18, 1942)
Dir: Seymour Kneitel; Paramount/Famous; Superman; The first "Superman" cartoon from Paramount's Famous Studios, which took over the series from Max Fleischer; Voices—Bud Collyer, Joan Alexander.

889 *Jasper and the Beanstalk* (October 9, 1945) †
Producer-Director: George Pal; Puppetoon, with Jasper; Oscar nominee.

890 *Jasper Goes Hunting* (July 28, 1944)
Producer-Director: George Pal; Puppetoon, with Jasper; Bugs Bunny (voiced by Mel Blanc and animated by Robert McKimson) makes a cameo appearance.

891 *Jasper in a Jam* (October 18, 1946)
Producer-Director: George Pal; Puppetoon, with Jasper; Musical instruments come to life in a pawnshop after hours; With the music of Charlie Barnett and voice of Peggy Lee (singing "Old Man Mose is Dead").

892 *The Jaywalker* (May 31, 1956) †
Dir: Robert Cannon; UPA; Oscar nominee.

893 *The Jazz Fool* (1929; b&w)
Producer-Director: Walt Disney; Mickey Mouse.

Jeepers and Creepers (series) **see** *The Boss Is Always Right* (1960)

894 *Jeepers Creepers* (September 23, 1939; b&w)
Dir: Bob Clampett; Warner Bros.; Looney Tune: Porky Pig; Fun Clampett short has Porky investigating a haunted house; Voices—Mel Blanc (Porky), Pinto Colvig (ghost).

895 *Jeff's Toothache* (April, 1916; b&w)
Dir: Bud Fisher; Mutt and Jeff Films; Mutt and Jeff (debut); First short in the cartoon series—one of the most popular of the silent era—based on the comic strip characters created in 1907 by Bud Fisher (1885–1954). The cartoons followed the two mustachioed friends, Archibald J. Mutt (the tall one) and Edgar Horace Jeff (the shorter, bald one), in a series of misadventures. Cartoonist Charles Bowers produced the series alone before joining with Raoul Barre in late 1916. (Fisher, incidentally, received sole credit on the cartoons even though he had little input in their actual production.) Over 500 "Mutt and Jeff" shorts were made (1916–26).

896 *Jerky Turkey* (April 7, 1945)
Dir: Tex Avery; MGM; A tubby pilgrim chases a Jimmy Durante–like turkey. Classic Avery.

897 *Jerry's Cousin* (April 7, 1951) †
Dir: William Hanna, Joseph Barbera; MGM; Tom and Jerry; Oscar nominee.

898 *Jimmy the C* (1977) †
Dir: Jimmy Picker; Motionpicker Prod; Oscar nominee; A clay-animated caricature of President Jimmy Carter sings "Georgia on My Mind"; Produced by Picker, Robert Grossman and Craig Whitaker.

899 *Johann Mouse* (March 21, 1953) AA
Dir: William Hanna, Joseph Barbera; MGM; Tom and Jerry; Oscar winner (the series' last); Enjoyable short about a cat and mouse living in the home of Johann Strauss; Narrated by Hans Conried.

John Doormat (series) **see** *Topsy TV* (1957)

900 *John Henry and the Inky Poo* (September 6, 1946) †
Producer-Director: George Pal; Puppetoon; Oscar nominee; Excellent puppet-animated telling of the famous folktale about a mighty black railroad worker and his battle with a steel-driving machine. One of Pal's best; Pal made the film partly in answer to charges of racism leveled at his "Jasper" shorts (which featured a little black boy); Voice— Rex Ingram (Preacher).

901 *Johnnie Fedora and Alice Bluebonnet* (August 15, 1946)
Dir: Jack Kinney; Walt Disney; The Andrews Sisters sing this lovely tale of two hats who fall in love, but are then separated; Part of the feature *Make Mine Music*; Rereleased May 21, 1954.

902 *Johnny Appleseed* (May 27, 1948; 18 mins)
Dir: Wilfred Jackson; Walt Disney; The story of the legendary folk hero (based on the real-life pioneer John Chapman), nicely sung and narrated by Dennis Day; Part of the feature *Melody Time*; Songs (by Kim Gannon and Walter Kent)—"The Lord Is Good to Me," "The Apple Song" and "The Pioneer Song"; Rereleased December 25, 1955.

903 *Johnny Smith and Poker-Huntas* (October 22, 1938)
Dir: Tex Avery; Warner Bros.; Merrie Melodie: Egghead.

Jolly Frolics (series) **see** *Ragtime Bear* (1949)

904 *Jolly Little Elves* (October 1, 1934) †
Walter Lantz; Cartune Classic (first in the series); Oscar nominee; The first Lantz cartoon in color (it was produced in early two-strip Cinecolor).

905 *Juke Box Jamboree* (July 27, 1942) †
Dir: Alex Lovy; Walter Lantz; Swing Symphony; Oscar nominee.

906 *Jumpin' Jupiter* (August 6, 1955)
Dir: Chuck Jones; Warner Bros.; Merrie Melodie: Porky Pig, Sylvester; While sleeping out on the desert, Porky and Sylvester are kidnapped by an alien spaceship; The pair's third spooky outing together, following *Scaredy Cat* (1948) and *Claws for Alarm* (1954); Voices—Mel Blanc.

907 *Jungle Drums* (March 26, 1943)
Dir: Dan Gordon; Paramount/Famous; Superman.

908 *Just Mickey* (March 14, 1930; b&w)
Producer-Director: Walt Disney; Mickey Mouse; Aka *Fiddlin' Around*; Mickey performs a violin solo in this early short; Voice — Walt Disney (Mickey).

909 *Kama Sutra Rides Again* (1972) †
Producer-Director: Bob Godfrey; Oscar nominee; A middle-aged couple follow a manual on sexual techniques.

910 *The Karnival Kid* (1929; b&w)
Producer-Director: Walt Disney; Mickey Mouse, Minnie Mouse; Hot dog vender Mickey falls for Minnie "the Shimmy Dancer"; Mickey speaks for the first time in this short.

Kartunes (series) **see** *Vegetable Vaudeville* (1951)

911 *Katnip Kollege* (June 11, 1938)
Dir: Ben Hardaway, Cal Dalton; Warner Bros.; Merrie Melodie; Lively musical short.

The Katzenjammer Kids (series) **see** *The Captain Is Examined for Insurance* (1917)

912 *Kick Me* (1975) †
Producer-Director: Robert Swarthe; Oscar nominee. Swarthe was later Oscar-nominated for his special effects work in *Star Trek: The Motion Picture* (1979).

913 *The Kids in the Shoe* (May 19, 1935)
Dir: Dave Fleischer; Max Fleischer; Color Classic.

914 *Kiko and the Honey Bears* (August 21, 1936; b&w)
Dir: Mannie Davis, George Gordon; Terrytoons; Kiko the Kangaroo (debut); The first of nine shorts (1936–37) starring the kangaroo first seen in the "Farmer Al Falfa" series.

Kiko the Kangaroo (series) **see** *Kiko and the Honey Bears* (1936)

915 *King for a Day* (October 18, 1940)
Dir: Dave Fleischer; Max Fleischer; Gabby; The first of eight shorts (1940–41) starring Gabby, the feisty little character who debuted in the Fleischer feature *Gulliver's Travels* (1939); Voice — Pinto Colvig (Gabby).

916 *King Neptune* (September 10, 1932)
Dir: Burt Gillett; Walt Disney; Silly Symphony; King Neptune and all the creatures of the sea come to the rescue of a mermaid kidnapped by pirates.

917 *King-Size Canary* (December 6, 1947)
Dir: Tex Avery; MGM; A bottle of Jumbo-Gro has an amazing effect on a dog, a cat, a mouse, and a canary in this wild Avery classic.

918 *Kings Up* (March 12, 1934; b&w)
Dir: Walter Lantz, William C. Nolan; Walter Lantz; Oswald the Rabbit; Operetta-style short casting Oswald as a medieval minstrel.

919 *Kitty Kornered* (June 8, 1946)

Dir: Bob Clampett; Warner Bros.; Looney Tune: Porky Pig, Sylvester; Porky has trouble putting the cats out at night; Voices—Mel Blanc.

920 *Kloot's Kounty* (January 19, 1973)

Dir: Hawley Pratt; DePatie-Freleng; Hoot Kloot (debut); The fat little western sheriff appeared in 17 shorts (1973–74); Voice—Bob Holt (Hoot Kloot).

921 *KnickKnack* (1989; 4 mins)

Dir: John Lasseter; Pixar; A snowman figure in a souvenir snow-globe journeys out among the other "knickknacks"; Computer-animated short, originally released as a 3–D stereoscopic film; Music by Bobby McFerrin.

922 *A Knight for a Day* (March 8, 1946)

Dir: Jack Hannah; Walt Disney; Goofy; Goofy is a medieval jouster.

923 *Knightmare Hare* (October 1, 1955)

Dir: Chuck Jones; Warner Bros.; Merrie Melodie: Bugs Bunny.

924 *Knighty Knight Bugs* (August 23, 1958) AA

Dir: Friz Freleng; Warner Bros.; Looney Tune: Bugs Bunny, Yosemite Sam; Oscar winner; Bugs tries to rescue the Singing Sword from the villainous Black Knight (Sam); The only "Bugs Bunny" cartoon to win an Academy Award; Voices—Mel Blanc.

925 *Knock Knock* (November 25, 1940)

Producer-Director: Walter Lantz; Andy Panda, Woody Woodpecker (debut); A looney woodpecker pesters Andy and his Pop, so Andy tries to catch him by putting salt on his tail; The first cartoon appearance of the little red-headed woodpecker who would become Walter Lantz's most popular cartoon star. His trademark "ha-ha-ha-HA-ha" laugh even spawned an Oscar-nominated hit song in 1948 called "The Woody Woodpecker Song" (from *Wet Blanket Policy*). Woody, who was voiced (from 1948 on) by Lantz's wife Grace Stafford (1904–92), appeared in 195 shorts (1940–72); Voice—Mel Blanc (Woody).

926 *Koko Makes 'Em Laugh* (February 10, 1927; b&w)

Dir: Dave Fleischer; Max Fleischer; The Inkwell Imps (series debut), with Koko the Clown; Popular Fleischer character Koko the Clown starred in this sequel series to the studio's innovative "Out of the Inkwell" series, which again combined live action and animation. 55 silent "Inkwell Imps" were produced (1927–29) before being replaced by the sound series "Talkartoons" (1929–32).

Koko the Clown (series) **see** *Out of the Inkwell* (1919)

927 *Koko's Earth Control* (March 31, 1928—copyright date; b&w)

Dir: Dave Fleischer; Max Fleischer; The Inkwell Imps, with Koko the Clown; Koko and his canine pal Fitz visit Earth's control center and, with the pull of one wrong lever, send the planet into turmoil; Imaginative visual effects and combination of live action and animation highlight this great Fleischer short.

Krazy Kat (series) **see** *Introducing Krazy Kat and Ignatz Mouse* (1916)

928 *La Salla* (September 7, 1996) †
Director: Richard Condie; National Film Board of Canada Oscar nominee computer-animated short—a comic tale of temptation—from Canadian animator Condie (*The Big Snit*); Premiered at the Toronto Film Festival; Produced by Condie and Chas Yetman.

929 *Lady Play Your Mandolin* (September 1931; b&w)
Dir: Frank Marsales; Warner Bros.; Merrie Melodie: Foxy (debut); The first "Merrie Melodie" and the first of three shorts (1931) starring the Mickey Mouse–like Foxy; Marsales was the studio's musical director.

930 *Lake Titicaca* (February 6, 1943)
Dir: Bill Roberts; Walt Disney; Donald Duck; Tourist Donald visits the land of the Incas; Part of the feature *Saludos Amigos*; Rereleased February 18, 1955; Voice—Clarence Nash (Donald), Fred Shields (Narrator).

931 *Lambert, the Sheepish Lion* (February 8, 1952) †
Dir: Jack Hannah; Walt Disney; Oscar nominee; Amusing tale about a lion who grows up among a flock of sheep. Catchy title song; Voice—Sterling Holloway (Narrator/Stork).

932 *Land of the Midnight Fun* (September 23, 1939)
Dir: Tex Avery; Warner Bros.; Merrie Melodie; Newsreel spoof looking at life in Alaska.

933 *A Language All My Own* (July 19, 1935; b&w)
Dir: Dave Fleischer; Max Fleischer; Betty Boop; Betty flies to Japan for a performance; Voice—Mae Questel (Betty).

934 *The Last Hungry Cat* (December 2, 1961)
Dir: Friz Freleng; Warner Bros.; Merrie Melodie: Sylvester, Tweety, Granny; Fine spoof of TV's *Alfred Hitchcock Presents*; Voices—Mel Blanc.

935 Laugh-O-Grams (series)
Walt Disney's earliest efforts were these cartoon gag reels on topical subjects which Disney first began to produce while he was working at Kansas City Film Ad. Though rather crudely-animated, the series (shown at the local Newman Theater) was popular enough for Disney to start his own company, Laugh-O-Gram Films. The only known titles in the series (1920–22) are the six fairy tales—*The Four Musicians of Bremen, Little Red Riding Hood, Puss in Boots, Jack and the Beanstalk, Goldie Locks and the Three Bears, Cinderella*—and *Alice's Wonderland*, the pilot film for his next series, "Alice Comedies," which would take Disney to Hollywood.

936 *The Legend of John Henry* (1973) †
Prod: Nick Bosustow, David Adams; Stephen Bosustow-Pyramid Films Prod; Oscar nominee.

937 *The Legend of Rock-a-Bye Point* (April 11, 1955) †
Dir: Tex Avery; Walter Lantz; Chilly Willy; Oscar nominee (Lantz's last); Chilly and a polar bear raid a fishing boat guarded by a vicious dog. Avery's second (and last) "Chilly Willy" short and one of the series' funniest; Aka *Rockabye Legend*.

938 *The Legend of Sleepy Hollow* (October 5, 1949; 31 mins)
 Dir: Clyde Geronimi; Walt Disney; Timid schoolteacher Ichabod Crane encounters the Headless Horseman on Halloween night. Delightfully scary Halloween treat, with first-rate animation and fine voice work by Bing Crosby; Part of the feature *The Adventures of Ichabod and Mr. Toad*; Based on the 1819 short story by Washington Irving; Songs—"Ichabod Crane," "Katrina" and "Headless Man" by Don Raye and Gene De Paul; Voices—Bing Crosby (Narrator/Singer), The Rhythmaires; Aka *Ichabod Crane*; Rereleased November 26, 1958.

939 *The Leghorn Blows at Midnight* (May 6, 1950)
 Dir: Robert McKimson; Warner Bros.; Looney Tune: Foghorn Leghorn, Henery Hawk.

940 *Leisure* (1976) AA
 Dir: Bruce Petty; Film Australia Prod; Oscar winner; A comical look at how people spend their free time; From Australian filmmaker and former cartoonist Petty; Produced by Suzanne Baker.

941 *Lend a Paw* (October 3, 1941) AA
 Dir: Clyde Geronimi; Walt Disney; Pluto; Oscar winner.

942 *Let's Get Movin'* (July 24, 1936; b&w)
 Dir: Dave Fleischer; Max Fleischer; Popeye the Sailor, Olive Oyl, Bluto; Popeye and Bluto help move Olive's furniture out of her apartment; Voices—Jack Mercer (Popeye), Mae Questel (Olive).

943 *Life Begins for Andy Panda* (September 9, 1939)
 Dir: Alex Lovy; Walter Lantz; Andy Panda; The debut of Andy Panda, who soon became a popular Lantz star and who would help introduce (in 1940's *Knock Knock*) the even more popular Woody Woodpecker. Andy appeared in 26 shorts (1939–49).

944 *Life with Feathers* (March 24, 1945) †
 Dir: Friz Freleng; Warner Bros.; Merrie Melodie: Sylvester (debut); Oscar nominee; An unhappy love bird wants Sylvester to eat him; The first cartoon appearance of the lisping, black-and-white alleycat Sylvester. In all, he would appear in 102 shorts (1945–66). For his teamings with Tweety see *Tweetie Pie* (1947); Voices—Mel Blanc.

Lil' Abner (series) **see** *Amoozin' but Confoozin'* (1944)

945 *The Lion Tamer* (February 2, 1934; b&w)
 Dir: George Stallings; Van Beuren; Amos 'n' Andy (second of two shorts); Amos, Andy and Kingfish visit the circus; Based on the popular radio series; Voices—Freeman Gosden (Amos), Charles Correll (Andy).

Little Audrey (series) **see** *Butterscotch and Soda* (1948)

946 *Little Boy Boo* (June 5, 1954)
 Dir: Robert McKimson; Warner Bros.; Looney Tune: Foghorn Leghorn.

947 *Little Dutch Mill* (October 26, 1934)
 Dir: Dave Fleischer; Max Fleischer; Color Classic (second in the series).

948 *Little Herman* (1915; b&w)
   Producer-Director: Paul Terry; Photographer/cartoonist Paul Terry's first animated short, caricaturing popular magician The Great Herrmann; The short got Terry a job at the Bray Studio, where he would develop the "Farmer Al Falfa" series (in 1916).

949 *Little Hiawatha* (May 15, 1937)
   Dir: David Hand; Walt Disney; Silly Symphony; Based on the Longfellow poem; Hand's last short (he continued at Disney as a feature supervisor); Other "Hiawatha" spoofs include Friz Freleng's *Hiawatha's Rabbit Hunt* (1941) and Tex Avery's *Big Heel-Watha* (1944).

950 *The Little Island* (1958; 30 mins)
   Producer-Director: Richard Williams; Fable involving the three figures of Truth, Beauty and Goodness; Williams' first animated short, produced in Great Britain. His later credits include the short *A Christmas Carol* (1972) and feature *Who Framed Roger Rabbit?* (1988); A three-year production.

951 *Little Johnny Jet* (April 18, 1953) †
   Dir: Tex Avery; MGM; Oscar nominee; A speedy little jet helps his father, an old B-29, win an around-the-world race; A variation on Avery's *One Cab's Family* (1952).

The Little King (series) **see** *The Fatal Note* (1933)

952 *The Little Lion Hunter* (October 7, 1939)
   Dir: Chuck Jones; Warner Bros.; Merrie Melodie: Inki (debut); The first of five shorts (1939–50) starring the jungle boy, Inki.

953 *The Little Lost Sheep* (October 6, 1939; b&w)
   Columbia/Screen Gems; Fable, with Krazy Kat (one of his last cartoon appearances); The first short in Columbia's "Fables" series (19 shorts, 1939–42).

Little Lulu (series) **see** *Eggs Don't Bounce* (1943)

954 *The Little Match Girl* (November 5, 1937) †
   Dir: Sid Marcus, Art Davis; Columbia/Screen Gems; Color Rhapsody; Oscar nominee; Haunting, beautifully produced version of the Hans Christian Andersen tale about a poor little girl trying to sell her matches on the snowy streets of a large city. One of Columbia's best cartoons.

955 *Little Nemo* (April 12, 1911; b&w)
   Producer-Director: Winsor McCay; Little Nemo, Impy, Flip; Groundbreaking animated film (employing 4,000 drawings) based on McCay's popular comic strip "Little Nemo in Slumberland" (which first appeared in *The New York Herald* in 1905); The first animated short from cartoonist/animation pioneer McCay (1871–1934), one of the leading figures in American comic art; The animated segment is introduced by a prologue featuring McCay and friends (one of whom is played by movie star John Bunny); McCay featured the short as part of a stage act (as he did with his later success *Gertie the Dinosaur*) with which he toured the vaudeville circuit; Premiered at William's Colonial Theater in New York; A feature version of *Little Nemo* was produced in 1992.

956 *The Little Orphan* (April 30, 1949) AA
Dir: William Hanna, Joseph Barbera; MGM; Tom and Jerry, Nibbles; Oscar winner; Jerry and Nibbles battle with Tom amidst the food of a Thanksgiving feast.

957 *Little Orphan Airedale* (October 4, 1947)
Dir: Chuck Jones; Warner Bros.; Looney Tune: Porky Pig, Charlie Dog (debut); Charlie, a wiseguy dog without a home, tries to convince Porky to be his new master; This color remake of Bob Clampett's *Porky's Pooch* (1941) was the first of five shorts (1947–51) starring Jones' Charlie Dog; Voices—Mel Blanc.

958 *Little Quacker* (January 7, 1950)
Dir: William Hanna, Joseph Barbera; MGM; Tom and Jerry.

959 *Little Red Riding Rabbit* (January 4, 1944)
Dir: Friz Freleng; Warner Bros.; Merrie Melodie: Bugs Bunny; Bugs must cope with a hungry wolf and an annoying Red Riding Hood. One of Freleng's funniest; Voices— Mel Blanc.

960 *Little Red Walking Hood* (November 6, 1937)
Dir: Tex Avery; Warner Bros.; Merrie Melodie: Egghead.

Little Roquefort (series) **see** *Cat Happy* (1950)

961 *Little Rural Riding Hood* (September 17, 1949)
Dir: Tex Avery; MGM; The Wolf and the Showgirl; A girl-crazy country wolf visits his big-city cousin in this typically zany Avery short; Includes reused animation (of the Showgirl) from *Swing Shift Cinderella* (1945).

962 *The Little Stranger* (March 13, 1936)
Dir: Dave Fleischer; Max Fleischer; Color Classic.

963 *Little Tinker* (June 15, 1948)
Dir: Tex Avery; MGM; A lonely skunk finds popularity by impersonating Frank Sinatra. Funny sendup of the '40s bobby-soxer craze, similar to Frank Tashlin's *The Swooner Crooner* (1944).

964 *Little Toot* (May 27, 1948)
Dir: Clyde Geronimi; Walt Disney; The Andrews Sisters sing the story of a little New York tugboat; Part of the feature *Melody Time*; Based on the 1939 children's story by Hardie Gramatky; Title song by Allie Wrubel; Rereleased August 13, 1954.

965 *The Little Whirlwind* (February 14, 1941)
Dir: Riley Thomson; Walt Disney; Mickey Mouse, Minnie Mouse; Raking Minnie's leaves is made more difficult for Mickey when a little whirlwind comes along, followed by a giant tornado!; Voices—Walt Disney (Mickey), Thelma Boardman (Minnie).

966 *Lonesome Ghosts* (December 24, 1937)
Dir: Burt Gillett; Walt Disney; Mickey Mouse, Donald Duck, Goofy; Mickey, Don-

ald and Goofy are called to rid a haunted house of ghosts. One of the trio's most memorable films; Voices—Walt Disney (Mickey), Clarence Nash (Donald), Pinto Colvig (Goofy).

967 *Lonesome Lenny* (March 9, 1946)
Dir: Tex Avery; MGM; Screwy Squirrel (last in the series); A big, dumb dog longs for a friend (he had one once, but "he don't move no more").

968 *The Lonesome Stranger* (November 23, 1940)
Dir: Hugh Harman; MGM; Funny send-up of "The Lone Ranger."

969 *The Lone Stranger and Porky* (January 7, 1939)
Dir: Bob Clampett; Warner Bros.; Great western spoof; Voices—Mel Blanc.

970 *Long-Haired Hare* (June 25, 1949)
Dir: Chuck Jones; Warner Bros.; Looney Tune: Bugs Bunny; Bugs disrupts the performance of a haughty opera singer in this classic Jones short; Voices—Mel Blanc.

Looney Tunes (series) **see** *Sinkin' in the Bathtub* (1930)

Loopy De Loop (series) **see** *Wolf Hounded* (1959)

971 *Loose Nut* (December 17, 1945)
Dir: James Culhane; Walter Lantz; Woody Woodpecker.

972 *Louvre Come Back to Me* (August 18, 1962)
Dir: Chuck Jones; Warner Bros.; Looney Tune: Pepe Le Pew; Pepe (in his last cartoon appearance) chases his unwilling love object through a museum; Voices—Mel Blanc.

973 *Love Me! Love Me! Love Me!* (1962)
Producer-Director: Richard Williams; Williams' second short, following *The Little Island* (1958).

974 *Lucky Ducky* (October 9, 1948)
Dir: Tex Avery; MGM; A little duck outsmarts two dopey hunters in this short filled with clever Avery gags.

975 *Lullaby Land* (August 19, 1933)
Dir: Wilfred Jackson; Walt Disney; Silly Symphony; A sleeping baby visits a magical dreamland where he meets three scary Boogeymen and a kindly Sandman. Lovely Disney fantasy.

976 *Lumberjack Rabbit* (November 13, 1954)
Dir: Chuck Jones; Warner Bros.; Looney Tune: Bugs Bunny; Bugs wanders into Paul Bunyan country and encounters a giant dog; The only Warner Bros. cartoon to be released in 3–D; Voices—Mel Blanc.

Luno (series) **see** *The Missing Genie* (1963)

977 *Luxo Jr.* (1986) †
Dir: John Lasseter; Pixar Prod; Oscar nominee; Computer-animated short (Pixar's first) about parent and child lamps; Produced by Lasseter (*Tin Toy, Toy Story*) and William Reeves.

978 *The Mad Doctor* (January 21, 1933; b&w)
Dir: David Hand; Walt Disney; Mickey Mouse, Pluto; Spooky short set in an old haunted house where Mickey has come to save Pluto from a mad doctor's evil experiments; Voice—Walt Disney (Mickey).

979 *The Mad Hatter* (February 1948)
Dir: Dick Lundy; Walter Lantz; Woody Woodpecker, Wally Walrus; Woody has trouble keeping hold of the top hat he bought at Wally's shop.

980 *Madeline* (November 27, 1952) †
Dir: Robert Cannon; UPA; Jolly Frolics; Oscar nominee; Based on Ludwig Bemelmans' children's stories (the first appeared in 1939).

Maggie and Sam (series) **see** *Crazy Mixed-Up Pup* (1955)

981 *The Magic Fluke* (March 27, 1949) †
Dir: John Hubley; UPA; The Fox and the Crow (in their second UPA short); Oscar nominee.

982 *The Magic Lamp* (September 15, 1924; b&w)
Dir: Walter Lantz; Bray Studios; Dinky Doodle (debut); Lantz (later of "Woody Woodpecker" fame) not only wrote and directed this silent cartoon series, which combined live action and animation, but also appeared alongside his characters—the little boy, Dinky, and his dog Weakheart; 23 "Dinky" shorts were produced (1924–26).

983 *The Magic Pear Tree* (1968) †
Prod: Jimmy Murakami; Murakami-Wolf Films/Bing Crosby Prods; Oscar nominee.

984 *Magical Maestro* (February 9, 1952)
Dir: Tex Avery; MGM; A magician, posing as a conductor, torments an opera singer ("The Great Poochini") with his magic wand. One of Avery's funniest films; Best bit—the stray hair that seemingly gets stuck in the film projector; Entered in the Library of Congress National Film Registry in 1993.

985 *Magician Mickey* (February 6, 1937)
Dir: David Hand; Walt Disney; Mickey Mouse, Donald Duck, Goofy; Donald heckles Mickey's magic act—until Mickey uses his wand on him; Voices—Walt Disney (Mickey), Clarence Nash (Donald).

986 *The Magnetic Telescope* (April 24, 1942)
Dir: Dave Fleischer; Max Fleischer; Superman.

987 *Magoo's Puddle Jumper* (July 26, 1956) AA
Dir: Pete Burness; UPA; Mr. Magoo; Oscar winner (the series' second and last); Magoo buys an electric car; Made in CinemaScope; Voices—Jim Backus (Mr. Magoo).

988 *The Major Lied Till Dawn* (August 13, 1938)
Dir: Frank Tashlin; Warner Bros.; Merrie Melodie.

989 *Make Me Psychic* (1978)
Producer-Director: Sally Cruikshank; Anita attends a party where she demonstrates her newly-acquired psychic powers; Sequel to Cruikshank's breakthrough short, *Quasi at the Quackadero* (1975); Cost of film—$14,000; Music by the Cheap Suit Serenaders; Voices—Sally Cruikshank (Anita), Kim Deitch (Quasi).

990 *Making 'Em Move* (July 5, 1931; b&w)
Dir: John Foster, Harry Bailey; Van Beuren; Aesop's Fables; Aka *In a Cartoon Studio*; A cat learns how drawings are animated during a visit to a cartoon studio. Classic Van Beuren short.

991 *Man in Space* (July 18, 1956) †
Producer-Director: Ward Kimball; Walt Disney; Oscar nominee (for Best Documentary Short); From the book by Heinz Haber.

992 *The Man Who Planted Trees (L'homme qui plantait des arbres)* (1987; 30 mins) AA
Dir: Frédéric Back; Société Radio–Canada/Canadian Broadcasting Corporation; Oscar winner; Moving, lyrical animated rendering of the short story by Jean Giono, which is read by Philippe Noiret/Christopher Plummer (English version); Music by Normand Roger; Back's followup (five years in the making) to his Oscar-winning short *Crac* (1981).

993 *Manipulation* (1991) AA
Producer-Director: Daniel Greaves; Tandem Films Prod; Oscar winner; An artist bends, twists and stretches his drawn character; Written and animated by Greaves.

Marc Antony and Pussyfoot (series) **see** *Feed the Kitty* (1952)

994 *The Martins and the Coys* (August 15, 1946)
Dir: Jack Kinney; Walt Disney; The last living members of two feuding hillbilly families fall in love; Part of the feature *Make Mine Music*; Sung by the King's Men; Rereleased June 18, 1954.

Marvin Martian (series) **see** *Haredevil Hare* (1948)

995 *Mask-A-Raid* (November 7, 1931; b&w)
Dir: Dave Fleischer; Max Fleischer; Talkartoon, with Betty Boop.

996 *Maw and Paw* (August 10, 1953)
Dir: Paul J. Smith; Walter Lantz; Maw and Paw (series debut); The first of four shorts (1953–55) starring the hayseed couple; Voices—Grace Stafford (Maw), Dal McKennon (Paw).

Meany, Miny and Moe (series) **see** *Monkey Wretches* (1935)

997 *Meatless Tuesday* (October 25, 1943)
Dir: James Culhane; Walter Lantz; Andy Panda; Andy chases a rooster whom he plans to eat for dinner. Fast-paced, with a lively musical score.

998 *The Mechanical Monsters* (November 21, 1941)
Dir: Dave Fleischer; Max Fleischer; Superman.

999 *Melody* (Adventures in Music) (May 28, 1953; 10 mins)
Dir: Charles Nichols, Ward Kimball; Walt Disney; A music lesson, given by birds, and animated in the flat, angular style of the UPA studio; The first cartoon released in 3–D; Followed by the Oscar-winning *Toot, Whistle, Plunk, and Boom* (1953); Songs by Sonny Burke (*Lady and the Tramp*) and Paul Webster.

1000 *Merbabies* (December 9, 1938)
Dir: George Stallings; Walt Disney; Silly Symphony.

1001 *Merlin the Magic Mouse* (November 18, 1967)
Dir: Alex Lovy; Warner Bros.; Merlin the Magic Mouse (debut); One of Warner Bros.' last cartoon characters, this W. C. Fields–like mouse appeared in five shorts (1967–69); Voice—Daws Butler (Merlin).

1002 *The Mermaid* (1997; 10 mins) †
Dir: Alexander Petrov; Dago/Shar/Panorama; Oscar nominee; Haunting short about an old monk and his long-lost love; From Petrov (*The Cow*), using his oil paint on glass technique; Awarded a special jury prize at the 1997 Annecy Animation Festival.

Merrie Melodies (series) **see** *Lady Play Your Mandolin* (1931)

1003 *The Merry Dwarfs* (1929; b&w)
Producer-Director: Walt Disney; Silly Symphony.

Merry Makers (series) **see** *Think or Sink* (1967)

1004 *Merry Mannequins* (March 19, 1937)
Dir: Ub Iwerks; Columbia/Screen Gems; Color Rhapsody; One of Iwerks' best shorts.

1005 *The Merry Old Soul* (November 27, 1933; b&w) †
Dir: Walter Lantz, William C. Nolan; Walter Lantz; Oswald the Rabbit; Oscar nominee (Lantz's first).

1006 *Mexicali Shmoes* (July 4, 1959) †
Dir: Friz Freleng; Warner Bros.; Looney Tune: Speedy Gonzales; Oscar nominee; Fine "Speedy" short pits the mouse against two dim-witted cats; Voices—Mel Blanc.

1007 *Mexican Boarders* (May 12, 1962)
Dir: Friz Freleng; Warner Bros.; Looney Tune: Speedy Gonzales, Sylvester.

1008 *The Mice Will Play* (December 31, 1938)
Dir: Tex Avery; Warner Bros.; Merrie Melodie.

1009 *Mickey and the Beanstalk* (September 27, 1947; 29 mins)
Dir: Bill Roberts, Hamilton Luske; Walt Disney; Mickey Mouse, Donald Duck and

Goofy climb the beanstalk to take back the Magic Harp stolen by Willie the Giant. Mickey and the gang's greatest adventure together and the last time Walt Disney provided the voice of his famous mouse; Highlight—the beanstalk's ascension into the sky; Part of the feature *Fun and Fancy Free*; Songs—"What a Happy Day," "Fe-Fi-Fo-Fum" and "In My Favorite Dream"; Voices—Walt Disney/James Macdonald (Mickey), Clarence Nash (Donald), Pinto Colvig (Goofy), Billy Gilbert (Willie), Anita Gordon (The Singing Harp), Edgar Bergen (Narrator).

1010 *Mickey and the Seal* (December 3, 1948) †
  Dir: Charles Nichols; Walt Disney; Mickey Mouse, Pluto; Oscar nominee; Mickey unknowingly brings a seal home from Seal Park; Voice—James Macdonald (Mickey).

1011 *Mickey Down Under* (March 19, 1948)
  Dir: Charles Nichols; Walt Disney; Mickey Mouse, Pluto.

Mickey Mouse (series) **see** *Steamboat Willie* (1928)

1012 *Mickey's Amateurs* (April 17, 1937)
  Dir: Pinto Colvig, Walt Pfeiffer, Ed Penner; Walt Disney; Mickey Mouse, Donald Duck, Goofy, Clara Cluck; Donald recites, Clara sings, and Goofy's a one-man band; Voices—Walt Disney (Mickey), Clarence Nash (Donald), Pinto Colvig (Goofy), Florence Gill (Clara).

1013 *Mickey's Birthday Party* (February 7, 1942)
  Dir: Riley Thomson; Walt Disney; Mickey Mouse, Donald Duck, Goofy, Minnie Mouse.

1014 *Mickey's Christmas Carol* (December 16, 1983; 25 mins) †
  Producer-Director: Burny Mattinson; Walt Disney; Mickey Mouse, others; Oscar nominee; Miserly Ebeneezer Scrooge is reformed when visited by four spirits on Christmas Eve in this classic tale featuring an all-star Disney cast; The first theatrical "Mickey Mouse" cartoon in 30 years (since 1953's *The Simple Things*); The idea for the film came from a 1974 Disneyland record of the same name; Based on the story by Charles Dickens; Music by Irwin Kostal; Song—"Oh, What a Merry Christmas Day" by Kostal and Frederick Searles; Voices—Wayne Allwine (Mickey Mouse as Bob Cratchit), Alan Young (Uncle Scrooge McDuck as Scrooge), Clarence Nash (Donald Duck as Fred), Hal Smith (Goofy as Jacob Marley), Will Ryan (Black Pete as Christmas Future/Willie the Giant as Christmas Present), Eddy Carrol (Jiminy Cricket as Christmas Past), Susan Sheridan (Morty as Tiny Tim), Patricia Parris (Daisy Duck as Isabel), Dick Billingsley; Note: Allwine takes over the voice of Mickey from James Macdonald (1906–91). Nash's last performance as Donald (he died in February 1985 at 80). Animator Tony Anselmo would take over the duck's famous voice.

1015 *Mickey's Fire Brigade* (August 3, 1935)
  Dir: Ben Sharpsteen; Walt Disney; Mickey Mouse, Donald Duck, Goofy, Clarabelle Cow; The trio struggle to put out a house fire in this funny, well-animated short.

1016 *Mickey's Follies* (1929; b&w)
  Dir: Wilfred Jackson; Walt Disney; Mickey Mouse; Mickey and his barnyard friends put on a show; Mickey sings his theme song "Minnie's Yoo-Hoo" (the studio's first origi-

nal song, written by Walt Disney and Carl Stalling); Jackson's directorial debut. One of Disney's leading animation directors, Jackson directed 54 shorts (1929–52) in addition to his feature work (*Snow White, Fantasia,* etc.). His classic shorts include *The Band Concert* (1935) and the Oscar winners *The Tortoise and the Hare* (1935) and *The Old Mill* (1937).

1017 *Mickey's Gala Premiere* (July 1, 1933; b&w)
    Dir: Burt Gillett; Walt Disney; Mickey Mouse, Pluto, Minnie Mouse; Mickey attends the star-studded premiere of his new film "Galloping Romance"; Features cartoon cameos by Laurel and Hardy, Jimmy Durante, Mae West, the Marx Brothers, and many others.

1018 *Mickey's Kangaroo* (April 13, 1935; b&w)
    Dir: David Hand; Walt Disney; Mickey Mouse, Pluto; The last Disney cartoon in black-and-white.

1019 *Mickey's Orphans* (December 14, 1931; b&w) †
    Dir: Burt Gillett; Walt Disney; Mickey Mouse, Pluto, Minnie Mouse; Oscar nominee; Orphan kittens show up on Mickey's doorstep in this holiday short; Voices — Walt Disney (Mickey), Marcellite Garner (Minnie).

1020 *Mickey's Parrot* (September 9, 1938)
    Dir: Bill Roberts; Walt Disney; Mickey Mouse, Pluto; A talking parrot pays a late-night visit to Mickey's home; Voice — Walt Disney (Mickey).

1021 *Mickey's Polo Team* (January 4, 1936)
    Dir: David Hand; Walt Disney; Mickey Mouse, Donald Duck, Goofy; Disney characters compete against a team of Hollywood stars (Laurel and Hardy, Charlie Chaplin and Harpo Marx).

1022 *Mickey's Revue* (May 12, 1932; b&w)
    Dir: Wilfred Jackson; Walt Disney; Mickey Mouse, Pluto, Goofy (debut), Minnie Mouse, Horace Horsecollar; The first cartoon appearance of Goofy (as the audience member with the goofy laugh). Starting off as a silly, skinny character named Dippy Dawg, Goofy developed (in the hands of animator Art Babbitt and, later, director Jack Kinney) into the loveable dope and great physical comedian known today. He would appear in 83 shorts (1932–65, '83, '90); Voices — Walt Disney (Mickey), Pinto Colvig (Goofy); Note: Vance "Pinto" Colvig (1892–1967), Goofy's main voice, was also a story man at Disney. One of his many other cartoon voices was that of Grumpy in Disney's *Snow White* (1937).

1023 *Mickey's Service Station* (March 16, 1935; b&w)
    Dir: Ben Sharpsteen; Walt Disney; Mickey Mouse, Donald Duck, Goofy, Pegleg Pete; The boys have ten minutes to get rid of a squeak in Pete's car; Voices — Walt Disney (Mickey), Clarence Nash (Donald), Pinto Colvig (Goofy), Billy Bletcher (Pete).

1024 *Mickey's Trailer* (May 6, 1938)
    Dir: Ben Sharpsteen; Walt Disney; Mickey Mouse, Donald Duck, Goofy.

1025 *Midnight in a Toyshop* (July 3, 1930; b&w)
    Dir: Wilfred Jackson; Walt Disney; Silly Symphony; A spider takes refuge from a snow storm inside a toyshop filled with fun and surprises; Aka *Midnite in a Toy Shop*.

1026 *The Midnight Snack* (July 19, 1941)
Dir: William Hanna, Joseph Barbera; MGM; Tom and Jerry; T & J's second short, following their debut in 1940's *Puss Gets the Boot.*

The Mighty Heroes (series) **see** *The Stretcher* (1969)

Mighty Mouse (series) **see** *The Mouse of Tomorrow* (1942)

1027 *The Mighty River (Le Fleuve aux grandes eaux)* (1993; 25 mins) †
Dir: Frédéric Back; Canadian Broadcasting Corporation/Société Radio–Canada; Oscar nominee; Animated tribute to the St. Lawrence River from Oscar winner Back (*Crac, The Man Who Planted Trees*); Produced by Back and Hubert Tison.

1028 *Milk and Money* (October 3, 1936; b&w)
Dir: Tex Avery; Warner Bros.; Looney Tune: Porky Pig.

1029 *The Milky Waif* (May 18, 1946)
Dir: William Hanna, Joseph Barbera; MGM; Tom and Jerry, Nibbles; The little mouse, Nibbles, makes his first appearance in this short.

1030 *Milky Way* (June 22, 1940) AA
Dir: Rudolf Ising; MGM; Oscar winner; The first MGM cartoon to win an Academy Award; Rereleased February 14, 1948.

1031 *The Miller's Daughter* (October 13, 1934; b&w)
Dir: Friz Freleng; Warner Bros.; Merrie Melodie; Little statues come to life in this musical short; Chuck Jones' first short as an animator. He would make his directorial debut in 1938 with *The Night Watchman.*

1032 *Million Dollar Cat* (May 6, 1944)
Dir: William Hanna, Joseph Barbera; MGM; Tom and Jerry.

1033 *Millionaire Droopy* (September 21, 1956)
Dir: Tex Avery; MGM; Droopy, Spike; CinemaScope remake of *Wags to Riches* (1949).

1034 *The Miner's Daughter* (May 25, 1950)
Dir: Robert Cannon; UPA; Jolly Frolics; The first UPA/Columbia short from Cannon. Robert "Bobe" Cannon (1901–64), a former Warner Bros. animator (1937–44), directed 18 shorts (1950–58), including the Oscar-winning classic *Gerald McBoing-Boing* (1951).

1035 *Minnie the Moocher* (March 1, 1932; b&w)
Dir: Dave Fleischer; Max Fleischer; Talkartoon, with Betty Boop, Bimbo; Betty runs away from home and into a haunted cave. Cab Calloway and his Orchestra perform the title song of this eerie Fleischer classic; Koko the Clown has a cameo (coming out of an inkwell); Voice—Mae Questel (Betty).

1036 *The Minute and a Half Man* (July, 1959)
Dir: Dave Tendlar; Terrytoons; Hector Heathcote (debut); The first of some 20 shorts

(1959–63, '70–71) starring the character who changes the course of events in history. The earlier shorts were shown on TV's *The Hector Heathcote Show* (1963–65), which also debuted the later releases; Made in CinemaScope; Voice—John Myhers (Hector).

1037 *Miss Glory* (March 7, 1936)
　　Dir: Tex Avery; Warner Bros.; Merrie Melodie; Fabulous art deco designs (by Leodora Congdon) highlight this entertaining Avery short (one of his earliest) about a grand hotel where everyone is awaiting the arrival of the lovely Miss Glory (voiced by Bernice Hansen); Title song by Harry Warren and Al Dubin, from the 1935 Warner feature *Page Miss Glory*.

1038 *The Missing Genie* (April 1, 1963)
　　Dir: Connie Rasinski; Terrytoons; Luno (debut); The white flying horse, Luno—and his young friend Tim—appeared in six theatrical shorts (1963–64), which were later shown on TV's *The Astronut Show* (1965, synd.).

1039 *Mr. Duck Steps Out* (June 7, 1940)
　　Dir: Jack King; Walt Disney; Donald Duck, Huey, Dewey and Louie, Daisy Duck; Donald's nephews accompany him on a date with Daisy in this entertaining musical short; Voice—Clarence Nash (Donald).

Mr. Magoo (series) **see** *Ragtime Bear* (1949)

1040 *Mr. Strauss Takes a Walk* (May 8, 1943)
　　Producer-Director: George Pal; Puppetoon; Followup to *Bravo, Mr. Strauss* (1943).

1041 *Modern Inventions* (May 29, 1937)
　　Dir: Jack King; Walt Disney; Donald Duck; Donald visits the Museum of Modern Marvels; The first "Donald Duck" cartoon, following his three years as a supporting player in "Mickey Mouse" shorts; King's Disney debut as director (he was a Disney animator before his stint as a Warner Bros. director, 1934–36); Voice—Clarence Nash (Donald).

Modern Madcaps (series) **see** *Right Off the Bat* (1958)

Molly Moo Cow (series) **see** *The Hunting Season* (1935)

1042 *Mona Lisa Descending a Staircase* (1992) AA
　　Producer-Director: Joan C. Gratz; Oscar winner; A clay-animated look at the history of art; Gratz is a former collaborator of Claymation pioneer Will Vinton (*Closed Mondays*).

1043 *The Monk and the Fish (Le Moine et le poisson)* (1994) †
　　Michael Dudok de Wit; Folimage Valence Prod; Oscar nominee.

1044 *Monkey Wretches* (November 11, 1935; b&w)
　　Producer-Director: Walter Lantz; Oswald the Rabbit, with Meany, Miny and Moe (debut); The comedic monkey trio Meany-Miny-Moe would appear in 13 shorts of their own (1936–37) see *Turkey Dinner*; Voice—Bernice Hansen (Oswald).

1045 *Monsieur Pointu* (1975; 12 mins) †
　　Dir: Bernard Longpré, André Leduc; National Film Board of Canada; Oscar nomi-

nee; A combination of live action and animation; Produced by Longpré, Leduc and René Jodoin; Cast—Paul Cormier.

1046 *Moonbird* (1959) AA
Producer-Director: John Hubley; Storyboard Inc; Oscar winner (the Hubleys' first); Charming, original Hubley short about two children's pursuit of a bird at night.

1047 *Moose Hunters* (February 20, 1937)
Dir: Ben Sharpsteen; Walt Disney; Mickey Mouse, Donald Duck, Goofy.

1048 *More Kittens* (December 19, 1936)
Dir: David Hand; Walt Disney; Silly Symphony; The kittens play with a large Saint Bernard in this sequel to the Oscar-winning *Three Orphan Kittens* (1935).

1049 *Morning Noon and Night* (October 6, 1933; b&w)
Dir: Dave Fleischer; Max Fleischer; Betty Boop, with Rubinoff and his Orchestra.

1050 *Morris, the Midget Moose* (November 24, 1950)
Dir: Jack Hannah; Walt Disney; A pint-sized moose teams up with another moose who has shortcomings of his own; Original story by Frank Owen.

1051 *Moth and the Flame* (April 1, 1938)
Dir: Burt Gillett; Walt Disney; Silly Symphony; Moths in a costume shop do battle with a candle flame.

1052 *Mother Goose Goes Hollywood* (December 23, 1938) †
Dir: Wilfred Jackson; Walt Disney; Silly Symphony; Oscar nominee. Movie stars populate a book of nursery rhymes (Katherine Hepburn as Little Bo-Peep, etc.).

1053 *Mother Goose Land* (June 23, 1933; b&w)
Dir: Dave Fleischer; Max Fleischer; Betty Boop; Betty visits the land of nursery rhymes; Voice—Mae Questel (Betty).

1054 *Motor Mania* (June 30, 1950)
Dir: Jack Kinney; Walt Disney; Goofy; Goofy plays Mr. Walker, mild-mannered pedestrian, who becomes Mr. Wheeler, maniacal driver, when he gets behind the wheel.

1055 *Mouse and Garden* (July 15, 1960) †
Dir: Friz Freleng; Warner Bros.; Looney Tune: Sylvester; Oscar nominee; Sylvester and another cat fight over a mouse; Voices—Mel Blanc (Sylvester), Daws Butler (Sam).

1056 *Mouse Cleaning* (December 11, 1948)
Dir: William Hanna, Joseph Barbera; MGM; Tom and Jerry; Hilarious "T & J" outing has Jerry trying to get Tom kicked out of the house by making the biggest mess he can.

1057 *The Mouse Comes to Dinner* (May 5, 1945)
Dir: William Hanna, Joseph Barbera; MGM; Tom and Jerry, Toots.

1058 *A Mouse Divided* (January 31, 1953)
    Dir: Friz Freleng; Warner Bros.; Merrie Melodie: Sylvester; Sylvester becomes father to a mouse; Voices—Mel Blanc.

1059 *Mouse in Manhattan* (July 7, 1945)
    Dir: William Hanna, Joseph Barbera; MGM; Tom and Jerry.

1060 *A Mouse in the House* (August 30, 1947)
    Dir: William Hanna, Joseph Barbera; MGM; Tom and Jerry.

1061 *Mouse Menace* (November 2, 1946)
    Dir: Arthur Davis; Warner Bros.; Looney Tune: Porky Pig; Porky tries to get rid of a troublesome mouse; Davis' first WB short as director. Davis (b. 1905), who had been an animator at WB since 1943, would direct 22 shorts (1946–49) then return to animating (for Friz Freleng). He directed one more WB short in 1962 and later worked at the studios of Walter Lantz and DePatie-Freleng; Voices—Mel Blanc.

1062 *The Mouse-Merized Cat* (October 19, 1946)
    Dir: Robert McKimson; Warner Bros.; Merrie Melodie: Babbit and Catstello; Babbit uses hypnosis on Catstello; Voices—Mel Blanc.

1063 *The Mouse of Tomorrow* (October 16, 1942)
    Dir: Eddie Donnelly; Terrytoons; Super Mouse (aka Mighty Mouse); The first cartoon appearance of Mighty Mouse (not billed as such until 1944's *Wreck of the Hesperus*), the rodent superhero who comes to the rescue of mice in trouble (usually from cats). The most popular cartoon star of Paul Terry's studio, Mighty Mouse appeared in 80 shorts (1942–61), which would also show up on TV's *The Mighty Mouse Playhouse* (1955–66); Voice—Tom Morrison (Mighty Mouse).

1064 *The Mouse That Jack Built* (April 4, 1959)
    Dir: Robert McKimson; Warner Bros.; Merrie Melodie; Jack Benny and the cast of his radio and TV series lend their voices to this amusing short about the mice who live in Benny's home; The real Jack Benny appears briefly at the end; Voices—Jack Benny, Mary Livingstone, Eddie "Rochester" Anderson, Don Wilson, Mel Blanc; Note: Warner Bros. voice artist Blanc had been a regular on Benny's radio and TV shows since 1939.

1065 *Mouse Trapped* (December 8, 1959)
    Dir: Alex Lovy; Walter Lantz; Doc (cat), with Hickory and Dickory (mice); When the police start rounding up black cats on Friday the 13th, Hickory and Dickory offer to help Doc hide; The debut of Lantz's bow-tied, top-hatted cat Doc, who would appear in seven shorts (1959–62); Voices—Paul Frees (Doc), Dal McKennon (Hickory/Dickory).

1066 *Mouse Trouble* (December 23, 1944) AA
    Dir: William Hanna, Joseph Barbera; MGM; Tom and Jerry; Oscar winner; Tom consults a book on mouse-catching.

1067 *Mouse Wreckers* (April 23, 1949) †
    Dir: Chuck Jones; Warner Bros.; Merrie Melodie: Hubie and Bertie, Claude Cat (debut); Oscar nominee; Two hobo mice remove a cat from their new home by driving

him insane. Great Jones short; Claude Cat (one of Warner's most unjustly overlooked comic characters) appeared in eight shorts (1949–54)—three with Hubie and Bertie; Voices—Mel Blanc.

1068 *Moving Day* (June 20, 1936)

Dir: Ben Sharpsteen; Walt Disney; Mickey Mouse, Donald Duck, Goofy, Black Pete; Mickey and friends are forced to move for not paying the rent. Comic bits include Goofy's trouble moving a piano and Donald getting his behind stuck in a plunger, then a goldfish bowl; Voices—Walt Disney (Mickey), Clarence Nash (Donald), Pinto Colvig (Goofy), Billy Bletcher (Pete).

1069 *Much Ado About Nutting* (May 23, 1953)

Dir: Chuck Jones; Warner Bros.; Merrie Melodie; A persistent squirrel tries to open a large nut.

1070 *The Mummy Strikes* (February 19, 1943)

Dir: I. Sparber; Paramount/Famous; Superman.

1071 *Munro* (1960) AA

Dir: Gene Deitch; Rembrandt Films; Oscar winner; A 4-year-old is drafted into the army. Stylishly-drawn short written by Jules Feiffer; Released by Paramount in their "Noveltoon" series (September 1961); American Deitch (a veteran of UPA and Terrytoons) directed a number of cartoons—including the revived "Tom and Jerry" series in the early '60s—for American distribution and television while working at Rembrandt Films in Prague, Czechoslovakia; Produced by William Snyder.

1072 *The Museum* (August 19, 1930; b&w)

Dir: Dick Huemer, Sid Marcus; Charles Mintz; Toby the Pup (debut); The mischievous little pup, Toby, appeared in 12 shorts (1930–31) in this series from producer Charles Mintz (head of Columbia's cartoon studio); Former Fleischer animators Huemer and Marcus went on to launch Columbia's "Scrappy" series.

1073 *Music Land* (October 5, 1935)

Dir: Wilfred Jackson; Walt Disney; Silly Symphony; A saxophone's love for a pretty violin starts a war between the Land of Symphony and the Isle of Jazz in this imaginative, splendidly-animated short; One of Disney's best.

1074 *Musical Memories* (November 8, 1935)

Dir: Dave Fleischer; Max Fleischer; Color Classic; Lovely Fleischer cartoon.

Musical Miniatures (series) **see** *The Poet and Peasant* (1946)

1075 *Musical Moments from Chopin* (February 24, 1947) †

Dir: Dick Lundy; Walter Lantz; Musical Miniature (second of four), with Andy Panda, Woody Woodpecker; Oscar nominee; Andy and Woody perform a duo-piano recital, playing "Polonaise" and other selections; Pianists Ted Saidenberg and Ed Rebner perform on the soundtrack; Aka *Chopin's Musical Moments*.

1076 *Mutiny on the Bunny* (February 11, 1950)

Dir: Friz Freleng; Warner Bros.; Looney Tune: Bugs Bunny, Yosemite Sam; Bugs is recruited to work on Sam's ship; Hilarious Freleng short; Voices—Mel Blanc.

Mutt and Jeff (series) **see** *Jeff's Toothache* (1916)

1077 *My Boy, Johnny* (May 12, 1944) †
Dir: Eddie Donnelly; Terrytoons; Terrytoon; Oscar nominee.

1078 *My Daddy, the Astronaut* (April 1, 1967)
Dir: James Culhane; Paramount; Fractured Fables (series debut); Six shorts were produced in the "Fables" series (1967–68), Paramount's last; Ralph Bakshi (of Terrytoons) was also a director on the series; The first Paramount short screened at France's International Animation Festival.

1079 *My Favorite Duck* (December 5, 1942)
Dir: Chuck Jones; Warner Bros.; Looney Tune: Daffy Duck, Porky Pig.

1080 *My Financial Career (Ma carrière financière)* (1963) †
Dir: Gerald Potterton, Grant Munro; National Film Board of Canada; Oscar nominee; Based on a Stephen Leacock story; Narrated by Stanley Jackson; Produced by Tom Daly and Colin Low.

1081 *My Little Duckaroo* (November 27, 1954)
Dir: Chuck Jones; Warner Bros.; Merrie Melodie: Daffy Duck, Porky Pig; Sequel to Jones' *Dripalong Daffy* (1951); Voices—Mel Blanc.

1082 *Nasty Quacks* (December 1, 1945)
Dir: Frank Tashlin; Warner Bros.; Merrie Melodie: Daffy Duck; A man tries to get rid of his daughter's obnoxious pet duck (Daffy). Hilarious Tashlin short; Voices—Mel Blanc.

1083 *Naughty but Mice* (May 30, 1939)
Dir: Chuck Jones; Warner Bros.; Merrie Melodie: Sniffles (debut); A drunk Sniffles makes friends with an electric shaver; The first of 12 shorts (1939–46) starring the sniffling, high-voiced little mouse created by Jones during his early years at Warner Bros.; Voice—Bernice Hansen (Sniffles).

1084 *Naughty but Mice* (October 10, 1947)
Dir: Seymour Kneitel; Paramount/Famous; Noveltoon, with Herman and Katnip (their debut together); The cat-and-mouse team, Herman and Katnip, appeared in 32 shorts (1947–59); Voices—Arnold Stang (Herman), Sid Raymond (Katnip).

1085 *Neighbours* (1952) AA
Producer-Director: Norman McLaren; National Film Board of Canada; Oscar-winner (for Documentary Short), also Oscar-nominated (for One-Reel Short); Acclaimed short shot in "pixillation," a stop-motion technique using live actors.

1086 *Nelly's Folly* (December 30, 1961) †
Dir: Chuck Jones; Warner Bros.; Merrie Melodie; Oscar nominee; A singing giraffe is brought to the city and becomes a star.

1087 *Never Bug an Ant* (February 2, 1966)

Dir: Gerry Chiniquy; DePatie-Freleng; The Ant and the Aardvark (debut); The comic adversaries appeared in 17 shorts (1966–71); Voices—John Byner (Ant/Aardvark).

1088 *The New Spirit* (January 23, 1942) †

Dir: Wilfred Jackson, Ben Sharpsteen; Walt Disney; Donald Duck; Oscar nominee (for Best Documentary); Wartime short promoting income tax payment; Produced for the U.S. Treasury Department; Voice—Clarence Nash (Donald).

The Newlyweds (series) **see** *When He Wants a Dog He Wants a Dog* (1913)

1089 *Night* (July 31, 1930; b&w)

Producer-Director: Walt Disney; Silly Symphony; The moon sings, owls dance, fireflies light up the sky, etc.

1090 *The Night Before Christmas* (December 9, 1933)

Dir: Wilfred Jackson; Walt Disney; Silly Symphony; Jolly old St. Nick pays a visit, bringing a bagful of toys (including a wind-up Mickey Mouse); Based on the Clement Moore poem.

1091 *The Night Before Christmas* (December 6, 1941) †

Dir: William Hanna, Joseph Barbera; MGM; Tom and Jerry; Oscar nominee.

1092 *Night of the Living Duck* (September 23, 1988)

Dir: Greg Ford, Terry Lennon; Warner Bros.; Merrie Melodie: Daffy Duck; Daffy dreams he is performing for monsters at a nightclub; Voices—Mel Blanc, Mel Torme.

1093 *Night on Bald Mountain / Ave Maria* (November 13, 1940; 13 mins)

Dir: Wilfred Jackson; Walt Disney; Brilliant animation brings to life two pieces of music—the dark, forceful 1866 tone poem by Modest Moussorgsky (1835–81) and the sacred song by Franz Schubert (1797–1828)—contrasting the forces of good and evil; Part of the feature *Fantasia*; Animation Supervisor—Vladimir "Bill" Tytla; Highlighted by Tytla's memorable animation of the devil Chernabog; One of the film's art directors was Danish-born illustrator Kay Nielson (*East of the Sun, West of the Moon*); Leopold Stokowski conducts the Philadelphia Orchestra; Voice—Julietta Novis (soloist).

1094 *The Night Watchman* (November 19, 1938)

Dir: Chuck Jones; Warner Bros.; Merrie Melodie; A gang of tough mice invade a kitchen guarded by little Tommy Cat; Jones' directorial debut. Charles M. Jones (b. 1912, Spokane, WA) joined the Warner studio in 1933 and would stay there for 30 years, creating such characters as the Road Runner, Wile E. Coyote, Pepe Le Pew and Marvin Martian, and directing many classic cartoons (*Duck Amuck, One Froggy Evening, What's Opera, Doc?*, etc.). Jones directed 208 theatrical WB shorts (1938–64), including two Oscar winners—*For Scenti-mental Reasons* and the documentary short *So Much for So Little* (both 1949). He returned to producing and directing WB shorts in 1994 (see *Chariots of Fur*) and in 1995 received a special Oscar for lifetime achievement.

1095 *Noah's Ark* (November 10, 1959; 18 mins) †

Dir: Bill Justice; Walt Disney; Oscar nominee; Musical telling of the Bible story using stop-motion puppet animation; Songs (by Mel Leven) include "The Good Ship Noah's Ark"; Voices—Jerome Courtland (Narrator), Jeanne Gayle, James Macdonald, Paul Frees.

1096 *Noah's Lark* (October 25, 1929–copyright date; b&w)
Dir: Dave Fleischer; Max Fleischer; Talkartoon; Debut short in the Fleischers' first "talking" cartoon series (their first sound series was the musical "Screen Songs"). The series featured former Fleischer stars Koko the Clown and Bimbo (a character evolved from Koko's dog Fitz) and launched a new one, Betty Boop (see *Dizzy Dishes*); 42 "Talkartoons" (1929–32) were produced.

1097 *No Barking* (February 27, 1954)
Dir: Chuck Jones; Warner Bros.; Merrie Melodie: Claude Cat, Frisky Puppy, Tweety (cameo); The puppy continues to bother Claude with his yelping; Claude and Frisky's third (and last) cartoon together.

1098 *No Hunting* (January 14, 1955) †
Dir: Jack Hannah; Walt Disney; Donald Duck; Oscar nominee; The spirit of Donald's ancestor sends him out on the hunt; Bambi and his mother make a cameo appearance (she solemnly tells him upon Donald's arrival, "Man is in the forest"); Filmed in CinemaScope; Voice—Clarence Nash (Donald).

1099 *No Mutton for Nuttin'* (November 26, 1943)
Paramount/Famous; Noveltoon, with Blackie the Lamb (debut); The first of 170 shorts in Famous Studio's long-running "Noveltoon" series (1943–67), which featured a variety of stories and characters (including Raggedy Ann, Little Audrey, Baby Huey, Buzzy the Crow, Herman and Katnip, Tommy Tortoise and Moe Hare); Blackie appeared in three "Noveltoon" shorts (1943–46).

1100 *Norman Normal* (February 3, 1968)
Dir: Alex Lovy; Warner Bros.; Cartoon Special; Animated satire with a rock score; Story and voices by Noel (Paul) Stookey (of the folk trio Peter, Paul and Mary) and Dave Dixon (as Norman); The title song appears on Peter, Paul and Mary's *Album* (1967).

1101 *Northwest Hounded Police* (August 13, 1946)
Dir: Tex Avery; MGM; Droopy, The Wolf; Droopy (as "McPoodle of the Mounted") effortlessly trails an escaped convict around the world; The Wolf's wild reaction shots are a highlight.

1102 *Nose Hair* (1994)
Producer-Director: Bill Plympton; It's man vs. nose hair in this short written and animated by Plympton; Music by Maureen McElheron.

1103 *Not Now* (February 28, 1936; b&w)
Dir: Dave Fleischer; Max Fleischer; Betty Boop, with Pudgy (her little dog).

1104 *Notes to You* (September 20, 1941; b&w)
Dir: Friz Freleng; Warner Bros.; Looney Tune: Porky Pig; Porky is kept awake by an alley cat singing outside his window; Color remake—*Back Alley Oproar* (1948) with Elmer Fudd and Sylvester; Voices—Mel Blanc.

Noveltoons (series) **see** *No Mutton for Nuttin'* (1943)

1105 *Now Hear This* (April 27, 1963) †
    Dir: Chuck Jones; Co-Dir: Maurice Noble; Warner Bros.; Looney Tune; Oscar nominee; Unusual, abstract film concerning an Englishman and his hearing aid; One of Jones' last Warner Bros. cartoons.

1106 *Nudnik No. 2* (1964) †
    Dir: Gene Deitch; Rembrandt Films; Nudnik; Oscar nominee; Produced by William L. Snyder.

1107 *The Nutcracker Suite* (November 13, 1940; 14 mins)
    Dir: Samuel Armstrong; Walt Disney; A visually-dazzling nature ballet set to the music of Pyotr Ilich Tchaikovsky (1840–93), from his 1892 *Nutcracker* ballet. Disney animation at its best; Segments—Dewdrop Fairies ("Dance of the Sugar Plum Fairy"), Mushrooms ("Chinese Dance"), Blossoms ("Dance of the Reed Flutes"), Fish ("Arab Dance"), Thistles ("Russian Dance"), Autumn-Winter ("Waltz of the Flowers"); Part of the feature *Fantasia*; Animators—Art Babbitt, Les Clark, Don Lusk, Cy Young, Robert Stokes; Highlight—the mushroom dance (animated by Babbitt); Leopold Stokowski conducts the Philadelphia Orchestra.

1108 *Odor-able Kitty* (January 6, 1945)
    Dir: Chuck Jones; Warner Bros.; Looney Tune: Pepe Le Pew (debut); Pepe (named Henry here) chases a male cat who is disguised as a skunk. Pepe's first cartoon appearance (and one of his funniest); The amorous French skunk (modeled after screen lover Charles Boyer) appeared in 17 shorts (1945–62), including the Oscar-winning *For Scentimental Reasons* (1949); Voices—Mel Blanc.

1109 *Of Fox and Hounds* (December 7, 1940)
    Dir: Tex Avery; Warner Bros.; Merrie Melodie; A dumb hunting dog named Willoughby (voiced by Avery) pursues a fox in this funny short.

1110 *Of Men and Demons* (1969) †
    Dir: John Hubley; Hubley Studios; Oscar nominee; A war erupts between nature and machines when a farmer confronts the gods of wind, rain and fire; Music by Quincy Jones.

1111 *Of Rice and Hen* (November 14, 1953)
    Dir: Robert McKimson; Warner Bros.; Looney Tune: Foghorn Leghorn, Miss Prissy; Foghorn tries to fend off the advances of the lonely Miss Prissy; Voices—Mel Blanc.

1112 *Often an Orphan* (August 13, 1949)
    Dir: Chuck Jones; Warner Bros.; Looney Tune: Porky Pig, Charlie Dog; Charlie needs a new master and sees one in farmer Porky; Voices—Mel Blanc.

1113 *Oh My Darling* (1978) †
    Dir: Borge Ring; Nico Crama Prod; Oscar nominee.

1114 *Old Glory* (July 1, 1939)
    Dir: Chuck Jones; Warner Bros.; Merrie Melodie: Porky Pig; Porky dreams of Uncle

Sam who recounts to him the history of America; Includes the use of rotoscoping (tracing from live-action footage); Won the Newsreel Theatre's award for best animated cartoon of the year; Voices—Mel Blanc (Porky), John Deering (Uncle Sam).

1115 *The Old Grey Hare* (October 28, 1944)
Dir: Bob Clampett; Warner Bros.; Merrie Melodie: Bugs Bunny, Elmer Fudd; Great Clampett short looks at Bugs and Elmer's relationship in their early and later years; Voices—Mel Blanc (Bugs), Arthur Q. Bryan (Elmer).

1116 *Old King Cole* (July 29, 1933)
Dir: David Hand; Walt Disney; Silly Symphony; Nursery rhyme characters gather at the palace of Old King Cole.

1117 *The Old Lady and the Pigeons* (*La Vielle Dame et les Pigeons*) (1997; 23 mins) †
Dir: Sylvain Chomet; Pascal Blais/Les Armateurs/Odec Kid Cartoons; Oscar nominee; Twisted tale about an old woman who feeds pigeons and a starving French policeman who disguises himself as one of the birds; A grand prize winner at the 1997 Annecy Animation Festival; Voices—Jim Pidgeon, Michoue Sylvain, Andrea Usher-Jones.

1118 *The Old Man of the Mountain* (August 4, 1933; b&w)
Dir: Dave Fleischer; Max Fleischer; Betty Boop, with the music of Cab Calloway and his Orchestra; Betty pays a visit to the title character in this terrific musical short; Calloway's third "Betty Boop" short, following *Minnie the Moocher* (1932) and *Snow White* (1933); Voice—Mae Questel (Betty).

1119 *The Old Mill* (November 5, 1937) AA
Dir: Wilfred Jackson; Walt Disney; Silly Symphony; Oscar winner (Disney's sixth); One of Disney Studios' most beautifully-animated shorts focuses on an old windmill and its little inhabitants on one stormy night; The first cartoon to use the multiplane camera, which gives the illusion of depth. Its design and application earned the studio a technical Oscar; Music by Leigh Harline.

1120 *Old Mill Pond* (March 7, 1936) †
Dir: Hugh Harman; MGM; Happy Harmony; Oscar nominee.

1121 *Old Rockin' Chair Tom* (September 18, 1948)
Dir: William Hanna, Joseph Barbera; MGM; Tom and Jerry.

1122 *The Olympic Champ* (October 9, 1942)
Dir: Jack Kinney; Walt Disney; Goofy; Goofy demonstrates various Olympic sports, including pole vaulting and javelin throwing.

1123 *On Ice* (September 28, 1935)
Dir: Ben Sharpsteen; Walt Disney; Mickey Mouse, Donald Duck, Goofy, Pluto, Minnie Mouse.

1124 *Once Upon a Wintertime* (May 27, 1948)
Dir: Hamilton Luske; Walt Disney; Pleasant tale of a young, ice-skating couple in

love; Frances Langford sings the title song (written by Bobby Worth and Ray Gilbert); Part of the feature *Melody Time*; Rereleased September 17, 1954.

1125 *One Cab's Family* (May 17, 1952)
Dir: Tex Avery; MGM; The young son of a proud taxi cab wants to be a hot rod.

1126 *One Droopy Knight* (December 6, 1957) †
Dir: Michael Lah; MGM; Droopy; Oscar nominee; Sir Droopy and a rival knight attempt to slay a fire-breathing dragon in this medieval reworking of Tex Avery's *Senor Droopy* (1949).

1127 *One Froggy Evening* (December 31, 1955)
Dir: Chuck Jones; Warner Bros.; Merrie Melodie; The story of a frog—discovered in the cornerstone of an 1892 building—whose amazing talent for singing and dancing brings nothing but misfortune to its owner. A Jones masterpiece, and one of the greatest cartoons of all time; The film's frog star (who has since acquired the name "Michigan J. Frog") later became the mascot of the WB (Warner Bros.) TV network; The name "Tregoweth Brown" on the 1955 cornerstone is a reference to Warner sound effects man Treg Brown; Animators—Abe Levitow, Richard Thompson, Ken Harris, Ben Washam; Musical Director—Milt Franklyn; Songs include "Hello, My Ragtime Gal," "Please Don't Talk About Me When I'm Gone," "Come Back to Erin" and an original song "The Michigan Rag"; Sequel—*Another Froggy Evening* (1995).

1128 *One Ham's Family* (August 14, 1943)
Dir: Tex Avery; MGM; A little pig fights off the Big Bad Wolf, who pays a visit disguised as Santa Claus.

1129 *One of Those Days* (1988)
Producer-Director: Bill Plympton; Great Plympton short in which the camera takes the point of view of a man who's having a *really* bad day (his hand catches fire, he's run over by a steamroller, and so on); Written and animated by Plympton.

1130 *One Quack Mind* (January 12, 1951)
Dir: I. Sparber; Paramount/Famous; Noveltoon, with Baby Huey (debut); The bumbling, oversized duck Huey appeared in 11 "Noveltoon" shorts (1951–59); Voice—Sid Raymond (Baby Huey).

1131 *The Oompahs* (January 24, 1952)
Dir: Robert Cannon; UPA; Jolly Frolics.

1132 *Opening Night* (February 10, 1933—copyright date; b&w)
Dir: Mannie Davis; Van Beuren; Cubby the Bear (debut); The first of 16 shorts (1933–34) starring Cubby the Bear (renamed "Brownie Bear" for TV).

1133 *Operation: Rabbit* (January 19, 1952)
Dir: Chuck Jones; Warner Bros.; Looney Tune: Bugs Bunny, Wile E. Coyote; Supergenius Wile E. Coyote—who debuted silent and nameless in 1949's *Fast and Furry-Ous*—now speaks and shifts his attention from the Road Runner to Bugs; Voices—Mel Blanc.

1134 *The Opry House* (1929; b&w)
Producer-Director: Walt Disney; Mickey Mouse.

1135 *The Orphan Duck* (October 6, 1939; b&w)
Dir: Connie Rasinski; Terrytoons; Dinky Duck (debut); The first of 15 shorts (1939–57) starring Terrytoons' Dinky Duck.

1136 *Orphans' Benefit* (August 11, 1934; b&w)
Dir: Burt Gillett; Walt Disney; Mickey Mouse, Donald Duck (in his second appearance), Goofy, Clara Cluck; Remade in color in 1941.

Oswald the Lucky Rabbit (series) **see** *Trolley Troubles* (1927)

1137 *Outfoxed* (October 12, 1949)
Dir: Tex Avery; MGM; Droopy; Droopy and a group of fox hounds chase a clever fox (who sounds a little like Ronald Colman).

1138 *Out of Scale* (November 2, 1951)
Dir: Jack Hannah; Walt Disney; Donald Duck, Chip 'n' Dale; The chipmunks make themselves at home in Donald's small-scale village-and-train set; Voice—Clarence Nash (Donald).

1139 *Out of the Inkwell* (1919; b&w)
Dir: Max Fleischer; Bray Studios; Out of the Inkwell, with Koko the Clown; Debut of the groundbreaking cartoon series (although experimental shorts were produced as early as 1916) created by Max Fleischer and produced by John R. Bray; Featuring a clown named Koko, the series ingeniously blended live action and animation by having Koko pop out of the inkwell on Max's animating desk and interact with him. It also used rotoscoping (patented, 1917), Fleischer's new technique of tracing live-action footage for more realistic movement in the animation (for this, Max's brother/collaborator Dave would dress and perform in a clown suit). Over 80 "Out of the Inkwell" shorts were produced (1919–27), followed by the "Inkwell Imps" series (1927–29) also with Koko. The Fleischers began producing the series through their own studio in 1921; Shown as part of the "Paramount-Bray-Pictograph" series.

1140 *Overture to William Tell* (June 16, 1947)
Dir: Dick Lundy; Walter Lantz; Musical Miniature (third of four), with Wally Walrus.

1141 *Ozzie of the Circus* (January 5, 1929; b&w)
Producer-Director: Walter Lantz; Oswald the Rabbit (sound debut); Silent cartoon star Oswald the Rabbit, whose original adventures were produced by Walt Disney (1927–28), appeared in some 170 shorts in this new sound series (1929–38, 43) which launched the Walter Lantz studio; The first seven shorts were unreleased silents with sound added; Oswald was originally voiced by Mickey McGuire (aka Mickey Rooney), then by Bernice Hansen.

1142 *Pablo, the Cold-Blooded Penguin* (February 3, 1945)
Walt Disney; Sterling Holloway narrates the story of a coldblooded penguin who sets sail from his antarctic home in search of a warmer climate; Part of the feature *The Three Caballeros*.

1143 *Pals* (December 22, 1933; b&w)
Dir: James Tyer; Van Beuren; The Little King; Aka *Christmas Night*.

1144 *Parade of the Wooden Soldiers* (December 1, 1933; b&w)
Dir: Dave Fleischer; Max Fleischer; Betty Boop, with the music of Rubinoff and his Orchestra; Betty, in doll form, arrives in a toy shop where she and other toys do battle with a stuffed gorilla; Voice—Mae Questel (Betty).

1145 *Paradise* (1984; 15 mins) †
Producer-Director: Ishu Patel; National Film Board of Canada; Oscar nominee; Visually-striking film from Patel (*The Bead Game*) using various techniques (cut-outs, double exposures, color pencil drawings, and so forth); Animated by Patel and George Ungar; Music by Gheorghe Zamfir.

1146 *Part-Time Pal* (March 15, 1947)
Dir: William Hanna, Joseph Barbera; MGM; Tom and Jerry.

1147 *Pass the Biscuits Mirandy* (August 23, 1943)
Dir: James Culhane; Walter Lantz; Swing Symphony; Culhane's first cartoon for Lantz. He would direct some of the studio's best shorts (19 in all, 1943–46), including the great "Woody Woodpecker" short *Barber of Seville* (1944). James "Shamus" Culhane (1908–96), a veteran animator (he worked at Bray, Fleischer, Disney, and Warner Bros.), later headed the Paramount cartoon studio (1965–67).

1148 *Past Perfumance* (May 21, 1955)
Dir: Chuck Jones; Warner Bros.; Merrie Melodie: Pepe Le Pew.

1149 *The Pastoral Symphony* (November 13, 1940; 21 mins)
Dir: Hamilton Luske, Jim Handley, Ford Beebe; Walt Disney; Mythical creatures (fauns, unicorns, winged horses, centaurs, cupids, and so on) frolic around Mount Olympus to the music of Ludwig van Beethoven's (1770–1827) Symphony No. 6 (1808). Colorful animation, beautifully choreographed to the music; Part of the feature *Fantasia*; The music originally selected for this short was the ballet "Cydalise and the Satyr" (1923) by Gabriel Pierne; Animation Supervisors—Fred Moore, Ward Kimball, Eric Larson, Art Babbitt, Oliver M. Johnston, Jr., Don Towsley; Walt Kelly (1913–73), who created the comic book/strip character "Pogo" (in 1942), was an animator on the film; Leopold Stokowski conducts the Philadelphia Orchestra.

1150 *Pastry Town Wedding* (July 27, 1934)
Dir: Burt Gillett, Ted Eshbaugh; Van Beuren; Rainbow Parade (series debut); The first of 27 musical fables (1934–36). The series was Gillett's second for Van Beuren (following the short-lived "Toddle Tales") and the studio's first in color.

1151 *Patient Porky* (August 24, 1940; b&w)
Dir: Bob Clampett; Warner Bros.; Looney Tune: Porky Pig.

1152 *Paul Bunyan* (August 1, 1958; 16 mins) †
Dir: Les Clark; Walt Disney; Oscar nominee; Entertaining tall tale about the towering lumberjack and his big blue ox; Great title song by George Bruns and Tom Adair, sung by The Mellomen (featuring Thurl Ravenscroft as Paul).

1153 *Paw's Night Out* (August 1, 1955)
    Dir: Paul J. Smith; Walter Lantz; Maw and Paw (last in the series); Milford the pig helps Paw sneak into the house late without Maw knowing; Voices—Grace Stafford (Maw), Dal McKennon (Paw).

1154 *Peace on Earth* (December 9, 1939) †
    Dir: Hugh Harman; MGM; Oscar nominee; The animals of a peaceful village look back on the time when men walked the Earth…and how they killed each other off. Excellent prewar short powerfully conveys the timely message of "peace on earth"; Remade in 1955 as *Good Will to Men*; Voices—Mel Blanc, Sarah Berner, Bernice Hansen.

1155 *The Peachy Cobbler* (December 9, 1950)
    Dir: Tex Avery; MGM; A group of magical (and very silly) elves help a poor cobbler by making his shoes.

1156 *Pecos Bill* (May 27, 1948; 22 mins)
    Dir: Clyde Geronimi; Walt Disney; Superbly rendered tale of the legendary cowboy, his trusty horse Widowmaker and the pretty Slue Foot Sue; Sung and told by Roy Rogers and the Sons of the Pioneers; Part of the feature *Melody Time*; Songs (by Eliot Daniel and Johnny Lange)—"Blue Shadows on the Trail" and the title song.

1157 *Pedro* (February 6, 1943)
    Dir: Hamilton Luske; Walt Disney; A little mail plane runs into trouble on his maiden flight over the Andes; Part of the feature *Saludos Amigos*; Narrated by Fred Shields; Rereleased May 13, 1955.

1158 *The Pelican and the Snipe* (January 7, 1944)
    Dir: Hamilton Luske; Walt Disney; The friendship of a pelican and a snipe, living atop a lighthouse, is strained by the pelican's habit of flying in his sleep; Narrated by Sterling Holloway.

1159 *The Penguin Parade* (April 16, 1938)
    Dir: Tex Avery; Warner Bros.; Merrie Melodie.

Pepe Le Pew (series) **see** *Odor-Able Kitty* (1945)

1160 *A Pest in the House* (August 3, 1947)
    Dir: Chuck Jones; Warner Bros.; Merrie Melodie: Daffy Duck, Elmer Fudd; Bellboy Daffy annoys a guest staying at Elmer's hotel. Very funny Jones short; Voices—Mel Blanc, Arthur Q. Bryan.

1161 *Pete Hothead* (September 25, 1952)
    Dir: Ted Parmelee; UPA; Jolly Frolics; Parmelee also directed the Oscar-nominated *The Tell-Tale Heart* (1953).

1162 *Peter and the Wolf* (August 15, 1946; 14 mins)
    Dir: Clyde Geronimi; Walt Disney; A young boy sets out to hunt a ferocious wolf. Delightful Disney telling of Serge Prokofieff's (1891–1953) popular musical fable, which was first performed in 1936; Each character is represented by a different musical instru-

ment—Peter (string quartet), Sasha the bird (flute), Sonia the duck (oboe), Ivan the cat (clarinet), Grandpa (bassoon), and the hunters' guns (kettledrums); Part of the feature *Make Mine Music* (it was originally intended to be part of a planned *Fantasia* sequel, which never came about); Disney first met with Prokofieff about making the film back in 1938; Voice—Sterling Holloway (Narrator); Rereleased September 14, 1955.

Phables (series) **see** *The Phable of Sam and Bill* (1915)

1163 *The Phable of Sam and Bill* (December 17, 1915; b&w)
Dir: Raoul Barre; Raoul Barre/International Film Service; Phables (debut); The first of seven silent shorts (1915–16) based on Tom E. Powers' comic strip. One of Barre's last efforts before joining with Charles Bowers on the "Mutt and Jeff" series.

Phantasies (series) **see** *The Charm Bracelet* (1939)

1164 *Philbert (Three's a Crowd)* (April, 1963; 26 mins)
Live-action Dir: Richard Donner; Animation Dir: Friz Freleng; Warner Bros.; A cartoonist's life is complicated by his little cartoon alter ego; Special fearurette combining live action and animation, originally made for TV as a pilot for a proposed series; Animation Co-directors—Hawley Pratt, Gerry Chiniquy; Opening titles animated by Art Babbitt. Title song by Sammy Fain and Sy Miller; Cast—William Schallert (Griff), Joanna Barnes (Angela); Voice—Trust Howard (Philbert).

1165 *The Philips Broadcast of 1938* (1938)
Producer-Director: George Pal; Early Pal "Puppetoon," an advertisement for Philips Radio, produced at his studio in Holland.

1166 *Pianissimo* (1963) †
Producer-Director: Carmen D'Avino; Oscar nominee; From American artist-animator D'Avino (b. 1918).

1167 *Pib and Pog* (1994)
Dir: Peter Peake; Aardman Animations; Two children's show characters (similar to *The Simpsons*' "Itchy and Scratchy") engage in violent combat with one another.

1168 *Picador Porky* (February 27, 1937; b&w)
Dir: Tex Avery; Warner Bros.; Looney Tune: Porky Pig; The first Warner Bros. cartoon to feature the amazing talent of voice artist Mel Blanc (1908–89) who, during his 32 years at the studio, would provide the voices for Bugs Bunny, Daffy Duck, Porky Pig, Yosemite Sam, Foghorn Leghorn, Pepe Le Pew, Sylvester, Tweety and others. In all he voiced 848 WB shorts.

1169 *The Pied Piper* (September 16, 1933)
Dir: Wilfred Jackson; Walt Disney; Silly Symphony; Fine Disney telling of Robert Browning's classic tale.

1170 *The Pied Piper of Guadalupe* (August 19, 1961) †
Dir: Friz Freleng; Warner Bros.; Looney Tune: Speedy Gonzales, Sylvester; Oscar nominee; Sylvester tries to lure mice by playing the "Pied Piper"; Voices—Mel Blanc.

1171 *Pigs in a Polka* (February 2, 1943) †
Dir: Friz Freleng; Warner Bros.; Merrie Melodie; Oscar nominee; The story of the "Three Little Pigs" is set to the music of Brahm's "Hungarian Rhapsody."

1172 *Pigs Is Pigs* (May 21, 1954; 9 mins) †
Dir: Jack Kinney; Walt Disney; Oscar nominee; In 1905, a railway station worker who does everything by the book gets stuck with some fast-multiplying guinea pigs. Delightful Disney short, drawn in the new flat, angular style; From the book by Ellis Parker Butler; Sung by The Mellomen.

1173 *Pink and Blue Blues* (August 28, 1952) †
Dir: Pete Burness; UPA; Mr. Magoo; Oscar nominee; Original title—*Pink Blue Plums*.

1174 *The Pink Blueprint* (May 25, 1966) †
Dir: Hawley Pratt; DePatie-Freleng; The Pink Panther; Oscar nominee.

The Pink Panther (series) **see** *The Pink Phink* (1964)

1175 *The Pink Phink* (December 18, 1964) AA
Dir: Friz Freleng, Hawley Pratt; DePatie-Freleng; The Pink Panther; Oscar winner; The first official "Pink Panther" cartoon (following the unreleased pilot short *Suspense Account*) featuring the skinny, silent character first introduced in the opening titles of Blake Edwards' spy spoof *The Pink Panther* (1964). The series (123 shorts, 1964–81) was the most popular ever produced by the company formed by David H. DePatie and director Friz Freleng, and featured the memorable theme music by Henry Mancini; Premiered at Grauman's Chinese Theatre in Hollywood.

1176 *Pixie Picnic* (May, 1948)
Dir: Dick Lundy; Walter Lantz; Musical Miniature (last of four).

1177 *Pizzicato Pussycat* (January 1, 1955)
Dir: Friz Freleng; Warner Bros.; Merrie Melodie; The story of an amazing mouse pianist and a cat who is mistaken to be the piano-playing miracle; Voices—Mel Blanc.

1178 *A Place in the Sun* (1959) †
Producer-Director: Frantisek Vystrcil; Oscar nominee; Debut short from Czech animator Vystrcil (b. 1923).

1179 *Plane Crazy* (March 17, 1929; b&w)
Producer-Director: Walt Disney; Mickey Mouse, Minnie Mouse; Mickey takes Minnie for a ride in his plane; The first "Mickey Mouse" cartoon ever produced (though not the first released, see *Steamboat Willie*), with superb animation by Ub Iwerks; Originally made in 1928 (along with *Gallopin' Gaucho*) as a silent short, then released a year later with sound; Music by Carl Stalling (of Warner Bros. fame, see *Porky's Poultry Plant*).

1180 *Plane Daffy* (September 16, 1944)
Dir: Frank Tashlin; Warner Bros.; Looney Tune: Daffy Duck; Daffy has to keep a military secret out of the hands of sexy spy Hatta Mari in this zany wartime short; Voices—Mel Blanc.

1181 *Plane Dippy* (April 30, 1936; b&w)
Dir: Tex Avery; Warner Bros.; Looney Tune: Porky Pig. Animator Virgil Ross' first WB short. Ross (1907–96) worked at the studio until 1967.

1182 *The Plastics Inventor* (September 1, 1944)
Dir: Jack King; Walt Disney; Donald Duck; Donald constructs a plastic airplane by following directions from a radio program; Voice—Clarence Nash (Donald).

1183 *Play Ball* (September 16, 1933; b&w)
Producer-Director: Ub Iwerks; Willie Whopper (debut); Iwerks followed his "Flip the Frog" series with this less successful one about a young teller of tall tales. Willie appeared in 13 shorts (1933–34).

1184 *Playful Pan* (December 28, 1930; b&w)
Dir: Burt Gillett; Walt Disney; Silly Symphony.

1185 *Playful Pelican* (October 8, 1948)
Dir: Dick Lundy; Walter Lantz; Andy Panda; Ship deckhand Andy has his hands full taking care of a baby pelican.

1186 *Playful Pluto* (March 3, 1934; b&w)
Dir: Burt Gillett; Walt Disney; Mickey Mouse, Pluto; Superior "Pluto" short. Highlights—Pluto's reaction to swallowing a flashlight and getting stuck to a piece of fly paper; Shown in Preston Sturges' 1941 classic *Sullivan's Travels* (it is the film the chain gang watches in the church).

1187 *Play Safe* (October 16, 1936)
Dir: Dave Fleischer; Max Fleischer; Color Classic; A careless boy plays on the railroad tracks with near-disastrous results.

Pluto (series) **see** *The Chain Gang* (1930)

1188 *Pluto at the Zoo* (November 20, 1942)
Dir: Clyde Geronimi; Walt Disney; Pluto.

1189 *Plutopia* (May 18, 1951)
Dir: Charles Nichols; Walt Disney; Pluto, Mickey Mouse.

1190 *Pluto's Blue Note* (December 26, 1947) †
Dir: Charles Nichols; Walt Disney; Pluto; Oscar nominee; Pluto becomes a dreamy crooner; Pluto sings (or, rather, lip-syncs) "You Belong to My Heart" (by Agustin Lara and Ray Gilbert), which was featured in Disney's *The Three Caballeros* (1945).

1191 *Pluto's Christmas Tree* (November 21, 1952)
Dir: Jack Hannah; Walt Disney; Pluto, Mickey Mouse, Chip 'n' Dale; The chipmunks play around in Mickey and Pluto's Christmas tree; Donald Duck, Goofy and Minnie appear briefly as carolers; Voice—Jim Macdonald (Mickey).

1192 *Pluto's Judgement Day* (August 31, 1935)
Dir: David Hand; Walt Disney; Mickey Mouse, Pluto; In Pluto's nightmare he is put on trial for his mistreatment of cats; Voice — Walt Disney (Mickey).

1193 *Pluto's Quin-Puplets* (November 26, 1937)
Dir: Ben Sharpsteen; Walt Disney; Pluto, Fifi; Pluto is left to take care of his mischievous pups.

1194 *Plymptoons* (1990)
Dir: Bill Plympton; Plympton/MTV; Twenty-seven comic vignettes — in 7 minutes — including "evolution" and "the car alarm." Very funny short from Plympton (*Your Face, How to Kiss*); Written and animated by Plympton.

1195 *The Poet and Peasant* (March 18, 1946) †
Dir: Dick Lundy; Walter Lantz; Musical Miniature (debut), with Woody Woodpecker, Andy Panda; Oscar nominee; Andy conducts a barnyard orchestra in a performance of the title overture by Suppe; One of Lantz's most successful cartoons and the first of four "Musical Miniatures" (1946–48), an expensive series of orchestral musical shorts; Soundtrack performed by a 50-piece symphonic orchestra.

1196 *The Pointer* (July 21, 1939) †
Dir: Clyde Geronimi; Walt Disney; Mickey Mouse, Pluto; Oscar nominee; Mickey and Pluto go quail hunting — but find a bear instead; Voice — Walt Disney (Mickey).

1197 *Polar Trappers* (June 17, 1938)
Dir: Ben Sharpsteen; Walt Disney; Donald Duck, Goofy.

Pooch the Pup (series) **see** *The Athlete* (1932)

1198 *Poor Cinderella* (August 3, 1934)
Dir: Dave Fleischer; Max Fleischer; Color Classic (debut), with Betty Boop; Charming version of the fairy tale, using the Fleischers' new 3–D process (in which the backgrounds were actually model sets on a revolving turntable) to stunning effect; The Fleischers' first (and Betty's only) color cartoon (filmed in two-strip Technicolor); 35 "Color Classics" were produced (1934–40); Song — "I'm Just a Poor Cinderella" by Charles Tobian, Murray Mencher and Jack Scholl; Voice — Mae Questel (Betty).

1199 *Poor Little Witch Girl* (April, 1965)
Dir: Howard Post; Paramount; Modern Madcap, with Honey Halfwitch (debut); The good little witch, Honey, appeared in 12 shorts (1965–67).

1200 *Popeye, the Ace of Space* (October 2, 1953)
Dir: Seymour Kneitel; Paramount/Famous; Popeye the Sailor; Famous Studios' first 3–D cartoon (the second was the 1954 "Casper" short *Boo Moon*).

1201 *Popeye the Sailor* (July 14, 1933; b&w)
Dir: Dave Fleischer; Max Fleischer; Betty Boop, with Popeye the Sailor (debut); Popeye takes Olive Oyl to a carnival where rival, Bluto, makes trouble and Betty performs as a hula dancer; The first cartoon appearance of Popeye the Sailor, based on Elzie C. Segar's

(1894–1938) popular comic-strip character (he first appeared in Segar's "Thimble Theatre" on January 17, 1929). Popeye's trademark can of spinach, famous catch phrases ("I yam what I yam," "Blow me down," and others) and great supporting cast (Olive Oyl, Bluto, Wimpy, etc.) helped make him the Fleischers' next major star. He appeared in 109 shorts (1933–42) for Fleischer, then another 122 shorts (1942–57), of lesser quality, for Famous Studios. He later starred on TV (1961–63, 78–82, 87–88) and in a live-action feature (1980) starring Robin Williams; Popeye sings his theme song "I'm Popeye the Sailor Man" (by Sammy Lerner); Voice—William Costello (Popeye); Note: Jack Mercer (1910–84) became Popeye's permanent voice a short time later. His funny mutterings (which he wrote or ad-libbed himself) were a highlight of the series.

1202 *Popeye the Sailor Meets Ali Baba's Forty Thieves* (November 26, 1937; 17 mins)
Dir: Dave Fleischer; Max Fleischer; Popeye the Sailor, Olive Oyl, Bluto; Popeye must rescue Olive from the sinister Abu Hassan (Bluto). Excellent Fleischer short, with Popeye's hilarious mutterings a highlight; The second of three special "Popeye" two-reelers (twice the length of a normal short); Song—"Abu Hassan" by Sammy Timberg, Tot Seymour, Vee Lawnhurst and Sammy Lerner; Voices—Jack Mercer (Popeye), Mae Questel (Olive), Gus Wickie (Bluto).

1203 *Popeye the Sailor Meets Sinbad the Sailor* (November 27, 1936; 16 mins) †
Dir: Dave Fleischer; Max Fleischer; Popeye the Sailor, Olive Oyl, Bluto, Wimpy; When Olive is kidnapped to the Isle of Sinbad (Bluto), Popeye is off to the rescue. One of the all-time greatest "Popeye" cartoons (the first in color), using the Fleischers' process of animating over a three-dimensional, revolving background; The first of three special two-reel "Popeye" featurettes. Followed by *Popeye the Sailor Meets Ali Baba's Forty Thieves* (1937) and *Aladdin and His Wonderful Lamp* (1939); Song—"Sinbad the Sailor" by Sammy Timberg, Bob Rothberg and Sammy Lerner; Voices—Jack Mercer (Popeye), Mae Questel (Olive), Gus Wickie (Bluto).

1204 *Porky and Daffy* (August 6, 1938; b&w)
Dir: Bob Clampett; Warner Bros.; Looney Tune: Porky Pig, Daffy Duck; Wacky boxing spoof; Voices—Mel Blanc.

1205 *Porky in Wackyland* (September 24, 1938; b&w)
Dir: Bob Clampett; Warner Bros.; Looney Tune: Porky Pig; Porky goes in search of the rare Do-Do Bird in this surreal Clampett classic; Remade in color in 1949 (*Dough for the Do-Do*); Voices—Mel Blanc.

Porky Pig (series) **see** *I Haven't Got a Hat* (1935)

1206 *Porky Pig's Feat* (July 17, 1943; b&w)
Dir: Frank Tashlin; Warner Bros.; Looney Tune: Porky Pig, Daffy Duck, Bugs Bunny (cameo); Daffy and Porky try to leave the Broken Arms Hotel without paying their bill. Hilarious gags and unique camera shots highlight this excellent short, which marked Tashlin's return to Warner Bros. following brief stints at Disney and Columbia; Voices—Mel Blanc.

1207 *Porky's Badtime Story* (July 24, 1937; b&w)
Dir: Bob Clampett; Warner Bros.; Looney Tune: Porky Pig, Gabby Goat; Clampett's

directorial debut. Robert Clampett (1913–84), who joined Warner Bros. in 1931, would become one of the studio's leading cartoon directors, famed for his wild comic style. He directed 80 WB shorts (1937–46), including such classics as *Porky in Wackyland* (1938), *A Tale of Two Kitties* (1942, Tweety's debut) and *The Great Piggy Bank Robbery* (1946).

1208 *Porky's Duck Hunt* (April 17, 1937; b&w)
    Dir: Tex Avery; Warner Bros.; Looney Tune: Porky Pig, Daffy Duck (debut); Out hunting with his dog, Porky encounters a crazy duck; The black-feathered Daffy Duck, who starts off here as a total loon, soon became an audience favorite and gradually evolved into the avaricious, loveable-loser of his '50s shorts. Among his best—*The Daffy Doc* (1938), *The Great Piggy Bank Robbery* (1946), *Duck Amuck* (1953) and *Duck Dodgers in the 24 1/2th Century* (1953). Daffy appeared in over 130 shorts (1937–68, 87—); One of the film's animators, Robert Cannon, later became a leading director at UPA (see *The Miner's Daughter*); Voices—Mel Blanc.

1209 *Porky's Hare Hunt* (April 30, 1938; b&w)
    Dir: Ben Hardaway; Warner Bros.; Looney Tune: Porky Pig; The hare Porky hunts in this cartoon is the earliest version of the rabbit who, in two years, would become that carrot-eating superstar Bugs Bunny. For Bugs' official debut see *A Wild Hare* (1940); Voices—Mel Blanc.

1210 *Porky's Hero Agency* (December 4, 1937; b&w)
    Dir: Bob Clampett; Warner Bros.; Looney Tune: Porky Pig; Greek hero Porky is hired to stop the Gorgon from turning people into stone; Voices—Mel Blanc.

1211 *Porky's Pooch* (December 27, 1941; b&w)
    Dir: Bob Clampett; Warner Bros.; Looney Tune: Porky Pig; A homeless dog tries to sell Porky on the idea of being his master; A precursor to Chuck Jones' "Charlie Dog" shorts, see *Little Orphan Airedale* (1947); Voices—Mel Blanc.

1212 *Porky's Poultry Plant* (August 22, 1936; b&w)
    Dir: Frank Tashlin; Warner Bros.; Looney Tune: Porky Pig; Porky fights to protect his poultry against a hungry hawk; Tashlin's directorial debut and the first Warner Bros. short to feature the work of famed cartoon music director and former Disney collaborator Carl Stalling (1891–1972), who stayed with the studio until 1958; Tashlin (1913–72), a cartoonist, gagman and future live-action director, first joined Warner Bros. as an animator in 1933. He became one of the studio's pioneering directors (with Tex Avery, Bob Clampett, etc.) who created a new, wilder, fast-paced style of cartoon comedy. He would direct 35 WB shorts (1936–38, '43–46), including the classics *Porky Pig's Feat* (1943) and *The Unruly Hare* (1945); Voices—Joe Dougherty (Porky).

1213 *Porky's Preview* (April 19, 1941; b&w)
    Dir: Tex Avery; Warner Bros.; Looney Tune: Porky Pig; Porky gives a preview of his own animated film, drawn with stick figures; Voices—Mel Blanc.

1214 *Porky's Romance* (April 3, 1937; b&w)
    Dir: Frank Tashlin; Warner Bros.; Looney Tune: Porky Pig, Petunia Pig; Great Tashlin short has Porky dreaming about married life with his love, Petunia.

Possible Possum (series) **see** *Freight Fright* (1965)

1215 *The Practical Pig* (February 24, 1939)
Dir: Dick Rickard; Walt Disney; Three Little Pigs; The Pigs' fourth cartoon, following earlier appearances in three "Silly Symphonies" (1933, 34, 36).

1216 *The Prince and the Pauper* (November 16, 1990; 23 mins)
Dir: George Scribner; Walt Disney; Mickey Mouse, Donald Duck, Goofy, others; A prince changes places with a look-alike peasant in this Disney version of the Mark Twain story; Mickey and the gang's first cartoon together since 1983's *Mickey's Christmas Carol*; Shown in theaters with the feature *The Rescuers Down Under*; Voices—Wayne Allwine (Mickey/Prince), Bill Farmer (Goofy/Horace/Weasel #1/Pluto), Arthur Burghardt (Captain Pete), Tony Anselmo (Donald), Charlie Adler (Weasel #2, #3/Pig Driver/Peasant/Man in Street), Frank Welker (Archbishop/Dying King), Elvia Allman (Clarabelle), Tim Eyster (Kid #1), Rocky Krakoff (Kid #2), Roy Dotrice (Narrator); Produced by Dan Rounds.

1217 *Private Pluto* (April 2, 1943)
Dir: Clyde Geronimi; Walt Disney; Pluto, Chip 'n' Dale (debut); Two chipmunks invade a military pillbox guarded by Pluto; The mischievous, squeaky-voiced chipmunks would appear in 23 shorts (1943–56), often bothering Donald Duck (see *Chip an' Dale*, 1947). They later starred in their own TV series, *Chip 'n' Dale's Rescue Rangers* (1989–93).

1218 *Prize Pest* (December 22, 1951)
Dir: Robert McKimson; Warner Bros.; Merrie Melodie: Porky Pig, Daffy Duck; Porky tries to get rid of his quiz show prize—a troublesome duck (Daffy) with a split personality; Voices—Mel Blanc.

1219 *Professor Small and Mister Tall* (March 26, 1943)
Dir: Paul Sommer, John Hubley; Columbia/Screen Gems; Color Rhapsody; The stars of this cartoon—whose names are the opposite of their actual sizes—also appeared in *River Ribber* (1945); Early Hubley short featuring the modern, stylized graphic design he would further explore at UPA.

Puddy the Pup (series) **see** *The Hot Spell* (1936)

1220 *Pulcinella* (1973) †
Producer-Directors: Emanuele Luzzati, Guilio Gianini; Oscar nominee; Italian filmmakers Luzzati and Gianini also directed the Oscar-nominated *The Thieving Magpie* (1965).

1221 *Pullet Surprise* (March 28, 1997)
Dir: Darrell Van Citters; Warner Bros./Chuck Jones Film Prods; Foghorn Leghorn, Pete Puma; Released in theaters with *Cats Don't Dance*; Voices—Frank Gorshin (Foghorn), Stan Freberg (Pete); Produced by Chuck Jones and Linda Jones Clough.

1222 *Punch Trunk* (December 19, 1953)
Dir: Chuck Jones; Warner Bros.; Looney Tune; Amusing tale of a five-inch-tall elephant roaming a city; Voices—Mel Blanc, June Foray.

1223 *Punchy De Leon* (January 12, 1950)
Dir: John Hubley; UPA; Jolly Frolics, with The Fox and the Crow (their last cartoon).

Puppetoons (series) **see** *Western Daze* (1941)

1224 *The Pups' Christmas* (December 12, 1936)
Dir: Rudolf Ising; MGM; Happy Harmony.

1225 *Push Comes to Shove* (1991)
Producer-Director: Bill Plympton; Two men in disagreement calmly bend, twist and mutilate each other's heads; Included in the 1992 feature *The Tune*; Winner of the Prix du Jury at the 1991 Cannes Film Festival; Animated by Plympton.

1226 *Puss Gets the Boot* (February 10, 1940) †
Dir: William Hanna, Joseph Barbera; MGM; Tom and Jerry (debut); Oscar nominee; Created by famed animating team Hanna-Barbera (though this short is credited to Rudolf Ising), the feuding, nonspeaking cat and mouse would go on to appear in 162 shorts (1940–67), becoming MGM's leading cartoon stars. The series, with its violent, fast-paced comedy style, would win the series would win seven Academy Awards (out of 13 nominations). Hanna-Barbera directed the series until 1958 (it was revived in 1961 by Gene Deitch and then by Chuck Jones in 1963). T & J also appeared in live-action features (*Anchors Aweigh, Dangerous When Wet*) and in their own 1993 feature (as talking friends!); Tom is named "Jasper" in this early short.

1227 *Puss N' Booty* (December 11, 1943; b&w)
Dir: Frank Tashlin; Warner Bros.; Looney Tune; The Last black-and-white "Looney Tune."

1228 *Quasi at the Quackadero* (1975; 10 mins)
Producer-Director: Sally Cruikshank; Anita and her friend Quasi visit the Quackadero, a futuristic amusement park with bizarre attractions; Unusual, imaginative short from independent animator Cruikshank, who spent two years and $6,000 on its production; Followed by a sequel, *Make Me Psychic* (1978); Music by the Cheap Suit Serenaders; Voices— Sally Cruikshank (Anita), Kim Deitch (Quasi).

1229 *Quest* (1996; 11 mins) AA
Dir: Tyron Montgomery; Oscar winner; Surreal puppet-animated short about a sandman's search for a drop of water; Made over a four-year period by Montgomery and producer-animator Thomas Stellmach; A 1997 WAC (World Animation Celebration) Award winner.

1230 *Quiet, Please!* (December 22, 1945) AA
Dir: William Hanna, Joseph Barbera; MGM; Tom and Jerry; Oscar winner.

1231 *Rabbit Every Monday* (February 10, 1951)
Dir: Friz Freleng; Warner Bros.; Looney Tune: Bugs Bunny, Yosemite Sam; Sam tries to roast an uncooperative Bugs; Voices—Mel Blanc.

1232 *Rabbit Fire* (May 19, 1951)
Dir: Chuck Jones; Warner Bros.; Looney Tune: Bugs Bunny, Daffy Duck, Elmer Fudd; The question of whether it is rabbit season or duck season is explored in the first of three classic Bugs-Daffy-Elmer cartoons, followed by *Rabbit Seasoning* (1952) and *Duck! Rabbit! Duck!* (1953); Voices—Mel Blanc, Arthur Q. Bryan (Elmer).

1233 *Rabbit Hood* (December 24, 1949)
Dir: Chuck Jones; Warner Bros.; Merrie Melodie: Bugs Bunny; Bugs outwits the Sheriff of Nottingham; Robin Hood makes a brief appearance (via live-action footage of Errol Flynn) at the end; Voices—Mel Blanc.

1234 *The Rabbit of Seville* (December 16, 1950)
Dir: Chuck Jones; Warner Bros.; Looney Tune: Bugs Bunny, Elmer Fudd; Elmer chases Bugs onto the stage of the Hollywood Bowl where they perform their own version of "The Barber of Seville." One of Jones' best; Voices—Mel Blanc (Bugs), Arthur Q. Bryan (Elmer).

1235 *Rabbit Punch* (April 10, 1948)
Dir: Chuck Jones; Warner Bros.; Merrie Melodie: Bugs Bunny; Great boxing spoof; Voices—Mel Blanc.

1236 *Rabbit Rampage* (June 11, 1955)
Dir: Chuck Jones; Warner Bros.; Looney Tune: Bugs Bunny, with a guest appearance by Elmer Fudd; Lesser remake of Jones' classic *Duck Amuck* (1953); Voices—Mel Blanc (Bugs), Arthur Q. Bryan (Elmer).

1237 *Rabbit Seasoning* (September 20, 1952)
Dir: Chuck Jones; Warner Bros.; Merrie Melodie: Bugs Bunny, Daffy Duck, Elmer Fudd; The trio's second cartoon together, following *Rabbit Fire* (1951); Voices—Mel Blanc, Arthur Q. Bryan (Elmer).

1238 *Rabbit's Feat* (June 4, 1960)
Dir: Chuck Jones; Warner Bros.; Looney Tune: Bugs Bunny, Wile E. Coyote.

1239 *Rabbitson Crusoe* (April 28, 1956)
Dir: Friz Freleng; Warner Bros.; Looney Tune: Bugs Bunny, Yosemite Sam; Sam is the shipwrecked Crusoe in this funny Freleng short; Voices—Mel Blanc.

1240 *Racketeer Rabbit* (September 14, 1946)
Dir: Friz Freleng; Warner Bros.; Looney Tune: Bugs Bunny; Bugs outwits two gangsters (caricatures of Edward G. Robinson and Peter Lorre) hiding out in an old house; Voices—Mel Blanc.

1241 *Raggedy Ann and Raggedy Andy* (April 11, 1941; 17 mins)
Dir: Dave Fleischer; Max Fleischer; A toy shop owner relates the story of the rag dolls' creation in Rag Land and their journey to the Castle of Names; Special two-reel short based on the classic children's stories (the first of which appeared in 1918) by Johnny Gruelle (1880–1938); Followed by two more shorts (*Suddenly It's Spring*, *The Enchanted Square*) produced by Famous Studios in the "Noveltoon" series. A feature based on the stories was made in 1977 by Richard Williams; Story by William Turner and Worth Gruelle; Songs (by Sammy Timberg)—"You're a Calico Millionaire," "You're Nobody Without a Name," "No Speak Merry-Can" and "Raggedy Ann I Love You"; Wrinkled Knees, the camel, is voiced by Pinto Colvig (voice of Disney's Goofy).

1242 *Ragtime Bear* (September 8, 1949)
Dir: John Hubley; UPA; Jolly Frolics, with Mr. Magoo (debut); Magoo mistakes a

grizzly bear for his nephew Waldo; The first cartoon appearance of the crotchety, near-sighted Mr. (Quincy) Magoo (voiced by Jim Backus). After the success of this "Jolly Frolics" short (the first of 17, 1949–53), he would go on to appear in 51 shorts of his own (1950–59) and on TV (1960–65, 77–79). Magoo's main director (Hubley directed only three) would be Pete Burness, whose first "Magoo" short was the Oscar-nominated *Trouble Indemnity* (1950). A live-action "Magoo" feature was produced in 1997 starring Leslie Nielsen; Note: Character actor Backus (1913–89) later played Thurston Howell III on TV's *Gilligan's Island* (1964–67).

Rainbow Parades (series) **see** *Pastry Town Wedding* (1934)

1243 *A Rainy Day* (April 20, 1940)
Dir: Hugh Harman; MGM; Superbly animated Harman short.

Ralph Phillips (series) **see** *From A to Z-Z-Z-Z* (1954)

Ralph Wolf and Sam Sheepdog (series) **see** *Don't Give Up the Sheep* (1953)

The Ranger (J. Audubon Woodlore) (series) **see** *Grin and Bear It* (1954)

1244 *The Rasslin' Match* (January 5, 1934; b&w)
Dir: George Stallings; Van Beuren; Amos 'n' Andy (the first of two); Cartoon version of the popular *Amos 'n' Andy* radio series (1926–58) and featuring the voices of its creators-stars, Freeman Gosden (Amos) and Charles Correll (Andy). Followed by *The Lion Tamer* (1934).

1245 *Ratskin* (August 15, 1929; b&w)
Dir: Manny Gould, Ben Harrison; Columbia/Screen Gems; Krazy Kat; The first of 98 sound shorts (1929–40) starring the comic-strip feline. The former silent screen star (1916–29) launched Columbia Pictures' cartoon studio (under producer Charles Mintz). The studio's later stars included Scrappy and the Fox and the Crow.

1246 *Really Scent* (June 27, 1959)
Dir: Abe Levitow; Warner Bros.; Merrie Melodie: Pepe Le Pew; Late entry in the "Pepe Le Pew" series (and one of the few not directed by Chuck Jones) in which the skunk's newest romance is ruined by his overpowering smell; Voices—Mel Blanc, June Foray (Narrator).

1247 *Reason and Emotion* (August 27, 1943) †
Dir: Bill Roberts; Walt Disney; Oscar nominee; Wartime propaganda short.

1248 *The Reckless Driver* (August 26, 1946)
Dir: James Culhane; Walter Lantz; Woody Woodpecker, Wally Walrus; Woody goes to renew his driver's license. Best bit—the eye chart Woody has to read spells: I CAN'T SEE A THING; Voice—Ben Hardaway (Woody).

1249 *Red Hot Mama* (February 2, 1934; b&w)
Dir: Dave Fleischer; Max Fleischer; Betty Boop.

1250 *Red Hot Rangers* (May 31, 1947)
Dir: Tex Avery; MGM; George and Junior; Forest rangers George and Junior try to put out a pesky little flame; Voices—Frank Graham (George), Tex Avery (Junior).

1251 *Red Hot Riding Hood* (May 8, 1943)
Dir: Tex Avery; MGM; The Wolf and the Showgirl (debut); Wild, big-city version of the fairy tale has the Wolf following sexy singer Red to "Grandma's"; The first of five hilarious Avery cartoons (1943–49) featuring the libidinous Wolf and the sexy Showgirl, which were very popular with wartime audiences; Red sings "Daddy."

1252 *Red Riding Hoodwinked* (October 29, 1955)
Dir: Friz Freleng; Warner Bros.; Looney Tune: Tweety, Sylvester.

1253 *Red's Dream* (1987; 4 mins)
Dir: John Lasseter; Pixar; Award-winning computer-animated short, written and animated by Lasseter (*Luxo Jr.*).

1254 *Redux Riding Hood* (1997; 15 mins) †
Dir: Steve Moore; Walt Disney Television Animation; Oscar nominee; A wolf's attempts to catch Red Riding Hood includes the use of a time machine; Debut short in Disney's "Totally twisted Fairy Tales" series; Combines cel and collage animation; Written by Dan O'Shannon; Voices—Lacey Chabert, June Foray, Garrison Keillor, Mia Farrow, Fabio, Michael Richards, Alan West.

1255 *The Reluctant Dragon* (June 20, 1941; 20 mins)
Dir: Hamilton Luske; Walt Disney; A gentle dragon would rather write poetry and sing songs than be ferocious. Wonderful Disney featurette based on the 1898 short story by Kenneth Grahame (1859–1932). Funny and superbly animated; Part of the 1941 feature of the same name; Voices—Barnett Parker (Dragon), Claud Allister (Sir Giles), Billy Lee (Little Boy), J. Donald Wilson (Narrator).

1256 *Rhapsody in Rivets* (December 6, 1941) †
Dir: Friz Freleng; Warner Bros.; Merrie Melodie; Oscar nominee; Workers construct a building to the music of Liszt's "Second Hungarian Rhapsody."

1257 *Rhapsody Rabbit* (November 9, 1946)
Dir: Friz Freleng; Warner Bros.; Merrie Melodie: Bugs Bunny; Bugs is a concert pianist in this first-rate Freleng short.

1258 *Rhythm in the Ranks* (December 26, 1941; 10 mins) †
Producer-Director: George Pal; Puppetoon; Oscar nominee (Pal's first); Toy soldiers go to war.

1259 *Rhythm on the Reservation* (July 7, 1939; b&w)
Dir: Dave Fleischer; Max Fleischer; Betty Boop (her last cartoon appearance).

1260 *Riding the Rails* (January 28, 1938; b&w)
Dir: Dave Fleischer; Max Fleischer; Betty Boop, with Pudgy (her dog).

1261 *Right Off the Bat* (November 7, 1958)
Dir: Seymour Kneitel; Paramount; Modern Madcap (series debut); The first of 56 shorts (1958–67) in the variety series "Modern Madcaps."

1262 *Rip Van Winkle* (1978; 28 mins) †
Producer-Director: Will Vinton; Oscar nominee; Claymation short, based on the Washington Irving story, from Oscar winner Vinton (*Closed Mondays*).

1263 *Rippling Romance* (June 21, 1945) †
Dir: Bob Wickersham; Columbia/Screen Gems; Color Rhapsody; Oscar nominee.

1264 *The Rite of Spring* (November 13, 1940; 22 mins)
Dir: Bill Roberts, Paul Satterfield; Walt Disney; The evolution of life on Earth, from the first one-celled organism to the extinction of the dinosaurs, is followed to the music from the 1913 ballet by Igor Stravinsky (1882–1971); Part of the feature *Fantasia*; Animation Supervisors—Wolfgang Reitherman, Joshua Meador; John Hubley (later of UPA) was one of the film's art directors; Leopold Stokowski conducts the Philadelphia Orchestra; Note: Stokowski conducted the American premiere of "Rite of Spring" in 1930.

1265 *River Ribber* (October 4, 1945)
Dir: Paul Sommer; Columbia/Screen Gems; Color Rhapsody, with Prof. Small and Mr. Tall (their second short).

1266 *The Riveter* (March 15, 1940)
Dir: Dick Lundy; Walt Disney; Donald Duck.

Road Runner-Coyote (series) **see** *Fast and Furry-Ous* (1949)

1267 *Robin Hood Daffy* (March 8, 1958)
Dir: Chuck Jones; Warner Bros.; Merrie Melodie: Daffy Duck, Porky Pig; A Jones classic, with Daffy as Robin Hood and Porky as a very jolly Friar Tuck. Daffy's failed attempts at swashbuckling ("Yoicks! And awayyyy!") are a riot; Voices—Mel Blanc.

1268 *Robin Hood Makes Good* (February 11, 1939)
Dir: Chuck Jones; Warner Bros.; Merrie Melodie; A hungry fox tricks a couple of squirrels who are playing Robin Hood; Voices—Bernice Hansen (Squirrels), Mel Blanc (Fox).

1269 *Robin Hoodlum* (December 23, 1948) †
Dir: John Hubley; UPA; The Fox and the Crow; Oscar nominee; The first UPA short released by Columbia Pictures and the first of seven UPA/Columbia shorts (1948–52) directed by animation great John Hubley (1914–77), a guiding light in the new, stylized approach to animation (making cartoons that were flatter, less natural in movement and simpler in drawing and design). Hubley started as an art director at Disney in the late '30s and, after taking part in the Disney animators strike of 1941, he worked briefly (1942–43) at Columbia/Screen Gems. At UPA he would launch the "Mr. Magoo" series (see *Ragtime Bear*) and direct one of the studio's best cartoons—*Rooty Toot Toot* (1952); Columbia/Screen Gem stars "The Fox and the Crow" appeared in only three UPA shorts (1948–50).

1270 *Rock-a-Bye Bear* (July 12, 1952)
Dir: Tex Avery; MGM; Spike; Spike housesits for a hibernating bear.

1271 *Rocket-Bye Baby* (August 4, 1956)
Dir: Chuck Jones; Warner Bros.; Merrie Melodie; A couple's new baby turns out to be from Mars; Voices—Daws Butler (Mr. Wilbur), June Foray (Mrs. Wilbur).

1272 *Rocket to Mars* (August 9, 1946)
Dir: Bill Tytla; Paramount/Famous; Popeye the Sailor; One of the better Famous-produced "Popeye" shorts.

Roger Rabbit (series) **see** *Tummy Trouble* (1989)

Roland and Rattfink (series) **see** *Hawks and Doves* (1968)

1273 *Roller Coaster Rabbit* (June 15, 1990)
Dir: Rob Minkoff; Disney/Amblin; Roger Rabbit, Baby Herman; Roger watches Baby Herman at a fair; Released with the feature *Dick Tracy*; Followed by *Trail Mix-Up* (1993); Voices—Charles Fleischer (Roger), April Winchell (Baby Herman); Live-action Dir: Frank Marshall; Produced by Don Hahn.

1274 *Roman Legion Hare* (November 12, 1955)
Dir: Friz Freleng; Warner Bros.; Looney Tune: Bugs Bunny, Yosemite Sam; Roman guard Sam is ordered to find a new victim to be thrown to the lions; Voices—Mel Blanc.

1275 *Romance of Transportation* (1953; 11 mins) †
Dir: Colin Low; National Film Board of Canada; Oscar nominee; Narrated by Max Ferguson; Produced by Tom Daly.

1276 *Rookie Bear* (May 17, 1941) †
Dir: Rudolf Ising; MGM; Barney Bear; Oscar nominee.

1277 *Room and Bird* (June 2, 1951)
Dir: Friz Freleng; Warner Bros.; Merrie Melodie: Tweety, Sylvester.

1278 *Room and Bored* (September 30, 1943)
Dir: Bob Wickersham; Columbia/Screen Gems; The Fox and the Crow; The Crow moves into the Fox's apartment building and soon wreaks havoc.

1279 *Rooty Toot Toot* (March 27, 1952) †
Dir: John Hubley; UPA; Jolly Frolics; Oscar nominee; First-rate animated version of the ballad of "Frankie and Johnny." This stylishly-animated work was Hubley's finest—and last—UPA short. A victim of blacklisting, Hubley was forced to leave the studio, after which he and his wife, Faith, would form their own production company; Designed by Paul Julian; Story adaption by Hubley and Bill Scott; Jazz score by Phil Monroe.

1280 *Rough and Tumbleweed* (January 31, 1961)
Dir: Paul J. Smith; Walter Lantz; Inspector Willoughby (debut); The bushy-mustached Inspector Willoughby (secret agent 6–7/8), last seen as Ranger Willoughby in *Hunger Strife* (1960), appeared in 11 shorts (1961–65); Voice—Dal McKennon (Willoughby).

1281 *Rudolph the Red-Nosed Reindeer* (1944)
Max Fleischer; Two years after the closing of his studio, Fleischer produced (in asso-

ciation with the Handy organization) this cartoon version of the Robert May story (1939), which later became a hit song (by Johnny Marks, 1949) and TV special (Rankin-Bass, 1964).

1282 *Rudy Vallee Melodies* (August 5, 1932; b&w)
Dir: Dave Fleischer; Max Fleischer; Screen Song, with Betty Boop.

1283 *Rugged Bear* (October 23, 1953) †
Dir: Jack Hannah; Walt Disney; Donald Duck, Humphrey Bear (debut); Oscar nominee; Humphrey hides out during hunting season by posing as Donald's bear rug; Loveable lunkhead Humphrey Bear appeared in six shorts (1953–56); Voice—Clarence Nash (Donald).

1284 *Runaway Brain* (1995) †
Producer-Director: Chris Bailey; Walt Disney; Mickey Mouse, Minnie Mouse, Pluto; Oscar nominee; In order to pay for a Hawaiian holiday with Minnie, Mickey offers his services to the evil Dr. Frankenollie; Voices—Wayne Allwine (Mickey), Russi Taylor (Minnie), Bill Farmer (Pluto), Kelsey Grammer (Dr. Frankenollie); Note: The name "Frankenollie" is a reference to veteran Disney animators Frank Thomas and Ollie Johnston, who appeared together in the documentary *Frank and Ollie* (1995).

1285 *Russian Rhapsody* (May 20, 1944)
Dir: Bob Clampett; Warner Bros.; Merrie Melodie; Adolf Hitler's plane is sabotaged by Russian gremlins (caricatures of the Warner studio's cartoon staff) in this wartime short; Working title—*Gremlins from the Kremlin*; Voices—Mel Blanc.

Sad Cat (series) **see** *Gadmouse the Apprentice Good Fairy* (1965)

1286 *The Saga of Windwagon Smith* (March 16, 1961; 12 mins)
Dir: Charles Nichols; Walt Disney; Capt. Smith's horseless windwagon runs into a mighty wind on its maiden voyage across the Kansas prairies; Nichols' last Disney short; Music by George Bruns, lyrics by Charles Nichols; Voices—Rex Allen and the Sons of the Pioneers.

1287 *Sahara Hare* (March 26, 1955)
Dir: Friz Freleng; Warner Bros.; Looney Tune: Bugs Bunny, Yosemite Sam.

1288 *Salt Water Tabby* (July 12, 1947)
Dir: William Hanna, Joseph Barbera; MGM; Tom and Jerry, Toots.

1289 *The Sand Castle (Le chateau de sable)* (1977; 13 mins) AA
Producer-Director: Jacobus Willem "Co" Hoedeman; National Film Board of Canada; Oscar winner; Creatures made out of sand build their own sand castle; Music by Normand Roger.

1290 *The Sandman* (1992) †
Producer-Director: Paul Berry; Batty Berry Mackinnon Prod; Oscar nominee.

1291 *Sandy Claws* (April 2, 1955) †
Dir: Friz Freleng; Warner Bros.; Looney Tune: Tweety, Sylvester; Oscar nominee;

Sylvester attempts to reach Tweety whose cage is stuck on a rock out at sea; Voices — Mel Blanc.

1292 *Santa's Workshop* (December 10, 1932)
Dir: Wilfred Jackson; Walt Disney; Silly Symphony.

1293 *Saturday Evening Puss* (January 19, 1950)
Dir: William Hanna, Joseph Barbera; MGM; Tom and Jerry.

1294 *Scalp Trouble* (June 24, 1939; b&w)
Dir: Bob Clampett; Warner Bros.; Looney Tune: Porky Pig, Daffy Duck; Porky and Daffy defend their fort against a horde of Indians; Color remake — *Slightly Daffy* (1944); Voices — Mel Blanc.

1295 *Scaredy Cat* (December 18, 1948)
Dir: Chuck Jones; Warner Bros.; Merrie Melodie: Porky Pig, Sylvester; Strange happenings at a spooky mansion where Sylvester spends a sleepless night; Followed by the similar *Claws for Alarm* (1954) and *Jumpin' Jupiter* (1955); Voices — Mel Blanc.

1296 *The Scarlet Pumpernickel* (March 4, 1950)
Dir: Chuck Jones; Warner Bros.; Looney Tune: Daffy Duck, Porky Pig, Sylvester, Elmer Fudd.

1297 *Scrap Happy Daffy* (August 21, 1943; b&w)
Dir: Frank Tashlin; Warner Bros.; Looney Tune: Daffy Duck; Daffy valiantly guards his scrap metal pile against a Nazi submarine — and also a Nazi goat — in this great wartime short; Voices — Mel Blanc.

1298 *Scrap the Japs* (November 20, 1942; b&w)
Dir: Seymour Kneitel; Paramount/Famous; Popeye the Sailor.

Scrappy (series) **see** *Yelp Wanted* (1931)

1299 *Scrappy's Ghost Story* (May 24, 1935; b&w)
Dir: Manny Gould, Ben Harrison; Columbia/Screen Gems; Scrappy; Superior "Scrappy" short, one of several from "Krazy Kat" directors Gould and Harrison.

1300 *Screen Play* (1992) †
Producer-Director: Barry J. C. Purves; Bare Boards Film Prod; Oscar nominee; A "Romeo and Juliet"–style tale is told through puppet-animated Kabuki theater.

Screen Songs (series) **see** *The Sidewalks of New York* (1929)

1301 *The Screwball* (February 15, 1943)
Dir: Alex Lovy; Walter Lantz; Woody Woodpecker; Woody sneaks into a baseball game without paying.

1302 *Screwball Football* (December 16, 1939)
Dir: Tex Avery; Warner Bros.; Merrie Melodie; Sports spoof.

1303 *Screwball Squirrel* (April 1, 1944)

Dir: Tex Avery; MGM; Screwy Squirrel (debut), Meathead; "Bird dog" Meathead chases a crazy squirrel; Highlight—Screwy's disposal of cute Sammy Squirrel at the film's beginning; The first of five shorts (1944–46) starring Avery's brash (and very violent) Screwy Squirrel.

1304 *The Screwdriver* (August 11, 1941)

Producer-Director: Walter Lantz; Woody Woodpecker (in his third cartoon appearance).

Screwy Squirrel (series) **see** *Screwball Squirrel* (1944)

1305 *The Screwy Truant* (January 13, 1945)

Dir: Tex Avery; MGM; Screwy Squirrel, Meathead (dog); Truant officer Meathead chases the hooky-playing squirrel.

1306 *Scrooge McDuck and Money* (March 23, 1967; 14 mins)

Dir: Hamilton Luske; Walt Disney; Uncle Scrooge McDuck (debut), Huey, Dewey and Louie; Uncle Scrooge teaches the boys about money and how to use it in this educational Disney short; Scrooge's next theatrical appearance was in *Mickey's Christmas Carol* (1983). He later starred in the *DuckTales* TV series (1987–92) and feature (1990); Uncle Scrooge McDuck (uncle of Donald Duck) first appeared in the comic book *Four Color (Donald Duck)* (#178) in December 1947 and was created by renowned artist-writer Carl Barks (b. 1901); Song—"Money's Got to Circulate"; Voices—Bill Thompson (Uncle Scrooge), The Mellomen.

1307 *Scrub Me Mama with a Boogie Beat* (March 28, 1941)

Producer-Director: Walter Lantz; Cartune Special; Musical short in which a young woman from Harlem brings jazz to Lazytown; Rarely shown on TV because of its racial stereotypes.

1308 *Sea Scouts* (June 30, 1939)

Dir: Dick Lundy; Walt Disney; Donald Duck, Huey, Dewey and Louie; Donald captains a ship, with his nephews as first mates; The directorial debut of Disney animator Lundy. He directed nine Disney shorts (1939–43) before leaving the studio for Walter Lantz (1945–49) see *The Sliphorn King of Polaroo.* He later worked at MGM (1952–54); Voice—Clarence Nash (Donald).

1309 *Season's Greetinks* (December 17, 1933; b&w)

Dir: Dave Fleischer; Max Fleischer; Popeye the Sailor.

1310 *Second Chance: Sea* (1977)

Dir: Faith Hubley; Hubley Studios; The first Hubley short released after John Hubley's death; Music by Dizzy Gillespie and William Russo.

1311 *Second Class Mail* (1984; 4 mins) †

Producer-Director: Alison Snowden; National Film and Television School; Oscar nominee.

1312 *Secret Agent* (July 30, 1943)

Dir: Seymour Kneitel; Paramount/Famous; Superman (last in the series).

1313 *See Ya Later, Gladiator* (June 29, 1968)
Dir: Alex Lovy; Warner Bros.; Looney Tune: Daffy Duck, Speedy Gonzales; Daffy's last theatrical cartoon until 1987's *The Duxorcist*; Voices—Mel Blanc.

1314 *Self-Defense—For Cowards* (1962) †
Prod: William L. Snyder; Rembrandt Films; Self-Help series; Oscar nominee.

1315 *The Selfish Giant* (1971) †
Dir: Peter Sander; Potterton Prods; Oscar nominee; Produced by Sander and Murray Shostak.

1316 *Señor Droopy* (April 9, 1949)
Dir: Tex Avery; MGM; Droopy; Droopy competes in a bullfighting contest; Lovely actress-singer Lina Romay makes a brief appearance at the end with the animated Droopy sitting on her lap; Droopy later battled a dragon in the similar *One Droopy Knight* (1957); Voice—Bill Thompson (Droopy).

1317 *Shanghaied* (January 13, 1934; b&w)
Dir: Burt Gillett; Walt Disney; Mickey Mouse, Minnie Mouse.

1318 *The Shanty Where Santy Claus Lives* (January 7, 1933; b&w)
Dir: Rudolf Ising; Warner Bros.; Merrie Melodie; A poor little boy is taken on Santa's sleigh to the North Pole where the toys put on a show for him. Tuneful holiday short.

1319 *She Reminds Me of You* (June 22, 1934; b&w)
Dir: Dave Fleischer; Max Fleischer; Screen Song, featuring the Eton Boys.

1320 *She Wronged Him Right* (January 5, 1934; b&w)
Dir: Dave Fleischer; Max Fleischer; Betty Boop; Betty plays the heroine in a stage melodrama; Voice—Mae Questel (Betty).

1321 *The Shepherd* (1970) †
Dir: Cameron Guess; Cameron Guess and Associates; Oscar nominee. Guess (1936–97) worked at the National Film Board of Canada before forming his own company in 1964.

1322 *Sh-h-h-h-h-h* (June 6, 1955)
Dir: Tex Avery; Walter Lantz; A nervous man finds peace and quiet at a mountain retreat—until a laughing, trombone-playing couple moves into the room next door; The neighbors' contagious laughter highlights this unusual Avery short (one of the few he made for Lantz); Avery's last theatrical effort.

1323 *The Shooting of Dan McGoo* (March 3, 1945)
Dir: Tex Avery; MGM; Droopy, The Wolf and the Showgirl.

1324 *Show Biz Bugs* (November 2, 1957)
Dir: Friz Freleng; Warner Bros.; Looney Tune: Bugs Bunny, Daffy Duck.

1325 *Showdown* (October 16, 1942)
Dir: Isadore Sparber; Paramount/Famous; Superman.

1326 *Shuffle Off to Buffalo* (July 8, 1933; b&w)
Dir: Friz Freleng; Warner Bros.; Merrie Melodie; Musical short set in the Heavenly land where babies come from; The title tune is from the 1933 hit film *42nd Street*.

1327 *Sick, Sick Sidney* (August 1958)
Dir: Art Bartsch; Terrytoons; Sidney the Elephant (debut); The insecure jungle elephant (created by Gene Deitch) appeared in 12 shorts (1958–63), which were later shown on TV's *The Hector Heathcote Show* (1963–65) and *The Astronut Show* (1965, synd.); Voices—Lionel Wilson (Sidney), Dayton Allen (Stanley the Lion/Cleo the Giraffe).

1328 *The Sidewalks of New York* (February 5, 1929; b&w)
Dir: Dave Fleischer; Max Fleischer; Screen Song (series debut); The Fleischers' first true sound series, following their experimental "Song Cartunes"; Like that series, the cartoons were built around popular songs of the day and used the "Bouncing Ball" to let audiences sing along; 108 Fleischer "Screen Songs" were produced (1929–38), followed by another 38 (1947–51, in color) from Famous Studios.

1329 *Sidney's Family Tree* (December 1958) †
Dir: Art Bartsch; Terrytoons; Sidney the Elephant (his second short); Oscar nominee (Terrytoons' first since 1945's *Gypsy Life*).

Sidney the Elephant (series) **see** *Sick, Sick Sidney* (1958)

1330 *Silly Scandals* (May 23, 1931; b&w)
Dir: Dave Fleischer; Max Fleischer; Talkartoon, with Bimbo, Betty Boop (an early appearance); Betty sings "You're Drivin' Me Crazy" (written by Walter Donaldson); Voice—Mae Questel (Betty).

Silly Symphonies (series) **see** *The Skeleton Dance* (1929)

1331 *The Simple Things* (April 18, 1953)
Dir: Charles Nichols; Walt Disney; Mickey Mouse, Pluto; Mickey and Pluto go fishing at the beach; Mickey's last theatrical cartoon until *Mickey's Christmas Carol* (1983).

1332 *Sinbad the Sailor* (July 30, 1935)
Producer-Director: Ub Iwerks; ComiColor.

1333 *Sink Pink* (April 12, 1965)
Dir: Hawley Pratt; DePatie-Freleng; The Pink Panther; The silent panther speaks for the first time in this short (he is voiced by Paul Frees).

1334 *Sinkin' in the Bathtub* (September 1930; b&w)
Producer-Directors: Hugh Harman, Rudolf Ising; Warner Bros.; Looney Tune (the very first): Bosko (debut), Honey (his girlfriend); Bosko makes music in the bathtub before taking Honey out for a ride; The first cartoon from Warner Bros. (following a 1929 pilot short *Bosko the Talk-Ink Kid*) and the debut of the studio's first cartoon star, Bosko, who appeared in 47 musical shorts (1930–38); Former Disney animators Hugh Harman (1903–82) and Rudolf Ising (1903–92) stayed at WB until 1933, then moved over to MGM (see *The Discontented Canary*), taking Bosko with them; Voices—Carmen Maxwell (Bosko), Rochelle Hudson (Honey).

1335 *The Sinking of the Lusitania* (July, 1918; b&w; 20 mins)
Producer-Director: Winsor McCay; McCay's first animated film since his successful *Gertie the Dinosaur* (1914) was this powerful, documentary-like depiction of the tragic wartime sinking of the British ship (in May 1915). Subtitled "An Amazing Moving Picture by Winsor McCay," the film consists of 25,000 drawings (15,000 more than *Gertie*) and begins with a live-action prologue.

1336 *Sisyphus* (1974; b&w) †
Producer-Director: Marcell Jankovics; Hungarofilms; Oscar nominee; Black-and-white animated drawings depict the efforts to push a boulder to the top of a mountain.

1337 *The Skeleton Dance* (July, 1929; b&w)
Producer-Director: Walt Disney; Silly Symphony (series debut); In a cemetery, skeletons rise from their graves and dance until dawn; The first short in Disney's classic "Silly Symphony" series, which gave him a chance to experiment outside of his "Mickey Mouse" shorts with different types of stories and new animation techniques. Highlights in the series (74 shorts, 1929–39), which won a total of seven Academy Awards, include *Flowers and Trees* (first Technicolor cartoon), *Three Little Pigs*, *The Wise Little Hen* (Donald Duck's debut), *Music Land* and *The Old Mill*; Animated by Ub Iwerks; Music by Carl Stalling (borrowing from Grieg's "March of the Dwarfs").

1338 *Ski for Two* (November 13, 1944)
Dir: James Culhane; Walter Lantz; Woody Woodpecker, Wally Walrus; Woody shows up at Wally's winter lodge without a reservation; Highlight—Woody's singing (of "The Sleigh") as he skis toward the lodge; Aka *Woody Plays Santa Claus*; Voice—Ben Hardaway (Woody).

1339 *Sky Princess* (March 27, 1942)
Producer-Director: George Pal; Puppetoon; The story of a beautiful princess held captive in a castle in the clouds; Music by Tchaikovsky.

1340 *Slap Happy Lion* (September 20, 1947)
Dir: Tex Avery; MGM; A ferocious lion is driven mad by a tiny mouse.

1341 *Sleeping Beauty* (1935)
Producer-Director: George Pal; Early advertising "Puppetoon" for Philips Radio in which the radio's music awakens the long-sleeping princess.

1342 *Sleepy Time Donald* (May 9, 1947)
Dir: Jack King; Walt Disney; Donald Duck, Daisy Duck; Donald's sleepwalking causes headaches for Daisy; Voice—Clarence Nash (Donald).

1343 *Slick Hare* (November 1, 1947)
Dir: Friz Freleng; Warner Bros.; Merrie Melodie: Bugs Bunny, Elmer Fudd; At the "Mocrumbo" restaurant, chef Elmer has to find a rabbit to cook for Humphrey Bogart; Includes a wonderful dance routine by Bugs; Voices—Mel Blanc (Bugs), Arthur Q. Bryan (Elmer).

1344 *Slightly Daffy* (June 17, 1944)
Dir: Friz Freleng; Warner Bros.; Merrie Melodie: Daffy Duck, Porky Pig; Daffy and

Porky fight off an Indian attack; Color remake of Bob Clampett's 1939 short *Scalp Trouble*; Voices—Mel Blanc.

1345 *The Sliphorn King of Polaroo* (March 19, 1945)
Dir: Dick Lundy; Walter Lantz; Swing Symphony; The Lantz debut of Disney animator-director Lundy. He directed 26 shorts (1945–49), including the Oscar-nominated *The Poet and Peasant* (1946) and *Musical Moments from Chopin* (1947), before moving over to MGM to revive the "Barney Bear" series (1952–54).

1346 *Sloppy Jalopy* (February 21, 1952)
Dir: Pete Burness; UPA; Mr. Magoo.

1347 *Small Fry* (April 21, 1939)
Dir: Dave Fleischer; Max Fleischer; Color Classic; Charming tale about a little fish who plays hooky from school to hang out at the pool hall.

1348 *The Small One* (December 16, 1978; 25 mins)
Producer-Director: Don Bluth; Walt Disney; Forced to sell his beloved donkey, a boy gives him to a couple traveling to Bethlehem on the eve of the first Christmas; One of Bluth's last Disney efforts before leaving to form his own production company; Based on the book by Charles Tazewell; Directing Animators—Cliff Nordberg, John Pomeroy, Gary Goldman; Songs (by Bluth and Richard Rich)—"Small One," "The Merchant's Song" and "A Friendly Face"; Voices—Sean Marshall, William Woodson, Olan Soule, Hal Smith, Joe Higgins, Gordon Jump; Note: Marshall also played the young lead in Disney's *Pete's Dragon* (1977).

1349 *Small Talk* (1993) †
Bob Godfrey, Kevin Baldwin; Bob Godfrey Films; Oscar nominee.

1350 *Smile, Darn Ya, Smile* (September 5, 1931; b&w)
Warner Bros.; Merrie Melodie: Foxy; Foxy is a trolley engineer in this early musical short; The title song was later featured in 1988's *Who Framed Roger Rabbit* (in the Toontown sequence).

1351 *Smoked Hams* (April 28, 1947)
Dir: Dick Lundy; Walter Lantz; Woody Woodpecker, Wally Walrus; Woody makes noise in the yard while Wally is trying to sleep; Voice—Ben Hardaway (Woody).

1352 *The Sneezing Weasel* (March 12, 1938)
Dir: Tex Avery; Warner Bros.; Merrie Melodie; A weasel (voiced by Avery) threatens a family of chicks.

Sniffles (series) **see** *Naughty but Mice* (1939)

1353 *Sniffles Bells the Cat* (February 1, 1941)
Dir: Chuck Jones; Warner Bros.; Merrie Melodie: Sniffles.

1354 *Snow Foolin'* (December 16, 1949)
Dir: Isadore Sparber; Paramount/Famous; Screen Song; Features the song "Jingle Bells."

1355 *Snow White* (March 31, 1933; b&w)
Dir: Dave Fleischer; Max Fleischer; Betty Boop, Bimbo, Koko the Clown; This sur-real, fast-paced short pits Betty and friends against an evil queen; The Fleischers' great-est "Betty Boop" cartoon, featuring the song "Saint James Infirmary Blues" performed by Cab Calloway, who last performed on Betty's *Minnie the Moocher* (1932). The film not only uses Calloway's voice but also his dance moves, which are rotoscoped (traced from live-action footage); Entered in the Library of Congress National Film Registry in 1994; Voice—Mae Questel (Betty).

1356 *The Snowman* (1982; 26 mins) †
Dir: Dianne Jackson; Snowman Enterprises/TVC London; Oscar nominee; Enchant-ing story, told through music and pantomime, about a young boy's snowman who comes to life one magical night; Based on the wordless 1978 book by author-illustrator Raymond Briggs (*When the Wind Blows*); Highlight—the pair's nighttime flight over the snowy countryside (to the song "Walking in the Air"); Jackson (1944–92) started as an anima-tor on TVC's *Yellow Submarine* (1968); Supervising Director—Jimmy T. Murakami; Music by Howard Blake; Won a British Academy of Film and Television Arts Award for Best Children's Drama; Produced by John Coates of Britain's TVC (TV Cartoons) London.

1357 *Snubbed by a Snob* (July 19, 1940)
Dir: Dave Fleischer; Max Fleischer; Color Classic, with Hunky and Spunky (don-keys).

1358 *So Much for So Little* (1949; 11 mins) AA
Dir: Chuck Jones; Warner Bros.; Oscar winner (for Best Documentary Short); Edu-cational short produced for the Federal Security Agency Public Health Service; The only animated short to win an Academy Award in the documentary category; Jones' *For Scent-imental Reasons* also won an Oscar that year.

1359 *Society Dog Show* (February 3, 1939)
Dir: Bill Roberts; Walt Disney; Mickey Mouse, Pluto; Pluto is ejected from a dog show competition only to become a hero in the short's spectacular fire finale; Voice—Walt Disney (Mickey).

1360 *Socko in Morocco* (January 18, 1954)
Dir: Don Patterson; Walter Lantz; Woody Woodpecker, Buzz Buzzard; Woody must rescue a beautiful princess from the villainous Sheik El Rancid (Buzz); Voice—Grace Stafford (Woody).

1361 *Solid Ivory* (August 25, 1947)
Dir: Dick Lundy; Walter Lantz; Woody Woodpecker; A protective mother hen thinks Woody's cueball is one of her eggs; Voice—Ben Hardaway (Woody).

1362 *Solid Serenade* (August 31, 1946)
Dir: William Hanna, Joseph Barbera; MGM; Tom and Jerry, Spike, Toots.

1363 *Somewhere in Dreamland* (January 17, 1936)
Dir: Dave Fleischer; Max Fleischer; Color Classic; Two poor, hungry children dream of a magical land where their every wish comes true. Delightful, beautifully animated fan-tasy; The Fleischer studio's first cartoon filmed in three-color Technicolor (full color),

which Disney had held exclusive rights to since 1932; Title song by Murray Mencher and Charles Newman; Voices—Mae Questel.

Song Cartunes (series) **see** *Goodbye My Lady Love* (1924)

1364 *The Song of the Birds* (February 27, 1935)
Dir: Dave Fleischer; Max Fleischer; Color Classic; Eerily moving short about a little bird, a boy, and a BB gun.

1365 *The Sorcerer's Apprentice* (November 13, 1940; 9 mins)
Dir: James Algar; Walt Disney; Mickey Mouse; A magician's assistant starts a spell he can't stop. Mickey's finest moment; Animated to the 1897 scherzo by Paul Dukas (1865–35); Part of the feature *Fantasia*; Walt Disney and famed conductor Leopold Stokowski combined their talents to make this outstanding short, which led to the production of an entire concert feature; Mickey and Stokowski (in silhouette) shake hands at the film's end; Mickey's eyes (formerly all-black) were given pupils for the first time in this short; Animation Supervisors—Fred Moore, Vladimir "Bill" Tytla; Stokowski conducts the Philadelphia Orchestra; Voice—Walt Disney (Mickey).

1366 *Sound of Sunshine—Sound of Rain* (1983) †
Eda Godel Hallinan; Hallinan Plus! Prod; Oscar nominee.

1367 *Southsea Sweethearts* (1938)
Producer-Director: George Pal; Early "Puppetoon" advertising Horlick's Malted Milk; Made at Pal's studio in Holland.

1368 *The Space Squid* (January 1, 1967)
Dir: James Culhane; Paramount; Go-Go Toons (series debut); The first of seven shorts (1967) in the "Go-Go Toons" series (one of Paramount's last), which featured a variety of stories and characters.

1369 *Speaking of the Weather* (September 4, 1937)
Dir: Frank Tashlin; Warner Bros.; Merrie Melodie; Magazine covers, including those of *Judge*, *Life* and *Liberty*, spring to life in this clever Tashlin short; Voices—Mel Blanc.

1370 *Special Delivery* (1978) AA
Producer-Directors: John Weldon, Eunice Macaulay; National Film Board of Canada; Oscar winner; Darkly comic short about a man who tries to hide the corpse of a mailman who slipped on his unshovelled front walk; Music by Karl Duplessis; Voice—Sandy Sanderson.

1371 *Speedy Gonzales* (September 17, 1955) AA
Dir: Friz Freleng; Warner Bros.; Merrie Melodie: Speedy Gonzales, Sylvester; Oscar winner (Warner Bros.' third for Best Animated Short); Speedy invades a cheese factory guarded by Sylvester; The first official "Speedy Gonzales" cartoon, following an earlier appearance in 1953's *Cat-Tails for Two*. Speedy, the "fastest mouse in all Mexico," appeared in 45 shorts (1953–68); Voices—Mel Blanc.

1372 *Spellbound Hound* (March 16, 1950)
Dir: John Hubley; UPA; Mr. Magoo; The first official "Mr. Magoo" cartoon, following his debut in 1949's *Ragtime Bear*; Voice—Jim Backus (Magoo).

1373 *The Spider and the Fly* (October 16, 1931; b&w)
Dir: Wilfred Jackson; Walt Disney; Silly Symphony.

Spike and Tyke (series) **see** *Dog Trouble* (1942)

1374 *Spooks* (December 21, 1931; b&w)
Producer-Director: Ub Iwerks; Flip the Frog.

1375 *Springtime* (1929; b&w)
Dir: Ub Iwerks; Walt Disney; Silly Symphony; Flowers, bugs and birds dance in celebration of spring; Includes music from Ponchielli's "Dance of the Hours," which Disney would use again, more memorably, in *Fantasia* (1940).

1376 *Springtime for Pluto* (June 23, 1944)
Dir: Charles Nichols; Walt Disney; Pluto; Nichols' directorial debut. Former animator Charles "Nick" (August) Nichols would direct 45 Disney shorts (1944–61), specializing in Pluto. Codirector of the Oscar-winning *Toot, Whistle, Plunk, and Boom* (1953), he later went to work for Hanna-Barbera (*Hey There, It's Yogi Bear, Charlotte's Web*, and so on).

1377 *Squatter's Rights* (June 7, 1946) †
Dir: Jack Hannah; Walt Disney; Pluto, Mickey Mouse, Chip 'n' Dale (their second appearance); Oscar nominee; Mickey and Pluto visit their log cabin, unaware that the chipmunks have made it their home; Voice—Walt Disney (Mickey).

1378 *The Squawkin' Hawk* (August 8, 1942)
Dir: Chuck Jones; Warner Bros.; Merrie Melodie: Henery Hawk (debut); Little chickenhawk Henery longs to eat a chicken; Henery would go on to costar with Foghorn Leghorn in nine shorts (1946–61); Voices—Mel Blanc.

1379 *Stage Door Cartoon* (December 30, 1944)
Dir: Friz Freleng; Warner Bros.; Merrie Melodie: Bugs Bunny, Elmer Fudd; Elmer chases Bugs onto the stage of a vaudeville theater; Voices—Mel Blanc (Bugs), Arthur Q. Bryan (Elmer).

1380 *Steamboat Willie* (November 18, 1928; b&w)
Producer-Director: Walt Disney; Mickey Mouse (debut), Minnie Mouse, Pegleg Pete; Steamboat deck hand Mickey brings Minnie on board where they perform "Turkey in the Straw" using (or abusing) animals as musical instruments; The first "Mickey Mouse" short (the first released but the third produced, see *Plane Crazy*) and the first cartoon produced with fully-synchronized sound; A landmark film starring the mouse that launched Walt Disney's illustrious career; Mickey, whose high-pitched voice was provided by Walt himself, became an international star and Disney's trademark character, earning his creator a special Academy Award in 1932; He would appear (often with girlfriend Minnie, dog Pluto and the villainous Pegleg Pete) in over 125 shorts (1928–53, '83, '90, '95); Animated by Ub Iwerks (who would open his own studio in 1930); Note: The name Mickey is said to have been the suggestion of Walt's wife Lillian (1899–1997) who disliked Walt's original name for the mouse: Mortimer. Premiered at the Colony Theater in New York.

1381 *The Stein Song* (September 5, 1930; b&w)
Dir: Dave Fleischer; Max Fleischer; Screen Song, with Rudy Vallee; Vallee sings the song of his alma mater, the University of Maine.

Stone Age Cartoons (series) **see** *Way Back When a Triangle Had Its Points* (1940)

1382 *Stop, Look and Hasten* (August 14, 1954)
Dir: Chuck Jones; Warner Bros.; Merrie Melodie: Road Runner, Coyote.

1383 *Stopping the Show* (August 12, 1932; b&w)
Dir: Dave Fleischer; Max Fleischer; Betty Boop; Vaudeville star Betty gives imitations of Fanny Brice (singing "I'm an Indian")and Maurice Chevalier (singing "Hello, Beautiful"); The first official "Betty Boop" cartoon, following some 15 appearances in the "Talkartoon" series; Voice—Mae Questel (Betty).

1384 *The Story of Anyburg, U.S.A.* (June 19, 1957)
Dir: Clyde Geronimi; Walt Disney; Automobiles are put on trial; Geronimi's last short; Voice—Hans Conried (prosecutor).

1385 *The Story of George Washington* (February 1965)
Dir: Jack Mendelsohn; Paramount; Noveltoon; Charming short presents a schoolboy's view of history, told through a series of child-like drawings; The first of two shorts Mendelsohn made at Paramount; Mendelsohn was a newspaper cartoonist who later cowrote the British feature *Yellow Submarine* (1968).

1386 *Stratos Fear* (November 11, 1933; b&w)
Producer-Director: Ub Iwerks; Willie Whopper; An overdose of dentist gas sends Willie floating off to a strange planet populated by weird scientists; Surreal entry in Iwerks' short-lived "Willie Whopper" series.

1387 *The Street* (1976; 10 mins) †
Dir: Caroline Leaf; National Film Board of Canada; Oscar nominee; Poignant family portrait centering around a dying grandmother; from acclaimed Seattle-born filmmaker Leaf, using a painted glass–style of animation; Based on a story by Montreal writer Mordecai Richler; Winner of over 20 awards; Voices—Mort Ransen, Vera Heitman, Sarah Dwight, John Hood, Howard Ryshpan; Produced by Leaf and Guy Glover.

1388 *The Stretcher* (April, 1969)
Dir: Ralph Bakshi; Terrytoons; The Mighty Heroes (theatrical debut); Created by Bakshi (who directed 1972's *Fritz the Cat*), this delightfully odd group of superheroes included Diaper Man, Strong Man, Tornado Man, Rope Man and Cuckoo Man; 10 shorts were released to theaters (1969–71) out of the 20 originally made-for-TV (1966–67); Voices—Herschel Bernardi, Lionel Wilson.

1389 *String Bean Jack* (August 26, 1938)
Dir: John Foster; Terrytoons; Terrytoons; The first Terrytoon short in color. The Terrytoons studio was one of the last to make the transition from black-and-white to color (it did not switch over completely until 1943).

1390 *Strings* (1991; 10 mins) †
Dir: Wendy Tilby; National Film Board of Canada; Oscar nominee; Moving film about two strangers who live in adjoining apartments; Written and animated by Tilby; Music by Chris Crilly; Produced by Douglas Macdonald, Barrie McLean and David Verrall.

1391 *The Stupid Cupid* (November 25, 1944)
Dir: Frank Tashlin; Warner Bros.; Looney Tune: Daffy Duck, Elmer Fudd; A cupid (Elmer) shoots an unwelcome arrow at Daffy; Voices—Mel Blanc (Daffy), Arthur Q. Bryan (Elmer).

1392 *Stupidstitious Cat* (April 25, 1947)
Dir: Seymour Kneitel; Paramount/Famous; Noveltoon, with Buzzy the Crow (debut); The wisecracking crow appeared in eight shorts (1947–54).

1393 *Stupor Duck* (July 17, 1956)
Dir: Robert McKimson; Warner Bros.; Looney Tune: Daffy Duck; Parody of TV's *Superman*; Voices—Mel Blanc.

1394 *Suddenly It's Spring!* (April 28, 1944)
Dir: Seymour Kneitel; Paramount/Famous; Noveltoon, with Raggedy Ann; The second of three "Raggedy Ann" shorts, following the Fleischer two-reeler *Raggedy Ann and Raggedy Andy* (1941).

1395 *Sufferin' Cat* (January 16, 1943)
Dir: William Hanna, Joseph Barbera; MGM; Tom and Jerry, Meathead.

1396 *Sugar and Spies* (November 5, 1966)
Dir: Robert McKimson; Warner Bros.; Looney Tune: Road Runner, Coyote (last short in the series until 1994's *Chariots of Fur*).

1397 *Sultan Pepper* (March 16, 1934; b&w)
Dir: George Stallings; Van Beuren; The Little King.

1398 *Summer* (January 6, 1930; b&w)
Dir: Ub Iwerks; Walt Disney; Silly Symphony; Bugs frolic in this early Disney short.

1399 *A Sunbonnet Blue* (August 21, 1937)
Dir: Tex Avery; Warner Bros.; Merrie Melodie.

1400 *Sundae in New York* (1983) AA
Producer-Director: Jimmy Picker; Motionpicker Prod; Oscar winner; Fine clay-animated short has Mayor Ed Koch singing "New York, New York" as he ponders the city's problems.

1401 *The Sunshine Makers* (January 11, 1935)
Dir: Burt Gillett, Ted Eshbaugh; Van Beuren; Rainbow Parade; Charming fantasy about happy elves who bottle sunshine and use it as a "happy" weapon against their gloomy foes.

1402 *Super Pink* (October 12, 1966)
Dir: Hawley Pratt; DePatie-Freleng; The Pink Panther; The usually-silent panther speaks in this short.

1403 *Super Rabbit* (April 3, 1943)
Dir: Chuck Jones; Warner Bros.; Merrie Melodie: Bugs Bunny; Classic Superman spoof; At the end of this wartime short Bugs turns into "a *real* Superman"—a U.S. Marine; Voices—Mel Blanc.

1404 *The Super Snooper* (November 11, 1952)
Dir: Robert McKimson; Warner Bros.; Looney Tune: Daffy Duck; Parody of private-eye films; Voices—Mel Blanc.

1405 *Superior Duck* (August 23, 1996)
Dir: Chuck Jones; Warner Bros./Chuck Jones Film Prods; Daffy Duck; New Warner Bros. cartoon from legendary WB director Jones; Released in theaters with the feature *Carpool*; Produced by Linda Jones Clough (Jones' daughter).

1406 *Superman* (September 26, 1941) †
Dir: Dave Fleischer; Max Fleischer; Superman (debut); Oscar nominee; An evil scientist threatens Metropolis with his "Electrothanasia Ray"; The first entry in the expensive, superbly-animated series (the Fleischers' last and most ambitious); Based on the comic book character (who first appeared in *Action Comics* No. 1 in June 1938) created by Jerry Siegel and Joe Schuster; The "Man of Steel" appeared in 17 shorts (1941–43); Voices—Bud Collyer (Superman), Joan Alexander (Lois Lane); Note: Collyer and Alexander also voiced the popular *Superman* radio series (which debuted in 1940).

1407 *Susie, the Little Blue Coupe* (June 6, 1952)
Dir: Clyde Geronimi; Walt Disney; An original story by Bill Peet, narrated by Sterling Holloway.

Swifty and Shorty (series) **see** *Without Time or Reason* (1962)

1408 *Swing Shift Cinderella* (August 25, 1945)
Dir: Tex Avery; MGM; The Wolf and the Showgirl; Hilarious, nonstop Avery madness which puts a sexy, modern twist on the old fairy tale. One of the director's best.

Swing Symphonies (series) **see** *$21.00 a Day Once a Month* (1941)

1409 *Switchin' Kitten* (September 7, 1961)
Dir: Gene Deitch; MGM; Tom and Jerry; The first "Tom and Jerry" cartoon since original creators William Hanna and Joseph Barbera left MGM in 1957; Deitch made 13 "T & J" shorts (1961–62), then Chuck Jones took over the series.

1410 *The Swooner Crooner* (May 6, 1944) †
Dir: Frank Tashlin; Warner Bros.; Looney Tune: Porky Pig; Oscar nominee; The chickens of Porky's egg-producing factory stop work to listen to a crooning rooster. Tuneful sendup of the bobby-soxer phenomenon featuring caricatures of Frank Sinatra, Bing Crosby, Cab Calloway and others; Tex Avery also parodied the crooner craze in his *Little Tinker* (1948); Voices—Mel Blanc.

Sylvester and Tweety (series) **see** *Tweetie Pie* (1947)

Sylvester the Cat (series) **see** *Life with Feathers* (1945)

1411 *Symphony Hour* (March 20, 1942)
Dir: Riley Thomson; Walt Disney; Mickey Mouse, Donald Duck, Goofy; Mickey and friends perform a radio concert with smashed instruments; Voices—Walt Disney (Mickey), Clarence Nash (Donald Duck), George Johnson (Goofy).

1412 *Symphony in Slang* (June 6, 1951)
Dir: Tex Avery; MGM; In Heaven, a man recounts the story of his life in slang.

1413 *A Symposium on Popular Songs* (December 19, 1962) †
Dir: Bill Justice; Walt Disney; Oscar nominee; The only theatrical appearance of Prof. Ludwig Von Drake, the German-accented duck and frequent host of Disney TV specials.

1414 *Tabasco Road* (July 20, 1957) †
Dir: Robert McKimson; Warner Bros.; Merrie Melodie: Speedy Gonzales, Sylvester; Oscar nominee; Speedy helps out two drunken mice who tangle with a hungry alleycat; Voices—Mel Blanc.

1415 *A Tale of Two Kitties* (November 21, 1942)
Dir: Bob Clampett; Warner Bros.; Merrie Melodie: Tweety (debut), Babbit and Catstello (debut); Two cats try to reach Tweety in his nest; Tweety, the little yellow canary who first uttered the immortal words "I tawt I taw a putty tat," appeared in three shorts before the first of his many teamings with Sylvester the Cat in *Tweetie Pie* (1947); The comic duo Babbit and Catstello—a feline version of Abbott and Costello)—reappeared (as mice) in *A Tale of Two Mice* (1945) and *The Mouse-Merized Cat* (1946); Voices—Mel Blanc.

1416 *A Tale of Two Mice* (June 30, 1945)
Dir: Frank Tashlin; Warner Bros.; Looney Tune: Babbit and Catstello; The comic mouse team Babbit and Catstello (last seen as cats in 1942's *A Tale of Two Kitties*) want some cheese but have to get past a cat first; Voices—Mel Blanc.

Talkartoons (series) **see** *Noah's Lark* (1929)

1417 *The Talking Magpies* (January 4, 1946)
Dir: Mannie Davis; Terrytoons; Heckle and Jeckle (debut); The first cartoon featuring the comical magpies, who became popular Terrytoons stars (second only to Mighty Mouse), appearing in 53 shorts (1946–66); Voices—Dayton Allen (Heckle/Jeckle).

1418 *Tall Timber Tales* (July, 1951)
Dir: Connie Rasinski; Terrytoons; Terry Bears (debut); Terrytoons' twin bears appeared in 17 shorts (1951–56).

1419 *Tango* (1982) AA
Producer-Director: Zbigniew Rybczynski; Film Polski Prod; Oscar winner; Grand-prize winner at the Annecy Animation Festival; Polish filmmaker Rybczynski has also directed American music videos.

Tasmanian Devil (series) **see** *Devil May Hare* (1954)

1420 *T-Bone for Two* (August 14, 1942)
Dir: Clyde Geronimi; Walt Disney; Pluto.

1421 *Tea for Two Hundred* (December 24, 1948) †
Dir: Jack Hannah; Walt Disney; Donald Duck; Oscar nominee; Donald is besieged by an army of ants while on a picnic; Voice—Clarence Nash (Donald).

1422 *Technological Threat* (1988) †
Bill Kroyer, Brian Jennings; Kroyer Films; Oscar nominee.

1423 *Tee for Two* (July 21, 1945)
Dir: William Hanna, Joseph Barbera; MGM; Tom and Jerry.

1424 *The Tell-Tale Heart* (December 27, 1953) †
Dir: Ted Parmelee; UPA; Oscar nominee; Excellent animated telling of Edgar Allen Poe's tale of murder and madness. A UPA classic, artistically rendered in the studio's best style; Art design by Paul Julian; Story adaption by Bill Scott and Fred Gable; Narrated by James Mason.

1425 *The Tender Tale of Cinderella Penguin* (1981; 10 mins) †
Producer-Director: Janet Perlman; National Film Board of Canada; Oscar nominee; Penguin version of the fairy tale.

1426 *Tennis Chums* (December 10, 1949)
Dir: William Hanna, Joseph Barbera; MGM; Tom and Jerry.

1427 *Tennis Racquet* (August 26, 1949)
Dir: Jack Kinney; Walt Disney; Goofy.

1428 *Termites from Mars* (December 8, 1952)
Dir: Don Patterson; Walter Lantz; Woody Woodpecker; Martian termites invade Woody's home in this imaginative, well-animated short. One of Woody's best; Voices—Grace Stafford (Woody).

1429 *Terrier Stricken* (November 29, 1952)
Dir: Chuck Jones; Warner Bros.; Merrie Melodie: Claude Cat, Frisky Puppy; Claude's attempts to get rid of Frisky are foiled by the little puppy's nerve-rattling barks; Claude and Frisky's second short together, following *Two's a Crowd* (1950).

1430 *Terror Faces Magoo* (July 9, 1959)
Dir; Chris Ishii; UPA; Mr. Magoo (last of series); The last theatrical UPA short, and the only one produced by the studio's commercial branch in New York.

1431 *Terror on the Midway* (August 30, 1942)
Dir: Dave Fleischer; Max Fleischer; Superman; The last short from the Fleischer studio (Famous Studios continued the "Superman" series into 1943); Voices—Bud Collyer, Joan Alexander.

Terry Bears (series) **see** *Tall Timber Tales* (1951)

Terrytoons (series) **see** *Caviar* (1930)

1432 *Tetched in the Head* (October 24, 1935)
Dir: uncredited; Columbia/Screen Gems; Barney Google (debut); Billy DeBeck's (1890–1942) comic-strip character was tried out in four shorts (1935–36).

1433 *There's Good Boos Tonight* (April 23, 1948)
Dir: Isadore Sparber; Paramount/Famous; Noveltoon, with Casper the Friendly Ghost (in his second cartoon appearance).

1434 *There's Something About a Soldier* (August 17, 1934; b&w)
Dir: Dave Fleischer; Max Fleischer; Betty Boop; Soldiers fight a war against giant mosquitoes; Voice—Mae Questel (Betty).

1435 *The Thieving Magpie (La Gazza Ladra)* (1965) †
Producer-Directors: Giulio Gianini, Emanuele Luzzati; Oscar nominee.

1436 *Think or Sink* (March, 1967)
Dir: James Culhane; Paramount; Merry Makers (series debut); Four shorts were produced in this variety series (1967), one of Paramount's last.

The Three Bears **see** *Bugs Bunny and the Three Bears* (1944)

1437 *Three Blind Mouseketeers* (September 26, 1936)
Dir: David Hand; Walt Disney; Silly Symphony.

3–D cartoons **see** *Melody* (1953), *Hypnotic Hick* (1953), *Popeye, The Ace of Space* (1953), *Working for Peanuts* (1953), *Boo Moon* (1954), *Lumberjack Rabbit* (1954).

1438 *Three Little Bops* (January 5, 1957)
Dir: Friz Freleng; Warner Bros.; Looney Tune; Great musical version of "The Three Little Pigs" has the Big Bad Wolf trying to join the pigs' "real cool" band; Narrated by Stan Freberg.

1439 *Three Little Pigs* (May 27, 1933) AA
Dir: Burt Gillett; Walt Disney; Silly Symphony; Oscar winner; Disney's most successful animated short and the first cartoon to produce a hit song—"Who's Afraid of the Big Bad Wolf?" (written by Frank Churchill, Ted Sears and Pinto Colvig)—which became a morale-boosting anthem for depression-era audiences; The film, which cost $60,000, grossed $150,000 in its first 15 months of release; The Three Pigs returned in *The Big Bad Wolf* (1934), *Three Little Wolves* (1936) and *The Practical Pig* (1939); Animators—Norm Ferguson, Dick Lundy, Fred Moore, Art Babbitt; Voices—Billy Bletcher (Big Bad Wolf), Pinto Colvig (Pig).

1440 *The Three Little Pups* (December 26, 1953)
Dir: Tex Avery; MGM; Droopy; Funny variation on "The Three Little Pigs" has Droopy and friends (Snoopy and Loopy) fighting off a dogcatcher (voiced by Daws Butler); Voice—Bill Thompson (Droopy).

1441 *Three Little Wolves* (April 18, 1936)
Dir: David Hand; Walt Disney; Silly Symphony, with the Three Little Pigs (and the Big Bad Wolf), in their third appearance.

1442 *Three Orphan Kittens* (October 26, 1935) AA
Dir: David Hand; Walt Disney; Silly Symphony; Oscar winner; Cute tale of three little kittens finding refuge from a blizzard and getting into all kinds of mischief; Followed by *More Kittens* (1936).

1443 *Thru the Mirror* (May 30, 1936)
Dir: David Hand; Walt Disney; Mickey Mouse; Mickey goes "through the looking glass" in this version of the Lewis Carroll tale; Voice—Walt Disney (Mickey).

1444 *Thugs with Dirty Mugs* (May 6, 1939)
Dir: Tex Avery; Warner Bros.; Merrie Melodie; Great spoof of gangster films; Voices—Mel Blanc.

1445 *Thumb Fun* (March 1, 1952)
Dir: Robert McKimson; Warner Bros.; Looney Tune: Daffy Duck, Porky Pig; Daffy hitches a ride with Porky; Voices—Mel Blanc.

1446 *Tick Tock Tuckered* (April 8, 1944)
Dir: Bob Clampett; Warner Bros.; Looney Tune: Porky Pig, Daffy Duck; Remake of Clampett's directorial debut, *Porky's Badtime Story* (1937); Voices—Mel Blanc.

1447 *Tiger Trouble* (January 5, 1945)
Dir: Jack Kinney; Walt Disney; Goofy; Goofy, riding on the back of an elephant, goes tiger hunting. First-rate "Goofy" short, ending in a wonderfully frantic chase involving tiger, elephant and Goof.

1448 *The Tijuana Toads* (August 6, 1969)
DePatie-Freleng; The Tijuana Toads (debut); The first of 17 shorts (1969–72) starring the toads, Poncho and Toro; Renamed "The Texas Toads" for TV.

1449 *Timber* (January 10, 1941)
Dir: Jack King; Walt Disney; Donald Duck, Black Pete; Logger Pierre (Pete) puts Donald to work for him; Voice—Clarence Nash (Donald).

1450 *Tin Toy* (1988; 5 mins) AA
Dir: John Lasseter; Pixar; Oscar winner; Computer-animated short (the first to win an Academy Award) about a windup toy and his young owner; Lasseter would later direct the full-length computer-animated feature *Toy Story* (1995); Produced by Lasseter and William Reeves.

1451 *To Duck or Not to Duck* (March 6, 1943)
Dir: Chuck Jones; Warner Bros.; Looney Tune: Daffy Duck, Elmer Fudd; Daffy and Elmer decide to settle their differences in the boxing ring; Voices—Mel Blanc, Arthur Q. Bryan (Elmer).

1452 *To Spring* (June 20, 1936)
Dir: William Hanna; MGM; Happy Harmony; Little worker elves gear up for the start of spring; Hanna's directorial debut. He would soon team up with Joseph Barbera to direct the long-running "Tom and Jerry" series (1940–58).

Toby the Pup (series) **see** *The Museum* (1930)

1453 *Toby Tortoise Returns* (August 22, 1936)
Dir: Wilfred Jackson; Walt Disney; Silly Symphony; Toby fights Max Hare in the boxing ring; Sequel to the Oscar-winning *The Tortoise and the Hare* (1935).

1454 *Toccata and Fugue in D Minor* (November 13, 1940; 9 mins)
Dir: Samuel Armstrong; Walt Disney; Abstract images illustrate Leopold Stokowski's symphonic transcription of the organ work by Johann Sebastian Bach (1685–1750); Part of the feature *Fantasia*; German abstract animator Oskar Fischinger (1900–67) contributed designs for this film; Stokowski conducts the Philadelphia Orchestra.

Toddle Tales (series) **see** *Grandfather's Clock* (1934)

1455 *Together in the Weather* (March 22, 1946)
Producer-Director: George Pal; Puppetoon; The story of Punchy and Judy, two figures on a weather clock who are unable to be together (one comes out when it's sunny, the other when it is rainy).

Tom and Jerry (MGM series) **see** *Puss Gets the Boot* (1940)

Tom and Jerry (Van Beuren series) **see** *Wot a Night* (1931)

1456 *Tom and Jerry at the Hollywood Bowl* (September 16, 1950)
Dir: William Hanna, Joseph Barbera; MGM; Tom and Jerry.

Tommy Tortoise and Moe Hare (series) **see** *Winner by a Hare* (1953)

1457 *Tom Thumb* (March 30, 1936)
Producer-Director: Ub Iwerks; ComiColor.

1458 *Tom Turk and Daffy* (February 12, 1944)
Dir: Chuck Jones; Warner Bros.; Looney Tune: Daffy Duck; Both Tom Turk and Daffy become the object of Porky's turkey hunt; Voices—Mel Blanc.

1459 *Toonerville Trolley* (January 17, 1936)
Dir: Burt Gillett, Tom Palmer; Van Beuren; Rainbow Parade; The first of three "Rainbow Parades" (1936) based on the popular "Toonerville Trolley" comic strip by Fontaine Fox (1884–1964).

1460 *Toot, Whistle, Plunk, and Boom* (Adventures in Music) (November 10, 1953) AA
Dir: Ward Kimball, Charles Nichols; Walt Disney; Oscar winner; Stylized animation highlights this entertaining history of music; The first cartoon to be filmed in widescreen CinemaScope; Follows *Melody* (1953) in the "Adventures in Music" series; Music by Joseph Dubin; Songs by Sonny Burke and Jack Elliot.

1461 *Topcat* (July, 1960)
    Dir: Seymour Kneitel; Paramount; The Cat (debut); The sleuthing British feline appeared in five shorts (1960–61); Voice—Dayton Allen (The Cat).

1462 *Topsy TV* (January 1957)
    Dir: Connie Rasinski; Terrytoons; John Doormat (debut); The first of four shorts (1957–59) starring average '50s suburbanite John Doormat. Writer-cartoonist Jules Feiffer contributed to later cartoons in the series; Voice—Lionel Wilson (John).

1463 *The Tortoise and the Hare* (January 5, 1935) AA
    Dir: Wilfred Jackson; Walt Disney; Silly Symphony; Oscar winner; First-rate animated version of the classic Aesop fable pits slowpoke Toby Tortoise in a race against fast and cocky Max Hare; Sequel—*Toby Tortoise Returns* (1936).

1464 *Tortoise Beats Hare* (March 15, 1941)
    Dir: Tex Avery; Warner Bros.; Merrie Melodie: Bugs Bunny, Cecil Turtle.

1465 *Tortoise Wins by a Hare* (February 20, 1943)
    Dir: Bob Clampett; Warner Bros.; Merrie Melodie: Bugs Bunny, Cecil Turtle; Bugs challenges Cecil to another race in this followup to *Tortoise Beats Hare* (1941); Voices—Mel Blanc.

1466 *Tot Watchers* (August 1, 1958)
    Dir: William Hanna, Joseph Barbera; MGM; Tom and Jerry; The last "Tom and Jerry" cartoon produced by Hanna-Barbera before the team left MGM to form their own production company (the series was revived by Gene Deitch with 1961's *Switchin' Kitten*).

1467 *Touché Pussycat* (December 18, 1954) †
    Dir: William Hanna, Joseph Barbera; MGM; Tom and Jerry, Nibbles; Oscar nominee.

1468 *Toy Tinkers* (December 16, 1949) †
    Dir: Jack Hannah; Walt Disney; Donald Duck, Chip 'n' Dale; Oscar nominee.

1469 *Toyland Broadcast* (December 22, 1934)
    Dir: Rudolf Ising; MGM; Happy Harmony.

1470 *Trader Mickey* (August 20, 1932; b&w)
    Dir: David Hand; Walt Disney; Mickey Mouse, Pluto; Hand's directorial debut. A former Bray Studio animator, Hand (1900–86) joined Disney in 1930 and directed 25 shorts (1932–37), including the Oscar winners *Three Orphan Kittens* (1935) and *The Country Cousin* (1936); He then supervised Disney features (*Snow White*, *Bambi*, etc.) into the mid–40s, leaving to head Britain's G. B. Animation (1944–49).

1471 *Traffic Troubles* (March 20, 1931; b&w)
    Dir: Burt Gillett; Walt Disney; Mickey Mouse, Minnie Mouse; Mickey's a taxi driver and Minnie's his fare; Voices—Walt Disney (Mickey), Marcellite Garner (Minnie).

1472 *Trail Mix-Up* (March 12, 1993)
    Dir: Barry Cook; Disney/Amblin; Roger Rabbit, Baby Herman, Jessica Rabbit; Roger

looks after Baby Herman in Yellowstain National Park. Jessica Rabbit appears as a sexy park ranger in this manic, fast-paced short; Released with the feature *A Far Off Place*; Third in the series, following *Tummy Trouble* (1989) and *Roller Coaster Rabbit* (1990); Voices—Charles Fleischer (Roger), April Winchell (Baby Herman).

1473 *Transylvania 6–5000* (November 30, 1963)
Dir: Chuck Jones; Co-Dir: Maurice Noble; Warner Bros.; Merrie Melodie: Bugs Bunny.

1474 *Trap Happy* (June 29, 1946)
Dir: William Hanna, Joseph Barbera; MGM; Tom and Jerry; Tom brings in a professional mouse exterminator to help him catch Jerry.

1475 *Trap Happy Porky* (February 24, 1945)
Dir: Chuck Jones; Warner Bros.; Looney Tune: Porky Pig; Porky hires a cat to rid his house of mice; Highlight—the hilarious drunken singing of the cat and his buddies; Voices—Mel Blanc.

1476 *Tree for Two* (October 4, 1952)
Dir: Friz Freleng; Warner Bros.; Merrie Melodie: Sylvester, Spike and Chester.

1477 *Trees* (May 27, 1948; 4 mins)
Dir: Hamilton Luske; Walt Disney; Beautiful Disney rendering of the 1913 Joyce Kilmer poem; Part of the feature *Melody Time*; Music by Oscar Rasbach, performed by Fred Waring and His Pennsylvanians; Rereleased with *Bumble Boogie* (as *Contrasts in Rhythm*) March 11, 1955.

1478 *Trees and Jamaica Daddy* (January 30, 1958) †
Dir: Lew Keller; UPA; Ham and Hattie (debut); Oscar nominee (UPA's last); The first in a series of four shorts (1958–59), each one featuring two separate stories.

1479 *The Trial of Donald Duck* (July 30, 1948)
Dir: Jack King; Walt Disney; Donald Duck; King's last short.

1480 *Triangle* (1994) †
Producer-Director: Erica Russell; Gingco Ltd Prod; Oscar nominee.

1481 *Trick or Treat* (October 10, 1952)
Dir: Jack Hannah; Walt Disney; Donald Duck, Huey, Dewey and Louie; On Halloween night the boys enlist the aid of Witch Hazel to play a trick on Donald; Voice—Clarence Nash (Donald).

1482 *Triplet Trouble* (April 19, 1952)
Dir: William Hanna, Joseph Barbera; MGM; Tom and Jerry; In this one, the fighting cat and mouse team up against three nasty little kittens.

1483 *Trolley Troubles* (September 5, 1927; b&w)
Producer-Director: Walt Disney; Oswald the Lucky Rabbit (debut); Walt Disney fol-

lowed his "Alice Comedies" with this series featuring a mischievous rabbit, who would appear in 26 silent shorts (1927–28). The series was a success, but after a dispute with his distributor (Charles Mintz) over profits, Disney lost Oswald—and four of his best animators—forcing him to create a new character—a mouse named Mickey (see *Steamboat Willie*); "Oswald" continued under Walter Lantz in a series of sound cartoons (1929–38), see *Ozzie of the Circus*; Premiered July 4, 1927, at the Criterion Theatre, Los Angeles.

1484 *Trouble Indemnity* (September 14, 1950) †
    Dir: Pete Burness; UPA; Mr. Magoo; Oscar nominee; Burness' directorial debut. Former Warner Bros. animator Burness (b. 1910) became Mr. Magoo's main director (taking it over from John Hubley), directing 36 shorts (1950–58) in the series, including the Oscar winners *When Magoo Flew* (1955) and *Magoo's Puddle Jumper* (1956). Burness was later a director on TV's *Rocky and Bullwinkle* in the early '60s; Voice—Jim Backus (Mr. Magoo).

1485 *Truant Officer Donald* (August 1, 1941) †
    Dir: Jack King; Walt Disney; Donald Duck, Huey, Dewey and Louie; Oscar nominee.

1486 *The Truce Hurts* (July 17, 1948)
    Dir: William Hanna, Joseph Barbera; MGM; Tom and Jerry, Spike.

1487 *The Truth About Mother Goose* (August 28, 1957) †
    Dir: Wolfgang Reitherman, Bill Justice; Walt Disney; Oscar nominee; Interesting look at the historical facts behind the famous nursery rhymes "Little Jack Horner," "Mary, Mary, Quite Contrary" and "London Bridge is Falling Down"; Written by Bill Peet; Music and lyrics by George Bruns, Tom Adair and Bill Peet; Sung by the Page Cavanaugh Trio.

1488 *Tubby the Tuba* (July 11, 1947; 10 mins) †
    Producer-Director: George Pal; Puppetoon; Oscar nominee; Charming tale about a tuba in an orchestra who longs to play his own melody. One of the last—and best—shorts in the "Puppetoon" series; Narrated by Victor Jory.

1489 *Tugboat Mickey* (April 26, 1940)
    Dir: Clyde Geronimi; Walt Disney; Mickey Mouse, Donald Duck, Goofy.

1490 *Tulips Shall Grow* (January 26, 1943) †
    Producer-Director: George Pal; Puppetoon; Oscar nominee; The Screwball Army (Pal's nuts-and-bolts parody of the Nazis) lays siege to a peaceful Dutch countryside; Entered in the Library of Congress National Film Registry in 1997.

1491 *Tummy Trouble* (June 23, 1989)
    Dir: Rob Minkoff; Disney/Amblin; Roger Rabbit, Baby Herman, Jessica Rabbit, Droopy (cameo); Roger rushes Baby Herman to the hospital after his little charge swallows a rattle; The first in a series of wild, Tex Avery–style cartoons featuring the animated stars of the hit feature *Who Framed Roger Rabbit* (1988); Released in theaters with the film *Honey, I Shrunk the Kids*; Followed by *Rollercoaster Rabbit* (1990); Live-action Dir: Frank Marshall; Voices—Charles Fleischer (Roger), Kathleen Turner (Jessica), April Winchell/Lou Hirsch (Baby Herman), Richard Williams (Droopy), Corey Burton (Orderly); Produced by Don Hahn.

1492 *Tup Tup* (1972) †
Producer-Director: Nedeljko Dragic; Zagreb Film/Corona Cinematografica Prod; Oscar nominee.

1493 *Turkey Dinner* (November 30, 1936; b&w)
Producer-Director: Walter Lantz; Meany, Miny and Moe; The nonspeaking monkeys' first "official" cartoon, following their debut in *Monkey Wretches* (1935).

1494 *TV of Tomorrow* (June 6, 1953)
Dir: Tex Avery; MGM; A gag-filled look at futuristic advances in TV technology; Live-action footage is shown on the TV screens (including a shot of actor Dave O'Brien).

1495 *Tweet Tweet Tweety* (December 15, 1951)
Dir: Friz Freleng; Warner Bros.; Looney Tune: Tweety, Sylvester.

1496 *Tweetie Pie* (May 3, 1947) AA
Dir: Friz Freleng; Warner Bros.; Merrie Melodie: Tweety, Sylvester; Oscar winner; Tweety and Sylvester's first cartoon together and the first Warner Bros. cartoon to win an Academy Award; Tweety (who debuted in 1942's *A Tale of Two Kitties*) and Sylvester (who debuted in 1945's *Life with Feathers*) became one of Warner Bros.' greatest cartoon teams (alongside Bugs and Elmer, and the Road Runner and Coyote), appearing together in 42 shorts (1947–64); Voices—Mel Blanc.

Tweety (series) **see** *A Tale of Two Kitties* (1942)

1497 *Tweety and the Beanstalk* (May 16, 1957)
Dir: Friz Freleng; Warner Bros.; Merrie Melodie: Tweety, Sylvester.

1498 *Tweety's S.O.S.* (September 22, 1951)
Dir: Friz Freleng; Warner Bros.; Merrie Melodie: Tweety, Sylvester, Granny.

1499 *25 Ways to Quit Smoking* (1989; 5 mins)
Producer-Director: Bill Plympton; One of Plympton's best shorts demonstrates various ways of kicking the habit; Written and animated by Plympton.

1500 *$21.00 a Day Once a Month* (December 1, 1941)
Producer-Director: Walter Lantz; Swing Symphony (series debut); The first short in Walter Lantz's jazzy musical series (15 shorts, 1941–45), which featured popular songs of the day.

1501 *Two Chips and a Miss* (March 21, 1952)
Dir: Jack Hannah; Walt Disney; Chip 'n' Dale; The chipmunks unknowingly have a date with the same girl, a singer at a club.

1502 *Two-Gun Mickey* (December 15, 1934; b&w)
Dir: Ben Sharpsteen; Walt Disney; Mickey Mouse, Minnie Mouse, Pegleg Pete; Sharpsteen's directorial debut. A veteran animator (of Hearst, Barre-Bowers, and Fleischer), he directed 22 Disney shorts (1934–42), including the classics *Mickey's Service Station* (1935) and *Clock Cleaners* (1937). He was also a director or supervisor on ten Disney features (1937–53); Voice—Walt Disney (Mickey).

1503 *Two Little Indians* (October 17, 1953)
Dir: William Hanna, Joseph Barbera; MGM; Tom and Jerry, Nibbles.

1504 *Two Mouseketeers* (March 15, 1952) AA
Dir: William Hanna, Joseph Barbera; MGM; Tom and Jerry; Oscar winner.

1505 *Two Scents Worth* (October 15, 1955)
Dir: Chuck Jones; Warner Bros.; Merrie Melodie: Pepe Le Pew.

1506 *Two Silhouettes* (August 15, 1946; 4 mins)
Dir: Robert Cormack; Walt Disney; Dinah Shore sings to the ballet dancing (in silhouette) of Tania Riabouchinska and David Lichine; Part of the feature *Make Mine Music*.

1507 *Two's a Crowd* (December 30, 1950)
Dir: Chuck Jones; Warner Bros.; Looney Tune: Claude Cat, Frisky Puppy; Claude's master brings home a yelping puppy; Claude and Frisky also costar in *Terrier Stricken* (1952) and *No Barking* (1954).

1508 *The Ugly Duckling* (April 7, 1939) AA
Dir: Jack Cutting; Walt Disney; Silly Symphony (last in series); Oscar winner; Disney's wonderful telling of the classic Hans Christian Andersen tale; Color remake of a 1931 "Silly Symphony"; The studio's eighth Academy Award–winning cartoon short in eight years.

1509 *Uncle Tom's Bungalow* (June 5, 1937)
Dir: Tex Avery; Warner Bros.; Merrie Melodie.

1510 *Uncle Tom's Cabana* (July 19, 1947)
Dir: Tex Avery; MGM; The Showgirl (Little Eva); Parody of the classic story.

1511 *Underground World* (June 18, 1943)
Dir: Seymour Kneitel; Paramount/Famous; Superman.

1512 *A Unicorn in the Garden* (September 24, 1953)
Dir: William Hurtz; UPA; Charming, faithful animated adaption of the story by *New Yorker* humorist James Thurber (1894–1961).

1513 *The Uninvited Pests* (November 29, 1946)
Dir: Connie Rasinski; Terrytoons; Heckle and Jeckle (in their second short).

1514 *The Unmentionables* (September 7, 1963)
Dir: Friz Freleng; Warner Bros.; Merrie Melodie: Bugs Bunny, Rocky and Mugsy (gangsters); Spoof of TV's *The Untouchables*; Voices—Mel Blanc.

Un-Natural History (series) **see** *How the Elephant Got His Trunk* (1925)

1515 *The Unruly Hare* (February 10, 1945)
Dir: Frank Tashlin; Warner Bros.; Merrie Melodie: Bugs Bunny, Elmer Fudd; Bugs

heckles railroad surveyor Elmer. Funny and fast-moving, this was the first of two "Bugs Bunny" shorts directed by Tashlin (followed by 1946's *Hare Remover*); Voices—Mel Blanc (Bugs), Arthur Q. Bryan (Elmer).

1516 *Unwelcome Guest* (February 17, 1945)
Dir: George Gordon; MGM; Barney Bear; Barney is pestered by a little skunk; In one scene, Barney reads a book titled "Red Hot Ridinghood" (after Tex Avery's racy 1943 cartoon).

1517 *Up a Tree* (September 23, 1955)
Dir: Jack Hannah; Walt Disney; Donald Duck, Chip 'n' Dale; The chipmunks take action when Donald starts cutting down their home. One of the last (and funniest) Donald-chipmunk shorts; Voice—Clarence Nash (Donald).

1518 *The Upstanding Sitter* (July 13, 1947)
Dir: Robert McKimson; Warner Bros.; Looney Tune: Daffy Duck; Daffy is hired to sit for an uncooperative baby chick; Voices—Mel Blanc.

1519 *The Vanishing Private* (September 25, 1942)
Dir: Jack King; Walt Disney; Donald Duck; Private Donald uses invisible paint to hide from his commanding officer; Voice—Clarence Nash (Donald).

1520 *Vegetable Vaudeville* (November 9, 1951)
Dir: Isadore Sparber; Paramount/Famous; Kartune; The first of 12 "Kartunes" (1951–53), a mixed-bag series of shorts similar to the studio's "Noveltoons."

1521 *Ventriloquist Cat* (May 27, 1950)
Dir: Tex Avery; MGM; Spike (the dog); A cat uses ventriloquism to fool Spike. Hilarious Avery short.

1522 *The Village* (1993) †
Producer-Director: Mark Baker; Pizazz Pictures Prod; Oscar nominee.

1523 *The Village Smithy* (December 5, 1936; b&w)
Dir: Tex Avery; Warner Bros.; Looney Tune: Porky Pig; Funny early short from Avery.

1524 *Vincent* (October 1, 1982; b&w)
Dir: Tim Burton; Walt Disney; Stop-motion short about a boy's obsession with Vincent Price; Narrated by Price; Burton (who joined Disney in 1980) later directed the live-action features *Batman* (1989) and *Edward Scissorhands* (1990, with Vincent Price); Animated by Stephen Chiodo; Produced by Rick Heinrichs.

1525 *The Violinist* (1959) †
Producer-Director: Ernest Pintoff; Oscar nominee; Pintoff had been a member of UPA and Terrytoons (where he directed *Flebus*).

1526 *Volcano* (July 10, 1942)
Dir: Dave Fleischer; Max Fleischer; Superman.

1527 *Voyage to Next* (1974; 10 mins) †
Dir: John and Faith Hubley; Hubley Studios; Oscar nominee; Music by Dizzy Gillespie; Voices—Maureen Stapleton (Mother Earth), Dizzy Gillespie (Father Time), Ella Fitzgerald, Benny Carter.

1528 *Wabbit Twouble* (December 20, 1941)
Dir: Bob Clampett; Warner Bros.; Merrie Melodie: Bugs Bunny, Elmer Fudd (chubby version); Bugs disrupts Elmer's restful stay at Jellostone National Park. Terrific "Bugs" short; Voices—Mel Blanc (Bugs), Arthur Q. Bryan (Elmer).

1529 *The Wabbit Who Came to Supper* (March 28, 1942)
Dir: Friz Freleng; Warner Bros.; Merrie Melodie: Bugs Bunny, Elmer Fudd (chubby version); Elmer will inherit $3 million from his Uncle Louie (or "Wouie," as Elmer says) if he doesn't harm any rabbits; Voices—Mel Blanc (Bugs), Arthur Q. Bryan (Elmer).

1530 *Wackiki Wabbit* (July 3, 1943)
Dir: Chuck Jones; Warner Bros.; Merrie Melodie: Bugs Bunny; Two starving castaways stranded on an island try to capture Bugs for their dinner. Classic "Bugs" short features stylized jungle backgrounds; The two castaways were modeled after Warner cartoon writers Michael Maltese and Tedd Pierce (they also voiced the characters); Voice—Mel Blanc (Bugs).

1531 *Wacky-Bye Baby* (May, 1948)
Dir: Dick Lundy; Walter Lantz; Woody Woodpecker, Wally Walrus; Woody poses as billionaire Wally's adopted son.

1532 *The Wacky Wabbit* (May 2, 1942)
Dir: Bob Clampett; Warner Bros.; Merrie Melodie: Bugs Bunny, Elmer Fudd (chubby version); Bugs heckles Elmer as he prospects for gold out on the desert. Hilarious Clampett classic; Voices—Mel Blanc (Bugs), Arthur Q. Bryan (Elmer).

1533 *The Wacky Weed* (December 16, 1946)
Dir: Dick Lundy; Walter Lantz; Andy Panda; A pesky weed keeps bothering (or, rather, strangling) Andy's new flower.

1534 *Wacky Wildlife* (November 9, 1940)
Dir: Tex Avery; Warner Bros.; Merrie Melodie.

1535 *The Wacky Worm* (June 21, 1941)
Dir: Friz Freleng; Warner Bros.; Merrie Melodie; A crow chases a Jerry Colonna–like worm; Followed by the Oscar-nominated *Greetings Bait* (1943).

1536 *Wagon Heels* (July 28, 1945)
Dir: Bob Clampett; Warner Bros.; Merrie Melodie: Porky Pig; Color remake of *Injun Trouble* (1938); Voices—Mel Blanc.

1537 *Wags to Riches* (August 13, 1949)
Dir: Tex Avery; MGM; Droopy, Spike; Spike tries to gain Droopy's inheritance by killing him off; Later remade in CinemaScope as *Millionaire Droopy* (1956).

1538 *Walking (En marchant)* (1968; 5 mins) †
Producer-Director: Ryan Larkin; National Film Board of Canada; Oscar nominee; A study of the different ways people walk, using various animation techniques; Animated by Larkin.

1539 *Walky Talky Hawky* (August 31, 1946) †
Dir: Robert McKimson; Warner Bros.; Merrie Melodie: Foghorn Leghorn (debut), Henery Hawk; Oscar nominee; Foghorn encounters a tough little chickenhawk; The large, loud-mouthed rooster (similar to the blustery Senator Claghorn character on radio's *Fred Allen show*) appeared in 29 shorts (1946–63, '97). His chief nemesis, besides Henery, was the Barnyard Dog; Voices—Mel Blanc.

Wallace and Gromit (series) **see** *A Grand Day Out* (1990)

1540 *War and Pieces* (June 6, 1964)
Dir: Chuck Jones; Co-Dir: Maurice Noble; Warner Bros.; Looney Tune: Road Runner, Coyote; Jones' last Warner Bros. cartoon (the "Road Runner" series continued under Robert McKimson and Rudy Larriva, 1965–66). Jones would move on to MGM, directing "Tom and Jerry" shorts (1964–67) and TV specials (*Dr. Seuss' How the Grinch Stole Christmas*).

1541 *Water Babies* (May 11, 1935)
Dir: Wilfred Jackson; Walt Disney; Silly Symphony; Colorful underwater fantasy, inspired by the Charles Kingsley story, which became a partly-animated feature film in 1978.

1542 *Water Water Every Hare* (April 19, 1952)
Dir: Chuck Jones; Warner Bros.; Looney Tune: Bugs Bunny; Jones' second cartoon pitting Bugs against a mad scientist and his hairy orange monster (following 1946's *Hair-Raising Hare*); Voices—Mel Blanc.

1543 *Wat's Pig* (1996; 11 mins) †
Producer-Director: Peter Lord; Aardman Animations; Oscar nominee; Medieval tale—told in clay animation and using a split-screen—about twins separated at birth, one becoming a king, the other a peasant (who has been raised by a pig); Ambitious production from Aardman cofounder Lord; Animated by Lord and Sam Fell; Music by Andy Price.

1544 *Way Back When a Triangle Had Its Points* (February 9, 1940)
Dir: Dave Fleischer; Max Fleischer; Stone Age Cartoon (series debut); A married man takes his young secretary out to dinner at the Cave Inn; This series, one of the Fleischers' last, presented a comical, pre–*Flintstones* look at prehistoric life; 12 shorts were produced (1940).

1545 *Way Down Yonder in the Corn* (November 25, 1943)
Dir: Bob Wickersham; Columbia/Screen Gems; The Fox and the Crow.

1546 *We Aim to Please* (December 28, 1934; b&w)
Dir: Dave Fleischer; Max Fleischer; Popeye the Sailor, Olive Oyl, Bluto, Wimpy; Restauranteurs Popeye and Bluto compete for Wimpy's patronage; Wimpy utters his famous phrase: "I'd gladly pay you Tuesday for a hamburger today"; Voices—Jack Mercer (Popeye), Mae Questel (Olive), Gus Wickie (Bluto).

1547 *The Weakly Reporter* (March 25, 1944)
    Dir: Chuck Jones; Warner Bros.; Merrie Melodie; Wartime newsreel spoof.

1548 *The Wearing of the Grin* (July 14, 1951)
    Dir: Chuck Jones; Warner Bros.; Looney Tune: Porky Pig; Porky encounters leprechauns at a spooky Irish castle; Voices—Mel Blanc.

1549 *We're on Our Way to Rio* (April 21, 1944)
    Dir: Isadore Sparber; Paramount/Famous; Popeye the Sailor; Rereleased October 20, 1950.

1550 *Western Daze* (January 7, 1941)
    Producer-Director: George Pal; Puppetoon (debut): Madcap Model; Before his successful feature film career in the '50s (*War of the Worlds*, *Tom Thumb*, etc.), Pal produced (for Paramount) 40 puppet-animated shorts (1941–47) called "Puppetoons." The shorts, each costing about $25,000, used a stop-motion technique known as replacement animation (the process of carving thousands of wooden figurines and filming them one frame at a time). The series received seven Academy Award nominations and earned Pal a special Oscar in 1943.

1551 *Wet Blanket Policy* (August 27, 1948) †
    Dir: Dick Lundy; Walter Lantz; Woody Woodpecker, Buzz Buzzard; Oscar nominee (for Best Song, "The Woody Woodpecker Song" by Ramey Idriss and George Tibbles); Insurance broker Buzz gets Woody to sign a life insurance policy, then tries to bump him off; The only cartoon short to receive an Oscar nomination in the song category.

1552 *The Whale Who Wanted to Sing at the Met* (August 15, 1946; 14 mins)
    Dir: Clyde Geronimi, Hamilton Luske; Walt Disney; A miraculous singing whale is hunted by impresario Tetti Tatti who thinks the whale has swallowed an opera singer. Imaginative, superbly animated Disney tale with a fine vocal performance by narrator-singer Nelson Eddy; Aka *Willie, the Operatic Whale*; Part of the feature *Make Mine Music*; Rereleased August 17, 1954.

1553 *The Whalers* (August 19, 1938)
    Dir: Dick Huemer; Walt Disney; Mickey Mouse, Donald Duck, Goofy.

1554 *What Makes Daffy Duck?* (February 14, 1948)
    Dir: Arthur Davis; Warner Bros.; Looney Tune: Daffy Duck, Elmer Fudd; Daffy is hunted by Elmer and a hungry fox; Voices—Mel Blanc, Arthur Q. Bryan (Elmer).

1555 *What on Earth! (La Terre est habitée!)* (1966; 9 mins) †
    Dir: Les Drew, Kaj Pindall; National Film Board of Canada; Oscar nominee; Visiting Martians see automobiles as Earth's true inhabitants; Narrated by Donald Brittain; Produced by Wolf Koenig and Robert Verrall.

1556 *What Price Fleadom?* (March 20, 1948)
    Dir: Tex Avery; MGM; A dog and a flea form a special friendship.

1557 *What's Bruin', Bruin?* (February 28, 1948)
Dir: Chuck Jones; Warner Bros.; Looney Tune: The Three Bears; Papa Bear can't get to sleep when the family hibernates for the winter; The first official "Three Bears" cartoon, following their debut in Jones' *Bugs Bunny and the Three Bears* (1944); Voices— Billy Bletcher (Papa Bear), Bea Benaderet (Mama Bear), Stan Freberg (Junior Bear); Note: Actor Bletcher (1894–1979) provided many cartoon voices, including that of Disney villain Pegleg (Black) Pete.

1558 *What's Buzzin' Buzzard?* (November 27, 1943)
Dir: Tex Avery; MGM; Out on the desert, two hungry buzzards scheme to eat one another.

1559 *What's Cookin'?* (November 24, 1941)
Producer-Director: Walter Lantz; Woody Woodpecker; Aka *Pantry Panic*.

1560 *What's Cookin' Doc?* (January 8, 1944)
Dir: Bob Clampett; Warner Bros.; Merrie Melodie: Bugs Bunny; Bugs campaigns for an Oscar at the Academy Award ceremony; Includes a clip from 1941's *Hiawatha's Rabbit Hunt* and live-action footage from *A Star Is Born* (1937); Voices—Mel Blanc.

1561 *What's Opera, Doc?* (July 6, 1957)
Dir: Chuck Jones; Warner Bros.; Merrie Melodie: Bugs Bunny, Elmer Fudd; Brilliant Jones short puts Bugs and Elmer in the roles of Brunhilde and Siegfried in a takeoff on Wagnerian opera. The spectacular art design (by Maurice Noble), unique camera angles, fine voice work, and clever use of the music make this one of the all-time classics; Memorable dialogue (sung)—"Kill the Wabbit! Kill the Wabbit! Kill the Wabbit!"; Entered in the Library of Congress National Film Registry in 1992; Animated by Ken Harris, Richard Thompson and Abe Levitow; Musical Director—Milt Franklyn; Song—"Return My Love" ("The Pilgrim's Chorus" from Wagner's *Tannhauser* with new lyrics by writer Michael Maltese); Voices—Mel Blanc (Bugs), Arthur Q. Bryan (Elmer).

1562 *What's Up, Doc?* (June 17, 1950)
Dir: Robert McKimson; Warner Bros.; Looney Tune: Bugs Bunny, Elmer Fudd; Bugs recalls his early career as a Broadway chorus boy and vaudeville headliner; Celebrity cameos include Al Jolson, Eddie Cantor and Bing Crosby; Voices—Mel Blanc, Arthur Q. Bryan.

1563 *When He Wants a Dog He Wants a Dog* (March 13, 1913; b&w)
Dir: Emile Cohl; Eclair Films; The Newlyweds; Debut of the silent series (one of the earliest) based on the comic strip "The Newlyweds and Their Baby" by George McManus (1884–1954), who also created the strip "Bringing Up Father." The series (13 shorts, 1913–14), which featured the baby Snookums, was directed and animated by French artist Cohl (*Fantasmagorie*), one of the early fathers of animation, and produced at the New Jersey branch of the Eclair Film Company.

1564 *When Magoo Flew* (January 6, 1955) AA
Dir: Pete Burness; UPA; Mr. Magoo; Oscar winner (the first of two for the series); Magoo boards a plane mistaking it for a movie theater; UPA's first CinemaScope cartoon; Voice—Jim Backus (Magoo).

1565 *Who Killed Cock Robin?* (June 29, 1935) †
Dir: David Hand; Walt Disney; Silly Symphony; Oscar nominee; A bird courtroom looks for the culprit who shot Cock Robin with an arrow (Cupid is found guilty); Features feathered caricatures of Mae West, Bing Crosby and Harpo Marx.

1566 *Who Killed Who?* (June 5, 1943)
Dir: Tex Avery; MGM; Funny parody of radio murder mysteries.

1567 *Whoa Be-Gone!* (April 12, 1958)
Dir: Chuck Jones; Warner Bros.; Merrie Melodie: Road Runner, Coyote.

1568 *Wholly Smoke* (August 27, 1938; b&w)
Dir: Frank Tashlin; Warner Bros.; Looney Tune: Porky Pig; Porky learns the hazards of smoking from a cigar-induced hallucination; Voices—Mel Blanc.

1569 *Wide Open Spaces* (September 12, 1947)
Dir: Jack King; Walt Disney; Donald Duck; Donald spends a sleepless night in the country; Voice—Clarence Nash.

1570 *Wild and Woolfy* (November 3, 1945)
Dir: Tex Avery; MGM; The Wolf and the Showgirl, Droopy; Droopy is part of a posse out to rescue a pretty saloon singer from an outlaw wolf. Zany western spoof.

1571 *Wild and Wooly Hare* (August 1, 1959)
Dir: Friz Freleng; Warner Bros.; Looney Tune: Bugs Bunny, Yosemite Sam; Bugs interferes with Sam's train robbing; Voices—Mel Blanc.

1572 *A Wild Hare* (July 27, 1940) †
Dir: Tex Avery; Warner Bros.; Merrie Melodie: Bugs Bunny, Elmer Fudd; Oscar nominee; The first official "Bugs Bunny" cartoon has Elmer in the woods "hunting wabbits"; Delightful Avery classic starring the wisecracking rabbit who first appeared (in his early form) in 1938's *Porky's Hare Hunt*, directed by Ben "Bugs" Hardaway (the rabbit was thus referred to as "Bugs' bunny"); Bugs' wiseguy personality, trademark phrase "Eh, what's up, Doc?," and association with some of the greatest cartoon directors of all time would make him Warner Bros.' top cartoon star and secure his popularity with audiences to this day; Bugs has appeared in over 180 shorts (1940–64, '90–); Voices—Mel Blanc (Bugs), Arthur Q. Bryan (Elmer).

1573 *Wild Waves* (1929; b&w)
Dir: Burt Gillett; Walt Disney; Mickey Mouse, Minnie Mouse; Lifeguard Mickey rescues Minnie from drowning; Gillett's Disney debut; A veteran of Hearst's and the Barre-Bowers studios, he would direct 50 early "Mickey Mouse" and "Silly Symphony" shorts (1929–34, '37, '38), including two Oscar-winning, landmark films—*Flowers and Trees* (1932) and *Three Little Pigs* (1933). From 1934 to 36 he supervised the "Toddle Tales" and "Rainbow Parade" series at Van Beuren.

Wile E. Coyote (series) **see** *Operation: Rabbit* (1952)

Willie Whopper (series) **see** *Play Ball* (1933)

1574 *The Wind in the Willows* (October 5, 1949; 33 mins)
Dir: Jack Kinney, James Algar; Walt Disney; The misadventures of the spoiled J. Thaddeus Toad of Toad Hall whose love of fast cars gets him into trouble. Delightful Disney adaption of the classic 1908 story by Kenneth Grahame (*The Reluctant Dragon*); Aka *The Madcap Adventures of Mr. Toad*; Part of the feature *The Adventures of Ichabod and Mr. Toad*; Rereleased December 25, 1975; Song—"Merrily on Our Way" by Frank Churchill, Charles Wolcott, Larry Morey and Ray Gilbert; Voices—Basil Rathbone (Narrator), Eric Blore (Mr. Toad), Pat O'Malley (Cyril), Colin Campbell (Mole), Campbell Grant (Angus MacBadger), Claud Allister (Rat), John McLeish (aka John Ployardt) (Prosecutor), Alec Harford (Winky); Note: Rathbone (1892–1967) is best known for playing Sherlock Holmes in 14 films (1939–46).

1575 *The Windblown Hare* (August 27, 1949)
Dir: Robert McKimson; Warner Bros.; Looney Tune: Bugs Bunny; Bugs gets involved with the Three Little Pigs and the Big Bad Wolf; Voices—Mel Blanc.

1576 *Window Cleaners* (September 20, 1940)
Dir: Jack King; Walt Disney; Donald Duck, Pluto.

1577 *Windy Day* (1968) †
Dir: John Hubley; Hubley Studios; Oscar nominee; Produced by John and Faith Hubley, and featuring the voices of their two daughters.

1578 *Winner by a Hare* (April 17, 1953)
Dir: Isadore Sparber; Paramount/Famous; Noveltoon, with Tommy Tortoise and Moe Hare (debut); Short-lived Famous series about dumb Tommy Tortoise who always manages to outwit the smarter Moe Hare. They appeared in four "Noveltoon" shorts (1953–57).

Winnie the Pooh (series) **see** *Winnie the Pooh and the Honey Tree* (1966)

1579 *Winnie the Pooh and a Day for Eeyore* (March 11, 1983; 25 mins)
Producer-Director: Rick Reinert; Walt Disney; Winnie the Pooh (last of four); When Pooh and friends realize they forgot Eeyore's birthday they prepare a great party for the melancholy donkey. Lesser entry in Disney's "Pooh" series (released nine years after the last one); Animated by Rick Reinert Productions; Based on the books by A. A. Milne and illustrations of Ernest H. Shepard; Songs by Richard and Robert Sherman; Voices—Laurie Main (Narrator), Hal Smith (Pooh/Owl), Ralph Wright (Eeyore), John Fiedler (Piglet), Will Ryan (Rabbit), Kim Christianson (Christopher Robin), Dick Billingsley (Roo), Julie McWhirter Dees (Kanga), Paul Winchell (Tigger); Note: Main took over the role of narrator from Sebastian Cabot (who died in 1977). Smith replaces Sterling Holloway.

1580 *Winnie the Pooh and the Blustery Day* (December 20, 1968; 25 mins) AA
Dir: Wolfgang Reitherman; Walt Disney; Winnie the Pooh; Oscar winner; A storm comes to the Hundred Acre Wood, toppling Owl's treehouse and giving Pooh nightmares. Disney's second—and arguably best—"Pooh" featurette; Later included in the compilation feature *The Many Adventures of Winnie the Pooh* (1977); Based on the books by A. A. Milne and illustrations of Ernest H. Shepard; Songs by Richard and Robert Sherman; Voices—Sebastian Cabot (Narrator), Sterling Holloway (Pooh), Ralph Wright (Eeyore), Hal Smith (Owl), Jon Walmsley (Christopher Robin), Barbara Luddy (Kanga), Clint Howard (Roo), Junius Matthews (Rabbit), Howard Morris (Gopher), Paul Winchell

(Tigger), John Fiedler (Piglet); Notes: Winchell had been on radio and television since the '40s as a ventriloquist (his dummy was Jerry Mahoney). Walmsley later played Jason on TV's *The Waltons* (1972–81).

1581 *Winnie the Pooh and the Honey Tree* (February 4, 1966; 25 mins)
　　　Dir: Wolfgang Reitherman; Walt Disney; Winnie the Pooh (debut); Pooh's search for honey leads him up a high tree and gets him stuck in Rabbit's hole; The first of four highly entertaining "Winnie the Pooh" cartoons from Disney concerning a boy named Christopher Robin and his stuffed animal friends in the Hundred Acre Wood; The characters interact with and within the pages of a book; Later included in the compilation feature *The Many Adventures of Winnie the Pooh* (1977); Based on the beloved children's books (1924–28) by A(lan) A(lexander) Milne (1882–1956) and the illustrations of Ernest H. Shepard; Songs by Richard and Robert Sherman (*Mary Poppins*); Voices—Sebastian Cabot (Narrator), Sterling Holloway (Pooh), Ralph Wright (Eeyore), Hal Smith (Owl), Bruce Reitherman (Christopher Robin), Barbara Luddy (Kanga), Clint Howard (Roo), Junius Matthews (Rabbit), Howard Morris (Gopher); Note: Holloway's Disney voice credits include the stork in *Dumbo* (1941) and the Cheshire Cat in *Alice in Wonderland* (1951). Child actor Howard (brother of Ron) starred in the television series *Gentle Ben* (1967–69).

1582 *Winnie the Pooh and Tigger Too* (December 20, 1974; 25 mins) †
　　　Dir: John Lounsbery; Walt Disney; Winnie the Pooh; Oscar nominee; Rabbit and the other animals of the Hundred Acre Wood try to take the bounce out of Tigger. Delightful third entry in Disney's "Pooh" series; Later included in the compilation feature *The Many Adventures of Winnie the Pooh* (1977); Based on the books by A. A. Milne and illustrations of Ernest H. Shepard; Songs by Richard and Robert Sherman; Voices—Sebastian Cabot (Narrator), Sterling Holloway (Pooh), Paul Winchell (Tigger), Junius Matthews (Rabbit), John Fiedler (Piglet), Barbara Luddy (Kanga), Dori Whitaker (Roo), Timothy Turner (Christopher Robin); Produced by Wolfgang Reitherman.

1583 *Winter* (November 5, 1930; b&w)
　　　Dir: Burt Gillett; Walt Disney; Silly Symphony.

1584 *Winter Storage* (June 3, 1949)
　　　Dir: Jack Hannah; Walt Disney; Donald Duck, Chip 'n' Dale; The chipmunks go after Donald's acorns in this amusing short; Voice—Clarence Nash (Donald).

1585 *The Wise Little Hen* (June 9, 1934)
　　　Dir: Wilfred Jackson; Walt Disney; Silly Symphony, with Donald Duck (debut); Seeking someone to help her plant her corn, a mother hen approaches Peter Pig and Donald Duck; The first cartoon appearance of the fiesty, sailor-suited white duck named Donald. His bad-tempered personality and distinctive voice endeared him to audiences and he soon rivaled Mickey Mouse in popularity. Donald would appear (often with girlfriend Daisy or nephews Huey, Dewey and Louie) in some 160 shorts (1934–61, '83, '90). But what about Peter Pig?; Voices—Clarence Nash (Donald), Florence Gill (Hen); Note: Nash would voice Donald until his death in 1985 (animator Tony Anselmo took over the role).

1586 *Wise Quackers* (January 1, 1949)
　　　Dir: Friz Freleng; Warner Bros.; Looney Tune: Daffy Duck, Elmer Fudd.

1587 *The Wise Quacking Duck* (May 1, 1943)
　　　Dir: Bob Clampett; Warner Bros.; Looney Tune: Daffy Duck; Daffy heckles a man who wants to cook the duck for his dinner; Voices—Mel Blanc.

1588 *The Wiseman* (1990; 5 mins)
Producer-Director: Bill Plympton; A wiseman delivers truths while strange things happen to his head; Included in the 1992 feature *The Tune*.

1589 *Without Time or Reason* (January 1962)
Dir: Seymour Kneitel; Paramount; Noveltoon, with Swifty and Shorty (debut); The comic duo, patterned after Paramount's dog team "Jeepers and Creepers," appeared in 19 shorts (1962–65). This was producer-director Kneitel's last series (he died in July, 1964); Voice—Eddie Lawrence (Swifty/Shorty).

1590 *Without You* (August 15, 1946; 3 mins)
Dir: Robert Cormack; Walt Disney; Sung by Andy Russell; Part of the feature *Make Mine Music*.

The Wolf and the Showgirl (series) **see** *Red Hot Riding Hood* (1943)

1591 *Wolf Hounded* (November 5, 1959)
Producer-Director: William Hanna, Joseph Barbera; Loopy De Loop (debut); Hanna-Barbera produced this series about a French wolf (who appeared in 49 shorts, 1959–65), the first theatrical series from their newly-formed studio (which would almost exclusively produce cartoons for television); Voice—Daws Butler (Loopy).

1592 *Woodland Cafe* (March 13, 1937)
Dir: Wilfred Jackson; Walt Disney; Silly Symphony; Tuneful Disney classic.

1593 *Woody Dines Out* (May 4, 1945)
Dir: James Culhane; Walter Lantz; Woody Woodpecker; Woody mistakes a taxidermist's shop for a restaurant; Voice—Ben Hardaway (Woody).

1594 *Woody the Giant Killer* (December 15, 1947)
Dir: Dick Lundy; Walter Lantz; Woody Woodpecker; A box of magic beans takes Woody to Giantland in this version of "Jack and the Beanstalk"; Voice—Ben Hardaway (Woody).

Woody Woodpecker (series) **see** *Knock Knock* (1940)

1595 *Woody Woodpecker* (July 7, 1941)
Producer-Director: Walter Lantz; Woody Woodpecker; The first official "Woody Woodpecker" cartoon, following his debut in *Knock Knock* (1940); Aka *The Cracked Nut*; Voice—Mel Blanc (Woody).

1596 *The Woody Woodpecker Polka* (October 29, 1951)
Producer-Director: Walter Lantz; Woody Woodpecker; Aka *The Gate Crasher*; The Starlighters sing the title song.

1597 *Words, Words, Words... (Reci, Reci, Reci...)* (1992) †
Producer-Director: Michaela Pavlatova; Kratky Film Prod; Oscar nominee; From Czech animator Pavlatova.

1598 *Working for Peanuts* (November 11, 1953)
    Dir: Jack Hannah; Walt Disney; Donald Duck, Chip 'n' Dale; The chipmunks attempt to take an elephant's peanuts; Disney's second cartoon released in 3–D (following *Melody*); Voice—Clarence Nash (Donald).

1599 *The Worm Turns* (January 2, 1937)
    Dir: Ben Sharpsteen; Walt Disney; Mickey Mouse, Pluto; Mickey tests his courage-building potion on various animals.

1600 *Wot a Night* (August 1, 1931; b&w)
    Dir: John Foster, George Stallings; Van Beuren; Tom and Jerry (debut); Taxi drivers Tom and Jerry take their fares to a haunted castle; The first (and probably best) cartoon starring Tom and Jerry (not the MGM cat-and-mouse team), who appeared in 27 shorts (1931–33). The two friends—one tall, the other short—were renamed "Dick and Larry" for TV; They were the first new characters to emerge from Van Beuren which, until then, had been producing only "Aesop's Fables."

1601 *Wreck of the Hesperus* (February 11, 1944)
    Dir: Mannie Davis; Terrytoons; Mighty Mouse; The superhero's first billing as "Mighty Mouse" (he had been called "Super Mouse" since his debut in 1942's *The Mouse of Tomorrow*); Voice—Tom Morrison (Mighty Mouse).

1602 *The Wrong Trousers* (1993; 30 mins) AA
    Dir: Nick Park; Aardman Animations; Wallace and Gromit; Oscar winner; Highly entertaining short (the second in the series) involves a penguin named "Feathers" McGraw who steals Wallace's new invention (mechanical trousers) to rob museums; Winner of more than 30 international awards; Animated by Park and Steve Box; Written by Park and Bob Baker; Music by Julian Nott; Voice—Peter Sallis (Wallace); Produced by Christopher Moll.

1603 *Wynken, Blynken and Nod* (May 27, 1938)
    Dir: Graham Heid; Walt Disney; Silly Symphony; Three young fishermen sail through the night sky in a large wooden shoe. Beautifully animated fantasy, based on the 1892 children's poem by Eugene Field (1850–95).

1604 *Yankee Doodle Daffy* (July 3, 1943)
    Dir: Friz Freleng; Warner Bros.; Looney Tune: Daffy Duck, Porky Pig; Daffy performs for talent agent Porky. Great voice work by Mel Blanc.

1605 *Yankee Doodle Mouse* (June 26, 1943) AA
    Dir: William Hanna, Joseph Barbera; MGM; Tom and Jerry; Oscar winner (the first of seven the series would win).

1606 *Ye Olden Days* (April 8, 1933; b&w)
    Dir: Burt Gillett; Walt Disney; Mickey Mouse, Minnie Mouse, Goofy (Dippy Dawg); Wandering minstrel Mickey fights a duel for Princess Minnie.

1607 *Yelp Wanted* (July 16, 1931; b&w)
    Columbia/Screen Gems; Scrappy (debut), Yippy (his dog); Scrappy needs to get some

of Dr. Woof's Dog Tonic for an ailing Yippy; The first short starring the little boy, Scrappy, who became Columbia's second cartoon star (after Krazy Kat). He would appear in over 100 shorts (1931–41). Dick Huemer, Sid Marcus and Art Davis (all former members of the Fleischer studio) produced the series.

Yosemite Sam (series) **see** *Hare Trigger* (1945)

1608 *You Ought to Be in Pictures* (May 18, 1940; b&w)
Dir: Friz Freleng; Warner Bros.; Looney Tune: Porky Pig, Daffy Duck; Clever combination of live action and animation has Porky quitting cartoons for features. This great Freleng short portrays "toons" as actual studio contract players 48 years before *Who Framed Roger Rabbit* (1988); Producer Leon Schlesinger appears as himself and Warner cartoon writer Michael Maltese plays the studio guard; Voices—Mel Blanc.

1609 *You Were Never Duckier* (August 7, 1948)
Dir: Chuck Jones; Warner Bros.; Merrie Melodie: Daffy Duck, Henery Hawk.

1610 *Your Face* (1987; 3 mins) †
Producer-Director: Bill Plympton; Oscar nominee; Wild facial contortions affect a vocalist in this cleverly animated short; Written and animated by Plympton; Music and vocals (slowed down) by Maureen McElheron.

1611 *You're an Education* (November 5, 1938)
Dir: Frank Tashlin; Warner Bros.; Merrie Melodie; Travel brochures come to life after hours; Tashlin's third "come-to-life" short, following *Speaking of the Weather* (1937) with magazines, and *Have You Got Any Castles?* (1938) with books.

1612 *Zipping Along* (September 10, 1953)
Dir: Chuck Jones; Warner Bros.; Merrie Melodie: Road Runner, Coyote.

1613 *Zoom and Bored* (September 14, 1957)
Dir: Chuck Jones; Warner Bros.; Looney Tune: Road Runner, Coyote; One of the series' best.

1614 *Zoot Cat* (February 26, 1944)
Dir: William Hanna, Joseph Barbera; MGM; Tom and Jerry, Toots; Tom wears a zoot suit to impress his girlfriend; One of the few cartoons in which Tom and Jerry speak.

APPENDIX: Animation Studios

Aardman Animations   (dist: various)

Formed in 1972 by Peter Lord and David Sproxton, this studio based in Bristol, England, specializes in stop-motion animation of plasticine puppets. Best known for the Oscar-winning "Wallace and Gromit" series.

Selected Shorts: *Creature Comforts* (1990), *The Wrong Trousers* (1993), *A Close Shave* (1995), *Wat's Pig* (1996).

Oscars: 1990, 1993, 1995; Oscar **nominations:** 1991, 1996.

Features: *Wallace and Gromit: The Best of Aardman Animation* (1996 / compilation), *Chicken Run* (set for 1998).

Selected TV work: *The Amazing Adventures of Morph* (1981–83 / Brit. Series), Peter Gabriel music video "Sledgehammer" (1986), commercials.

Producer-Directors: Rob Copeland, Richard Goleszowski, Peter Lord, Christopher Moll, Nick Park, Peter Peake, Michael Rose, Carla Shelley, David Sproxton.

Amblimation   (dist: Universal Pictures)

Producer-director Steven Spielberg formed this London-based studio in 1988 following the success of his Amblin Entertainment production *An American Tail* (1986). He closed it in 1995 when he cofounded Dreamworks SKG and began setting up that company's new L.A.-based animation studio.

Features (1991–95): *An American Tail: Fievel Goes West* (1991), *We're Back! A Dinosaur's Story* (1993), *Balto* (1995).

Producers: Steven Spielberg (exec), Robert Watts, Stephen Hickner.

Directors: Nancy Beiman, Bibo Bergeron, David Bowers, Sahin Ersoz, Rodolphe Guenoden, Nicolas Marlet, Patrick Mate, Phil Nibbelink, Borge Ring, William Salazar, Thierry Schiel, Kristof Serrand, Rob Stevenhagen, Jeffrey J. Varab, Simon Wells, Dick Zondag, Ralph Zondag.

Barre-Bowers **see** *Raoul Barre*

Bill Plympton   (dist: various)

Talented animator of comic shorts whose drawn characters usually undergo (or suffer) some bizarre physical transformation. His most typical work is the Oscar-nominated *Your Face* (1987).

Selected Shorts (1985–): *Your Face* (1987), *One of Those Days* (1988), *How to Kiss* (1989), *25 Ways to Quit Smoking* (1989).

Oscar nomination: 1987.

Features (animated): *The Tune* (1992), *Mondo Plympton* (1997 / compilation), *I Married a Strange Person* (1997).

Selected TV work: *The Edge* (1992–93 / series / inserts).
Producer-Director: Bill Plympton.

Bray Studios   (dist: Paramount Pictures, various)

Animation pioneer J(ohn) R(andolph) Bray (1879–1978) formed this early cartoon studio, which would launch the careers of such future animation giants as Max Fleischer and Walter Lantz.

Shorts (1913–27): Series/characters—Colonel Heeza Liar, Dinky Doodle, Out of the Inkwell, Bobby Bumps, Un-Natural History, Goodrich Dirt, Pete the Pup, Jerry on the Job, Quacky Doodles, Otto Luck, Police Dog, Hardrock Dome, The Trick Kids, Glackens Cartoons, Historical Cartoons, Bud and Susie, Miss Nanny Goat, Ink-Ravings, Silhouette Fantasies, US Fellers, Technical Romances, Lampoons.
Producer: J. R. Bray.
Directors: Carl Anderson, Wallace A. Carlson, Max Fleischer, Clyde Geronimi, Burt Gillett, W. L. Glackens, F. Lyle Goldman, Milt Gross, David Hand, Earl Hurd, Gregory La Cava, Walter Lantz, Ashley Miller, Frank Moser, Grim Natwick, J. A. Norling, Vernon Stallings, Pat Sullivan, Paul Terry.

Columbia / Screen Gems   (dist: Columbia Pictures)

Producer Charles Mintz signed with Columbia in 1929 to distribute his new sound series of "Krazy Kat" shorts, and other series followed. Mintz died in 1940 and in 1948 Columbia closed down his studio and became the distributor for UPA (United Productions of America).

Shorts (1929–49): Series/characters—Krazy Kat, Scrappy, Color Rhapsodies, Fox and the Crow, Barney Google, Phantasies, Li'l Abner, Fables, Flippy, Professor Small and Mr. Tall, Tito, Willoughby Wren.
Oscar nominations: 1934, 1937, 1941, 1943, 1944, 1945.
Producers: Charles Mintz (1929–39), Jimmy Bronis, George Winkler, Frank Tashlin, Dave Fleischer, Paul Worth, Hugh McCollum, Raymond Katz, Henry Binder.
Directors: Art Davis, Paul Fennell, Alec Geiss, Manny Gould, Ben Harrison, John Hubley, Dick Huemer, Ub Iwerks, Lou Lilly, Harry Love, Alex Lovy, Sid Marcus, Don Roman, Allen Rose, Paul Sommer, Howard Swift, Frank Tashlin, Bob Wickersham.

DePatie-Freleng   (dist: United Artists, Warner Bros. [1964–67])

After the closing of Warner Brothers' cartoon studio in 1963 (it re-opened in 1967), director Friz Freleng joined with executive David H. DePatie to form their own production company. One of their first projects—providing the opening animation for the 1964 film *The Pink Panther*—would launch their studio's most famous cartoon star.

Shorts (1964–81): Series/characters—The Pink Panther, The Ant and the Aardvark, The Inspector, Roland and Rattfink, Tijuana Toads, Hoot Cloot, The Blue Racer, The Dogfather.
Oscar: 1964; Oscar **nomination**: 1966.
Selected TV work: *Dr. Suess' The Cat in the Hat* (1971 / special), *Dr. Suess' Halloween Is Grinch Night* (1977 / special / Emmy-winner).
Producers: David H. DePatie, Friz Freleng.
Directors: Bob Balser, Durward Bonaye, Brad Case, Gerry Chiniquy, Art Davis, Dave Detiege, Friz Freleng, George Gordon, Cullen Houghtaling, Rudy Larriva, Arthur Leonardi, Sid Marcus, Robert McKimson, Roy Morita, Hawley Pratt, Bob Richardson, George Singer.

Don Bluth (Don Bluth Productions / Sullivan Bluth)   (dist: various)
In 1979, animator Don Bluth led a mass defection from the Disney studio and (with partners Gary Goldman and John Pomeroy) began producing his own features. In 1985, he moved his newly-formed Sullivan Bluth Studios to Ireland and, with films like *An American Tail* and *The Land Before Time*, became Disney's leading competitor in the field of feature animation. In 1994 Bluth joined 20th Century–Fox's new animation studio (located in Phoenix, Arizona). His first effort for Fox was *Anastasia* (1997).

Features: *The Secret of NIMH* (1982), *An American Tail* (1986), *The Land Before Time* (1988), *All Dogs Go to Heaven* (1989), *Rock-A-Doodle* (1992), *Hans Christian Andersen's Thumbelina* (1994), *A Troll in Central Park* (1994), *The Pebble and the Penguin* (1995).

Oscar nomination: 1986.

Selected TV work: *Banjo, the Woodpile Cat* (1982 / special).

Producers: Don Bluth, Gary Goldman, John Pomeroy.

Directors: Don Bluth, also Richard Bazley, Piet Derycker, Ken Duncan, Jeff Etter, Gary Goldman, John Hill, T. Daniel Hofstedt, Cathy Jones, Dan Kuenster, Dave Kupczyk, Linda Miller, Jean Morel, Ralf Palmer, John Pomeroy, Lorna Pomeroy-Cook, Len Simon, Jeffrey J. Varab, Dick Zondag, Ralph Zondag.

Fables Studio (Fable Pictures, Inc.) (dist. Pathe Film Exchange)
Paul Terry (1887–1971), whose first series, "Farmer Al Falfa," debuted in 1916, formed this studio (with the backing of the Keith-Albee theater circuit) to produce the "Aesop's Fables" series. In 1928, the studio was taken over by Amadee J. Van Beuren and Terry left a year later to form Terrytoons.

Shorts: Series — Aesop's Fables (1921–29).

Producer: Paul Terry.

Director / Animators: Fred Anderson, Harry Bailey, Mannie Davis, John Foster, Frank Moser, Jerry Shields, Vladimir "Bill" Tytla.

Famous Studios **see** *Paramount / Famous Studios*

Filmation (dist. various)
California-based company, formed in 1962 and specializing in cartoons for Saturday morning television.

Features: *Treasure Island* (1972), *Journey Back to Oz* (1974), *Oliver Twist* (1974), *The Great Space Chase* (1983), *The Secret of the Sword* (1985), *Pinocchio and the Emperor of the Night* (1987), *Bravestarr* (1988), *Happily Ever After* (1990).

Selected TV work: *Fat Albert and the Cosby Kids* / *The New Fat Albert Show* (1972–84 / series), *He-Man and the Masters of the Universe* (1983, synd. / series).

Producers: Lou Scheimer (head), Norman Prescott, Arthur Nadel.

Directors: Gian Celestri, John Celestri, Ed Friedman, Chuck Harvey, John Howley, Lou Kachivas, Marsh Lamore, Amby Paliwoda, Bill Reed, Kamoon Song, Hal Sutherland, Tom Tataranowicz, Gwen Wetzler, Lawrence White, Kay Wright, Lou Zukor.

Fleischer Studios **see** *Max Fleischer*

George Pal Puppetoons (dist. Paramount Pictures)
When Hungarian-born producer-director George Pal (1908–80) came to the United States in 1940, his first Hollywood project was a series of puppet-animated short films called "Puppetoons" (similar to the advertising puppet shorts he made in Holland during the '30s). Pal received a special Academy Award for the series in 1943

and later went on to a successful career in sci-fi / fantasy features (*War of the Worlds*, etc.).

Shorts: Series—Puppetoons (1941–47); Titles include: *John Henry and the Inky Poo* (1946), *Jasper in a Jam* (1946), *Tubby the Tuba* (1947).
Oscars nominations: 1941, 1942, 1943, 1944, 1945, 1946, 1947.
Feature: *The Puppetoon Movie* (1987 / compilation).
Producer-Director: George Pal.

Halas and Batchelor Cartoon Films (dist. various)

Britain's leading animation studio, formed in 1940 by husband-and-wife animators John Halas (1912–95) and Joy Batchelor (1914–91), best known for producing the first feature-length British cartoon, *Animal Farm* (1954).

Selected Shorts (over 2,000): *Automania 2000* (1963).
Oscar nomination: 1963.
Features: *Animal Farm* (1954).
Selected TV work: *Foo Foo* (1961 / synd. Series).
Also produced many educational, advertising and military instructional films.
Producer-Directors: John Halas, Joy Batchelor.

Hanna-Barbera (dist. various)

After 17 years of directing "Tom and Jerry" shorts for MGM, famed animators William Hanna (b. 1910) and Joseph Barbera (b. 1911) opened their own studio in 1957, becoming leaders in the field of television animation.

Shorts: Series—Loopy De Loop (1959–65).
Features: *Hey There, It's Yogi Bear* (1964), *The Man Called Flintstone* (1966), *Charlotte's Web* (1973), *Heidi's Song* (1982), *GoBots: Battle of the Rock Lords* (1986), *Jetsons: The Movie* (1990).
Selected TV work: *The Huckleberry Hound Show* (1958–62 / series / Emmy-winner), *Yogi Bear* (1961–63 / series), *The Flintstones* (1960–66 / series).
Producers: William Hanna, Joseph Barbera, Kay Wright.
Directors: Hal Ambro, Joseph Barbera, Janine Dawson, Charlie Downs, William Hanna, David Michener, Charles A. Nichols, Ray Patterson, Paul Sabella, Iwao Takamoto, Robert Taylor.

Harman-Ising **see** *Warner Bros, MGM*

Hearst International Studio **see** *International Film Service*

Hubley Studios (Storyboard Productions) (dist. Paramount Pictures, various)

Formed in 1955 by former UPA director John Hubley (1914–77) and his wife, writer-producer Faith (Elliott) Hubley (b. 1924), this studio produced a series of highly original, thought provoking short films, which tackled many social and philosophical issues.

Selected Shorts: *Moonbird* (1959), *The Hole* (1962), *Herb Alpert and the Tijuana Brass Double Feature* (1966).
Oscars: 1959, 1962, 1966; Oscar **nominations:** 1968, 1969, 1974, 1977.
Features: *Of Stars and Men* (1961), *The Cosmic Eye* (1985).
Selected TV work: *Dig* (1972 / special), *Everybody Rides the Carousel* (1976 / film), commercials.

Producers: John Hubley, Faith Hubley.
Directors: John Hubley, Faith Hubley, William Littlejohn, Gary Mooney.

International Film Service (dist. various)

This company (1915–18), formed by William Randolph Hearst, turned the comic strips syndicated in Hearst newspapers into animated cartoons to be shown at the end of the popular newsreel *The Hearst-Vitagraph News Pictorial.*

Shorts (1915–18): Series/characters—Krazy Kat, The Katzenjammer Kids, Happy Hooligan, Judge Rummy, Joys and Gloom, Maud the Mule, Phables, Little Jimmy, Abie the Agent.
Executive Producer: William Randolph Hearst.
Producer: Gregory La Cava.
Directors: Raoul Barre, Burt Gillett, Manny Gould, H. E. Hancock, Ben Harrison, Jack King, Gregory La Cava, Grim Natwick, William C. Nolan, Ben Sharpsteen.

Lee Mendelson—Bill Melendez (dist. various)

Production team best known for bringing Charles M. Schulz's "Peanuts" comic strip to the big and small screens.

Features: *A Boy Named Charlie Brown* (1969), *Snoopy, Come Home* (1972), *Race for Your Life, Charlie Brown* (1977), *Bon Voyage, Charlie Brown (and Don't Come Back!)* (1980).
Oscar nomination: 1969.
Selected TV work: *A Charlie Brown Christmas* (1965 / special / Emmy/Peabody-winner), *Garfield on the Town* (1983 / special / Emmy-winner), *Cathy* (1987 / special / Emmy-winner).
Producers: Lee Mendelson, Bill Melendez.
Directors: Bill Melendez, Phil Roman.

Max Fleischer (Out of the Inkwell Films, 1921–28 / Fleischer Studios, 1928–42) (dist. Red Seal Pictures, Paramount Pictures)

Famed cartoon studio, formed in 1921 by cartoonist-inventor Max Fleischer (1889–1972), based on the success of his "Out of the Inkwell" series (originally produced for Bray Studios). With his brother Dave (1894–1979) as supervising director, the Fleischer studio became Disney's main competition during the 1930s, producing funny, technically innovative shorts starring the likes of Betty Boop and Popeye the Sailor.

Shorts (1921–42): Series/characters—Out of the Inkwell, Betty Boop, Popeye the Sailor, Superman, Screen Songs, Talkartoons, Koko the Clown, Bimbo, Color Classics, Inkwell Imps, Song Cartunes, Stone Age Cartoons, Gabby, Animated Antics.
Oscar nominations: 1936, 1937, 1938, 1941.
Features: *Gulliver's Travels* (1939), *Mr. Bug Goes to Town* (1941).
Oscar nominations: 1939 (2).
Producer: Max Fleischer.
Directors: Dave Fleischer (supervising), Willard Bowsky, Orestes Calpini, Roland Crandall, James Culhane, H. C. Ellison, William Henning, Winfield Hoskins, Thomas Johnson, Frank Kelling, Seymour Kneitel, Robert Leffingwell, Grim Natwick, Tom Palmer, Graham Place, Stan Quackenbush, David Tendlar, Myron Waldman.

MGM (dist. MGM (Metro-Goldwyn-Mayer))

MGM first entered the cartoon business with their releasing of two series (1930–34) from Ub Iwerks, after which the studio signed with producer-directors

Hugh Harman and Rudolf Ising (the team who had launched Warner Bros.' cartoon studio). Beginning in the early '40s, MGM would join Warner Bros. in the forefront of cartoon comedy with their Tex Avery and Hanna-Barbera ("Tom and Jerry") shorts. The studio closed in 1957, but began releasing more "Tom and Jerrys" in the '60s.

Shorts (1934–58, 1961–67): Series/characters—Tom and Jerry, Droopy, Screwy Squirrel, Barney Bear, The Wolf and the Showgirl, Spike and Tyke, George and Junior, Captain and the Kids, Bosko.

Oscars: 1940, 1943, 1944, 1945, 1946, 1948, 1951, 1952, 1965; Oscar **nominations:** 1935, 1936, 1939, 1940, 1941 (2), 1942, 1947, 1949, 1950, 1952, 1954, 1955, 1957.

Features: *Invitation to the Dance* (1956 / part anim.), *The Phantom Tollbooth* (1969 / part live action).

Selected TV work: *Dr. Seuss' How the Grinch Stole Christmas* (1966 / special).

Producers: Hugh Harman and Rudolf Ising (1934–40), Fred Quimby (1941–55), William Hanna and Joseph Barbera (1955–58), Gene Deitch (1961–62), Chuck Jones and Les Golden (1963–67).

Directors: Robert Allen, Hal Ambro, Tex Avery, Joseph Barbera, Preston Blair, Gene Deitch, Friz Freleng, George Gordon, Milt Gross, William Hanna, Hugh Harman, Rudolf Ising, Chuck Jones, Michael Lah, Abe Levitow, Dick Lundy, George Nicholas, Jim Pabian, Tom Ray, Ben Washam.

The National Film Board of Canada (dist. National Film Board of Canada, various)

The animation unit of the National Film Board of Canada, formed in 1943 under Scottish animator Norman McLaren (1914–87), has nurtured the talents of many top artists and produced a string of award-winning shorts.

Selected Shorts: *Neighbours* (1952), *The Street* (1976), *The Sand Castle* (1977), *Special Delivery* (1978), *Every Child* (1979), *The Big Snit* (1985), *Bob's Birthday* (1994).

Oscars: 1952, 1977, 1978, 1979, 1994; Oscar **nominations:** 1952, 1963, 1964, 1966, 1967, 1968, 1969, 1971, 1974 (2), 1975, 1976, 1977, 1981, 1984, 1985, 1987, 1988, 1991 (2).

Producers/Directors: Cordell Barker, Richard Condie, Tom Daly, Les Drew, Eugene Fedorenko, David Fine, Peter Foldes, Guy Glover, Jeff Hale, Christopher Hinton, Co Hoedeman, René Jodoin, Wolf Koenig, Derek Lamb, Ryan Larkin, Caroline Leaf, André Leduc, Bernard Longpré, Colin Low, Eunice Macaulay, Douglas Macdonald, Jim MacKay, Yvon Mallette, Carlos Marchiori, Norman McLaren, Barrie McLean, Michael Mills, Grant Munro, Ishu Patel, Janet Perlman, William Pettigrew, Kaj Pindall, Gerald Potterton, Michael Scott, Alison Snowden, Wendy Tilby, Ron Tunis, David Verrall, Robert Verrall, John Weldon, Ches Yetman.

Nelvana (dist. various)

Canada's leading animation studio, based in Toronto.

Features: *Rock and Rule* (1983), *The Care Bears Movie* (1985), *Care Bears Movie II: A New Generation* (1986), *The Care Bears Adventure in Wonderland* (1987), *Babar: The Movie* (1989), *Pippi Longstocking* (1997).

Selected TV work: *The Care Bears Family* (1986–88 / series).

Producers: Michael Hirsh, Patrick Loubert, Clive A. Smith.

Directors: Anne Marie Bradwell, Charles Bonifacio, Robin Budd, Alan Bunce, John Lawrence Collins, Bill Giggie, Raymond Jafelice, Ute V. Munchow-Pohl, Dale Schott, Arna Selznick, Clive A. Smith.

Out of the Inkwell Films see *Max Fleischer*

Paramount / Famous Studios (dist. Paramount Pictures)

After closing the Fleischer studio in 1942, Paramount formed their own, New York–based studio, keeping most of the Fleischers' staff. Famous Studios (changed to Paramount Cartoon Studio in 1956) lasted 25 years (closing in 1967), but its output was largely undistinguished.

Shorts (1942–68): Series/characters—Casper the Friendly Ghost, Popeye the Sailor, Little Lulu, Noveltoons, Superman, Little Audrey, Herman and Katnip, Buzzy the Crow, Screen Songs, Baby Huey, Raggedy Ann, Tommy Tortoise and Moe Hare, Kartunes, Modern Madcaps, Blackie the Lamb, Honey Halfwitch, Jeepers and Creepers, The Cat, Swifty and Shorty, Spunky, Go-Go Toons, Merry Makers, Fractured Fables, Goodie the Gremlin, Comic Kings.

Producers: Sam Buchwald, Seymour Kneitel, Isadore "Izzy" Sparber, Howard Post (1964–65), James "Shamus" Culhane (1965–67), Ralph Bakshi (superv. dir, 1967).

Directors: Ralph Bakshi, James "Shamus" Culhane, Gene Deitch, Dan Gordon, Chuck Harriton, Seymour Kneitel, Jack Mendelsohn, Howard Post, Isadore "Izzy" Sparber, Dave Tendlar, Bill Tytla.

Pat Sullivan (dist. Universal Pictures, Paramount Pictures, various)

Australian-born artist Patrick O'Sullivan (1887–1933) opened his studio in 1915 and, during the '20s, produced the popular "Felix the Cat" series, created and animated by the studio's creative force, Otto Messmer.

Shorts (1916–31): Series/characters—Felix the Cat, Nervy Cat, Boomer Bill, Box Car Bill, Charlie Chaplin Cartoons, Sammie Johnsin.

Producer: Pat Sullivan.

Directors: Raoul Barre, Bill Cause, Burt Gillett, Louis Glackens, Otto Messmer, William Nolan, Dana Parker, George Stallings, Pat Sullivan.

Pixar (dist. various)

Computer animation studio (formerly a division of Lucasfilm Ltd., it was bought in 1986 by Apple Computers' Steven Jobs) which has won acclaim for its award-winning shorts and commercials and which, in 1995, produced the first fully computer-animated feature, *Toy Story*.

Selected Shorts (1986–): *Luxo Jr.* (1986), *Red's Dream* (1987), *Tin Toy* (1988), *Knick-Knack* (1989), *Geri's Game* (1997).

Oscars: 1988, 1997; Oscar **nomination:** 1986.

Feature: *Toy Story* (1995).

Oscar nominations: 1995 (3); Special Oscar: 1995.

Selected TV work: commercials for GummiSavers (1993 / Clio Award-winner), Listerine (1994 / Clio Award-winner), others.

Exeutive Producer: Steven Jobs (studio head).

Producers/Directors: Bonnie Arnold, Peter Docter, Ralph Guggenheim, John Lasseter, William Reeves.

Ralph Bakshi (dist. various)

Ralph Bakshi (b. 1938), an animator-director at Terrytoons in the 1960s, first gained fame with his X-rated feature debut, *Fritz the Cat* (1972). Since then he has directed a number of adult-oriented, often controversial films.

Features: *Fritz the Cat* (1972), *Heavy Traffic* (1973 / part live action), *Coonskin* (1975/ part live action), *Wizards* (1977), *Lord of the Rings* (1978), *American Pop* (1981), *Hey, Good Lookin'* (1982), *Fire and Ice* (1983), *Cool World* (1992 / part live action).

Selected TV work: *Mighty Mouse: The New Adventures* (1987–89 / series), *Tattertown* (1988 / special), The Rolling Stones' "Harlem Shuffle" (music video).
Producers: Ralph Bakshi, Frank Frazetta, Steve Krantz, Frank Mancuso, Jr., Albert S. Ruddy, Saul Zaentz.
Director: Ralph Bakshi.

Rankin—Bass (dist. various)

Formerly Videocrafts International, this studio, headed by Arthur Rankin, Jr., and Jules Bass, produced many high-quality specials for television since the early '60s, often using their "Animagic" process (stop-motion animated puppets).

Features: *The Daydreamer* (1966 / part live action), *Mad Monster Party?* (1967), *The Wacky World of Mother Goose* (1967), *The Last Unicorn* (1982).
Selected TV work: *Rudolph the Red-Nosed Reindeer* (1964 / special), *Little Drummer Boy* (1968 / special), *The Hobbit* (1977 / film / Peabody-winner).
Producer-Directors: Arthur Rankin, Jr., Jules Bass.

Raoul Barre / Barre—Bowers (Mutt and Jeff Film Exchange / Bud Fisher Films Corp / Jefferson Film Corp / Associated Animators) (dist. various)

Early New York–based studio formed in 1914 by French Canadian cartoonist Raoul Barre (1874–1932). In 1916, after producing "Animated Grouch Chasers" (for the Edison Company) and "Phables" (in association with Hearst's International Film Service), Barre joined with fellow cartoonist Charles R. Bowers (1889–1945) to produce a cartoon series based on Bud Fisher's popular "Mutt and Jeff" comic strip. The new studio and series lasted until 1926 under several studio heads (Barre had left in 1918, returning to animation only briefly in 1926 on Pat Sullivan's "Felix the Cat").

Shorts (1915–26): Series/characters—Mutt and Jeff, Animated Grouch Chasers, Phables, The Boob Weekly.
Executive Producer: Bud Fisher.
Producers: Raoul Barre (1915–18), Charles R. Bowers (1916–19), Dick Friel (1921–25), Burt Gillett (1925–26).
Animators: Mannie Davis, Burt Gillett, Manny Gould, Milt Gross, Ben Harrison, Dick Huemer, Albert Hurter, I. Klein, Gregory La Cava, Frank Moser, William Nolan, George Rufle, Ted Sears, Ben Sharpsteen, (Vernon) George Stallings, Pat Sullivan, Vladimir "Bill" Tytla.

Richard Williams (dist. various)

Canadian animator Richard Williams (b. 1933) has directed shorts, film titles (including *Return of the Pink Panther*) and TV commercials at his studio in England since the mid-'50s. His most notable feature work was the animation for 1988's *Who Framed Roger Rabbit*.

Selected Shorts (1958–): *The Little Island* (1958), *Love Me! Love Me! Love Me!* (1962), *A Christmas Carol* (1972).
Oscar: 1972.
Features: *Raggedy Ann and Andy* (1977), *Who Framed Roger Rabbit* (1988 / part live action / a Robert Zemeckis film), *Arabian Knight* (1995 / re-edited version of the unfinished *The Thief and the Cobbler*).
Oscars: 1988 (Special Award, Visual Effects).
Selected TV work: *Ziggy's Gift* (1982 / special / Emmy-winner), commercials.
Producer-Director: Richard Williams.

Storyboard Productions **see** *Hubley Studios*

Sullivan Bluth **see** *Don Bluth*

Terrytoons (dist. Educational Pictures (Fox Pictures), 20th Century–Fox)

Following the success of his silent "Aesop's Fables" series (1921–29), produced through Fables Studios, Paul Terry formed his own studio (with partner Frank Moser). After introducing such cartoon stars as Mighty Mouse and Heckle and Jeckle, Terry sold the studio to CBS in 1955 and retired.

Shorts (1929–68): Series/characters — Terrytoons (umbrella title for all shorts), Mighty Mouse, Heckle and Jeckle, Farmer Al Falfa, Gandy Goose, Little Roquefort, Dinky Duck, Terry Bears, Possible Possum, Hector Heathcoate, The Mighty Heroes, Sidney the Elephant, Puddy the Pup, Astronut, Hashimoto, Kiko the Kangaroo, James Hound, Sad Cat, Luno, Gaston Le Crayon, Clint Clobber, John Doormat, Sourpuss, Percy the Cat, Willie the Walrus, Dimwit, Foofle, Phoney Baloney, Good Deed Daily, Nancy and Sluggo.

Oscar nominations: 1942, 1944, 1945, 1958.

Selected TV work: *Tom Terrific* (1957–61 / series), *Deputy Dawg* (1960, synd. / series / some shorts released theatrically).

Producers: Paul Terry (1929–55), Frank Moser (1929–36), William M. Weiss (1955–68), Gene Deitch (artistic superv. / 1956–58), Ralph Bakshi (superv. dir / 1966–67).

Directors: Cosmo Anzilotti, Ralph Bakshi, George Bakes, Art Bartsch, Al Chiarito, Mannie Davis, Eddie Donnelly, John Foster, Dan Gordon, George Gordon, Win Hoskins, Al Kouzel, Bob Kuwahara, Frank Moser, Ernest Pintoff, Connie Rasinski, Martin B. Taras, Bob Taylor, Dave Tendlar, Paul Terry, Bill Tytla, Volney White, Jack Zander.

Ub Iwerks (dist. MGM [1930–34], Celebrity Pictures)

Ub Iwerks (1901–71), Walt Disney's chief collaborator in his early years (*Steamboat Willie*), produced his own cartoons for Pat Powers' Celebrity Productions from 1930 to 1936. After producing shorts for Warners and Columbia, he returned to Disney in 1940 as a special effects supervisor and worked there until his death, winning two Oscars (1959, 1965).

Shorts (1930–36): Series/characters — Flip the Frog, ComiColor, Willie Whopper.
Producer-Director: Ub Iwerks.

UPA (United Productions of America) (dist. Columbia Pictures [1948–59])

Formed in 1943 by a group of talented young animators, headed by Stephen Bosustow (1911–81), who had defected from Disney Studios. UPA's first project was the FDR campaign short *Hell Bent for Election* (1944). In 1948, after striking a distribution deal with Columbia Pictures, the studio put out a string of successful, highly innovative shorts noted for their new, stylized look and inventive storylines. Bosustow retired in 1961 and the studio (under Henry G. Saperstein) turned full-time to television production.

Shorts (1944–59): Series/characters — Mr. Magoo, Gerald McBoing-Boing, Jolly Frolics, Ham and Hattie, Fox and the Crow, Specials.

Oscars: 1951, 1954, 1956; Oscar **nominations:** 1948, 1949, 1950, 1951, 1952 (2), 1953 (2), 1956 (2), 1957.

Features: *1001 Arabian Nights* (1959), *Gay Purr-ee* (1962).

Selected TV work: *The Gerald McBoing-Boing Show* (1956–57 / series), *Mr. Magoo's Christmas Carol* (1962 / special).

Producers: Stephen Bosustow, Dave Hilberman, Zachary Schwartz, Henry G. Saperstein.

Directors: Art Babbitt, Pete Burness, Robert Cannon, Osmond Evans, John Hubley, William Hurtz, Chris Ishii, Paul Julian, Lew Keller, Jack Kinney, Rudy Larriva, Abe Levitow, Abe Liss, Tom McDonald, Ted Parmelee, Gil Turner, Alan Zaslove.

Van Beuren (dist. RKO Radio Pictures)

Lesser-known cartoon studio formed in 1928 after Amadee J. Van Beuren bought the Fables Studio, which, since 1921, had been producing Paul Terry's "Aesop's Fables" series. The studio never produced a truly standout series or character, however, and closed in 1936. Van Beuren died the following year.

Shorts (1928–36): Series/characters—Aesop's Fables, Rainbow Parades, Cubby the Bear, The Little King, Tom and Jerry (not the cat and mouse), Toddle Tales, Toonerville Trolley, Molly Moo Cow, Amos 'n' Andy, Felix the Cat.
Producer: Amadee J. Van Beuren.
Directors: Harry Bailey, James Culhane, Mannie Davis, Eddie Donnelly, Ted Eshbaugh, John Foster, Burt Gillett, Dan Gordon, Rollin Hamilton, Hugh Harman and Rudolf Ising, Tom McKimson, J. J. McManus, Steve Muffati, Tom Palmer, George Rufle, Frank Sherman, George Stallings, Frank Tashlin, Paul Terry, James Tyer.

Walt Disney (The Disney Brothers Studio, 1923–26 / The Walt Disney Studio) (dist. M. J. Winkler [1924–27], Universal Pictures [1927–28], Columbia Pictures [1929–32], United Artists [1932–37], RKO Radio Pictures [1937–56], Buena Vista [1956–])

Kansas City cartoonist Walt Disney (1901–66) came out to Hollywood in 1923 and, with brother Roy, founded his now famous studio. After several years of middling success he hit it big with his first "Mickey Mouse" short, *Steamboat Willie* (1928), which was also the first sound cartoon. A shrewd businessman, and finder of talent, Disney built his studio into a leading force in animation which, in 1937, would produce the first feature-length cartoon, *Snow White and the Seven Dwarfs*. More animated classics followed and, in the 1950s, he moved with equal success into television and theme park production. By the time of his death in 1966 Disney had personally won 32 Academy Awards and made his name synonomous with quality family entertainment and top-notch animation.

Shorts (1920–): Series/characters—Mickey Mouse, Donald Duck, Goofy, Pluto, Silly Symphonies, Oswald the Lucky Rabbit, Alice Comedies, Laugh-O-Grams, Winnie the Pooh, Minnie Mouse, Huey Dewey and Louie, Chip 'n' Dale, Humphrey Bear, Daisy Duck, Figaro the Cat, Uncle Scrooge McDuck, Pegleg (Black) Pete, Fifi, Cleo the Goldfish, Ranger, Joe Carioca, Willie the Giant, Clara Cluck, Clarabelle Cow, Horace Horsecollar.
Oscars: 1932–39 (eight in a row), 1941, 1942, 1953, 1968, 1969; Oscar **nominations:** 1932, 1933, 1935, 1938 (3), 1939, 1941, 1942 (doc.), 1943, 1944, 1945, 1946, 1947 (2), 1948 (2), 1949, 1951, 1953, 1954, 1955, 1956 (doc.), 1957, 1958, 1959, 1959 (doc.), 1960, 1961, 1962, 1974, 1983, 1995.
Features: *Snow White and the Seven Dwarfs* (1937), *Pinocchio* (1940), *Fantasia* (1940), *The Reluctant Dragon* (1941 / part live action), *Dumbo* (1941), *Bambi* (1942), *Saludos Amigos* (1943 / part live action), *Victory Through Air Power* (1943 / part live action), *The Three Caballeros* (1945 / part live action), *Make Mine Music* (1946), *Song of the South* (1946 / part anim.), *Fun and Fancy Free* (1947 / part live action), *Melody Time* (1948 / part live action), *So Dear to My Heart* (1949 / part anim.), *The Adventures of Ichabod and Mr. Toad* (1949), *Cinderella* (1950), *Alice in Wonderland* (1951), *Peter Pan* (1953), *Lady and the Tramp* (1955), *Sleeping Beauty* (1959), *101 Dalmatians* (1961), *The Sword in the Stone* (1963), *Mary Poppins* (1964 / part anim.), *The Jungle Book* (1967), *The Aristocats*

(1970), *Bedknobs and Broomsticks* (1971 / part anim.), *Robin Hood* (1973), *The Rescuers* (1977), *Pete's Dragon* (1977 / part anim.), *The Many Adventures of Winnie the Pooh* (1978), *The Fox and the Hound* (1981), *The Black Cauldron* (1985), *The Great Mouse Detective* (1986), *Oliver and Company* (1988), *The Little Mermaid* (1989), *The Rescuers Down Under* (1990), *DuckTales: The Movie—Treasure of the Lost Lamp* (1990 / TV-based), *Beauty and the Beast* (1991), *Aladdin* (1992), *The Lion King* (1994), *Pocahontas* (1995), *A Goofy Movie* (1995 / TV-based), *The Hunchback of Notre Dame* (1996), *Hercules* (1997).

Oscars: 1940 (2), 1941, 1946, 1964 (5), 1971, 1988 (3), 1989 (2), 1991 (2), 1992 (2), 1994 (2), 1995 (2); Oscar **nominations:** 1937, 1941, 1942 (3), 1943 (4), 1945 (2), 1946, 1949, 1950 (3), 1951, 1959, 1963, 1964 (8), 1967, 1971 (4), 1973, 1977 (3), 1989, 1991 (4), 1992 (3), 1994 (2), 1996.

Producers: Walt Disney (1920–66), also Howard Ashman, Ron Clements, Jerome Courtland, Alice Dewey, Don Hahn, Joe Hale, Winston Hibler, Burny Mattinson, Ron Miller, John Musker, James Pentecost, Wolfgang Reitherman, Dan Rounds, Thomas Schumacher, Art Stevens, Bill Walsh.

Directors: James Algar, Ruben A. Aquino, Sam Armstrong, Art Babbitt, Chris Bailey, Tony Bancroft, James Baxter, Ford Beebe, Nancy Beiman, Ted Berman, Aaron Blaise, Don Bluth, Jasper Blystone, Chris Buck, David Burgess, Tim Burton, Hendel Butoy, Bob Carlson, Randy Cartwright, Michael Cedeno, Les Clark, Ron Clements, Pinto Colvig, Robert Cormack, William Cottrell, David Cutler, Jack Cutting, Marc Davis, Andreas Deja, Anthony DeRosa, Walt Disney, Ken Duncan, Russ Edmonds, Norman Ferguson, Will Finn, Tony Fucile, Michael Gabriel, Clyde Geronimi, Burt Gillett, Eric Goldberg, Ed Gombert, Joe Grant, David Hand, Jim Handley, Jack Hannah, T. Hee, Graham Heid, Mark Henn, T. Daniel Hofstedt, Dick Huemer, Ron Husband, Ub Iwerks, Wilfred Jackson, Oliver M. Johnston, Jr., Bill Justice, Milt Kahl, Glen Keane, Ward Kimball, Hal King, Jack King, Jack Kinney, Doug Krohn, Alex Kupershmidt, Eric Larson, John Lounsbery, Dick Lundy, Hamilton Luske, Duncan Marjoribanks, Burny Mattinson, Joshua Meador, Dave Michener, Robert Minkoff, Fred Moore, Larry Morey, John Musker, Charles Nichols, Cliff Nordberg, Matthew O'Callaghan, Perce Pearce, Ed Penner, Walt Pfeiffer, John Pomeroy, David Pruiksma, Nik Ranieri, Rick Reinert, Wolfgang Reitherman, Richard Rich, Dick Rickard, Bill Roberts, Paul Satterfield, Milt Schaffer, George Scribner, Ben Sharpsteen, Art Stevens, Michael Surrey, Frank Thomas, Riley Thomson, Don Towsley, Gary Trousdale, Vladimir "Bill" Tytla, Darrell Van Citters, Erwin Verity, Chris Wahl, Kirk Wise, Ellen Woodbury, Norman Wright, Kathy Zielinski.

Walter Lantz (dist. Universal Pictures, United Artists [1947–49])

Walter Lantz (1899–1994), a veteran of Hearst and Bray studios, opened his own studio at Universal in 1928, with his first task being the continuation of the "Oswald the Rabbit" series (Walt Disney's former property). But over the course of the studio's long history a number of other stars would emerge, including Andy Panda, Chilly Willy and, most notably, Woody Woodpecker (whose voice was provided by Lantz's wife, Grace Stafford). Lantz recieved a special Academy Award for his work in 1978.

Shorts (1929–72): Series/characters—Woody Woodpecker, Andy Panda, Chilly Willy, Oswald the Rabbit, Musical Miniatures, Maw and Paw, Inspector Willoughby, The Beary Family, Swing Symphonies, Pooch the Pup, Meany Miny Moe, Maggie and Sam, Doc, Baby Face Mouse, Wally Walrus, Buzz Buzzard, Gabby Gator, Sugarfoot, Foolish Fables, Li'l Eightball, Windy and Breezy, Hickory, Dickory, Homer Pigeon, Nertsery Rhymes.

Oscar nominations: 1933, 1934, 1941, 1942, 1943, 1944, 1945, 1946, 1948 (song), 1954, 1955.

Selected TV work: *The Woody Woodpecker Show* (1957–58, 1970–71 / series).

Producer: Walter Lantz.

Directors: Tex Avery, James "Shamus" Culhane, Burt Gillett, Jack Hannah, Ben

Hardaway, Emery Hawkins, Lester Kline, Fred Kopietz, Walter Lantz, Patrick Lenihan, Alex Lovy, Dick Lundy, Sid Marcus, William Nolan, Don Patterson, Ray Patterson, Elmer Perkins, Milt Schaffer, Paul J. Smith, Rudy Zamora.

Warner Bros. (Harman-Ising / Leon Schlesinger Prods / Warner Bros Cartoons) (dist. Warner Bros.)

The Warner Bros. cartoon studio was launched in 1930 when producer Leon Schlesinger (1884–1949) joined with former Disney animators Hugh Harman and Rudolf Ising to produce an early sound series starring "Bosko, the Talk-Ink Kid." Over the next three decades, with the help of such great directors as Tex Avery, Bob Clampett, Friz Freleng and Chuck Jones and their cartoon creations (Bugs Bunny, Daffy Duck, Porky Pig, and so on), the studio emerged as one of the leading producers of comedy cartoon shorts. The studio closed in 1963 and briefly reopened again in 1967 (Warner shorts released from 1964–67 were produced by DePatie-Freleng and Format Films). With the late '70s came compilation features and TV specials, followed by more cartoon shorts starting in the late '80s.

Shorts (1930–69, 1987–): Series/characters—Merrie Melodies and Looney Tunes (umbrella titles for all shorts), Bugs Bunny, Daffy Duck, Porky Pig, Elmer Fudd, Tweety, Sylvester the Cat, Yosemite Sam, Pepe Le Pew, Foghorn Leghorn, Speedy Gonzales, Road Runner and (Wile E.) Coyote, Bosko, Buddy, Beans, Sniffles, Tasmanian Devil, Inki, Egghead, Henery Hawk, The Three Bears, Charlie Dog, Marvin Martian, Goofy Gophers, Hubie and Bertie, Hippety Hopper, Claude Cat, Frisky Puppy, Beaky Buzzard, Ralph Wolf and Sam Sheepdog, Goopy Geer, Foxy, Marc Antony and Pussyfoot, Ralph Phillips, The Honey-mousers, Conrad Cat, Merlin the Magic Mouse, Cool Cat, Babbit and Catstello, Michigan J. Frog, Pete Puma, Sylvester Junior, Spike and Chester, Cecil Turtle, Rocky and Mugsy, Gabby Goat, Petunia Pig, Piggy, Ham and Ex, Bobo, Bunny and Claude.

Oscars: 1947, 1949, 1949 (doc.), 1955, 1957, 1958; Oscar **nominations:** 1932, 1939, 1940, 1941 (2), 1942, 1943, 1944, 1945, 1946, 1948, 1949, 1953, 1954, 1957, 1959, 1960 (2), 1961 (3), 1962.

Features (compilations): *The Bugs Bunny / Road Runner Movie* (1979), *The Looney, Looney, Looney Bugs Bunny Movie* (1981), *Bugs Bunny's 3rd Movie: 1001 Rabbit Tales* (1982), *Daffy Duck's Movie: Fantastic Island* (1983), *Daffy Duck's Quackbusters* (1988), *Space Jam* (1996 / original story / part live action).

Selected TV work: *The Bugs Bunny Show* (1960–62 / series), *Carnival of the Animals* (1976 / special), *Bugs Bunny's Looney Christmas Tales* (1979 / special).

Producers: Hugh Harman and Rudolf Ising (1930–33), Leon Schlesinger (1930–44), Edward Selzer (1944–57), John W. Burton (1957–60), William Hendricks (1967–69), Friz Freleng, Chuck Jones, Linda Jones Clough, Kathleen Helppie-Shipley, Timothy Cahill, Julie McNally, Bill Exter.

Directors: Tex Avery, Ted Bonnicksen, Bernard Brown, Gerry Chiniquy, Bob Clampett, Cal Dalton, Arthur Davis, Dave Detiege, Earl Duvall, Greg Ford, Friz Freleng, Ben Hardaway, Hugh Harman, Ken Harris, Rudolf Ising, Ub Iwerks, Chuck Jones, Jack King, Terry Lennon, Abe Levitow, Alex Lovy, Norman McCabe, Robert McKimson, Phil Monroe, Maurice Noble, Tom Palmer, Bil Perez, Hawley Pratt, Irv Spector, Frank Tashlin, Richard Thompson, Darrell Van Citters.

Will Vinton (dist. various)

Pioneer in the field of clay animation (or "Claymation"), best known for his California Raisins TV commercials (from 1986). Vinton, whose studio is located in Portland, Oregon, received an Oscar nomination for his Claymation work in *Return to Oz* (1985).

Selected Shorts: *Closed Mondays* (1974), *Rip Van Winkle* (1978), *The Creation* (1981), *The Great Cognito* (1982).

Oscar: 1974; Oscar **nominations:** 1978, 1981, 1982.

Features: *The Adventures of Mark Twain* (1986), *Will Vinton's Festival of Claymation* (1987 / compilation).

Selected TV work: *A Claymation Christmas Celebration* (1987 / special / Emmy-winner), *A Claymation Easter* (1992 / special / Emmy-winner), commercials.

Producer-Director: Will Vinton.

Selected Bibliography

Beck, Jerry and Will Friedwald. *Looney Tunes and Merrie Melodies: A Complete Illustrated Guide to the Warner Bros. Cartoons.* New York: Henry Holt, 1989.

Bendazzi, Giannalberto. *Cartoons: One Hundred Years of Cinema Animation.* London: John Libbey, 1994.

Blanc, Mel and Philip Bashe. *That's Not All Folks!: My Life in the Golden Age of Cartoons and Radio.* New York: Warner Books, 1988.

Cabarga, Leslie. *The Fleischer Story.* New York: DaCapo Press, 1988.

Crafton, Donald. *Before Mickey: The Animated Film 1898–1928.* Cambridge, Massachusetts: MIT Press, 1982.

Culhane, John. *Walt Disney's Fantasia.* New York: Harry N. Abrams, 1983.

Finch, Christopher. *The Art of Walt Disney: From Mickey Mouse to the Magic Kingdom.* New York: Harry N. Abrams, 1975.

Jones, Chuck. *Chuck Amuck: The Life and Times of an Animated Cartoonist.* New York: Farrar, Straus & Giroux, 1989.

Katz, Ephraim. *The Film Encyclopedia,* 2nd ed. New York: HarperCollins, 1994.

Lenburg, Jeff. *The Encyclopedia of Animated Cartoons.* New York: Facts on File, 1991.

Maltin, Leonard. *Of Mice and Magic.* New York: McGraw-Hill, 1980.

McNeil, Alex. *Total Television: The Comprehensive Guide to Programming from 1948 to the Present.* New York: Penguin Books, 1996.

Index

References are to entry numbers

St. Louis Community College
at Meramec
LIBRARY